T5-DGW-028

TRADE CONDITIONS AND LABOR RIGHTS

Trade Conditions and Labor Rights

U.S. Initiatives, Dominican and Central American Responses

HENRY J. FRUNDT

University Press of Florida

Gainesville · Tallahassee · Tampa · Boca Raton
Pensacola · Orlando · Miami · Jacksonville

03 02 01 00 99 98   6 5 4 3 2 1

Library of Congress Cataloging-in-Publication Data

Frundt, Henry J.
Trade conditions and labor rights: U.S. iniatives, Dominican and
Central American responses / Henry J. Frundt
        p. cm.
Includes bibliographical references and index.
ISBN 0-8130-1621-5 (alk. paper)
1. Employee rights—Central America. 2. Employee rights—
Caribbean Area. 3. Foreign trade and employment—Central
America. 4. Foreign trade and employment—Caribbean Area.
 5. Tariff preferences—United States. 6. Caribbean Basin Initiative,
1983–
HD6971.8.F78   1998
331′.01′109728—dc21   98–8512

The University Press of Florida is the scholarly publishing agency for
the State University System of Florida, comprising Florida A & M
University, Florida Atlantic University, Florida International
University, Florida State University, University of Central Florida,
University of Florida, University of North Florida, University of
South Florida, and University of West Florida.

University Press of Florida
15 Northwest 15th Street
Gainesville, FL 32611
http://nersp.nerdc.ufl.edu/~upf

This book is dedicated to my grandfather Henry, who researched worker compensation and equitable wage scales in Europe after World War I, and to my children, Michael, Laura, James, Daniel, Janine, and Paul, all workers in the United States, for whom I also have great affection.

CONTENTS

TABLES

ABBREVIATIONS

ACILS	American Center for International Labor Solidarity
ACTWU	Amalgamated Clothing and Textile Workers Union
ADOZONA	Asociación Nacional de Zonas Francas de Exportación
AFL-CIO	American Federation of Labor-Congress of Industrial Organizations
AIFLD	American Institute for Free Labor Development
AIP	Apparel Industry Partnership
ANACH	Asociación Nacional de Campesinos de Honduras
ANC	Asociación Nacional Campesina
ANEP	Asociación Nacional de Empleados Publicos [Costa Rica]
ANEP	Asociación Nacional de la Empresa Privada [El Salvador]
ANTA	Asociación Nacional de Trabajadores Agropecuarios
ANTEL	Asociación Nacional de Telecomunicaciones [El Salvador]
ARENA	Alianza Republicana Nacionalista [El Salvador]
ASI	Asociation Salvadoreña de Industriales
ASTTEL	Asociación Salvadoreña de Trabajadores de Telecomunicaciones
ATC	Asociación de Trabajadores del Campo [Nicaragua]
ATMOP	Asociación de Trabajadores de Ministerio de Obras Publicas [El Salvador]
AVANSCO	Asociación para el Avance de las Ciencias Sociales en Guatemala
CACIF	Comité Coordinador de Asociaciones Agricolas, Comerciales, Industrias y Financieras [Guatemala]
CAMI	CENTRO de Actividades Multiplef y Investigaciones
CASC	Confederación Autonoma Sindical Clasista
CATI	Confederación Auténtica de Trabajadores Independientes [Panama]
CBERA	Caribbean Basin Economic Recovery Act
CBI	Caribbean Basin Initiative
CENOC	Consejo Nacional de Organizaciones Campesinas [Guatemala]

CENTRA	Centro de Estudios del Trabajo [El Salvador]
CEA	Consejo de Estatal de Azúcar [Dominican Republic]
CERJ	Consejo de Comunidades Ethicas Runujel Junam [Guatemala]
CGS	Confederación General de Sindicatos [El Salvador]
CGT	Central General de Trabajadores
CGT	Confederación General de Trabajadores [Dominican Republic, Honduras]
CGT	Confederación General del Trabajo [El Salvador]
CGT	Confederación Gremial de Trabajadores [Panama]
CGTG	Central General de Trabajadores de Guatemala
CGTP	General Autonoma de Trabajadores de Panama
CIEP	Centro de Investigación y Educación Popular
CLAT	Central Latinoamericana de Trabajadores
CMT	Confederación de Trabajadores de Mexico
CNT	Confederación Nacional de Trabajadores
CNTC	Consejo Nacional de Trabajadores de Campo
CNTD	Confederación Nacional de Trabajadores Dominicanos
COCENTRA	Confederación Centroamericana de Trabajadores
COLPROSUMAH	Colegio Profesional de Superación Magisterial Hondureño
CONIC	Coordinación Nacional Indígena y Campesina [Guatemala]
COSEP	Consejo de Sector de Empresa Privados [Nicaragua]
CPT	Congreso Permanente de Trabajadores [Nicaragua]
CST	Central Sandinista de Trabajadores
CTC	Confederación de Trabajadores de Costa Rica
CTC	Central de Trabajadores Clasista [Dominican Republic]
CTC	Central de Trabajadores de Campo [Guatemala]
CTCA	Confederación de Trabajadores de Centro América
CTD	Confederación de Trabajadores Democraticos [El Salvador]
CTH	Confederación de Trabajadores de Honduras
CTM	Central de Trabajadores Mayoritaria [Dominican Republic]
CTRN	Confederación de Trabajadores de Rerum Novarum [Costa Rica]
CTRP	Confederación de Trabajadores de la República de Panama
CTU	Confederación de Trabajadores Unitaria [Dominican Republic]
CUC	Comité de Unidad Campesina

CUS	Confederación de Unificación Sindical [Nicaragua]
CUSG	Confederación Unidad de Sindicatos de Guatemala
CUT	Confederación de Trabajadores [Paraguay]
CUT	Central Unitaria de Trabajadores [Dominican Republic]
DGFP	Dirección General de Formación Profesional
ECLAC	Economic Commission on Latin America and the Caribbean
EPZ	Export Processing Zone
FCG	Federación Campesina de Guatemala
FEASIES	Federación de Asociaciones y Sindicatos Independientes de El Salvador
FECETRAG	Federación Central de Trabajadores de Guatemala
FENASEP	Federación Nacional de Servidores Publicos [Guatemala]
FENASTEG	Federación Nacional de Trabajadores del Estado [Guatemala]
FENASTRAS	Federación Nacional Sindical de Trabajadores Salvadoreños
FENATRAM	Federación Nacional de Trabajadores Municipales [Guatemala]
FENATRAZONAS	Federación Nacional de Trabajadores de Zonas [Dominican Republic]
FESEBS	Federación Sindical de Empleados Bancarios y de Seguros de Guatemala
FESINCONSTRANS	Federación de Sindicatos de Industria, Construcción, Transportación y Similares [El Salvador]
FESINTRABS	Federación de Sindicatos de Trabajadores de Alimentos, Bebidas y Similares
FESITRANH	Federación de Sindicatos de Trabajadores Nacionales de Honduras
FESTRAES	Federación Sindical de Trabajadores de El Salvador
FESTRAS	Federación Sindical de Trabajadores de la Alimentación, Agroindustria y Similares [Guatemala]
FITH	Federación Independiente de Trabajadores de Honduras
FLACSO	Facultad Latinoamericana de Ciencias Sociales
FMLN	Frente Faribundo Martí Para la Liberación Nacional
FNT	Frente Nacional de Trabajadores [Nicaragua]
FOES	Fundación Obrero Empresarial Salvadoreña
FSLN	Frente Sandinista de Liberación Nacional
FTS	Federación de Trabajadores de Salud [Nicaragua]

FUSS	Federación Unitaria Sindical Salvadoreña
FUTG	Frente Unitario de Trabajadores de Guatemala
FUTH	Federación Unitaria de Trabajadores de Guatemala
GATT	General Agreement on Tariffs and Trade
GDP	gross domestic product
GNP	gross national product
GSP	Generalized System of Preferences
HTS	Harmonized Trade Schedule
ICFTU	International Confederation of Free Trade Unions
ICIC	Iniciativa Civil para la Integración Centroamericana
ICO	International Coffee Organization
IGSS	Instituto Guatemalteco de Seguridad Social
ILGWU	International Ladies Garment Workers Union
ILO	International Labour Organisation
ILRF	International Labor Rights Fund
IMF	International Monetary Fund
INPEP	Instituto Nacional de Pensiones de Empleados Publicos [El Salvador]
INSAFORP	Instituto Salvadoreño de Formación Profesional
INCAP	Instituto de Nutrición de Centroamérica y Panama
ISCREL	Instituto Superior de Central America de Relaciones Laborales
ISSS	Instituto Salvadoreño del Seguro Social
IUF	International Union of Food and Allied Workers
LAWG	Latin (Central) American Working Group
NACDC	Netherlands National Advisory Council for Development Co-operation
NAFTA	North American Free Trade Agreement
NGO	non-governmental organization
NIE	newly industrializing economy
NISGUA	Network in Solidarity with the People of Guatemala
NLC	National Labor Committee in Support of Democracy and Human Rights in Central America
NYLC	New York Labor Committee
OAS	Organization of American States
OPIC	Overseas Private Investment Corporation
ORIT	Organización Regional Interamericana de Trabajadores
PAN	Partido de Avanzado Nacional [Guatemala]
PCD	Partido Communista Dominicana
PDC	Partido Democratica Cristiano [El Salvador]
PLD	Partido de Liberación Dominicana

PLD	Partido Revolucionario Democratico [Panama]
PLN	Partido de Liberación Nacional [Costa Rica]
PRD	Partido Revolucionario Dominicano
PREALC	Programa Regional del Empleo para América Latina y el Caribe [ILO]
PRI	Partido Revolucionario Independiente [Dominican Republic]
PRSC	Partido Reformista Social Cristiana [Dominican Republic]
PVH	Phillips-Van Heusen
SETMI	Sindicato de Empleados y Trabajadores de Mandarin Internacional [El Salvador]
SITRAIHSS	Sindicato de Trabajadores del Instituto Hondureño de Seguridad Social
SITRAMEDHYS	Sindicato de Trabajadores de Medicina, Hygenica y Similares
SITRASS	Sindicato de Trabajadores de Servicios de Salud [Guatemala]
SITRATERCO	Sindicato de Trabajadores de la Tela Railroad Company [Honduras]
SOICSES	Sindicato de Obreros de Industrias de Construcción, Similares y Connexos de El Salvador
STEG	Sindicato de Trabajadores del Estado de Guatemala
STIBYS	Sindicato de Trabajadores de Bebidas y Similares
STINDE	Sindicato de Trabajadores de Instituto Nacional de Electrificación [Guatemala]
STISSS	Sindicato de Trabajadores del Instituto Salvadoreño de Seguro Social
STITAS	Sindicato de Trabajadores de Industria Textil de Algodón, Sintéticos, Acabados Textiles, Similares y Connexos [El Salvador]
SUTC	Sindicato Unión de Trabajadores de la Construcción
TPC	Tripartite Commission
UASP	Unidad Accion Sindical y Popular
UCA	Universidad de Centro America [El Salvador]
UE	United Electrical Workers
UFCW	United Food and Commercial Workers Union
UGTD	Unión General de Trabajadores Dominicanos
UITA	Unión Internacional de Trabajadores de Alimentos
UNE	Unión Nacional de Empleados [Nicaragua]
UNITE	Union of Needletrades, Industrial and Textile Employees
UNO	Uníon Nacional Opositora [Nicaragua]

UNOC	Unión National Obereo-Cambesina [El Salvador]
UNSITRAGUA	Unión Sindical de Trabajadores de Guatemala
UNTS	Unión Nacional de Trabajadores Salvadoreños
URNG	Unidad Revolutionaria Nacional Guatemalteca
USAID	U.S. Agency for International Development
U.S./GLEP	U.S./Guatemala Labor Education Project
USITC	United States International Trade Commission
USTR	United States Trade Representative
UTE	Unidad de Trabajadores de Escuintla
UTESP	Unión de Trabajadores del Estado y Sectors Populares de San Marcos
UTQ	Unión de Trabajadores de Quetzaltenango
WFTU	World Federation of Trade Unions
WTO	World Trade Organization

PREFACE

In 1976, while working at the offices of the Interfaith Center on Corporate Responsibility in New York, I received a tape smuggled out of Guatemala from workers attempting to organize a union at a local Coca-Cola plant. This began my journey into the world of trade unionists in developing nations and their painful struggle for a measure of respect. My journey took me through the horrible deaths of so many—labor leaders at Coca-Cola and elsewhere—and the exile of thousands of their compatriots. It also revealed the dramatic success of a small group of workers, who with the help of international labor, religious, and human rights groups gained a degree of dignity and autonomy. In Guatemala, the local Coca-Cola franchise remains an example of effective labor-management relations in the midst of a cauldron of economic dislocation and abusive work conditions. It has served as a model of how non-governmental organizations can work cooperatively to confront the social injustices that working people face everywhere.

In 1987, I documented this story in a book entitled *Refreshing Pauses*. During the years since the Coca-Cola story was told (by others as well as myself), much has changed in the international political economy, especially concerning the global coordination of production and consumption. Corporations have freely expanded their offshore operations, either directly or through subcontracting. To complement their efforts, governments have shifted away from state-led investment policies toward massive deregulation and privatization. Despite the pro-and-con debate over the North American Free Trade Agreement (NAFTA) and "fast-track" trade legislation, public attention has largely focused on the benefits of globalization. Only in the mid–1990s did the unconscionable treatment of women and children workers in maquila plants resurrect the Coca-Cola example. Corporate campaigns for international employee standards regained media interest. U.S. unions, historically quite protectionist in their solutions to world competition, finally joined the effort, realizing that if basic worker rights were to be protected, the labor movement needed to pay better attention to the needs of people in other countries as well as at home.

In a contested election, the AFL-CIO elected new leadership in Fall 1995. By 1997 the federation had begun to articulate a fresh approach to international labor issues. In the same year, at White House urging, labor joined with human-rights activists and business representatives to form an apparel industry partnership known as the "No Sweat Task Force," which established guidelines and independent monitoring regarding the treatment of employees by outside contractors. Results testified to the importance of corporate campaigns and non-governmental efforts as antidotes to the dislocation and workplace abuse associated with international corporate expansion.

However, the intervening period has also suggested that when voluntary measures prove insufficient, government pressure has a role to play. During the 1980s, this realization led labor-rights proponents to another approach. They sought clauses in free-trade agreements that would improve local labor laws and compliance. A requirement to respect basic freedoms to organize and bargain would allow for local differences in culture and levels of development, argued these advocates, but it would also assure that international competition proceeded fairly. While there would be worker dislocations, they would be much less brutal. Ultimately, they hoped for a global mechanism that would assure compliance with basic labor rights.

Conventional economists have nevertheless been reluctant to emphasize the "employment impact" of "free global trade" much less to endorse any international standards or enforcement agency. Their view has had far-reaching influence on U.S. and European policy makers. For them, international mechanisms imply state interference in the market, which benefits a favored "labor aristocracy" and downgrades the commonweal. Until an economic crisis struck in 1997, such economists customarily cited several economically liberalized nations in Southeast Asia that had demonstrated growth and increased equality for their citizens.

Such controversies demand clear thinking. They motivated me to undertake further research on the social impact of global trade. Who was more correct: those who advocated greater state action to enforce international labor rights or those who believed the market would deliver a fairer outcome? The market argument certainly appeared more persuasive to many policy makers. Let me explain, however, why my previous experience had oriented me to the first approach. I credit my sustained interaction with workers who were struggling to form unions in Guatemala, El Salvador, and other nearby countries. Their experiences, encapsulated recently in Thomas Reed and Karen Brandow's *The Sky Never Changes,* revealed how ordinary folks organize to protect themselves from horrendous abuse—a far cry from the "labor aristocracy" or "entrenched bureaucracy" characterization often applied toward labor unions in Latin America and Asia. With few exceptions, active labor leaders in the countries I was annually visiting appeared often to be in danger and were always laboring to obtain dignity and basic necessities. They labored not only on behalf of their own unions but for everyone around them, unionized, non-unionized, underemployed, or unemployed. For most of their waking hours they urged workers facing difficult conditions to hold on a little longer, if not to win a union contract at least to demand a limited measure of justice in the way they were spoken to, in how they were treated when they were sick, in how they were informed when contracts were slow, and in how they were paid relative to what it cost them to live.

Most of their co-workers led simple but demanding lives. They were often unfamiliar with the intricacies of trade debates and policy. They became frightened when businessmen and government officials warned them of being manipulated by foreign agents. It was not that they believed such charges, but they felt their livelihoods were threatened. They understood mistreatment, however. They understood exploitation. They readily sensed basic class loyalties even when they knew overt repression and competing interests and personalities suggested caution.

So, integral to the principles of trade policy, I must acknowledge that it was the perceptions of these workers that motivated my search for an answer. I was especially interested in how they viewed changes over the past ten years—in their attitudes, for example, toward fresh investments and opportunities for industrial employment. Perhaps they agreed with conventional economists that they too benefited substantially from unbridled markets. Maybe, despite new forms of potential exploitation, they saw themselves as much better off.

I found myself overwhelmed by what these workers did and said. In the following pages I have tried to pass on to the reader a sample of their perspectives on labor rights and trade conditions. I discovered, as the reader will, that their responses demonstrate a range of complexity. Since I am testing the impact of state intervention on labor rights, I have attempted to integrate these testimonies with relevant statistical data and expert commentary. I must confess to finding the views of workers and their representatives especially persuasive. I also have attempted to present the views of businesspeople and government officials in as straightforward a manner as I could. Now I invite the reader to consider the evidence at hand.

Note on Sources

This work is based on three types of sources. The first is an extensive set of personal interviews, often in Spanish, that I conducted between 1993 and 1997. Quotations are credited in the notes. English translations of the interviews are available from the author. I also consulted petitions and supportive documents filed with the GSP Subcommittee of USTR, and related labor union and USAID documents. Full references to these sources are in the notes. Most petition-related documents are stored in the USTR Archive, 600 17th St. NW, Washington, D.C. 20506. Related materials are held at the ILRF, 733 15th Street N.W., no. 920, Washington, D.C. 20005; U.S./GLEP, Box 268–290, Chicago, Ill., 60626; CENTRA, Av. Sierra Nevada 615, Colonia Miramonte, San Salvador. Finally, I consulted much of the available published material on U.S. labor relations in Central America; those sources are cited in the notes and listed in the bibliography.

Acknowledgments

I must first acknowledge the working men and women in Central America and the Caribbean, especially those who agreed to be interviewed. It is difficult to single out certain people, but I must mention those who led me to others: Roberto Robles of the Federación Sindical de Trabajadores de la Alimentación, Agroindustria y Similares (FESTRAS) has been a sounding board in the fight for labor justice in Guatemala for many years. Sergio Guzman and Byron Morales, of the Unión Sindical de Trabajadores de Guatemala (UNSI-TRAGUA), and Luis Merida deserve special thanks, as do Juan Francisco Alfaro of the Confederación Unidad de Sindicatos de Guatemala (CUSG) and Thelma del Cid. I am particularly indebted to Reynaldo González of the Federación Sindical de Empleados Bancarios y de Seguros de Guatemala (FESEBS), who was forced for a time into exile, no doubt in part because of his efforts on behalf of international worker rights, and I thank Rigoberto Dueñas of the Central General de Trabajadores de Guatemala (CGTG), Francisca Chinik of the Coordinación Nacional Indígena y Campesina (CONIC), and Miguel Aczoc. Frank LaRue of the Center for Human Rights and Legal Action has offered his insightful analyses of labor issues since the late 1970s. The views of Gabriel Aguilar Peralta, Luis Padilla, Dinorah Azpuru, Karin Erbsen de Maldonado, Eduardo Mazarieagos, and Alicia Rodriguez have also been helpful, as has the personal support given to me from former students and faculty at the Universidad Rafael Landivar (Arlena Cifuentes, Rolando Cabrerra, Lorena Cabrerra, Veronica González, and Hugo Solares) and the Universidad Mariano Gálvez. From El Salvador, I extend my appreciation to Roger Gutiérrez of the Federación de Asociaciones y Sindicatos Independientes de El Salvador (FEASIES), Soida Alvarez and Carlos Hurtado of the Confederación de Trabajadores Democraticos (CTD), and Carlos Ochoa of the Unión Nacional de Trabajadores Salvadoreños (UNTS).

I also express my gratitude to the many officials from local governments and the private sector who agreed to extensive discussions, especially Fernando Rivera, Carlos Moran, Guillermo Palma, Carlos Arias, and Juan Hector Vidal. Karen Delaney, Randall Peterson, and Donald Knight from the U.S. mission were also very cooperative. Mario Aníbal González and Raul and Maria Elena Anzuelo supplied essential insights and lasting friendship.

There is a second group from my own country that deserves much credit for this effort. Key contributors to this study include Stephen Coats, the highly capable director of the U.S./Guatemala Labor Education Project (U.S./GLEP), which has played such a leadership role in the Guatemala trade actions; its very knowledgeable and skilled former and current staffers Rhett Doumitt, Karen Brandow, Bruce Fieldman, Erich Hahn, Hannah Frisch, and Bob Perillo; Mark Anner, whose groundbreaking work in El Salvador has brought code monitoring to a new level; and Barbara Briggs and Charles Kernaghan, whose creative leadership on the National Labor Committee is well recognized. I extend my appreciation to other members and former members of the U.S./GLEP board: its founder, John Ruthrauff; early petitioner Lance Compa, who schooled me in how labor petitions work with local unions (see his fine summary of current trade and rights issues, *Human Rights, Labor Rights, and International Trade,* co-edited with Stephen F. Diamond); U.S./GLEP's early leader Peter Hogness; its chair Gail Lopez-Henriquez; and its members and supporters from UNITE and elsewhere: Noel Beasley, Paul Filson, Brent Garren, Nancy Lorence, Jeff Hermanson, and Alan Howard. I also thank Joy Anne Grune, Lisa Haugaard of LAWG, and Pamela Vossenas. Pharis Harvey, the able director of the International Labor Rights Fund, is also on that board, and constantly provides national leadership on this issue as well as to this study. I also thank Stan Gacek, now Latin American Regional Director in the AFL-CIO International Affairs Department. My colleagues in the Guatemala Scholars Network, so capably coordinated by Marilyn Moors, helped arrange many events at meetings of the Latin American Studies Association, where I have also depended on research on labor and politics by Susanne Jonas, Robert Trudeau, Kurt Petersen, Rachael Garst and others. Arthur and Joan Domike's hospitality and Brenda Webb's assistance at USTR made my Washington, D.C., research viable. Yolanda Prieto, Suzy Suarez, Behzad Yaghmaian, Judith Jeney, Donna Crawley, Robert Becklen, Diana Alspach, and our associates at the School of Social Science of Ramapo College and AFT Local 2274 offered their strong shoulders.

Finally, I am also indebted to a third group of those who have critiqued the material in specific chapters: Mark Hager and Hoby Spalding, who offered general comments; Ben Davis on El Salvador; Jeff Hermanson on the Dominican Republic; Sharon Phillipps on Panama; Richard Stahler-Sholk on Nicaragua; Gene Miller on Costa Rica. Of course, the interpretations and errors are mine alone. I wish to thank Ramapo College and its foundation for providing me with a sabbatical and some travel funds to carry out this research, the Centro de Investigaciónes Regionales de Mesoamérica for office space and assistance, and Edward Page of the UN Commission on Disarmament Education for his encouragement. I must convey my special appreciation to the editors of the University Press of Florida, especially Meredith Morris-Babb, editor in chief, Jacqueline Kinghorn Brown, project editor, and Michael Senecal, copy editor, for their firm corrections and friendly suggestions. My wife, Bette, who carefully read and corrected the manuscript, and our six children always remain my greatest source of support.

Introduction

In November 1997, U.S. president Bill Clinton was forced to withdraw his requested renewal of fast-track trade authority after congressional leader Newt Gingrich could not deliver the necessary votes. Despite White House pleas that non-renewal would undermine the international stature of the American presidency, and despite President Clinton's promotional free-trade tour to major countries in South America, Congress had heard from too many constituents about the failed promises of the North American Free Trade Agreement (NAFTA), the persistent international violations of labor and environmental standards, and their own economic fears. The canceled authorization was reminiscent of November 1995, when Congress refused to grant other southern neighbors the "benefits of free trade" and tariff reductions enjoyed by Mexico. Critics then elaborated the dismal record of Latin nations in implementing environmental and worker rights. In a close vote, Congress failed to pass the Caribbean Basin Security Act, which would have extended trade parity to most other North American nations. Nevertheless, with the renewal of the General Agreement on Tariffs and Trade (GATT) and the creation of the World Trade Organization (WTO), free-trade advocates retain a forceful position in policy circles. In December 1996, despite U.S. objections, the WTO rejected the inclusion of labor standards for GATT's next round of debate. At the second Summit of the Americas, held in Chile in April 1998, the hemisphere's heads of state reaffirmed their commitment to a "Free Trade Area of the Americas" by 2005, although they also accepted a parallel program to improve social conditions (Sims 1998). As negotiations progress in the years ahead, the specific design of unregulated trade between the U.S. and Latin and Caribbean Basin countries will assuredly spark heated exchange.

This book is about labor standards and augmented trade in the Caribbean region.[1] In 1996, the equity of labor standards gained notoriety when TV celebrity Kathie Lee Gifford tearfully denied knowledge of the abusive conditions endured by underaged workers who sewed her labels on clothing produced in Honduras. (She later had to face similar charges about clothing made in New York City.) But Kathie Lee became a cause célèbre because the U.S.

public had already been educated about the low wages, long hours, minuscule benefits, and sexual harassment faced by maquila workers beyond U.S. borders. Shoppers took notice when labor solidarity organizations such as the National Labor Committee or the U.S./Guatemala Labor Education Project (U.S./GLEP) distributed leaflets at stores requesting that retailers adopt a minimum code of employee standards for their contracting producers. Journalists devoted sympathetic programs and columns to the issue of sweatshop conditions abroad. While occasionally the publicity generated opposite claims—that sweatshop workers were happier to have jobs than to be without them (Rohter 1996a)—global discussion mounted.

Publicity efforts began to show positive results when the Phillips–Van Heusen shirt company agreed to abide by a corporate code and recognize a Guatemalan union in 1992; Levi Strauss Co. voluntarily announced a code for contractors in 1993; then Starbucks Coffee promised to enforce purchasing standards, and GAP Clothing committed to honor outside monitoring of its producing companies in 1995. In 1997, ten major U.S.-based maquila contractors assented to the White House "No Sweat Task Force" recommendations. Other name-brand companies were expected to soon follow.

But while solidarity leaflets and purchaser efforts to remedy oppressive labor conditions remained essential, others sought to reach beyond visible targets and grapple with less visible subcontractors and local firms that persistently mistreated their employees with little consequence. They advocated attaching conditions to trade that the U.S. (or any nation) extends to exporting countries. In effect they said, if you want favorable access to U.S. markets, then you must take steps to improve national observance of basic labor rights. The question this study asks is whether that approach is effective.

The Argument

While the trade condition argument appears simple, it has not been easily accepted by a significant number of people, including those who believe that workers in developing countries are glad to get a job. They point out that work conditions there cannot be compared to standards in advanced nations. The definition of labor rights can be elusive. Workers have much lower food and housing costs, and life has less elaborate requirements. Indeed, their less-adorned, enjoyable livelihoods are something to be admired.

U.S. workers know that there is more to life than "living standards" can measure. On wintry days they might even wistfully dream of trading places with those living simpler lives in warmer climes. But they also know that increased trade attracted by the low wages of campesinos and seamstresses and the unhealthy and undignified circumstances of their work have made comparison more of an issue.

The struggle to reconcile standards reflects a fundamental debate between those who believe each culture or nation will naturally evolve appropriate standards as its economy develops through trade with its neighbors and those who deny that this "market process" is sufficient to assure worker protection. To put the matter academically, neo-liberal (also called neo-classical) economists argue that imposed labor standards interfere with the market, thereby inhibiting overall national growth; neo-institutional economists insist that without standards, worker exploitation will remain. Decent treatment may motivate worker productivity and increase consumer demand, but market-driven companies can still choose intimidation and bare-subsistence wages.

U.S. workers also believe labor conditions abroad are increasingly tied to similar conditions at home, and the unrestricted ability of publicly chartered corporations to shift high-paying, unionized jobs to low-paying, non-unionized locations outside the U.S. They wonder who really benefits when untrammeled trade allows jobs to be relocated from industrial to developing nations with no controls to assure worker dignity. Again, in explaining this trend, neo-liberal economists stress the benefits of "market factors": Seeking a "comparative advantage," companies are simply obeying the law of supply and demand. Since modern communications and transport systems now make it possible to coordinate production and distribution on a worldwide basis, any firm that desires to remain competitive must take advantage of lower labor costs wherever it can locate them. If this means having its shirts or auto parts assembled abroad, then of course that is what a company will choose to do, but its investments will convey substantial gains for workers in all countries.

However, neo-institutionalists emphasize that it is not just a matter of corporations relocating for the best market advantage (see Dietz 1995). They also justify economic systems that perpetuate a small minority of wealthy families and a large underclass ready to work for pittance remuneration. Consciously or unconsciously they thereby help formulate political policies that encourage enclaves of low-wage opportunity. Under the rationalization of national security, they support authoritarian governments and quasi-military dictatorships that guarantee stability. In the process, even within "market" conditions, they cultivate a breeding ground for anti-union sentiment that inhibits the natural ability of working people to demand their own work requirements.

Background: Changing Economies of Caribbean Basin Nations

To contribute to this debate, our study focuses on labor standards in the Caribbean region as they relate to augmented trade. We will evaluate the merits of the neo-classical and neo-institutional arguments. The historical transformation of work in this region remains a key factor in such evaluation.

Over the last fifteen years (1983–98), largely due to trade, a growing number of the still mostly agricultural workers in Caribbean Basin nations have been transformed into wage laborers in foreign industries. Far from setting their own pace of life, they have quickly been forced into tasks previously performed by assembly workers in U.S. factories.

As with work conditions in the U.S., the transformation of trade is not solely responsible for converting the work process in Caribbean Basin nations. The other factors, while stimulated by trade, are also operative: augmented mechanization of agriculture, land concentration, urbanization, improvements in communications technology, enhanced industrialization, and consumer substitution of formulated products (such as corn syrup for sugar, and coffee substitutes). But among these factors, the export/import decisions of both national and international upper classes have a significant influence, as our study will discover.

Until the 1980s, the pace of change was slower in the Caribbean Basin than in much of Latin America. Some have attributed this to the conservative policies of a relatively isolated elite which has controlled the political and economic system. Satisfied with traditional export income, they were reluctant to reinvest to improve output, offering minuscule opportunities to the vast number of poor, landless peasants and part-time workers who sustained production (see Debray 1975). However, others stress that international class interests were complicitous in maintaining the region's dependent state. The Caribbean Basin's strategic value became defined as an area for corporate sourcing and investment and for political alliances against the Soviet Union. Although structural imbalances persisted, policy makers were oriented to protect U.S. interests and property (see Coleman and Herring 1991; Hamilton et al. 1988; Weaver 1994).

For many years the region's peasants and workers, sometimes separately, sometimes jointly, demanded change. Occasionally, as in Guatemala between 1944 and 1954 and in Cuba after 1959, they enjoyed periods of control and improved conditions. However, neither the local nor the North American upper classes envisioned peasant/worker revolutions as an acceptable formula for advancement (Paige 1997). Critics charge that international and national elites coordinated their forces to brutally repress any indigenous efforts at national freedom: U.S. officials would not tolerate an independent Guatemala, so they encouraged CIA operatives to overthrow its elected government (Immerman 1982; Gleijeses 1991). They isolated and blockaded Cuba, whose autonomy might inspire similar efforts elsewhere (Franklin 1997). They evolved a double-pronged approach: Thoughtful northern development theorists realized that peasant/worker solutions to inequality had to be replaced by an Alliance for Progress for improved land redistribution and employment. At the same time, U.S. government operatives infiltrated every free-spirited, democratically chosen alternative to the structure of power. They would either divide it or eliminate it directly, as they did with Juan Bosch's brief presidency of the Dominican Republic.

From this perspective, these interventions protected traditional class privileges, but they also created fresh institutional forces which unleashed a counterinsurgency monster that viewed all reform efforts as "communistic." Military henchmen schooled in Panama or Fort Benning, Georgia, returned to rule their nations with unapologetic blood and torture. Any activity to improve local conditions was suspect. Not only did this halt grassroots development, it also stymied the proper functioning of traditional structures of justice. As they became subjected to the brutalizing authority, government ministries, police, and courts surrendered previous legitimacy. They hesitated to apply established principles of human rights and labor standards, and abuses persisted.

Although they are open and generous, Central American and Caribbean peoples were not prone to accept injustice, and pockets of resistance persisted. Other endeavors via the U.S. Agency for International Development failed to mitigate conditions, and inequalities exacerbated. Campesinos, intellectuals, and even disillusioned military officers fled to the mountains to organize their rebellions.

The "Guerilla Wars" of Central America and other movements in the Caribbean began as a thirty-year struggle to redress the gross imbalances in land and power and the resulting grinding poverty and mistreatment (Burbach and Flynn 1984; LaFeber 1984; Landau 1995; PACCA 1984; Pearse 1982; Walker 1985, 1997; see also Berryman 1984, 1987, 1995 and Lernoux 1992 for religious influence). In the late 1970s, these paramilitary forces won important victories in Guatemala (Jonas 1991) and El Salvador (Armstrong and Shenk 1982). The Sandinistas celebrated the achievement of state power in Nicaragua in 1979 (Vilas 1986; Walker 1985). In the Caribbean, the New Jewel movement gained office in Grenada. Rather than dealing with such changes constructively, once again U.S. policy makers chose ideology over humanity. They flooded the region with military aid and advisors. In Central America, local armies unleashed a reign of terror against virtually all popular organizations and indigenous communities. They would stop the guerillas, as one

Guatemalan general put it, "killing the fish by draining the sea." For reasons partly related to the war effort, prices which these nations received for their traditional agricultural exports dropped significantly.

U.S. Policy Promotes Regional Job Shift

In the early 1980s, North American strategists again reached the consensus that brute force alone would not bring order to the region's population. They could not wean themselves from military force, since they blamed the region's social and political crisis on "Cuba's regime and the presence of other anti-democratic forces in Nicaragua, Grenada, and other parts of the region." The U.S. overt/covert war would still have to deal with them. However, they also admitted that "this crisis was triggered by escalating costs of imported oil and declining prices of the Basin's major traditional exports" (USITC 1994). To remedy this, they urged an economic development strategy that stepped beyond the designated assistance programs of USAID. In 1982, President Ronald Reagan proposed the Caribbean Basin Initiative (CBI) and invited Henry Kissinger to head the National Bipartisan Commission on Central America. The commission gave a fresh emphasis to freer regional trade: Along with overt military force and other forms of development aid, trade would become the solution for improving living standards in Central America and the Caribbean (see U.S. Department of State 1986 and U.S. National Bipartisan Commission on Central America 1984).

To implement this plan, Congress in August 1983 enacted the Caribbean Basin Economic Recovery Act (CBERA). The U.S. hoped that the CBI and CBERA (which are often equated) would mollify the mushrooming economic and political crisis in the region. The programs were designed to promote regional stability "principally by providing incentives to foreign and domestic private investors in non-traditional economic sectors" (USITC 1994). The package of trade preferences and tax incentives was geared to diversify production and exports away from traditional Caribbean Basin commodities (see appendix).

Twenty-four of the region's twenty-nine nations were eventually included. CBERA made it possible for Central American and Caribbean nations to dramatically increase their duty-free exports to the U.S., and the Reagan administration reorganized its many aid agencies to offer advice and financial assistance (see Johnson 1993). All told, over the next twelve years CBI programs spent nearly $16 billion to transform the region into an agro-industrial complex valued at 12 percent of overall regional exports to the U.S.

From Cane Cutter and Coffee Picker to Stitcher and Seamstress

CBI stimulated a new pattern of exports. This pattern expanded after 1986 when President Reagan announced a "Special Access Program" for textiles and apparel, which brought a crucial shift in regional employment. Apparel, which constituted only 5.5 percent of overall U.S. imports from the area in 1984, reached 39.8 percent in 1993, making "Caribbean countries collectively the fastest growing U.S. supplier in 1989–93," followed by Mexico and China (USITC 1994). At the same time, similar job opportunities developed in footwear, instruments, and sporting goods. Most were products that lent themselves to the final assembly of components produced in the U.S. Eyeing an opportunity to industrialize, observed USITC (1994), "regional policy-makers recruited export-oriented assembly operations" known as maquilas. The number of factories and export-processing zones in the region magnified dramatically.

Jobs were also available in the region's traditional export industries, in bananas, coffee, sugar, and beef, and—from several Caribbean islands—aluminum ore and petroleum products. But even here new export growth came from seafood and such "nontraditional" agricultural export crops as vegetables and fruit sold to the U.S. market. Jobs in these areas did not pull people toward urban areas, but they transformed life in the countryside (see Burnham et al. 1992 and Green 1997 on changes in family roles).

The CBI legislation contained references both to human rights in general and labor rights in particular, as elaborated below. However, in their promotion of the new maquila assembly plants or the nontraditional agricultural sector, U.S. policy makers minimized references to this aspect of the policy. The subject also remained verboten among their counterpart basin technocrats, who often informally agreed that the local labor laws would not be enforced in export-related facilities. Thus, an aspect of the promotion of trade in place of autonomous development was an insistence on maintaining labor control.

Impact on U.S. Workers

At the time that the Caribbean Basin neighbors of the U.S. experienced a massive transformation in employment, U.S. working families faced a drop in income (Ehrenreich 1990; Sklar 1995). Despite more of its members joining the workforce, the average U.S. family had less buying power in 1994 than it enjoyed in 1964. Social scientists offered several reasons for this loss of U.S. family income, including the changing value of the American dollar, job-displacing technology (Rifkin 1995), longer work hours (Schor 1992) and the growing importance of lower paid service sector occupations (Labor Institute 1995). But, in a growing national debate, the runaway corporation and increased exports from abroad remained the most popular rationale.[2]

Affected by the job-transfers argument, U.S. policy makers justified their actions by claiming that increasing trade abroad meant more jobs for the U.S.

In any case, CBI imports did not account for much loss. Aside from apparel, said USITC, CBI-produced goods rarely surpassed 10 percent of U.S. production in any category. Those over 5 percent included luggage, leather apparel, frozen vegetables, and cigars. Medical instruments were highest (12 percent) followed by electrical resistors (11 percent). USITC unconvincingly argued that these figures did not constitute a job-displacement effect.[3]

Nevertheless, especially from industrial areas, the U.S. public demanded restrictions on the ability of corporations to relocate to Mexico, the Caribbean Basin, and elsewhere. "It is not just a question of free market economics," they insisted. "U.S. workers have devoted their lives to the construction of corporate America. Their sweat and tears helped create the investment potential of these companies. Their families should not be treated as a commodity that can simply be moved about at will. Both family and community health depend on a stable and lasting environment which deserves protection."[4]

During the 1980s, these "populists" developed several strategies to prevent corporate dislocation (see Ramney 1987). Some sought restrictive clauses in corporate charters; others demanded early warning legislation so that workers might have an opportunity either to collaborate with a company to achieve desired savings or to buy it with some government financing. The official labor movement remained wary of these solutions, preferring laws that would specify domestic product content. The AFL-CIO urged the public to "Buy American," thereby preserving U.S. jobs and living standards. In the 1990s, public figures like Ross Perot and Pat Buchanan capitalized on widespread popular discontent over factory closings by promising to redraft U.S. trade policies to retard plant dislocations. While such efforts won notoriety, the trend toward corporate globalization and job transfers accelerated.[5]

The Labor Rights Argument

Another approach to the workforce impact of corporate globalization also emerged in the 1980s (see Cavanagh et al. 1988). Rank-and-file trade unionists as well as an articulate group of social scientists postulated the linkage: Uncontrolled transnational investment and trade was detrimental to workers in the U.S., *and* it did not necessarily improve the living standards of those working in other countries. In fact, argued the group, most of the countries where jobs were transferred had highly authoritarian governments that tightly controlled the income levels of the population. They would often summon their U.S.-trained armies to enforce local laws prohibiting strikes, factory occupations, and even organizing—activities designed to improve the quality of life of the nation's workforce. In other words, it was not just market factors that stimulated the transfer of U.S. industrial jobs elsewhere; the attraction of "labor repressive" regimes also made it possible for transnational corporations to exploit their workforce more easily. These advocates challenged the "protectionist" AFL-CIO "Buy American" campaign as both ineffective and insensitive to the genuine needs of workers abroad, who needed jobs but were also being persecuted. Instead, they promoted an enforced requirement for labor rights in all countries.

In 1984, this perspective won a sufficient number of adherents to win legal recognition for the principle of labor rights as an element of fair trade: U.S. trade benefits such as those of the CBI program must arrive in the context of a nation's respect for labor rights. Requirements for worker standards were elaborated in the Generalized System of Preferences (GSP), a trade program that grants tariff reductions to "most-favored nations." If a country's exports were to obtain favored-nation treatment, the country would have to show that it was "taking steps" toward full respect of worker dignity and free organizational rights. GSP contained a provision that permitted interested parties to petition for review of participating nations to verify that they were complying with five core areas of labor rights: freedom of association; the right to negotiate and bargain; prohibitions against child labor and slave labor; and humane working conditions. At first, few people comprehended the potential effect of this new legislative requirement. By the early 1990s, however, a significant number of countries had been cited for labor abuses and "labor rights trade conditionality" had emerged as a major public issue.

By the time of Kathie Lee Gifford's dramatic televised confession, calls for "labor rights" had become a primary union response to the expansion of hemispheric free trade. The voices had an effect: In 1990, GSP worker-rights provisions were attached to the Caribbean Basin Initiative. Such monitoring provisions were excluded in the final round of NAFTA, and the side agreement on labor issues was much weaker than advocates had hoped. Nevertheless, it did contain important provisions that could generate pressure (see Compa 1996; Cook et al. 1997; Herzenberg 1996). The Miami Summit of the Americas promoted labor rights in 1994. That same year, the U.S. won a commitment that labor rights would be on the agenda of the World Trade Organization preparatory committee created to implement the General Agreement on Tariffs and Trade. Although the U.S. remained ambivalent on trade conditionality for China (see Tonelson 1996), it did take stronger actions vis-à-vis Japan for non-labor-related market protections. In 1997, partly because of labor-rights concerns, the U.S. Congress balked at renewing fast-track treatment of trade legislation. Unions remained adamant about "social-contract" provisions in future agreements. The issue of trade conditionality promised to remain on the public policy agenda in the years ahead.

Through this study I hope to enlighten debate by examining the impact of

U.S. labor-rights trade provisions on labor standards in Central America and the Caribbean. The region is constituted by a number of small economies, most of which have historically resisted trade-union rights more so than their larger neighbors to the south. Central American and Caribbean nations are also more dependant on U.S.-based trade, and potentially more affected by labor-rights conditions. While the area has been subjected to considerable worker-rights pressure, up to this point policy advocates have had virtually no scientifically assessed results.

Basic Propositions: Labor Rules Help

The basic hypothesis of this study is that in Central America and the Caribbean, labor-rights provisions positively influence national labor-rights legislation and enforcement. To put it another way, were it not for the application of trade-based conditions, Central American and Caribbean countries would be much slower to legislate trade-union protections. Specifically, if GSP requirements were not invoked, these nations would still be governed by antiquated labor codes and little enforced monitoring.

Corollary to this fundamental hypothesis is another important principle: Enforced labor rights improve a society's labor conditions. This subsequent proposition will test the claim that enforced labor standards are counterproductive, that they serve as a barrier to market forces which would more rapidly lead to better conditions for a larger number of people. To examine this possibility, we will probe other potential causes of labor-standards improvement which could serve as "intervening variables" and affect this relationship. These include economic development, political forces, *private*-sector flexibility, and union strength.

The two hypotheses bear on the neo-classical/neo-institutional debate about the role of market forces in improving labor conditions. The hypotheses will motivate an exploration of the nuances of these theories as they affect conditions in Central American and Caribbean nations, where corporations have few restrictions on investment and trade. One such nuance is the admission by some neo-institutionalists that enforcement of labor standards might stimulate corporate scofflaws to clandestinely transfer production to the lower-paying informal sector.

Research Design

Economists may be inclined to study the impact of labor rights by examining econometric outcomes on export income, job creation, wage increases, and overall economic growth (see Rodrik 1995). However, we believe that the above hypotheses require a much broader approach that integrates several types of evidence: comparative historical examination of the changes in national labor legislation, its compliance in specific countries, and personal testimonies by those affected. While testimonies are not always objective, they do convey the experience of trade impact as a *social* reality. This study proposes to reconcile various forms of evidence. It will look at the results of imposed trade requirements in seven Caribbean Basin nations: Costa Rica, the Dominican Republic, El Salvador, Guatemala, Nicaragua, Panama, and Honduras. All seven have been subjected to GSP petitions. Then, the study will give special emphasis to the development of labor rights in El Salvador, Guatemala, Honduras, and the Dominican Republic since these nations have exemplified extreme labor-rights violations on the one hand and clearly delineated government and private-sector responses to labor-rights trade provisions on the other.

To test the specific impact of GSP on local labor-rights practice, the project is organized into two parts and thirteen chapters. The first part examines the arguments surrounding labor rights and specific aspects of labor legislation in Latin America. The second part constitutes case studies. A final chapter summarizes the results.

Chapter 1, "Caribbean Basin Workers Search for Decent Treatment," serves as a vehicle for individual workers to tell their own stories about conditions resulting from increased global trade. While they recount experiences at specific work sites, they also tell of challenging repressive work conditions through moribund legal systems, and of their recent frustration with unilateral decisions by their governments to privatize public services. Chapter 2, "The Debate over Methods of Achieving Labor Rights," presents the story of how worker rights came to be codified through the International Labour Organisation (ILO), beginning with the early conventions on hours and mandated rest in 1919. The dispute between neo-classical and neo-institutional economists regarding labor-rights standards is examined in detail, as well as the beneficial and detrimental roles of the market, the government, and an enlightened private sector in redressing employee grievances. Finally, the chapter focuses on the utility of trade requirements for gaining observance of such rights.

Chapter 3, "Implementing Labor Rights Through Trade Conditions," briefly details the history and legal mechanisms used to tie trade conditions to labor rights. It then reviews the evolution and function of U.S. GSP trade legislation. GSP is the most concrete example of a policy that limits trade with nations less committed to improving respect for such rights. The discussion addresses the selection of rights to be enforced, procedures for reviewing these rights, and measures of trade condition effectiveness. It then proposes an approach for testing the usefulness of labor rights requirements on corporate and government behavior.

Chapter 4, "The Record of GSP Petitions in Latin America," briefly summarizes the economic and labor conditions extant in Latin America countries prior to the introduction of GSP petitions. After some introductory comments describing the evolution of labor rights in Latin America in general, it describes the process in which the AFL-CIO invoked GSP to review labor conditions in Chile and Paraguay. Then it places Central American and Caribbean national conditions within the overall context of world trade. It also traces the past and present role of U.S. trade on Central American and Caribbean economies. The chapter then questions the effect of the GSP petition process in Central America and the Caribbean, asking how the process has affected specific national labor policies over the past ten years.

The first chapter in part 2, "The Labor Petitions in El Salvador: A Weak Labor Code," recounts what happened following the first major drive in Central America to tie together trade and labor rights. In the midst of a relatively upbeat national mood following the implementation of the 1992 peace accords, it reveals how business interests succeeded in substituting a relatively weak code for genuine private-sector reform and substantive labor dialogue. Chapter 6, "Structural Implications of GSP Pressure in El Salvador," scrutinizes institutional behavior to assess changes following passage of El Salvador's code. Included are the Labor Ministry, the courts, and tripartite dialogue.

Chapter 7, "The Guatemalan Case: Reluctant Compromise," deals with a more complex outcome of labor-rights observance. The chapter presents the step-by-step chronology of the legal petitions, government/corporate responses, and trade-union assessment. Utilizing statistical tables and expert appraisal, chapter 8, "Structural Residues of the Guatemalan Case: An Analysis," examines modifications in Guatemala's Ministry of Labor, courts, wage structure, health services, tripartite discussions, and broader social transformations that are linked to labor-rights conditions.

After discussing the failure of a New York union-sponsored petition, chapter 9, "GSP and Labor Changes in Honduras," focuses on an agreement between the government and the AFL-CIO to equitably apply labor law in the maquila sector. The chapter considers the evolution of labor activism in Honduras.

In chapter 10, "Petitions in the Dominican Republic: Stronger Maquila Unions," the trade-condition strategy achieved its most substantial victory—the actual functioning of maquila unions. The chapter answers why, among many misses, the GSP strategy brought success. It examines the evolution of labor rights, petition antecedents, the Haitian question, the passage of a new labor code, and the battle over code implementation in the free zones.

Chapter 11, "Regional GSP Efforts in Costa Rica, Panama, and Nicaragua," briefly chronicles the impact of the trade-conditions approach with three additional nations. AFL-CIO–sponsored petitions stimulated important, though reluctant, improvements in Costa Rican labor legislation and prevented a major backsliding in Panama. Results from the Nicaraguan case also offer salient insights on the application of labor-rights principles under divergent types of governments.

In chapter 12, "Workers Evaluate Trade-based Labor Strategies," trade-union leaders who have participated in GSP actions reflect on the lessons of a labor-conditioned approach to regional trade. In addition to their insights and reservations, they discuss what this portends for future trade-union cooperation and for "social charters" that affect trade.

The concluding chapter reflects on the results of my 1994–96 fieldwork in Guatemala and El Salvador and includes data from more than eighty lengthy interviews with businessmen, trade-union leaders, and government officials. It also incorporates data from other nations in Central America and the Caribbean and abstracts of GSP-related labor-reform legislation. While the results are largely drawn from qualitative research and the reconciliation of conflicting views, quantitative data that test relationships and measure institutional performance add legitimacy to qualitative findings. Finally, after discussing the complexities of testing the two hypotheses about the impact of trade conditions on worker rights, the study suggests policy implications that combine state and non-governmental approaches to achieve a more humane model for trade.

Part 1

General Considerations on Labor Rights

CHAPTER 1

Caribbean Basin Workers Search
for Decent Treatment

Juan José Antonio García is not one to take up radical causes. He works hard. In the evenings he prefers a quiet life with his family; on Sunday he plays soccer with his friends. In early 1994, the twenty-six-year-old and his co-workers at La Exacta Ranch were aroused to action. Carlos Blanco, the ranch owner, had refused to pay them the legal minimum wage of 11.60 quetzals ($2.00). In fact, Sr. Blanco would only promise half of that amount—6 quetzals ($1.06) per day. So in early February, Juan José and several other workers endured the six-hour ride on the bus from their home near Coatepeque, Quetzaltenango, to Guatemala City. There, they visited the offices of the independent union confederation UNSITRAGUA, seeking advice about what to do.

Shortly thereafter, with the confederation's help, Juan José and several other ranch hands filed a court complaint concerning their pay along with an injunction that made it illegal to fire any worker until the wage question was resolved. They also took their first steps to organize a union. This infuriated Carlos Blanco and his managers, who not only disregarded the court injunction but demanded retribution from the organizers and sympathizers. "They fired 78 of us and replaced us with other workers, simply because we demanded our minimum wages," explained Juan José in a firm, sad voice. So after the July firings and nearly five months of court inaction on the wage issue or the protective injunction, "we finally determined that our only recourse was public attention." On July 17, the La Exacta campesinos occupied the *finca* (farm) in a sit-down action to protest the unfair terminations and their employer's refusal to pay minimum wages. Several weeks later, representatives from the Human Rights Procurator and Labor Ministry arrived to negotiate a settlement, but the company would accept no interference or compromise.

Yet few anticipated ranch owner Carlos Blanco's August 24 revenge. With guns blazing and helicopters hovering overhead, five hundred Guatemalan police and private security agents descended on the small group of La Exacta ranch hands. "When we heard the helicopters, we were terrified," recounts Juan José. "We wanted to run but we were there with women and children. The soldiers surrounded us and started to fire tear gas and bullets." Swat teams immediately killed Efraín Recinos Gómez and Basilio Pedro Carreto, shooting the latter in the back. They wounded eleven others and captured more than a hundred, including Diego Orozco García, a member of the union executive committee. Some hours later, they tossed his mutilated body from a helicopter furnished by a nearby landlord.

The La Exacta killings represent old-style traditional violence in the agro-export sector. However, they occurred less than two years after Guatemala had reformed its labor code to increase penalties against those violating mini-mum-wage laws. The code also purportedly improved court procedures to fine those blocking labor organizing. Despite the labor code, the group-imposed rules of Guatemala's traditional elite prevailed. After the occupation began, the ranch owner refused any agreement with national government officials and instead won a judgment for eviction from a local court. When the case became widely publicized, the police cited the eviction notice to justify their behavior, claiming that the campesinos had illegally occupied the land. The authorities were quick to brutally remove the workers, but not to enforce the wage law or court injunction.

In October 1994, the fired trade unionists elected Juan José as their leader. When he arrived in the U.S. to present his case to the United States Trade Representative (USTR), Juan José reflected on the union's status: "Because of the attack, four of the seventy-eight fired are now dead. Forty-four have left for other employment, and thirty of us continue to struggle for our union rights. Should we give up our demands, the ranch owner has offered to rein-state us and pay 19 quetzals a day which is what they are now paying the replacement workers. Of course we would have no protection in the future should they decide to lower the pay or do whatever they want to us. They don't want to recognize us. Our union has been granted legal status [*personalidad juridica*] that we want to preserve. So we have not accepted their offer."

To counteract Carlos Blanco's refusal, the union waged a national effort, meeting with Monica Pinto, special delegate from the United Nations; Osvaldo Clayton of the Organization of American States; and Labor Minister Gladys Morfin. The parties made an attempt at reconciliation, but the talks broke off. During Spring 1995, Juan José and the La Exacta committeemen took the long bus ride to the capital to testify in labor-court proceedings. "We asked the government to investigate since the lives of our campesinos are at stake. Our children are hungry and we need work. They say we are to have free organization in this country, but in reality it is not free."[1] As of 1998, the unionized workers at La Exacta were still unemployed. Although the Organization of American States (OAS) had taken up their case, the local court petition for redress and back pay remained in limbo. While the Quetzaltenango police chief had been detained for questioning, no officials remained in custody for perpetrating the attack.

Far from being unique, the killings at La Exacta Ranch are but one of many similar military attacks in rural areas, for example against the Consejo Nacional de Trabajadores de Campo (CNTC), an organization of itinerant farmers in Honduras. "There are 160,000 landless families in Honduras, and we are starving to death" explained CNTC general secretary Oscar Mejía. "The landless peasant has nothing; no food, no water, no electricity, no health care, nothing. And yet there are huge amounts of land, much of it owned by the multinationals, which is left uncultivated." Because of this, the campesinos had no choice but to occupy the unused tracts, even though over the past several years Honduran security forces had killed twenty CNTC members for doing so (NLC 1991:27).

But even when campesinos do hold title to the land, this is no protection from abuse. On May 3, 1991, more than a dozen uniformed troops under the command of Honduran Colonel Leonel Galindo opened fire on members of the Asociación Nacional de Campesenas de Honduras (ANACH). Court victory in hand, they had just settled a small plot of 28 hectares near Agua Caliente. The troops machine-gunned the unarmed ANACH unionists, killing five and seriously wounding seven more. "While lying there wounded and pleading for help, two of those killed were shot in the head at point-blank range" (NLC 1991:35).

Parallel with killings with impunity, threats also remain a traditional form of rural oppression in Central America (see Delgado González 1994). In another well-publicized Guatemalan occupation in August 1994, campesinos at the huge Spanish-owned San Gregorio rubber plantation acted after two and a half years of ineffectual court judgments. The Supreme Court itself had decreed that they had been fired unjustly, but no agency would enforce the remedy, so the workers finally occupied the finca. For several weeks, vitriolic diatribes in defense of private property filled Guatemala's public media, with virtually no mention of the underlying issues or supportive court judgments. The plantation owner equated the union to "Basque terrorists." Guatemalan President Ramiro de León Carpio threatened to expel any foreign supporters who ventured near the plantation. Army swat teams poised to attack. At the last moment, the dispute was resolved.

Likewise, in March 1998 more than 300 anti-riot police descended on workers attempting to organize unions at several banana plantations that supply Del Monte Fresh Produce. Twenty-two workers had been illegally fired the previous month after obtaining a protective injunction. Firings also occurred on plantations producing for Chiquita. Following a work slowdown by sympathetic unions on other plantations, the police began house-to-house searches to locate and evict workers that sought affiliation with SITRABI banana union. After they left, a work stoppage led to more firings and a strike. It required considerable international pressure and personal visits by the vice ministers of labor and government to temporarily resolve the standoff, although workers remained vulnerable to arrest (NISGUA 1998; U.S./GLEP 1998).

La Exacta, Agua Caliente, San Gregorio, and Del Monte/Chiquita are all symptomatic of the enduring conflict between landholders claiming their privileges and workers evoking their rights to decent treatment. The cases reflect a much larger pattern of abuse of both rural and urban working people throughout Central America and the Caribbean. Despite legislated labor reforms in the early 1990s, workers in most Central American nations have questioned their usefulness. When employees invoked the law as a safeguard, they found that the institutions established to provide protection (the police, the courts, the ministries of labor) remained enmeshed in a system that encouraged private owners (and public managers) to disregard basic standards of worker treatment.

But La Exacta, Agua Caliente, San Gregorio, and Del Monte/Chiquita represent the traditional agricultural sector. As global trade and investment in *non*-traditional sectors increase, work conditions are projected to improve. This is one of the questions that is central to our investigation. Will trade modify the linkage between employer power and institutional subservience that has previously penetrated all segments of the society? When we consider labor activities in these areas of fresh investment, stretching from rural land and wage conflicts, to attempts at maquila union organizing, to privatization efforts of state enterprises, do we find changes from prior patterns, fewer delays in processing worker petitions, and reduced abuse, official bribery, and corruption? Has labor legislation and implementation proved a measure of success for non-traditional-sector workers? How do the workers themselves respond—those in the rural areas, in manufacturing, in maquila organizing and in state enterprises?

Rural Land and Wage Conflicts

Some Central American workers who labor in non-traditional export crops have earned higher incomes than in previous rural production. Nevertheless, many have not (see Burnham et al. 1992; W. Ramírez et al. 1994). In 1995, for example, the $2.70-per-day pay *standard* for Guatemalan agricultural workers remained among the lowest in the hemisphere and less than half of what most agricultural unions said they needed to meet living costs. However, all unions agree that *payment* of the legally required standard remains the primary issue. Rafael Can Chabac and Francisca Chinik of the Coordinación Nacional Indígena y Campesina (CONIC) and Carlo Lobos, who worked with the Centro de Investigación y Educación (CIEP), cited extensive noncompliance with current minimal standards throughout the country. CONIC has provided documentary evidence to successive Guatemalan labor ministers that at least sixty fincas in six departments paid below $2.00 a day. In many, women were paid half the men's wage. Many of the fincas produced nontraditional crops.

Lobos had been threatened with death countless times because of his organizational activities. He told of the "Fincas Cadanom, and La Chote where they raise cardamom and peppers. Workers receive between three and four quetzals a day."[2] "Even less attention is paid to women in the countryside," pointed out CIEP's Adelia del Gado. "Often there is only one salary received in the family, and it goes to the man. Women are also not registered in government statistics for rural workers."[3]

Organizing Plant Workers

For many years, workers within the Central American and Caribbean industrial sectors have been valiantly struggling to organize. In Guatemala in the late 1970s and early 1980s, Coca-Cola workers led one of the most inspiring efforts against intimidation, arbitrary firings, and below-minimum standard pay. Before they solidified an effective contract in 1985, they had to endure two extensive plant occupations and the slaughter of eight of their leaders. In 1980, many of their brother and sister trade unionists in the Confederación Nacional de Trabajadores (CNT) were kidnapped and disappeared (see Albizúrez 1988; Frundt 1987b; Levenson-Estrada 1994). "To this date, I suffer," says the wife of one CNT leader who was taken in 1980. "I dream that he comes and looks for us. I don't dream of his being dead. . . . I only dream of him alive . . . a terrible anguish" (Reed and Brandow 1996:68).

Angel was another who lost a sister in that onslaught against CNT trade unionists. Angel remained active in labor activities. In 1988, two men and two women followed him to a picket line where they drugged and beat him and threatened him with death. A number of times since, he and members of his family have been followed and assaulted. He was forced to be vigilant "of the children's security twenty-four hours a day. When they go to school, my wife and I are thinking of the hour they're going to leave and the hour they're going to arrive. . . . If at all possible, we pick them up" (quoted in Reed and Brandow 1996:43). Such consciousness still characterized the lives of many active trade unionists in Central America in the 1990s.

What also characterizes their lives is the society's disregard for the labor rights that *are* legally granted. From the day that women workers at one apparel plant won a dispute with management over forming a union in 1987, "management began to separate us from the rest of the plant. We were put into a kind of alleyway behind the factory, which we called 'the chicken coop' because it really wasn't suitable for 65 people to work in. . . . They even made us leave by another door. The supervisor told our other work mates not to associate with us because we unionists had leprosy and they could catch it!" (Hooks 1993:32). Tomas Jolón and twenty-three other unionists had a similar experience after winning union recognition at the Lunafil thread plant in 1988. Following a 410-day occupation and many death threats against union family members, the company recognized the union but isolated its members. "It becomes more difficult to negotiate a contract," explained Jolón. "We are at a disadvantage, because we haven't reached the number of members required by the law; 25% of the workers must be affiliated with the union to negotiate. . . . We now see that we can't have any hope. What the company did was to give the (wage) increase . . . to everyone . . . but no increase to union members" (Reed and Brandow 1996:138). Then, in May 1994, the company closed without paying salaries to anyone.

Inspired by the victory at Coca-Cola in Guatemala City, workers won union recognition in late 1992 at INCASA, a Coca-Cola franchise in Puerto Barrios on Guatemala's Atlantic Coast. The owner immediately fired the thirty-six activists. The case came before a local judge for what was usually a routine reinstatement pending a full hearing, but the owner offered the official an incentive sufficient to deny the workers' request. After eighteen months of legal battles, Rodolfo Robles, at the time leader of the Guatemala City Coca-Cola Union and general secretary of the Food Workers Federation, frustratingly described the outcome: "Twenty of the fired workers still out of work, accused of theft, and a phony plant bombing set off by the Puerto Barrios management. We have now lost in two courts. The union continues to exist as a legal entity, even though all members have been fired, some of their most important files have been lost, and the people are fearful because of the psychological pressure."[4]

Despite an agreement with the International Union of Food and Allied Workers (IUF) and Coca-Cola International in 1995, the INCASA owner never recognized the union. His intimidations prevented any fresh organizing drive or favorable court decisions. This time, a modern manufacturer was able to subvert the law in face of considerable international pressure.

The labor picture in the Caribbean Basin's industrial sector is not bright. As recently as 1994 in Guatemala there were hundreds of death threats and more than thirty executions of union leaders. In Central America "there is a great force against unions," commented Enrique Alvarez, former head of the CIEP labor training Center. "Only one organizing campaign succeeds out of five or six, allowing many companies to function without unions. Many other unions have been destroyed. While there are fewer outright deaths and death threats than in the early 1980s when 80 percent of the trade-union leadership disappeared, now employers exert economic and psychological pressure to force employees to leave unions. Tactics encompass buy-outs (indemnization), employer-sponsored solidarity associations, and other benefits designed to divide unions. Leaders with less experience are facing these new tactics."[5]

Organizing in the Maquila Sector

Abuses have become especially pronounced in the rapidly growing apparel assembly factories. A few workers among the many, Lesley Rodriquez, Judith Yaniera Viera, Soida Alvarez, and the workers at Gabo Industries recount typical treatment.

Lesley Rodriguez

In 1994, fifteen-year-old Lesley Rodriguez reported to a U.S. Senate subcommittee about conditions at the Galaxy plant in Honduras.[6] Since age thirteen she had been sewing sweaters and other apparel there for subcontractors like Liz Claiborne.

"We start at 7:30 A.M. until 7:00 P.M. Some days we work until 9:30 P.M. and even until 10:00 P.M. . . . Sometimes we work 80 hours a week. Management has set up a production quota so high that it is impossible for us to fill it. When we manage to do it, they increase it again the following day, so we are always behind the quota and under a lot of pressure. Many workers are forced to take their work home to be able to fill the quota set up by management. Where I work now, around 70 or 80 workers take their work home. Sometimes they work until 1:00 A.M. to finish it and they are not paid overtime. To go to work we have to get up at 5:30 A.M.

"We are searched when we arrive . . . we cannot talk during the day; if we do they scream at us and send us home with no pay, for four or five days. The supervisors are always shouting to work faster and faster. Sometimes they beat us on the head or on the back. Some supervisors like to touch the girls' behinds or breasts; some girls let them do it because they can get more money per week.

"We have no breaks during the day except for the half hour lunch. To go to the bathroom we have to raise a hand and ask permission. Bathrooms are locked. We are allowed to go to the bathroom only twice a day . . . if we stay long they punish us.

"Because this factory produces sweaters, there is a lot of dust in the air and we cough a lot. Many workers have respiratory problems such as asthma or bronchitis. We have no health coverage and when we get sick they put us on leave without pay."

Lesley had left school in the third grade to work and help her family. Although the factory managers promised her she could finish school, they did not end the work shift until 9:00 P.M. Finally, in 1993 she had enough and joined the union to force management "to treat us better and respect our rights." When management found out, they dismissed thirty-five of Lesley's co-workers and threatened the others.

But the employees fought back: "We went on strike; 600 workers participated." Management reacted by firing more workers and "made a lot of promises that they did not keep." They would "not allow Labor Inspectors to enter the factory."

Lesley and her co-workers "would like the American people to know how much we suffer making these sweaters." She learned "Liz Claiborne's sweaters are sold for $90. Here, I am paid $.38/hour just to make them," which works out to about $21.50 a week. Honduras labor minister Cecilio Zavala responded that Lesley's was an isolated case, not an indication of massive violations (*El Tiempo*, Nov. 25, 1994). But the young apparel worker said, "We have not just a hundred but thousands of testimonies like mine."

Judith Yaniera Viera

Eighteen-year-old Judith Yaniera Viera tells a very similar story about her experience at the Mandarin maquiladora in El Salvador that assembles shirts for the GAP, Eddie Bauer, and J.C. Penney (quoted in Briggs and Kernaghan 1996:36–37). "From Monday to Thursday, our work shift went from seven in the morning until nine at night. On Fridays, we would work straight through the night, starting at 7 A.M. and working until 4 A.M. We would sleep overnight at the factory on the floor. The following day, we would work from 7 A.M. until 5 P.M." With all these hours Judith would occasionally earn over $40.00 a month.

"The supervisors often screamed at the women. They would slap us with the shirts and tell us to work faster. Even though we worked a 14-hour day, we were only permitted to go to the bathroom twice. Each time, we had to get a ticket from the supervisor, and then we were allowed no more than three to five minutes. It gets very hot in the plant, and the ventilation is poor. In the factory, the drinking water they give us is contaminated."

Viera spoke of many underage women workers at Mandarin who were not allowed to go to school and of special punishments for those who did not agree to work overtime. Women were also "not allowed to go to an outside health clinic even though they deduct medical insurance from our pay." They would have to go to the plant's doctor, who often simply prescribed contraceptives so they wouldn't become pregnant. Yet Viera also recounted being thoroughly frightened by Mandarin's head of personnel, an ex-colonel who first propositioned and then followed her: When "the workers formed a union, the colonels hired thugs to beat up the union leaders. In June, 1995, the company fired more than 350 workers." Thugs went to unionists' homes and "demanded that they quit the union, saying that if they didn't they would suffer the consequences."

Finally, they tortured the union general secretary, and fired Judith and her two sisters. "We've all been blacklisted," she reported the following month. "We cannot find new jobs."

Soida Alvarez

Soida Alvarez is also out of work, even though she serves as union president of SEC Apparel Ltd., a company that employs 1,200 women in El Salvador's Santa Bartolo Free Zone. They were able to organize "with great difficulty. I worked with these women to form a union and demand negotiations. The reason we wanted a union was because of the way we were treated. They beat us and then called us names like 'stupid!' 'brute!'

"We made jackets and overalls. They were always introducing new styles. Because each style was distinct, we often had to change over the machines, putting in fresh thread, etc. This was a special problem for the recent hires. The managers would not allow sufficient time for the trainees to learn how to operate these machines or get up to speed in production quantity. This is when they would call us names. But then they took it a step further.

"Without us realizing it, they set us up in thirteen lines, sixty machines to a line. One line did special projects, but the rest of us were usually on the same project. When we finally did gain experience with a style, they would change the production goals and incentives from one day to another. For example, they might set a goal of 200 for a line for a day, and offer to pay an incentive over and above that: 'move it up from 200 to 300 pieces,' they would say, 'and the extra pay is yours.' Then once they got the production up, they would put a new goal in place, or they would do 'efficiency studies' and move the new base to 300, with no extra pay unless one did 400. So sometimes workers would refuse to increase their production. Then the supervisors would hang a watch around their neck, and say to them, 'You *can* make the new goal!'"

They had twelve '*manuales*,' one for each line, who would circulate and ideally give each of the sixty a bathroom break. This had to be between 9:30 and 11:00 A.M. or 1:00 and 4:00 P.M., for at other times the lavatories were closed for cleaning. Yet only two could be excused at one time, since the management had issued two 'fichas' for each line, and they had to be returned before others could go. So we were allowed four minutes to go to the bathroom, which was difficult to accomplish. If we returned late, we risked having to pay a 'damage' payment of 36 colons per minute. With everyone from the various lines crowding into the bathrooms, this could sometimes be difficult to avoid.

"While on the line, we needed to ask to have water. When permission came, the water was often not potable; sometimes it was very yellow and would make us sick. Occasionally, they would put in chlorine, but that did not change its composition. We also could not have fans (except for a few in the ceiling). The heat sometimes would become so intense, we would ask to be excused at noon; they always said 'no.'

"So this is why we began to form a union in October 1993. They did not find out about it for another year, but then, on October 26, 1994, they fired 200 on the spot, using the excuse that we did not have enough raw materials to work with. But they only let go those in the union, and we discovered plenty of basic material in the warehouse. We went to the minister of labor, the procurator of human rights, and to the various courts to demand justice. We were able to get seven of our directors rehired but the company does not want to rehire the rest of us."

The Gabo Case

Workers at Gabo del Salvador describe how they came to form a union in Spring 1995. Gabo's 500 workers produce apparel for export in a complex of five huge semicircular prefabricated sheds that take up nearly a third of the San Marcos Export Processing Zone (EPZ) compound. Normally, their work shift is from 7:00 A.M. to 7:00 P.M. Bertha, a young mother of a six-year-old, recounted rising at 5:00 A.M. each day to catch the bus to work, and returning home at 8:30 P.M. Her costs, including round trip and baby care, totaled 39 colons (almost $5.00), nearly equivalent to her salary, but there was no other work to be found where she lived. Work requirements were stringent; in years previous the company fired at least two women for becoming pregnant. Then, in March 1995 a woman died of a burst appendix. At first Gabo management denied her permission to leave to see the doctor. When they finally allowed her to leave during her lunch break, she discovered that the hospital clinic would not accept her insurance card. Although the company had deducted medical coverage costs from her pay, it had not submitted those payments to El Salvador's Institute for Social Security. During the previous six months, Gabo had failed to send in funds for half of its employees. The government investigated and allegedly found that ten companies in the free zone were not forwarding the fee. The workers believed the number was undoubtedly higher.

When the workers discovered the cause of their co-worker's death, their anger deepened to anguish. To make matters worse, the company refused to allow them to attend her funeral. When eighteen disregarded management's mandate, they were summarily fired. Gabo also balked at complying with the labor-code requirement that the company must pay two months' salary to cover funeral expenses and education of the deceased's offspring. Anguish broadened. The workers blocked the EPZ gates where Gabo was located, permitting no one to enter. At the same time, the eighteen who were fired also formed a union.

The company agreed to rehire those fired and to provide 1,000 colones ($125.00) for funeral and education expenses. This minimal response infuriated other workers, and soon a hundred signed up. In turn, Gabo management retaliated, "enticing the workers with other things, such as an excursion to the beach on Saturdays or extending work hours to keep them away from attending our assembly," said one organizer. As the cluster waited for the 7 P.M. shift to let out, security police sauntered by, eyeing the group suspiciously. The young woman organizer quickly responded about how important the Saturday meeting was: It would take another 151 union members before they could demand negotiations on a contract.[8]

The testimonies from the three women and those at Gabo are not universally shared. Some workers view maquila work as preferable to hard labor on the farm. Eber Orellana Vásquez gives "thanks to the maquila . . . my monthly income is seven times what I made in the countryside." Vásquez had milked cows on a dairy ranch, and every time he visited, everyone wanted "to come back with me. The work there is very hard . . . and the bosses are always mean" (Rohter 1996a:A14).

Most researchers and labor leaders agree, however, that the women's experiences are typical in regional maquila (see Safa 1995, 1997 on the Dominican). In the last half of the 1990s, "violations repeat themselves over and over," elaborated Nelson González, textile organizing director at the Federación de Asociaciones y Sindicatos Independientes de El Salvador (FEASIES), the labor federation that helped to organize the Gabo workers. "Workers face mandatory overtime, and they are not even paid for the extra hours. If they don't work extra hours, companies dock their "Sunday" pay.[9] Companies also are not contributing to the government-sponsored health plan, or any plan. Like Gabo, the Hang Chung plant with 1,000 workers and Lindo Text with 500 would prefer to offer pregnant women 3,000 colones to resign."

"The majority of workers suffer violations of both labor and human rights, especially firings," stressed Carlos Hurtado, a leader of the Confederación de Trabajadores Democraticos (CTD). "As at Mandarin International, other companies have also increased production speed-ups. We have documented sexual mistreatment and striking of women. Some have died while working."[10]

"When maquila employers seek to justify their firings, they say they need to reduce their work force," said Mario Lutini of the Guatel Union, "but really they turn over their workforce to avoid facing a *pliego de peticiones* [list of complaints]. This is because they demonstrate the greatest human rights and labor rights violations—against women who have children to care for." As Adelia del Gado noted, "70% of those working in the maquila are women," and they find "it very difficult" to blow any whistles.[11]

"In 1990 they were paid 57c/hour; in 1995 it had fallen to 27c," explained Miguel Ramírez, head of the Federación Sindical de Trabajadores de El Salvador (FESTRAES). There is great corruption. They rob workers of their assigned quotas. Only 40% pay minimum salary, or they pay the minimum for eight hours, but they require work for two to four more. Out of 1,800,000 workers in the country, only 350,000 have daily employment."[12]

Perhaps the greatest fear of owners is "labor insurgence" in the maquila factories, something they publicly linked to the occupations at La Exacta, San Gregorio, and other instances of union militancy, whether in traditional or non-traditional sectors.

"We have a large number of workers and five export processing zones (EPZs) that are unorganized," emphasized Nelson González. "The government is threatening to open up more where they won't permit free organization. Our object is to organize so that we can motivate the free zone employers to respect the labor laws. While the majority of owners are Korean and Japanese, a small number are from the U.S. In any case, the Koreans etc. also have distribution houses in Miami and New York. We are in favor of generating employment, but not without guaranteeing labor rights. The companies respond that if we organize they will go to Guatemala, Honduras, Nicaragua, and ultimately to Haiti, so many are afraid."[13]

"Abuses have definitely increased in the last year, and many women are attempting to form unions," stated Carlos Hurtado of the CTD, which backed the union organizing efforts of Soida Alvarez and Judith Yaniera Viera.[14] Hurtado and González, as well as Lesley Rodriquez, Judith Yaniera Viera, Soida Alvarez, and the Gabo workers all admit that under current conditions, this is something very difficult to accomplish (see also U.S. Department of Labor 1990).

Carlos González Méndez works at the textile plant Industrial Nacional (INSINCA). Because of a conflict in 1989, the owners there fired 250 employees, including Carlos and other members of the union executive committee. "For the past seven years, we have been trying to get back to work," said Carlos. After a court order, the company agreed to pay salaries to four members of the committee, including Carlos. "But they won't let us enter the plant, afraid we will convince others. The Minister of Labor has decreed that it is illegal to prevent contact with other workers in the company, but the company continues to do so. The case has gone back to the Ministry, but it has not taken further action."[15]

Concerns of Public Workers

Despite globalization, death threats and kidnappings remain a primary method of discouraging labor participation in Caribbean Basin societies; firings and intimidation also play an important role. However, the more apparently benign but often arbitrary modification of work structures can also have far-reaching implications, especially among the largely unionized public-sector workers. Nowhere is the change more apparent than in recent government decisions to "privatize" traditional areas of state services. Popular among conservative U.S. lawmakers, the sale of government properties (telephones, airlines) and the contracting out of activities (from road building to health) are suddenly becoming expedient ways of reducing state budgets in Central America and the Caribbean as they have in South America (see Accolla 1989).

Privatization Without Negotiations

While state-sector unions realize the potential damage that privatization portends, they also allow for possible social benefits. Their main concern is that the workers are completely excluded from any discussions that would afford them an opportunity to present their perspectives on cost-savings and assurances of employment. Both they and private-sector unions also fear the impact on services. "They want to privatize education in a country largely illiterate, to privatize health, telecommunications, essential services, even natural resources such as rivers . . . all will favor the rich," insisted Nery Barrios, former leader of the Guatemalan grassroots coalition Unidad Accion Sindical y Popular (UASP) and current labor advisor to the Congressional Labor Committee.[16]

"Since the end of 1995, they have reinforced decree 471 to allow terminations to make the public sector 'more suitable,'" reported Mario Vasquez, director of public information for the Salvadoran labor federation FEASIES.
"Some were voluntary retirements, but the objective was to eliminate the
union leadership.

"Public sector strikes and marches helped obtain some benefits; but the goal
of decree 471 is to prevent union resistance in all institutions: the telephone
workers, the electrical workers, the workers in pensions and social security—all
among the strongest unions. Fear among workers is high. The government is
investing 400,000 colones to promote privatization and advertise what is good
for the workers, but the sale of properties [e.g., the Asociación Nacional de
Telecomunicaciones telephone company, ANTEL] will go to friends of the
ARENA party now in power. We don't have the funds to show how these institutions guarantee that certain basic services reach more people. The government seeks short-term funds; but does not consider the longer term benefits that
will help the people. It is an ugly situation; after the signing of the peace accords,
they are moving against both the maquila workers and the public sector workers. It is not easy to reinforce union solidarity."

In Guatemala, Alvaro Arzú, elected president in 1996, gave greater attention to human rights (see Garst 1996). However, in line with the presidents
in El Salvador and Costa Rica, he also committed his administration to large
scale privatization. "Fundamentally, we find ourselves in a new world economic situation, and Guatemala is not an exception," explained Sergio
Guzman, leader of the Unión Sindical de Trabajadores de Guatemala (UNSI-
TRAGUA). "Some of the state institutions, supposedly created to benefit
workers, have passed to private control such as INCAP and the Banco de
Trabajadores. The neo-liberal government imposed an anti-strike law on the
public sector to achieve 'flexibility,' not only opposing the right to strike, *but
also* challenging the right to unionize. In Guatemala, as on a world level,
unions are seen as an obstacle. The current government is doing nothing regarding poverty, much less the living conditions of workers, while business
seeks even lower taxes."[17]

Case in Point: Privatization at a Public Hospital
The Esquintla Regional Hospital in Guatemala offers a complex but revealing
example of workers being excluded from the privatization process, and the
consequent impact this portends for services to the poor. The hospital was
constructed in 1981, a four-story modern building of about a hundred beds on
the regional capital's outskirts along the road to El Salvador. In just over a
decade, it was in disrepair, with ceilings falling, Formica peeling from nurs-
ing-station counters, and no backup water system. By 1995, the hospital did

not have sufficient medicines or materials to meet the needs of southern coast workers, many of whom were admits from accidents in the sugar fields. The half-full men's ward smelled of urine. Little babies at risk were supplied with oxygen, but by the end of the week, the supplies had been depleted.

According to registered nurse Ericka Aziza Tuch, general secretary of the Esquintla Hospital Workers Union, and several of her companions, conditions had worsened after 1991 when the government cut back funding for its four regional hospitals. Besides general deterioration at the Esquintla facility, the sweltering heat in the operating area caused acute concern. Engineers from Fundazucar, a private foundation supported by the nation's wealthy landowners and sugar producers, offered to install air conditioning. At first the hospital staff appreciated their involvement, but according to Sra. Aziza Tuch, soon Fundazucar rehabilitated and took control of the hospital's outpatient building.[18] None of the new employees in outpatient services were members of the union.

Union workers say Fundazucar signed a pilot agreement with the Ministry of Health to set up the outpatient clinic as a self-financed unity in exchange for tax breaks on sugar: "In spite of a guarantee for health services under the constitution, each patient is required to pay $1 [or half a day's minimum salary] for the first consultation. Then they have to pay additional fees for clinic-related expenses. Thus, the sugar owners are making money from the takeover," explained Ericka Aziza. "Japan donated an electrocardiogram machine to the hospital, yet the clinic uses it and charges the patients well beyond cost for each use." The union leaders claimed that Fundazucar also used state-funded buildings and hospital services and equipment (such as telephone, light, water, medical services, laundry, laboratories, supplies such as photocopying, anesthesiology, and several other services), reducing funds available for hospital operations. Some doctors also received double salaries, even though they only work in the clinic area. When confronted, the local hospital administrator would neither confirm nor deny the charges.[19]

The situation was exacerbated in March 1994 during a national public-workers' strike that shut down the entire Esquintla facility. Ericka Aziza received threats for her organizing efforts. "We have great fear about what will happen to us, to all the workers here!" she said. "We know they are planning to cut personnel, but they have not discussed anything with us. Several times, we have sought meetings with the Minister, Vice Minister and Attorney for the health department, but they refuse to see us. Most of all, we want to offer our positions and have our questions answered. What are the Fund's expenses, and its plans for the future? We are willing to discuss what is good and bad about the present situation, but wish to protect our rights."[20]

For working people, hospital "privatization" is just one example of excluding union members from discussing plans to reorganize state agencies. Like others, the 130 union members at the Esquintla Regional Hospital foresaw greater privatization ahead, with potential job losses to themselves. Major regional hospitals in Coban, Chiquimula, and Quetzaltenango became involved in similar arrangements, often with Fundazucar. In 1997, the Guatemalan Congress passed a revised health code that imposed fees for all services, with subsidies for the poor.

Other Areas of Privatization

Workers had similar reactions to other types of privatization. In 1993, Carlo Lobos, general secretary of the Public Workers Union in the department of Alta Verapaz, Guatemala, anticipated privatization and union disappearances in road construction. The ministry stated the workers lacked "sufficient business skills." When his union protested, "services awarded to outside contractors, many were illicitly fired."[21] In December 1992, fifty-four workers were ordered reinstated from the Coban Public Works Department; union activity was the cause of their firing, and in violation of accords that the government of Guatemala signed with the ILO. Lobos explained that "union activists, including myself, have been persistently threatened with claims that we are members of guerilla organizations."[22] By July 1996, the Arzú government had laid off 2,500 public-sector workers.

Rail, electric, and telephone companies also went on the privatization block. "We have shown what we can do," elaborated Mario Lutini from the Guatel (telephone) Workers Union. "We earned 242 million quetzals [$450,000] in 1993, and have used it on 18 new projects. Between 1994 and 1995 we expanded our lines from 235,000 to 288,000 customers. The telephone company is one of the most profitable, so they all want it. The company's president has not answered our requests for a direct discussion." Lutini predicted that under privatization, services would be cut in rural areas.

Structural Factors in the Enforcement of Labor Rights

These experiences of Caribbean Basin workers in rural, urban, maquila, and state sectors all reveal a persistent pattern of rights abuse unaffected by increased trade. As one municipal unionists puts it, "When a worker knows the labor laws, employers don't let them keep their jobs because they say they're going to organize the people."[23] But underlying this pattern is the failure of social institutions. It is difficult for readers north of the Rio Grande to appreciate the virtual paralysis of state funded institutions in carrying out and enforcing the basic labor rights that legally exist in Basin countries. Unionists describe the courts and the labor ministry as an instance.

Judicial Bottlenecks

When facing direct threats or privatization, or simply when thwarted by the refusal of business to negotiate, unions are citing constitutional requirements that collective bargaining is obligatory. However, there is no effective institutional mechanism to assure this will happen.

As an illustration, Guatemala's 1992 reformed labor code separated labor or "collective" cases from individual cases in an effort to improve court procedures. For the former, it mandated "Tribunals of Conciliation and Arbitration" that would be conducted by representatives from management and labor. Instead of creating parallel courts as the labor-code reform stipulated, by 1994 the Supreme Court had only established one court, located in several offices on one floor of a building, to resolve the entire nation's labor disputes. Facing a single court brought all labor conflict cases to a standstill since virtually no disputes could be resolved. Many union leaders thought the change had been purposefully rigged to fail. "The system is insufficient to handle the volume of cases.[24] The courts have become more and more behind in their work," said Mario Lutini. "Even if they weren't afraid, campesinos can't travel to the offices here. It is hard enough for us to do so. Thus nothing moves."

Judge Raul Alfredo Pimentel Afreed acknowledged the problems, including the "lack of funding" and "failure of the tribunals." The court administrator and staff openly admitted that it was impossible for those who depended on daily wages to travel to the capital from all over the country to participate in lengthy deliberations. The administrator also cited the lack of direct phone lines or proper equipment necessary for handling the cases. Labor representatives demanded budget modifications and funding so that the court system would begin to function (see chapter 8).

Court conditions may differ in other countries of the region. In Panama, for example, labor representatives believe current procedures are effective and are striving to protect them. But in most area nations, leaders say that court processes are entangled in political pressures and are notoriously encumbered.

Slow Reform at the Ministry of Labor

Workers also believed that most labor ministries were not seriously enforcing the labor laws. Common complaints were that when the labor inspectors did in fact travel to a labor site, they were easily threatened or bribed. Unions sought a purging of corrupt inspectors. In 1995, the Guatemalan minister herself acknowledged the legitimacy of these complaints.

The Guatemalan Economic Ministry had also taken no action to deny export licenses to corporate violators. Guatemalan law encourages consultation if companies violate worker rights, an action the ministry could take without having to rely on the judicial system. "How many export licenses have been denied to worker rights violators in the export sector since July? In 1994 overall? If none, why?" Congressman George Brown asked these questions of USTR ambassador Michael Kantor on September 9, 1995. "It seems a good indicator of how committed the government is to promoting respect for worker rights."[25]

Labor Rights and the Private Sector

Underlying the key immediate issues of threats, arbitrary firings, minimum-wage violations, court bottlenecks, mandated privatization, and dilatory ministry reform is the negative attitude toward labor rights in the private sector. Labor advisor Enrique Alvarez defines the lack of political will as a regional problem for both government officials and employers, something globalization has not changed "except for appearances. In the maquila, they still fire women if they are pregnant, or they give medicines that causes abortions or eliminate sexual interest." Alvarez also offered the example of a coffee agreement that agro-exporters signed with several Guatemalan campesino unions in 1994. "It seems like a change, but in fact, it was designed to prevent a bigger wage increase. The agro-exporters often still didn't pay the salaries anyway."[26]

Most government officials and union leaders agree that the number of enlightened businessmen remains minuscule. "When we sign an agreement," notes labor leader and former congressman Juan Francisco Alfaro, "the employers say all is well, but in fact little is well. Union liberty is jeopardized. Potential leaders are fired. . . . They seek to make sure there are only a minimum number of union members so they will not have to negotiate."[27]

Rather than seek agreements for labor peace, the hope among many exporters is that Guatemala will soon become part of NAFTA or a similar regional trade agreement that will eliminate GSP labor-rights requirements. From 1994 through May 1997, Guatemalan businesspeople mounted an intensive lobbying campaign to remove GSP scrutiny, but local leaders say they made little effort to talk with labor. Most Guatemalan trade unions gave up their hope for any tripartite business-government-labor dialogue.

This chapter reviews how labor leaders and workers in Central America and the Caribbean perceive employment conditions. They make few distinctions between practices in traditional and nontraditional sectors, suggesting that enhanced trade has not conveyed labor-rights improvements. For example, they report widespread intimidation against union organizing, especially in the maquila sector.

Do the thwarted expectations of these trade unionists present a biased assessment of trade impact throughout the Caribbean Basin? While their views reflect a broad survey of opinion from major labor confederations (notably in Guatemala and El Salvador), they may not accurately reflect the full reality. The answer leads us to the debate about how labor rights are best achieved.

CHAPTER 2

The Debate over Methods
of Achieving Labor Rights

In chapter 1 the Central American and Caribbean workers from modern as well as traditional sectors poured forth, recounted the abuses they experienced in their workplaces and the need for improved labor conditions in their countries. Few readers would be unmoved by their testimonies of tedious hours, low pay, threats, and even death. Nevertheless it remains a challenging step to translate their subjective experiences into a clear definition of what rights are at stake and how they are best achieved. This chapter attempts to clarify these two questions.

Others have eloquently discussed the philosophical and cultural bases of human rights (Rawls 1971) and human-rights policy in Latin America (Schoultz 1981; Crahan 1982). The remaining task is to delineate the consensus about what rights people deserve in the workplace.[1] During the first half of the twentieth century, many of the world's nations established basic employee rights via the International Labour Organisation (ILO), which now represents governments, workers, and employers from nearly 200 countries. Despite political and bureaucratic compromises, the best summary of these rights can be found among the ILO's first hundred "conventions." While it may seem tedious, the sorting out of ILO "instruments" can lead us to those core rights that have achieved quasi-universal acceptance. Despite their monitoring, ILO conventions and recommendations are only acknowledged and implemented voluntarily. Nothing can force nations to comply, and their violations remain at a significant level. Thus the second, more controverted, question emerges: How are these codified rights best assured? This chapter is an examination of the debate over whether these basic rights are best achieved through market forces or through other institutional mechanisms. Chapter 3 then takes up the question of using trade requirements for obtaining observance of worker rights.

ILO Standards

The primary institutional proponent of current labor standards is the ILO, based in Geneva. Begun in 1919, the ILO evolved from a focus on industrial conditions to the general conditions that all workers faced (see Valticos 1979; French 1994). Its purpose remained normative—to promote a regulatory framework that assures employee rights in the world of work.

Constituted by equitably proportioned tripartite representatives from government, business, and labor who convene annually, the ILO proposes conventions designed to improve work conditions in conjunction with increased productivity and earnings. ILO economists "stress the potential benefits of interventions, holding that regulated markets adjust better than unregulated labor markets to shocks." They endorse "tripartite consultations and collective bargaining as the best way to determine labor outcomes" (Plant 1994:10). The ILO also approves non-binding recommendations that detail methods of compliance. Member states vote some instruments a higher rate of endorsement than others. They all commit themselves to integrate the ratified conventions and recommendations into their own legal systems and to monitor implementation or report on why they cannot do so. The function of the ILO's three major committees is to report on government implementation of their own ratified agreements.[2]

Basic Rights Evolve under the ILO, 1919–1952

The chronology of ILO instruments illustrates how a global consensus has developed around basic labor rights. Conventions restricting work time were passed during the early years of the ILO's existence and received widespread acceptance. The agreements limited work hours, mandated rest, created minimum-wage-setting mechanisms, and prohibited forced labor and the hiring of below-age children. In other words, there was widespread agreement that humane work should not extend beyond certain hours and should be paid equitably. The very first ILO convention, the Hours of Work (Industry) Convention (1919), stated that working hours ought not go beyond eight in a single day, or 48 in a week. The fourteenth, the Weekly Rest (Industry) Convention (1921), called for workers to be granted twenty-four consecutive hours of rest within each week.

From the beginning (1919), Convention 5 established minimum ages for children in industry. Convention 26 (1928) created procedures for setting minimum wages. It is important to emphasize that the convention did not establish any specific wage, but rather allowed for each state to create its own wage-fixing system.[3] The Forced Labor Convention, no. 29 (1930), prohibited such type of employment. The Holidays and Pay Convention, no. 52 (1936), guaranteed six days of paid vacation following one year of continuous employment. While these conventions received significant backing from member states, their coverage only extended to industrial workers.

In 1944, the ILO reached a major turning point. Its Declaration of Philadelphia emphasized the dignity of labor and stressed that labor was not to be treated as a commodity under any circumstances. Thus the declaration broadened the organization's constitution to cover general conditions of life for working populations (Valticos 1979; French 1994). In post–World War II planning, this perspective on work and worker freedom was accepted by policy makers as an essential component of other global economic institutions linked to the United Nations. As Pursey (1994:367) argues, "They saw sound money, free trade, trade union rights and social security as shared commitments that would bind nations together . . . [to] prevent a resurgence of militaristic nationalism." Since employers had been granted limited organizational liability via corporate rights, the rights of workers to organize and bargain became the "balancing mechanism between the twin imperatives of economic flexibility and social [and political] security."

Thus, by the conclusion of the ILO's first period, the world community had accepted worker autonomy as well as limited hours and health protections as basic rights. It accepted the ability of workers to freely organize as essential. As productivity rises, wages should not be artificially kept down, explained Pursey (1994:372), but the best means available of reconciling aspirations for social progress with productive potential was to assure that workers had a right to bargain.

This key insight spurred the ILO to pass its two most important conventions guaranteeing labor union functions. The Freedom of Association and Protection of the Right to Organize Convention, no. 87 (1948), stated that workers (and employers) can establish organizations of their own choosing in order to defend their interests. They may create constitutions, elect representatives, establish administrative bodies, and carry out activities free from interference from public and private authorities. The Right to Organize and Collective Bargaining Convention, no. 98 (1949), prevented acts of anti-union discrimination and encouraged voluntary collective bargaining. It rejected employer financing and control of worker associations.[4]

Several other important conventions passed in the early postwar period were meant to reinforce these two essential areas of worker rights. The Labor Inspection Convention, no. 81 (1947), assured implementation of legal regulations regarding industrial work conditions; and the Protection of Wages Convention, no. 95 (1949), monitored timely payment of full wages. The ILO ratified Convention 100 on equal remuneration in 1951, assuring agricultural workers minimum wages and ILO protections. It passed the Social Security

(Minimum Standards) Convention, no. 102, in 1952. That convention consolidated a number of earlier conventions directed at specific sectors. For example, the ILO had afforded women maternity protection via Convention 3 in 1919. The Social Security Convention specified nine types of benefits: medical, sickness, unemployment, pension, injury, family, maternity, invalids, and survivors. Ratifying states had to agree to provide three of the nine benefits for at least half of their employees or 20 percent of their residents.

Mid-century Achievement and Subsequent Reinforcement

Thus, by mid-century, ILO representatives from many participant countries had established the core principles of labor rights, detailing decent working conditions and union freedom. As Plant (1994) suggests, the ILO actions were influential in codifying labor rights within the United Nations Universal Declaration on Human Rights, passed in 1948, and the United Nations International Covenant on Economic, Social, and Cultural Rights, passed in 1966. The Universal Declaration stipulated that everyone had a right to employment, to form and join trade unions, and to adequate standard of living.[5] Neither the ILO conventions nor the UN covenant were rigid in content. They allowed for adaptation to local conditions. For example, they did not address job security as a fundamental right, but they did oppose arbitrary firings due to trade-union involvement. The ILO did not directly confront unemployment, but its conventions promoted a rational employment policy and made employment agencies accessible.[6]

During the last half of the century, ILO conventions and recommendations refined and updated these basic principles and also emphasized important new ones, such as non-discrimination and workplace safety. For example, conventions 87 and 98 enhanced the right to organize and bargain, and the Workers' Representatives Convention, no. 135 (1971), reiterated freedom of association at the plant level. The Labor Relations (Public Service) Convention, no. 151 (1978), assured the public sector's right to organize and settle disputes; the Collective Bargaining Convention, no. 154 (1981), adapted collective bargaining to national situations; convention no. 125 further protected workers' representatives. The Labor Inspection (Agriculture) Convention, no. 129 (1969), extended parallel protections to agricultural workers, and convention 141 supported rural workers' organizations.

The Abolition of Forced Labor Convention, no. 105, passed in 1959, elaborated concerns already expressed in convention 29. Addressing child labor, the Minimum Age Convention, no. 138 (1973), stated that the employment age must not be less than the age for finishing one's required education, usually not less than fifteen years. (In its 1998 annual conference, the ILO opened debate on a new convention that would protect children from hazardous and harmful work. Although many developing nations resisted ratifying conventions that governed child labor, it was expected to pass in 1999.) In 1970, convention 131 strengthened "wage fixing machinery" in developing countries, whereby each nation would set minimum-wage standards for groups of workers that would assure humane living conditions within local contexts. Such wage payments would be appropriately adjusted and inspected. Agencies administering standards would maintain full consultations with unions and business. The maximum forty-eight-hour week had already received reaffirmation via convention 116 (1963), which urged a reduction to forty hours where possible. In 1970, convention 122 guaranteed holidays (ILO 1992b).

In 1960, the ILO reaffirmed the principle of equal opportunity via the Convention Concerning Discrimination in Respect of Employment and Occupation, no. 111, which many nations subsequently ratified. Social security and other health-related conventions were updated by a variety of instruments, beginning with the Equality of Treatment (Social Security) Convention, no. 118 (1962), which extended benefits to refugees and non-nationals.[7]

Employers Object to the Proliferation of Regulations

Nevertheless, in the years following the ILO's mid-century achievement, employers grew disgruntled over certain instrument stipulations. In 1976, the Tripartite Consultation (International Labor Standards) Convention, no. 144, promoted communication between business, labor, and government, as states convened representatives of the three groups to collaborate on international labor standards (Trebilcock et al. 1994; see also Simpson 1994). Some remained dissatisfied, however. For example, Hans-Goran Myrdal, head of the Swedish Employers Association, claims that cold-war pressures forced many employers and first-world governments to agree to postwar ILO conventions. He argues that communist-bloc nations formulated conventions with no intention of implementing them, "to cause problems for companies and governments in market economies . . . [which] the workers' group within the ILO found it difficult to decline." Although the instruments passed, they were opposed by a large minority, mainly employers and Western governments (1994:341). To Myrdal, this explains why only 10 percent of nations ratified the forty-one ILO conventions passed between 1970 and 1990 compared with the 25 percent ratification rate between 1919 and 1969. He advocates replacing the more than 175 conventions with a fewer number of more basic ones and removing outdated language that impedes economic and social development. If employers and governments could eliminate the multiplicity of standards, the ILO measures could focus on helping members achieve optimal growth.[8]

Myrdal's description may accurately reflect certain less-subscribed "category 1" conventions passed in the 1980s, such as those promoting occupational safety and health. The Occupational Safety and Health Convention, no. 155 (1981), committed participating states to develop and monitor comprehensive national and workplace health and safety policies. The Indigenous Peoples Conventions, nos. 107 (1957) and 169 (1989), assured the right of peoples to determine their own priorities in the development process, some of which might inhibit "growth." Nevertheless, Myrdal himself advocates the six conventions that the ILO has declared support "basic worker rights": nos. 87 and 98 on union rights; nos. 29 and 105 opposing forced labor; no. 138 opposing child labor; and no. 111 on non-discrimination. He admits that all were ratified by two-thirds of ILO member states before 1970 (1994:345). Most postwar conventions, as noted above, simply specify these rights further.

Consensus over Basic Rights

The above chronology reveals discussion over a wide spectrum of rights but also a consensus around those rights considered most basic, even among employer representatives. Many other researchers validate this point. The Netherlands National Advisory Council for Development Cooperation distilled twelve ILO basic conventions into seven principles(NACDC 1984).[9] Four had been ratified by two-thirds of ILO member states: the conventions on forced labor, nos. 29 and 105; on collective bargaining, no. 98; on discrimination, no. 111; and on equal remuneration, no. 100.[10] Three additional ones, in its view, would not adversely affect the competitive position of developing countries: on freedom of association, no. 87; on protections for child labor, no. 138; and on employment policy, no. 122. In his review of eight major legislative proposals, including the NACDC, ILO economist Gijsbert van Liemt (1989) found universal mention of the rights to organize, to bargain collectively, and to prevent the employment of young children. Three-fourths of the proposals added freedoms from forced labor, from poor health and unsafe conditions, and from discrimination. David Montgomery (1996) emphasized freedom of association as the sine qua non of all other rights, and Virginia Leary (1996) stressed the right to strike in particular. Brocas et al. (1990) traced the growing acceptance of equal treatment for women. What has emerged is what ILO deputy director-general Heribert Maier (1994) calls a body of minimum international labor standards agreed on by all parties concerned. They present a global alternative to the variety of minimum standards for different regions and cultures that respectfully accomplishes the same objective (see also Sweptson 1994).

Many businessmen have adopted Maier's broader view. General Electric executive Frank Doyle believes it would be a mistake for business not to engage in a debate on labor standards (1994:43f). Recalling a dictum from ILO deputy director Maier, he favors widely recognized standards set through negotiations that guarantee benefits for all parties. For Doyle, a single set of rules for all countries would minimize information and compliance costs. He believes the ILO would be the likely agency to bring groups together, even though its conventions need updating.

The Debate over Achieving Labor Rights

Most policy makers and social scientists agree with the core listing of basic worker rights developed through the ILO. Despite this basic agreement, however, they differ over how best to achieve those rights. While the ILO urges nations to ratify key conventions and to report on compliance, it often does not specify mechanisms for implementation. In the next chapter we will assess the impact of trade conditionality in promoting respect for worker rights, but before we do that it is important that we understand the terms of debate: Can market forces achieve rights, or are other institutional interventions required?

Most scholars and activists would not disagree that, broadly understood, the market is the optimal way of achieving rights. In a certain sense, Freeman is correct that world labor standards ultimately depend on what the members of global society want them to be. They can vote for these rights through the "market" of their political and economic choices (1994:79f). But there are many intervening "market" stages before political institutions are sufficiently developed to reflect such "votes." We offer the following possibilities improving rights:

1. Market forces through increased corporate investment. In this scenario, comparative advantages such as a low-cost labor pool attract companies to enter a country and hire workers. As investments expand, the supply of workers grows limited, placing them in a position to demand higher wages and better treatment. This becomes increasingly true as their input affects product quality.

2. Labor union demands. Here, the workers organize themselves into a group strong enough to negotiate the terms under which they will labor. A forceful social-union movement may improve benefits for the entire workforce.

3. Corporate responsiveness. Enlightened managers realize that respectful treatment of employees improves productivity. Shareholder actions and publicity have accelerated this enlightenment.

4. Consumer pressure. Because of international consumer interest, corporations develop and monitor their own codes of employee rights and treatment. Certain business groups even accept independent monitoring.

5. State-imposed standards. In this case, national governments legislate and enforce certain rules about minimum wages, union rights, and so on.

Of course, these possibilities can exist in various combinations. States, companies, and labor and human-rights groups can jointly agree on voluntary standards. Governmental influence can extend beyond single state boundaries such as when several nations penalize another nation that does not implement globally recognized worker rights. Let us evaluate the pros and cons of these five approaches designed to improve worker conditions before examining possible combinations.

Market Forces and Corporate Investment

For classical and neo-classical economists, labor standards are best achieved by economic market forces alone. Such economists believe that minimum-wage standards develop organically in tandem with economic expansion. Artificially disrupting this process could reduce worker benefits (see Cordova 1984; Flanigan 1987). This argument rests on the principle of comparative advantage, whereby companies respond to incentives to increase productivity in a certain country. Higher output leads to improved living standards for all. As Kochan and Nordlund (1989a) note, comparative advantage is determined by factor endowments, including low-cost labor. However, as productivity rises and demand for labor increases, wage standards will naturally rise and workers will be better off.

Classical theorists therefore oppose an "artificial" improvement in labor standards, since this would raise wages and/or other costs associated with labor inputs. Mandated standards are rigid and can distort the labor market's healthy operation. For example, job security protections benefit specialized groups but discourage investors from increasing employment. Government intervention to support higher standards can threaten general economic efficiency. Imposed standards also inhibit the global market and thereby ultimately fail to benefit the nations that would otherwise share in its expansion.

Labor scholar Gary Fields (1990) offers a convincing statement of the market proponents' position. Fields bases his argument on four newly industrializing economies (NIEs) in Asia that experienced several decades of remarkable growth before their dramatic economic crisis in Fall 1997. In South Korea, Singapore, Hong Kong, and Taiwan, where labor standards were not imposed, worker conditions showed greater improvement. The rapid economic growth in these countries between the 1960s and the 1980s accelerated the demand for labor. At first, pay increases were modest, but once these nations approached full employment a bidding up of wages occurred, increasing the competition for the scarce labor supply.

Fields admits that in the four "Asian Tigers" labor unions did not do well. They were de-registered in Singapore. They could form in Korea, but firms were not obligated to bargain with them. While the law did require arbitration of employee-employer disputes, Fields notes that the "abuse of labor standards is in the eye of the beholder." He believes collective bargaining or minimum wages may lead to divisions between better-off and worse-off workers. This condition of "labor market segmentation" results in lower formal-sector employment and lower wages in uncovered sectors. While Fields would accept certain basic ILO standards,[11] he says that ambitious labor codes have caused adverse outcomes. What really benefits workers is the opportunity to sell to open markets such as the U.S. Implicit in Fields's argument is that employers would improve worker conditions to compete with a better quality product.

Many economists across the globe agree with Fields. T. N. Srinivasan (1994: 34f) believes that workers in developing countries would choose employment without standards in place of non-employment. Mexican scholar Adalberto García-Rocha (1990) reaffirms Fields's point about the disadvantages of labor legislation, which excluded many when it was applied in Mexico. As the government enforced high labor costs, producers compensated via mechanization. Wage earners represented two-thirds of the labor force but only brought in one-third of the nation's income. Speaking from his experience in India, Datta-Chaudhuri (1990) notes that wages are less important to workers than job security. Advocates of employment standards have introduced expensive government policies that prevent firms from going out of business simply to preserve jobs. Economically, more people are worse off.

These economists have no doubt that labor standards are best left to market processes and the private sector. They appear less comfortable when the market strengthens worker unions that in turn demand rights.

Union Strength

Thus, a second possibility for improving labor standards is an energized labor movement. Forceful unions can negotiate basic ILO standards in their contracts. As a political force, they also can demand enforcement from governments. Current labor standards in many nations are often the result of bitter struggles by trade unions seeking better treatment. Peter Dorman, who has carefully investigated the question, finds "vigorous action by workers in developing countries . . . indispensable if they are to attain procedural and substantive rights identified by the ILO; similar struggles, after all, were required of workers in the advanced countries during comparable historical periods" (1989:3; see also Bergquist 1986 and Collier and Collier 1991 for further examples).

Neo-classical economists like Fields do not believe union action is a guarantee for generalized labor rights. Fields blamed labor's demands in Jamaica and Columbia for those nations' lack of success in manufacturing exports (Chernick 1978). Others, like Alejandro Portes, believe that unions in Mexico, Brazil, Peru, and other countries form protected enclaves, gaining advantages that do not extend to the working class (1990:229). García-Rocha argues that Mexican labor standards resulted from government courting the unions, which increased labor-market dualism and increased the low-wage informal sector.[12]

Other labor economists say these worn arguments bypass the total benefits brought to all societal members by labor coalitions. Jong-il You describes the overall benefits in Korea (one of Fields's examples of market success), where wages responded to labor militancy. At first the historical weakness of workers' organizations meant that the government was not constrained to protect workers rights, but their bargaining power rose over time as export-led industrialization encouraged industrial employment. While repression retarded union power, the government still had to acquiesce to various rights for broad segments of the population.

You insists that the South Korean government's actions did not stem from a corporatist tradition (as in Singapore) but rather were attributable to union strength, including company unions. Female-headed unions became especially strong in the late 1970s, during a period when the labor market was tight and real wages were rising steeply. Then, when a new government crackdown came in 1980, unions reverted to male leadership, as the labor movement accelerated in high-skill, heavy-manufacturing industries. Both male- and female-led unions organized many strikes after 1986 (such as in 1995) as the country took more steps toward democracy. They demanded minimum wages for all and a national health and pension system. What could polarize (and weaken) the labor movement, admits You, would be the imposition of enterprise unionism.

The ability of unions to assure labor rights often depends on the juncture of local and international conditions. The context stimulates crucial linkages between national and international trade unions. Under the banner of labor solidarity, for both ideological and practical reasons international unions have advocated adoption of global labor standards (see ILRF 1991 and Waterman 1995). However, unions are increasingly discovering that they cannot achieve this goal without the cooperation of a wider constituency.[13]

Corporate Responsiveness

A third possibility for implementing employee rights is for large transnational companies to become more responsibly involved. Management is often aware of the economic and social benefits of a trained workforce. Many corporations have also come to understand that employees with a sense of their own rights have a greater stake in the organization's success, and will help to maintain its competitive position in a changing marketplace. As production becomes globally coordinated, a product's quality becomes an even more visible benchmark. These managers are convinced that contented employees positively affect product standards. Because employers have been involved in the ILO since its inception, this understanding could encourage their participation in the codification and monitoring of specific ILO instruments at the national level.

Corporate commitment was given impetus in the 1970s by the shareholder responsibility movement, which exerted media publicity to alter corporate behavior (see ICCR 1973). Labor-related examples of corporate responses include corporate investors in South Africa who accepted a code of conduct toward workers; Sears, which disclosed its promotion record for women and minorities (Vogel 1978; Post 1978); and Coca-Cola, which intervened to prevent labor abuses at its Guatemalan franchise (Frundt 1987b). Following socially aware shareholders, investment funds such as Working Assets, Franklin Research, and Development, Calvert, and Parnassus began to evaluate companies according to social criteria.

A combination of enlightened management and shareholder publicity motivated companies and employers associations to address employment issues voluntarily. Compa and Darricarrère (1996:185f) trace the resulting "codes of conduct" exemplified by the Sullivan principles, the MacBride Code, and Levi Strauss and Co.'s Terms of Engagement. Richard Edwards (1994a) offers a sophisticated version of one such corporate strategy that contains legal remedies for employees but also eliminates unions. Edwards advocates an approach called "choosing rights" through which worker protections could be achieved without compromising employer competitiveness. In Edwards's "market-based" approach, company-produced employee handbooks would guarantee worker rights. As legally binding contracts, they would transfer the formulation of rules and rights from regulatory agencies to the private sector. This would provide benefits to both workers and employers, but it would also replace collective bargaining and protective legislation.

During President Clinton's first term, administration policy makers articulated similar thoughts. For example, the Dunlop Commission in 1994 reduced the role of organized labor in settling future disputes. The Clinton administration also formed an ad hoc group, staffed by the National Economic Council and the National Security Council but virtually no labor representatives, to formulate ethical guidelines for doing business in China (see also Sciolino 1998).

Nevertheless, in the 1990s, corporate executives have paid more attention to employee rights for sound managerial reasons. With greater frequency, business publications are trumpeting the issue. In one example, RMI Marketing and Advertising urges an "Employee's Bill of Rights" advocating the treatment of each worker as a unique individual, with respect and fairness, as someone to be challenged, appreciated, and informed, as someone who has the opportunity to fail, to express himself or herself freely, to determine the best way to achieve goals, and to approach management and receive confidence.[14] Kinni (1994:37) reports that even small businesses are in agreement about extending employee rights. As one headline put it, "Workers' rights are the gateway to better bottom line" (Hopkins 1994:23).

Consumer Pressure

Despite the efforts of enlightened managers and shareholder pressure, a most important impetus toward responsible corporate behavior has been direct consumer action. Corporations respond to publicity about their products. Consumer pressure for improved rights backed up with potential or actual boycotts has achieved results (see Munves 1974; Green 1976; Ermann and Clements 1986). Freeman (1994) argues that labor standards can be a normal consumer good, meaning that consumers can set labor standards. The demand curve depends on how much more customers are willing to pay for goods that are produced by people working under decent conditions. Product publicity affects this demand. Freeman contends that sufficient information, conveyed through product labeling, should be all that is necessary to ensure improved conditions. If goods are not properly certified, consumers will force producers out of business.

One example that fits Freeman's vision is the campaign against the use of child labor, represented by the Child Labor Coalition's advocacy for the Rugmark label (see, for example, Ramey 1994:30). The coalition's objective is to persuade appropriate retail stores to sell rugs from India, Pakistan, and Nepal only if they carry the label showing they were made by adults. In 1994, Senator Tom Harkin introduced legislation to ban products produced by child labor (*New York Times*, Dec. 5, 1994). By September 1997, Congress had prohibited the importation of any product made by "forced or indentured child labor" (see Collingsworth 1997).

At one point, Freeman himself saw no additional need for enforced international standards. A well-functioning market that allows for consumer-corporate pressure would eliminate abuses of labor standards. More recently, Freeman has admitted that labeling could be inaccurate and misused, and thus legal requirements also might be needed. He concludes, "Standards governing how the market works, such as those regulating labor contracts and guaranteeing freedom of association, may be more efficaciously set by legal regulations, whereas standards for actual market outcomes, such as wages and hours or occupational health and safety conditions, may possibly be more efficaciously determined through providing consumers with information about those outcomes" (1994:85).

Customer advocacy has begun to address the nature of labor contracts. Recently, because of consumer actions coordinated by the U.S./Guatemala Labor Education Project, companies like Starbucks coffee and shirtmaker Phillips–Van Heusen have acquiesced to employee codes that include freedom of assembly (Coats 1996; Cogan 1995; Frundt 1996; Armbruster 1997; Interhemispheric Resource Center 1997). In late 1995, after a campaign organized by the National Labor Committee, the GAP clothing outlet announced independent monitoring of its code of conduct.[15] Less than a year later, under White House sponsorship, representatives from ten major companies, six human-rights groups, and several union representatives collaborated in a U.S. Apparel Industry Partnership (AIP) to create a set of common guidelines. They reaffirmed the freedom of association and the right to bargain. Rules also prohibited a workweek beyond sixty hours and the hiring of children under age fourteen (Greenhouse 1997a; Schilling 1997). The agreement reconciled U.S. corporate policies on child employment in the offshore apparel industry surveyed by the U.S. Department of Labor.[16]

Whether it is from enlightened managers and stockholders or from consumer interest, corporate action is crucial in the implementation of labor standards. As Dorman notes, "the role of private employers in the determination of worker rights should not be underestimated." They influence state policy and often control actual implementation of labor regulations. Adopting a code is only the first step, as a *Wall Street Journal* report has cautioned: While a growing number of U.S. companies have adopted codes of conduct setting minimum standards for their suppliers abroad, "virtually no one applauds the way the codes are enforced." Yet few companies actually monitor compliance (Ortega 1995). For example, a U.S. apparel self-monitoring program to police domestic sweatshops has proved inadequate (see Greenhouse 1997b). The AIP has yet to fully implement a satisfactory outside-monitoring program that guarantees input from labor and human-rights organizations (see Coats 1998 on outside monitoring). This failure necessitates an important role for a final element of compliance, the oversight of government.

National Government Regulation

People who select market forces to implement employee rights often ultimately turn to legislation—and the institution of the state—to enforce standards. "Institutional" economists and social scientists contend that govern-

ment-enforced labor standards encourage respect and understanding between workers and business. Legislated labor codes also aid local economies
in adjusting to technological change.

Since the turn of the century, institutionalists have argued that the state
could act as a positive force for promoting human progress (Kochan and
Nordlund 1989a). Prosperity required industrial peace. In the U.S., a painful
depression, government response, and the 1935 National Labor Relations Act
bolstered labor's dealings with employers. Despite restrictive court interpretations in the 1950s and 1960s (Craver 1995), the New Deal coalition successfully promoted collective bargaining as the mechanism for settling wages,
hours, and working conditions. During the 1970s political concerns developed around equal employment, occupational safety, and pension security.
Neo-classical economists worried that bargaining over these issues would
feed inflation, especially as the economic crisis widened. In addition to inherent morality, neo-institutionalists stressed the function of labor standards in
encouraging productive efficiency. For example, Servais (1989) argued that
safety standards could bring economic savings by reducing the cost of accidents. Conflict resolution standards could increase the utilization of plant
capacity by avoiding disruptions and retraining expenses. Others urged job-
security regulations for their role in stabilizing employment relations and
enhancing productivity, thereby contributing to competitiveness (see
Sengenberger and Campbell 1994). In general, labor markets have become
"deeply segmented by power relationships." In consequence, labor is under-
valued and wages "bear little or no relationship to the value contributions of
individual workers" (Sengenberger and Wilkinson 1994:119). In the face of
rising poverty, reality dictated the need for government activism. Otherwise,
lower aggregate demand would threaten prosperity. In 1996, certain U.S.
congresspersons even proposed tax breaks for companies that treated workers better (see Clymer 1996a, 1996b).

Singapore, often cited as a free-market success, illustrates government intervention since it gave social development and distribution priority over economic development and growth (Lim 1987). In 1986, for example, while the
government advocated selective wage restraint, its expenditures on education helped bring recovery.[17] Lim concludes that the state played a crucial role
in mediating the country's economic integration and encouraging beneficial
export manufacturing. Were it not for government-mandated wage increases
and incentives to improve technology and skills, the private sector might not
have moved as quickly toward more highly productive industries. State-guar-
anteed social welfare won popular support. Companies had to make significant compulsory contributions to employee pension funds, and savings plans
for buying medical coverage and property. The government also promoted

subsidizing housing, cheap transportation, and other policies that supported a healthy, educated workforce with high female participation. Official policy encouraged child care, job sharing, and tax breaks for working mothers. High safety standards were monitored by a relatively efficient bureaucracy—the welfare state.

Theoretical Issues in Comparing the Five Mechanisms

We have examined five sources of potential achievement of labor rights: the economic market, union strength, corporate responsiveness, consumer pressure, and government intervention. Each source conveys advantages for certain *types* of rights. The economic market may be most effective at determining wages, although this does not hold true for every case. At times, its advocates appear oblivious to the human need for freedom and dignity. A democratic union movement articulates what workers perceive as most realistic for their own situation. It develops when workers are free to organize and choose their own representatives "on the ground." However, unions are most effective at gaining wage equity and fair treatment when they have the backing of the larger community (Fantasia 1988). They need what has perhaps unfortunately been characterized as "consumer" backing. For example, when unions have simply sought job security or an improved economic package, they have been less successful at obtaining this support. When they have stressed the importance of dignity, the difficulty of long hours (see Schor 1992), or part-time work assignments and loss of benefits, they have won considerable sympathy. Such was the case in the U.S. when American Airline flight attendants struck in 1992 and when UPS workers went out in 1997.

However, corporate mergers and global expansion are destabilizing work hours and job-security conditions. As consumer interest over these conditions heightens, some state regulation also seems inevitable. In South Korea, Jong-il You (1989) postulates that state intervention and market forces have had varying results on productivity, at times enhancing healthy competition while at times fostering destructive competition via wage-cutting work intensification. She argues that productivity is prompted by rising wages, not vice versa. Labor repression, usually motivated by political considerations, can inhibit both.

Following the restrictions of labor autonomy implemented in 1963, the ratio between Korean capital and labor declined until the late 1960s. Further legislated restrictions continued until 1986 as the government suppressed independent unions. On the other hand, government intervention in the economy enabled the manufacturing sector to grow rapidly. Ironically, says You, export-led industrialization generated employment that strengthened workers' power (a development also noted in Park 1993). In a process parallel to that in Singapore, the expanding industrial workforce bolstered the underlying vitality of the union movement despite its repression in the 1970s. Union membership grew until 1979; the government was forced to promote labor management councils as an alternative, and it expanded health coverage for accidents and strengthened penalties for unfair labor practices. The wage share of manufacturing value added rose from 37 percent to 47 percent or more. While Korea retained the world's longest workweek (54.7 hours in 1986), the fast growth of wages and worker organizations accelerated productivity growth. When that growth became jeopardized, the government felt it necessary to apply wage restraints and union repression. Beginning in the late 1980s, Korea experienced a revitalized union organizing effort along with enhanced strike actions.

A closer look at two of the Asian Tigers challenges Fields's interpretation of the importance of unrestricted free-market forces in improving labor standards. It points instead to the key role of government and other determinants.[18] In a review of national policies in twelve developing countries, labor-market institutions did not contravene stabilization, and wages showed amazing flexibility (Horton et al. 1991). These examples reinforce the positive function of government controls and the neutral role of union demands.

Mechanisms in Operation in Latin America

Latin American social scientists are also in agreement that no single mechanism will achieve labor rights in the hemisphere, but rather it will require some type of combination. Sociologist Alejandro Portes believes labor legislation in many Latin nations would win the envy of workers in advanced countries for accident protection, job security, unemployment compensation, old-age pensions, and rights to unionization. He attributes this both to working-class mobilization and to values diffused from the industrialized world (1994:163). However, Portes finds some Latin American labor codes so stringent that they drive business and workers into the informal sector. He cites evidence (1994:164) that competitive pressures have lead firms to bypass regulations (Beneria 1989; Bromley 1978) and turn to intermediaries and temporary workers (Beneria and Roldan 1987; Birkbeck 1979; Davies 1979), which perpetuates a dualistic economy. He especially eschews the rigid standards in Columbia, Peru, and Mexico, where he says it is legally more difficult to fire workers than it is in the U.S.[19]

To encourage new export-led industrialization, many Latin governments surreptitiously disregard these laws. However, their approach confuses North American firms accustomed to labor-legislation compliance. They find themselves saddled with costly, inflexible arrangements and a "prisoners dilemma in which full observance . . . leads to competition at high cost levels, but . . . surplus profits by those who by-pass the rules" (Portes 1990:222).[20] The solution of North American companies is to meet minimum requirements to avoid sanctions and to expand subcontracted production via the informal economy. Portes says a high proportion of the informal labor force is really "disguised" wage workers hired by such firms. With substantial formal-informal articulation, an increasing number of workers go unprotected.

However, others believe Portes's analysis is too simplistic. An expanded informal sector is not simply due to the imposition of formal-sector labor codes but is also caused by corporations pumping "western" resources into the modern sector (Banuri 1990). Such investors neglect small-scale indigenous producers, increasing their poverty level and forcing them to search for informal employment.

World Bank economists Peter Fallon and Luis Riveros (1990) examined employment creation in the formal sector of twenty-three countries. They found that the informal sector grew when job creation was inadequate, whether or not investment expanded.[21] Most countries were experiencing a reallocation of employment from primary production (where labor productivity was high) to secondary and tertiary areas, and from agriculture and mining to informal services. Simply put, the growth of the modern industrial/commercial sector in Latin America was insufficient to absorb the expanding workforce.

Thus, Fallon and Riveros offer solid empirical data that disputes that labor standards, no matter how they are enforced, are responsible for increasing the informal sector. Minimum-wage policies in the 1980s were largely "ineffective" in raising wages sufficiently to create distortions in labor markets. In fact, wages dropped in many countries. Within the public sector, most nations opted to reduce wages rather than cut jobs. They also relaxed job-security regulations.

In her examination of the market impact, A. Marshall (1994) also discovered no direct association between permissive (versus stronger) labor legislation and worker improvements in Mexico and six southern cone nations, suggesting that other factors were controlling. Her findings suggest that government codes under varying degrees of enforcement do not in and of themselves harm workers as a group or force them into the informal sector. Marshall's research challenges any definitive assertion that labor protections in Latin America bring economic harm. Protective Latin American legislation may or may not be associated with economic improvement as such. The results also imply that labor-code passage has little directly to do with code enforcement.[22] Rodrik's research on child-labor standards (1995) may prove an exception to these results; however, OECD data (1996) are more supportive of Marshall's findings. So is ILO specialist Arturo Bronstein, who emphasizes that de facto flexibility has always existed in Latin America. But Bronstein believes the debate has shifted toward those aspects "really useful to enterprises and those which merely serve . . . free market ideologies" (1997:26).

In some Latin nations, labor policies may have prevented migration to the informal sector, as happened in Singapore (Lim 1987). That "society based on effort and merit, not wealth and privilege," vastly reduced its informal sector, largely owing to government policy. Government-mandated working conditions and wages were meshed with other strategies to accelerate development and labor welfare.[23]

Sweat Exceptionalism

The strategy of combining mechanisms to achieve labor standards in Latin America is augmented by the arguments of Michael Piore (1990) and others. Piore offers a challenging thesis to explain why government-induced labor standards improve economic efficiency and why the lack of standards locks some companies and nations into low-productivity production with low economic results.

The market today encourages less capital-intensive production techniques, or more "flexible production."[24] There has been a consequent move away from government labor-market regulation. Thus there is an increased danger that investors opting for flexible production will choose a sweatshop process. Until twenty years ago, sweatshops were in retreat, kept in check by transport costs and inferior products. Now they are expanding.[25]

"What's at stake here is not simply a list of discrete characteristics but a whole way of doing business," states Piore. Entire countries can permit sweatshop systems that are relatively immune to the market. The sweating strategy means employers use low fixed-capital costs. They pay workers as little as possible per unit, thereby minimizing the need to attend to worker productivity or even the production process itself. Since a sweatshop owner does not care how or how much the industrious worker produces, the owner is prone to hire low-production workers and even children. Since the employer is not motivated to reorganize production, s/he ignores work-process layout and improvements to reduce health and safety violations (1990:36ff.).

Transport and communications technologies have encouraged low-wage (sweatshop) producers to invade industrial markets served by both mass production and flexible production (Banuri 1990, 1991). While flexible specialization is the theoretical opposite of the sweatshop since it emphasizes skill and quality, it also *encourages* the sweatshop's reemergence because it eats into mass markets, reduces economies of scale, and thereby makes mass production vulnerable to sweat. With the mass-marketing strategy reduced and costs increased, sweatshops proliferate. Sociologist Alejandro Portes believes conditions in developing-country Export Processing Zones (EPZs) combine sweatshop practices and piece rates with speedups and specialization. This results in levels of labor exploitation even higher than the minimal compensation of traditional offshore producers investigated by Fernandez-Kelly (1993), Deyo (1993), Petersen (1992), Sklair (1993), and others.

However, Piore believes labor standards can "push business strategy toward structures of production that are most likely to lead to cooperative economic production systems" (1994:21). Sweatshop conditions disappear as soon as governments introduce a minimum hourly rate high enough to create an employer interest in productivity. As wage standards stimulate business to enhance productivity, owners will employ fewer young children. They will be forced to reorganize the workplace to gain control over its pace and more easily meet government requirements.[26]

Thus Piore (1994) advocates a new kind of regulation to meet the flexible technologies of low-wage modern sweatshops, such as computerized machines that unload variable costs onto workers. Standards will help boost aggregate demand and foster economic growth by encouraging stability in production relationships and by ensuring that firms develop high-productivity strategies. While rigid labor standards may interfere with flexible responses to dynamic production processes, labor costs are only part of a nation's "comparative advantage." Contrary to the neo-classical view of labor as a commodity, production systems have a social structure that must be respected.

With the mass market in retreat, standards are also more essential (Banuri 1990). Without standards, low-cost producers will not increase world demand. Standards help maintain a balance between aggregate demand and supply, encouraging the efficient utilization of flexible technologies. But standards must be implemented carefully. Rules can stifle or stimulate productive behavior, such as protecting sunset industries, but they are important for encouraging innovative craft-production (Banuri 1990). They work best where there is a web of interdependence between economic, social, and cognitive exchanges. Reciprocal obligations help balance cooperation and competition that might otherwise degenerate into sweating. Mediating takes into account national circumstance, culture, and history—not just policy variables to suit a national development strategy. It reconciles dynamic development and social peace. Guided by standards, businesspeople can better evaluate how alternative strategies will not only affect the conditions of work but also the entire society.

In this chapter, we have considered the generally accepted basis for global labor rights. We have also examined five potential agents for actualizing those rights: the market, unions, consumers, corporations, and government action. Both theoretically and empirically, each option has certain strengths and weaknesses. It is their combination that offers the greatest promise. As Dorman points out, governments have difficulty with standard enforcement under three conditions: when they do not have full control because of interference from paramilitary or privately employed forces; when they lack funds for implementation; and when private employers can evade their directives. Relations between the state and private interests are crucial to attain worker rights (1989:3).

In the next chapter we will outline how to test the success of a sixth option for assuring standards: trade conditionality.

CHAPTER 3

Implementing Labor Rights
Through Trade Conditions

In chapter 2 we outlined an emerging consensus regarding core labor rights but found less agreement on how to implement them. We encountered the benefits and difficulties of relying on an unrestricted market, unions, corporations, and consumers as guarantors of labor standards. We were also cautioned to avoid rigid state-imposed requirements. In this chapter, we face an even more controverted question: Do imposed trade sanctions benefit workers? The answer bears upon the central thesis of this book.[1]

Of the five implementing agents considered in chapter 2, the state has greatest control over trade. This chapter explores how "neo-institutionalists" have challenged the "neo-liberal" market approach opposing trade restrictions, and what the ILO has determined about the matter. We will review the evolution and function of the U.S. General System of Preferences (GSP) trade legislation as the most concrete example of limiting trade from nations that avoid steps to improve labor rights. The topic leads us to consider GSP procedures for selecting the rights to be enforced, for reviewing these rights, and for determining trade-condition effectiveness.

The Trade Condition Debate

Trade sanctions represent an aspect of government-imposed labor standards discussed in chapter 2. They generate a similar debate between neo-classical thinkers who oppose state intervention in the market and neo-institutionalists who favor imposed controls.[2] Neo-classicists emphasize the mutual (win-win) aspects of free trade. All members of participating states benefit from specialization in production and increases in productivity (see Weintraub 1993; Irwin 1996). Inevitable temporary losers can be compensated from the trade largesse.

But to neo-institutionalists, free-market supporters share a utopian vision that open trade will simultaneously increase investment, jobs, and growth and reduce inflation and political instability (Bowman 1993). Yet free trade can only occur in a basic context of fairness. The market advantages cited by classical economists also usually assume full employment and balanced trade in reciprocating countries (Sanford 1993). Since these conditions rarely occur, the protection of global standards requires market intervention. Nations should be as willing to do this as they are to write intellectual property rights protections into trade agreements. They do not assume that free trade will assure business interests either (Adams and Turner 1994; Cavanagh et al. 1988; Collingsworth 1989; Collingsworth et al. 1994; R. Marshall 1987; Nader et al. 1993; Piore 1990, 1994; Rosen 1992).

Neo-institutionalists also eschew the conceptual distinction between tariffs and subsidies: State assistance or inaction can be positive or negative with similar trade effect. For example, the government that requires the purchase of pollution abatement equipment or the provision of day-care facilities needs to be measured against the government that does not impose such requirements. Non-regulation "is as much a subsidy in the eyes of foreign producers saddled with costly regulatory requirements as direct funding" (Langille 1994:331). Thus, "natural" or "neutral" trade does not exist. As companies with lower standards and enforcement gain unfair competition, regulatory competition replaces comparative advantage as the new global strategy. It leads to a transfer of power from government to the market (Elmslie and Milberg 1996). However, while capital has slipped the boundaries of the nation state, labor has not.

To encourage nations to meet basic labor standards, neo-institutionalists advocate that a social condition be added to trade arrangements. Such a clause would set a floor of minimum standards that would preserve comparative advantage. It would encourage fair competition among exporters by guaranteeing that those who honor worker rights would not be placed at a disadvantage. Importing nations could reduce or stop receiving an offender's products. Producers would be forced to choose between improving conditions or losing trade. Those opting for the former would be assured that competition would bring balanced development, not cutthroat competition (Pursey 1994:375). In this context, working people would gain from growth in trade (van Liemt 1989:435).

The Debate for Developing Nations

For developing countries, institutional-oriented social scientists also believe national standards evolve more reliably when guided by labor-rights initiatives embedded in cross-border trade agreements (Banuri 1991; Cavanagh

1988; Collingsworth 1989; Piore 1990). Otherwise, countries that follow the export-led growth model are more likely to disregard worker rights: They face intense competition from countries not subject to labor standards, and they are reluctant to raise wages in a labor-intensive economy (Dorman 1989). Without standards, there could be what many call "a race to the bottom" (Langille 1994:334). Trade liberalization may deflate wages and conditions worldwide, since the "gap between conditions of work remains uncomfortably large . . . increasing social inequality between a well-educated and skilled section of the population and a large but marginalized mass." The resulting instability could be "fertile ground for extremist nationalist, religious, ethnic and anti-democratic forces . . . [that] feed on a pervasive sense that forces beyond their control are undermining jobs, their communities or culture" (Pursey 1994:370). Likewise, an absence of labor standards in developing countries undermines standards in advanced countries, whereas a rise in labor requirements may stimulate productivity gains and trade surpluses for all (Mead 1988; Singh 1990). Freer trade with protections assures a more orderly economic adaptation. Workers in both developing and developed nations can buy what they *and* others produce, thereby maintaining global demand.

However, in developing countries where trade is the primary hope for advancement, government officials remain skeptical. They attribute the fascination with their working conditions to their success at exporting and to rising unemployment and protectionist sentiments in importing countries. Improved standards could prevent the less-industrialized nations from exercising their primary comparative advantage: productive low-cost labor. Government intervention to support higher standards would threaten economic efficiency, inhibit the market, and ultimately fail to benefit their nation (van Liemt 1989:435). These sentiments were reflected in the December 1996 WTO vote to reject labor standards: Representatives from Malaysia, India, and Pakistan branded them as sanctimonious protections for developed country industries (see WTO 1996; Elmslie and Milberg 1997).

Developing-country spokespersons also question the types of sanctions and rights considered and the consequences for non-unionized and informal-sector workers (Perez-López and Schoepfle 1993). They believe proponents of labor standards often do not take into account the very real benefits that rapid growth may confer upon their workers (Portes 1994:160). Such workers would prefer employment without standards to non-employment.[3] In any case, trade sanctions are virtually impotent to affect human rights abuses (Srinivasan 1994:34).

Developing nations also view the imposition of standards by a handful of powerful countries as an interference in their domestic affairs.[4] These latter countries boast an average income that is twenty-four times greater than the rest of world, and they account for 55 percent of the world's output and 75 percent of world trade (Pursey 1994:367, citing 1993 data). The smaller nations wonder why the more powerful raise labor issues while they neglect other imbalances in world trade, such as market access, raw materials prices, and economic restructuring.[5] Finally they question the unbalanced treatment accorded larger developing countries, China for example, that can get by with continual rights violations without losing trade privileges (see Devroy 1994; Tonelson 1996).

Nevertheless, labor leaders in developing nations have a somewhat divergent perspective. In Latin America, many are persuaded that new investment and trade will improve their societies. They often distrust U.S. unions and agencies for placing their own political and economic interests ahead of everyone else. They recall the historically divisive tactics of the U.S. government–sponsored American Institute for Free Labor Development (AIFLD) (see Armstrong et al. 1987; Barry and Preusch 1990; Cantor and Schor 1987; Sims 1992; Spalding 1988a, 1988b, 1993; Weinrub and Bollinger 1987). However, in the face of abuses like those at La Exacta ranch (see chapter 1), they remain suspicious of arguments opposing trade-based labor standards. What they hear are justifications advanced by entrenched aristocratic interests and rabid anti-union businessmen to avoid action on worker rights (Moody and McGinn 1992). They also affirm the need to redress past damage to labor unions and worker conditions brought by U.S. military interventions (see the introduction). Confronting free trade, workers in both exporting and importing nations face transformed lives, unprotected habitats, and broken communities. Claimed benefits for poorer sectors may be ideological manipulations rather than honest and compassionate assessments of real people.

Evaluating the Arguments

Certain scholars have sought to balance neo-liberal and institutional arguments on trade conditions. To the former, international trade-based labor standards increase protectionism, destroy comparative advantage, aggravate a dual economy, and interfere in a nation's internal affairs. The latter hold that intervention would keep social progress in line with economic progress, build solidarity between working people by preventing the lowering of standards around the globe, and reduce further protectionism (Emmerij 1994:324–25).[6]

"At its core," argues Charnovitz, "the idea of fair labour standards is not protectionist. It is anti-protectionist. While workers everywhere would benefit from the further division of labour made possible by international commerce, freer trade is stymied whenever any trading partner questions the underlying fairness of the labour practices used by another. Establishing a floor for worker rights has the potential of removing one of the chief justifications for import restrictions" (1987:581).

In weighing neo-classical and neo-institutional arguments, there is some consensus that a trade clause with minimum standards might be beneficial but must be carefully applied. Much is at stake: In highly competitive, labor-intensive conditions, buyers easily switch, making markets difficult to regain. A social clause must be verifiable, universal, and flexible: "A loose and less than universal application might pose an immediate threat to the economic and employment situation in these countries" (van Liemt 1989:436; see also Cagatay 1990). To address the concerns of developing nations that trade conditions are not simply protective mechanisms for larger powers, the clause must create an open forum that would help air issues of debt and economic policy. It also could serve to reward complying nations with enhanced import quotas or delay requirements for structural adjustment (Pursey 1994:375). In that case, a minimum package of labor standards in international agreements "would have no adverse effect on the international economic position of developing countries" (Emmerij 1994:324–25) as several empirical studies have posited (OECD 1996; Swinnerton and Schoepfle 1997). In addition, developed nations could pay compensation for short-term imbalances, as through a "Tobin Tax" assessed at roughly .05 percent value of all shipments (see Elmslie and Milberg 1997:78).

Selecting and Implementing Enforceable Rights

Neo-classicists and neo-institutionalists also debate the choice of rights to be promoted, the manner in which sanctions are chosen, and what body or agency is best suited to carry them out.

Hierarchies of Rights Enforcement

While opposed to trade conditions as a general principle, neo-classical economists sympathetic to the observance of labor rights would still be more inclined to use sanctions in some cases more than in others. For example, labor economist Gary Fields, who advocates market forces as the primary mechanism responsible for the improvement of labor rights, also finds "certain actions abusive anywhere . . . slavery, prohibitions on freedom of association or on collective bargaining, exposure of workers to unsafe or unhealthy working conditions, and the employment of children for long work hours." Fields leaves unspecified how he would honor these rights, but he is clear that "minimum wages, hours etc. are other issues" that would best be left to market forces (1990:20).

Neo-institutionalists could agree with this approach, which identifies rights in rough parallel with the hierarchy of human needs identified by psychologist Abraham Maslow (1954). Alejandro Portes ranks basic, survival, security, and civic rights. Basic rights (from servitude, violence) and civic rights (for association, collective representation) lend themselves to international standards, but survival rights (wages, health benefits) and security rights (job protection, pension)—that is, work condition rights—are best locally bargained between workers, employers, and governments (see Portes 1994:171).[7] Former U.S. secretary of labor Robert Reich (1994) called this second set of rights a "vast gray area" where "we cannot expect [every country] to reach our level." As nations reach higher levels of economic development, these standards should show observable improvement.

One "labor right" debated among neo-institutionalists regarded workers who could not be fired. Portes argued that the drive for businesses to informalize their operations (that is, to utilize sweatshop techniques) was motivated by a desire to avoid adding workers who could not be let go (1990:231). Countries should be able to prevent such an "immobile" labor force by restricting survival and security rights. Nevertheless, while acknowledging the problem of labor aristocracies, others, such as Fallon, Riveros, and A. Marshall, questioned the extent to which worker protection contributed to an expansive informal sector (see chapter 2).

While this debate provokes academic interest, it nevertheless bypasses the primary experiences of rights abuses we encountered in chapter 1: violence directed at individuals and groups who attempt to organize unions; reticence of government institutions to prevent such activity or to investigate and bring to justice the perpetrators; and the dilatory functioning of labor ministries and courts in processing union recognitions, contract negotiations, arbitrations, and grievances. Many governments also have little interest in enforcing shorter hours and school regulations for children (Krueger 1996). In the trade debate, it is these latter experiences of rights—that is, basic human and survival rights—which are often at issue (see *L.A. Labor News,* var; Rosen 1992; U.S. Department of Labor 1990). These rights should receive more attention than wages or job security. If the courts function appropriately, then unions can organize and unjustly fired members can receive due process.

By focusing attention on wages and job security, the trade debate attacks a straw man. As we saw in chapter 2, while ILO instruments include mechanisms for countries to set minimum wages, and while the ILO debated the idea of "fair wages" during the 1950s, its conventions suggest no specific wages. Job security as such has also never been a basic ILO codified right. However, as we argued in chapter 2, ILO standards can be used to establish a basic list of rights appropriate for a multilateral social clause affecting trade.

ILO Standards and Trade Conditionality

ILO conventions or recommendations do not specifically address trade conditionality, and there has been substantial dispute among ILO members about the use of such sanctions. Nevertheless, the ILO deliberated trade sanctions as it developed its original charter (Charnovitz 1987:576).[8] At least since the 1930s, nations have appealed to ILO standards in formulating trade policy. A 1943 ILO study advocated international requirements as "a condition . . . of shares of the export quota allotted to the country concerned" (Charnovitz 1987). The ILO Declaration of Philadelphia sought to prevent socially unacceptable conditions created by trading relationships (Caire 1994:298).

It was not until the 1980s that certain ILO participants urged that labor-rights principles should be incorporated into multilateral trading agreements. In 1983, the European parliament unsuccessfully proposed that GATT adopt a new article that members "respect ILO Conventions on freedom of association and collective bargaining, on discrimination in employment, and on forced labour" (Charnovitz 1987:573). The U.S. Caribbean Basin Initiative, which requires participants to observe reasonable workplace conditions and the right to organize and bargain collectively, "was also implemented with these standards in mind" (Charnovitz 1987:573). In 1989, the European Social Charter established a common set of labor rights for all countries except Britain.

While not calling for specific conditions on trade, the ILO Committee of Experts has recently sought "closer coordination between international agencies involved in advising and assisting governments on economic and employment policy" (Plant 1994:40; see also Hansenne 1994; ILO 1994b). It has admonished specific governments (such as Peru, discussed in chapter 4) that policies interfering in collective bargaining over wage rates should be imposed only as an exceptional measure. The ILO Committee on Freedom of Association challenged Costa Rica on similar grounds.

In 1994, ILO deputy director-general Maier suggested discussions about the need for supranational institutions to replace national institutions weakened by increased global integration. He urged that the ILO's 1977 Tripartite Declaration of Principles Concerning Multinational Enterprises and Social Policy be invoked to prevent competitive bidding wars for foreign investment. Discretionary clauses in trade agreements that relied on persuasion from organizations such as the ILO were preferable to binding clauses (Maier 1994:9f).

Certain employer representatives challenged the deputy general's plea, believing that any social clause would constitute a threat reminiscent of the U.S. Smoot-Hawley Act which raised U.S. tariffs to save American jobs in response to union demands (Myrdal 1994:339f). Such power would turn the

ILO into a weapon directed at developing countries, which might retaliate by making it more difficult to replace obsolete conventions. These proponents view its voluntary character as the key asset of the ILO: The body cannot be both legislator and judge! "The ILO's decision-making body, the International Labour Conference, and the ILO's Governing Body have never stated that they were in favor of a social clause and are unlikely to do so in the future" (Myrdal 1994:350).

Edward Potter of the U.S. Council for International Business insists that opposition to linking standards with trade "has been widespread in the ILO and GATT." "Many developing countries simply do not have the economic or political ability to implement ILO standards. . . . With the possible exception of the human rights conventions, there is no international consensus that ILO standards should be used to 'level the playing field.'" But while Potter prefers the weight of international opinion to sanctions, he agrees that ILO human rights standards do not depend on level of economic development, and that the ILO Tripartite Committee on Freedom of Association and its investigations provide a model for impartiality (1994:362–64).

Nevertheless, ILO members are searching for consensus in three areas. Most agree with (1) the ILO reporting on government compliance. They have less consensus about (2) regional groups restricting imports; and (3) GATT developing a social clause that includes a one-year suspension for violators with voluntary ILO mediation (see Caire 1994:313f). For many years, the International Confederation of Free Trade Unions (ICFTU) has been refining this last approach. Contracting parties would "agree to take steps to ensure the observance of the minimum labor standards specified by an advisory committee to be established by the GATT and the ILO, and including those on freedom of association and the right to collective bargaining, the minimum age for employment, discrimination, equal remuneration and forced labor" (Pursey 1994:374). If the GATT/ILO advisory body located a violation, it would recommend that a nation take measures to improve performance such as a strengthened labor inspectorate and it would offer that nation technical assistance. Only if the failing persisted would it recommend the nation to the WTO for direct sanctions.

The adoption of such ideas has been laboriously slow, frustrating the U.S. and certain other nations. Ironically, the U.S., which failed to ratify many of the ILO conventions, turned to unilateral mechanisms to enforce trade sanctions.[9] Thomas Donahue, at that time AFL-CIO Secretary, said he would prefer to use ILO standards in the enforcement of labor rights, but "compliance requires a stronger enforcement mechanism" (1994:46f).

U.S. Support for Trade Conditions

As the ILO developed standards recognizing labor rights, a parallel historical process incorporated such standards into U.S. trade legislation (see Charnovitz 1987; Hansson 1983; Lyle 1991; Rothstein 1993; Tucker et al. 1988). In 1890, the U.S. banned imports of all foreign goods made by "convict" labor. Congress expanded the law in 1930 to include all forced labor, but despite continued congressional pressure, it was rarely enforced.[10] In 1927, U.S. Caribbean neighbor Cuba became the first government to propose a tariff on nations that violated wage and hour standards. However, it was the union movement, especially the CIO and Textile Workers Union of America in the early 1940s, which originated "the idea of adding labour standards to international trade rules" (Charnovitz 1987:575). In 1947, the U.S. subsequently became the primary proponent of including fair labor standards in GATT. Although unsuccessful at winning trade prohibitions for goods made by forced or child labor,[11] in 1953 the U.S. proposed that unfair labor standards could be sanctioned under Article XXIII (Charnovitz 1987:574). The following year, it urged aiming trade restrictions on countries paying wages "well below accepted standards in the exporting country" (Charnovitz 1987:572). President Eisenhower endorsed a policy to withhold reductions in tariffs on products made by workers receiving wages that are substandard (Charnovitz 1987:572).

Following several earlier efforts by others, in 1979 the U.S. unsuccessfully argued for a minimum labor standard in GATT that included "certain working conditions that are dangerous to life and health." (Charnovitz 1987:572). It was the U.S. that pushed the hardest for minimum labor standards in trade, says French labor law professor Guy Caire (1994:83). However, the U.S. explained that it did not wish to be chastised for acting unilaterally. In the mid-1980s, it sought a multilateral approach (GATT doc., quoted in van Liemt 1989:442). The rebuff that the U.S. received there gave impetus to its adoption of unilateral measures, such as the GSP. Its "aggressive unilateralism" continues to receive criticism (Alston 1996).[12]

Despite the U.S. lack of success in embedding labor standards in the GATT in 1996, it has won backing from several European and Third World nations. These nations remain committed to the principles of enforceable, universal, but flexible standards applied multilaterally. In his keynote address to a 1994 U.S. Labor Department–sponsored symposium, then secretary of labor Robert Reich asserted that standards related to fundamental human rights are absolute, to be upheld regardless of a country's level of economic development. They address "slavery, forced labor, the suppression of freedom of association, and the employment of very young children." Other standards require higher levels of economic development, which go hand in hand with an emergence of democratic institutions. Reich argued that responses should be multilateral, pragmatic, and selected from a range of options (1994:1f).

GSP Incorporation of ILO Standards

The U.S. has ratified very few ILO Conventions. However, its trade conditionality legislation is based on core ILO principles and the UN Universal Declaration of Human Rights. In the 1980s, the International Labor Rights Fund (ILRF) helped draft trade legislation,[13] later supported by the AFL-CIO, which incorporated five specific areas of rights: organizing, bargaining, prohibitions against child labor, against forced or slave labor, and humane working conditions.[14]

1. Right of Association (ILO convention 87). In certain countries, besides psychological intimidation, such a right is often violated by the killings, death threats, kidnappings, attempted kidnappings, and other forms of physical intimidation directed at labor union members.

2. Right to Organize and Bargain Collectively (convention 98). This right is often denied by the refusal to negotiate in good faith and the firing of workers without sufficient cause (they are often the ones demanding negotiations). Another common violation is the failure to develop and implement effective labor legislation that includes reasonable requirements for union recognition and penalties for employers that do not comply.

3. Prohibition Against Forced Labor (convention 29). This provision includes mandated civil patrols, forced migration, the locking of workers in plants, and so on.

4. Prohibition Against Child Labor (convention 138).

5. Right to Acceptable Working Conditions (convention 1 on hours; convention 14 on mandated rest; convention 26 on minimum-wage machinery; convention 102 on social security, and so on). This condition could be violated by exceedingly low wages in comparison with the cost of living with no wage adjustment review, lengthy hours, and unsafe and unhealthy work environments.

The list did not include the principle of anti-discrimination (by gender, race, or religion). Despite the high number of nations that ratified ILO convention 111, the principle was judged to be more susceptible to cultural and economic conditions.

Ohio congressman Donald Pease inserted these five labor-rights standards in the renewed GSP—that is, the Trade and Tariff Act of 1984. For Pease and those of like mind, the basic argument behind such inclusion was not protectionist but rather that the U.S. should not be offering preferential trade advantages to nations that mistreat or penalize their own workforces. Pease cited both economic and political rationales for linking trade and labor rights: Unfairly low standards are inconsistent with stable economic growth in the developing nations. They suppress wealth and job creation in the U.S. It is unfair for workers to lose jobs due to competition from labor whose wages and working conditions have been politically suppressed. Artificially low standards are unfair to workers in the trading countries. Finally, the U.S. public will not support trade liberalization unless standards are addressed (1994:51f).

In passing the bill, Congress did not cut off trade. Rather, it removed the special advantages it normally gave to countries it judged deserving an economic boost. It stressed that the denial of worker rights in these countries tends "to perpetuate poverty, to limit the benefits of economic development," while also being "a powerful inducement for capital flight and overseas production by U.S. industries."[15] Such laws ought not be an incentive for transnational firms to exploit repressed workers and trade unions elsewhere.

The renewed act did allow flexibility in applying GSP labor standards. Recognizing "that acceptable minimum standards may vary from country to country," Congress did not expect that "developing countries come up to the prevailing labor standards of the U.S. and other highly industrialized countries." It only expected them to be "taking steps." Countries should encourage fair treatment of employees, not promote the reverse. Congress did insist that basic human rights were "universal and that all governments are required to respect basic human rights, which include the first three cited worker rights, irrespective of social systems or stage of economic development."

Provisions similar to GSP were included in the Caribbean Basin Economic Recovery Act of 1983 (specifically referencing ILO standards noted above).[16] Over the next few years, they were added to other trade legislation including the Omnibus Trade and Competitiveness Act (1988), the Andean Trade Preference Act (1991), and several other related aid and investment programs.[17] Even the World Bank, the International Monetary Fund (IMF), and the Interamerican Development Bank were subjected to certain labor-rights conditions in 1994.[18] GSP became the "benchmark" of trade legislation because it alone provided interested parties with a mechanism for registering a complaint. The U.S. Trade Representative (USTR) could then review and sanction a U.S. trading partner that allowed worker repression.

Under GSP legislation, a party with appropriate interest in labor violations petitions the USTR to consider possible removal of a nation from the roster of those enjoying tariff reductions. When a petitioner requests a review, the USTR has the authority to accept or deny the request.[19] If it accepts, USTR investigates and holds public hearings. Following this, USTR can decide a nation is "taking steps" to improve labor rights. It can maintain the nation under further review, or it can eliminate a nation's preferential tariffs. In the years following the program's general review in 1986, USTR's GSP subcommittee has removed trade benefits from only nine countries, but it has prolonged the review of many more.

It is the enforcement procedures through USTR that have tied other trade and development legislation such as the Caribbean Basin Initiative and the Overseas Private Investment Corporation Amendment Act to GSP. Thereafter, the labor-rights observance of all program recipients could be evaluated. Although rarely employed, program participants could invoke the GSP mechanism to review labor conditions.

USTR's Reserved Views Toward Labor Rights

Attitudes among unions and government agencies employing labor-rights conditionality have undergone change. In chapter 12, we discuss reactions to GSP effectiveness among workers abroad. Here we examine the transformation that occurred within the U.S. labor movement and within USTR itself.

As indicated above, the impetus toward GSP conditions arose from international "neo-institutionalist" perspectives, not from protectionist sentiments. Since the early 1980s, human-rights and labor groups collaborating with the ILRF argued "that an open trading system can be sustained only if workers are given as much of a stake in it as consumers and financiers" (ILRF 1986). Other nations had the right to develop and expand, even though this might place U.S. workers at some competitive disadvantage. Rather than restricting imports and control investments, advocates preferred to raise labor standards elsewhere so that producers in those countries would be less prone to compete unfairly with U.S. producers. While it would admittedly take many years for other nations to approximate U.S. living standards, that was no reason to allow competition with U.S. workers to be based on gross violations of basic worker rights. Countries that routinely intimidated their workforces with arbitrary firings, anti-union repression, and violence (along with excessively low wages) had an inhumane "advantage" in lower production costs. Standards would help prevent union oppression and encourage just wages. A secondary argument was that better paid workers abroad could afford to buy more U.S. imports.

Nevertheless, support for trade conditionality also arose from protectionist advocates. These included large segments of the U.S. labor movement and other political and labor conservatives who simply sought to protect U.S. jobs. They had good reason for concern about the annual loss of 200,000 jobs from the U.S. and the downgrading nature of new jobs, which often paid substantially lower wages (Labor Institute 1995). Both supporters of ILRF and more protectionist advocates opposed what came to be called "low-wage internationalism," meaning the freedom of transnational corporations to shift their factories to countries that had cheap labor. Disagreements emerged, however, over the extent to which trade barriers would stem job loss, since they could provoke retaliation against U.S. exports. Within the U.S. labor movement, debate evolved between those labeled as "high-wage nationalists" and "high-wage internationalists" (see Cavanagh 1988:42; Pereira and Welch 1995; Garver 1989). This difference influenced the manner in which petitions were brought to USTR. Through much of the 1980s, high-wage internationalists associated with ILRF emphasized labor abuses, while high-wage nationalists of the official U.S. labor movement often endorsed petitions for protectionist reasons. This conflict provided USTR with an additional rationale to delay its judgments.

Politics added another complication. Both the U.S. administration and the AFL-CIO were more likely to support USTR action for political purposes than for labor-related reasons. Their thinking developed amidst the stringent national debate about U.S. policy in Central America. A host of human-rights groups and many rank-and-file members within the union movement urged the U.S. to cease offering military aid to both the El Salvador military and the Nicaraguan contras (see Cantor and Schor 1987). However, attitudes at USTR paralleled administration perspectives. "The first country, Nicaragua, was a give-away," noted one State Department observer, referring to the GSP review of the country most on the outs with the U.S. administration. On the other hand, USTR consistently rejected petitions from human-rights groups. Between 1986 and 1993, the AFL-CIO filed twenty-one petitions, while ILRF and human-rights groups filed nineteen petitions requesting review of Latin nations (see table 4.1). USTR rejected only 29 percent of the federation's petitions but quashed 79 percent of those from rights groups.[20]

Until 1989, USTR rarely found abuses to be labor related. "Especially of petitions not sponsored by the AFL-CIO, the GSP Subcommittee looked for any loophole to deny petitions, including the linkage between violations in human rights [kidnappings, extra-judicial killings] and those of labor rights."[21] It would simply dismiss the petition, saying it contained "insufficient information relevant to the statutory provision" or was not "appropriately related to the five statutory worker-rights criteria clearly delineated."[22] Or USTR would chide petitioners for listing union leaders threatened or executed without clearly showing that the victims were specifically involved in union business or that the perpetrators had acted for that reason.

The U.S. State Department investigations, when they took place, were in sync with USTR's attitude. Part of this was political: Secretary of Interameri-

can Affairs Elliot Abrams eschewed any linkage between human-rights violations and labor rights. Part was because of inexperience: "Most of the embassy
attaches were young junior officers with no labor background, even perhaps
suspicious of labor. They were asked to make decisions about the new GSP
law, and it took a long time for it to sink in."[23]

USTR inaction generated substantial criticism for adopting "a broad definition of 'taking steps' and a narrow interpretation of 'worker rights.' While
USTR has found that even minimal progress on worker rights constitutes 'taking steps,' it has concluded that assassinations of union leaders are not worker
rights violations" (Davis 1995). USTR rejected most petitions by rights advocates without explanation, but then shifted the burden of enforcement to them
and assumed "the role of counsel to the beneficiary developing country" (Collingsworth 1989). If finally forced to review a country, it carried out the U.S.
administration's political agenda, for example ordering withdrawal for Nicaragua, which was hardly the worst offender of labor rights. It also denied
Chile, but quickly accepted its reapplication as a free-market supporter (see
Amato 1990:116). Even the AFL-CIO objected to USTR's "cracking down on
left-wing governments . . . while taking a more lenient attitude toward right-
wing dictatorships" (*AFL-CIO News,* July 11, 1987).[24]

Transformation of GSP

Labor-rights proponents received an unanticipated boost from the disinte-
gration of the Soviet Union. When cold-war politics no longer served any
purpose, U.S. trade-union leaders understood more clearly that unrestricted
overseas expansion posed a real danger for workers everywhere. In 1988, the
AFL-CIO signaled its new emphasis with Lane Kirkland's commemoration of
the fortieth anniversary of ILO convention 87 on freedom of association: "The
denial of basic worker rights should be clearly defined as the unfair trading
practice that it is."[25] Subsequently, the federation took a more expansive view
of the petition process.

Gradually, the State Department and USTR also modified their positions.
"It took awhile for the local embassies to understand that the law on trade
was the law," explained Anthony Freeman. "But the embassies became accustomed to [AIFLD director] Doherty whom they saw as speaking for the AFL-
CIO. They had to learn that the freedom of association is a basic human right,
no matter what a nation's level of development. On the other hand, minimum-wage standards do depend on its level of development. AIFLD was
very adroit at what it did, but it was a four- or five-year education process to
get our house in order before we could apply the law."[26]

In the 1990s, USTR also became much more sensitive to specific labor violations. The shift preceded the arrival of the Clinton administration, but hav-

ing a Democrat in the White House and a new head of USTR with a labor background was certainly a benefit. So were the more clearly defined AFL-CIO objectives. USTR also faced considerable publicity because of its mishandling of petitions on Central America (elaborated below), and ILRF's otherwise unsuccessful lawsuit against it in 1990 (see Davis 1995). Gradually, it became more professionally responsive in appraising petitions.

Still, the difference between GSP's affect on smaller versus larger countries remained a vexing problem. "USTR has bent over backwards to avoid protectionism," noted Freeman. "This made it easier to apply the law to the smaller and weaker nations, not larger countries" where it has a potentially heavy economic effect.[27] It also carried a political message as an indicator of "advanced country displeasure." So small nations viewed the loss of GSP benefits not only as affecting their trade but also their aid, credit, and security. They criticized GSP's unilateral nature, especially since it disproportionately punished local economies. The small nation could not retaliate, yet found its own ability to reduce indebtedness and balance of payments difficulties limited (van Liemt 1989:443–44).

The Byzantine nature of the tariff system also complicated the determination of the precise outcomes of trade sanctions. GSP legislation only covers certain types of products. Certain categories, for example textiles and apparel, fall under their own agreements,[28] while GSP benefits largely accrue to producers and exporters of vegetables, fruit, grains, and sugar. On the other hand, labor violations are not usually restricted to the production of these products. For example, many complaints emanate from treatment in the free-zone apparel maquilas. To put limited pressure on a country or sector, GSP petitioners would sometimes request denial of product-specific benefits. Nevertheless, it took a GSP analysis by the General Accounting Office (GAO 1994) to convince USTR to drop its reluctance.[29] It finally interpreted GSP law to allow penalties on one specific product area.

Perhaps the most vexing problem facing USTR was whether or not a country receiving preferential treatment was "taking steps" to achieve labor rights. "Taking steps" is not an objective standard. USTR has developed pragmatic criteria assessing "steps" in specific countries and conditions. In one country, "steps" might mean that a labor code must be reformed; in another, that certain private sector conflicts be resolved.

In addition, the GSP subcommittee has often interpreted the meaning of "taking steps" differently under different U.S. administrations. In one example in 1995, USTR made the unprecedented decision to send a mission to Honduras, El Salvador, and Guatemala to verify compliance. It even invited trade unionists and labor-rights groups to participate. "The backdrop was an upcoming election year," explained one delegate. "The Democratic Party was assessing its constituencies, including labor and consumers sensitive to sweatshop conditions. It was also concerned about low wages of high-profile retailers. So it was much easier to say, 'this is the trade law and it should be enforced,' than if there had not been an upcoming election."

As Dorman (1989:8) suggests, such quasi-subjective USTR actions must confront at least four difficulties: unstable governments unable to carry out reforms; unpredictable results, such as the strengthening of anti-union actions; lack of public scrutiny of informal government-to-government commitments; and GSP legalese that justifies further delays. USTR's often clandestine determinations of how a national labor code incorporates internationally recognized labor rights can raise questions about objectivity and accountability. They risk the same cultural and economic biases of U.S. labor standards. "Resolving" a particular conflict without public participation can engender lasting resentments.

By 1997, U.S. tariffs had been reduced to near-negligible levels. The GSP program was renewed only until June 30, 1998. "When it receives such short term renewals, it isn't particularly effective," stated one USTR official.[30] Nevertheless, key elements of the GSP process will prove essential for future labor-enforcement trade mechanisms, as we will explore in the chapters ahead.

Empirical Issues in the Measurement of Rights Improvement

The determination of whether trade conditions bring changes in the labor standards of specific countries remains a daunting challenge. It is a challenge that scholars have neglected. "Unfortunately," notes a joint report by the U.S. Department of Labor and the Overseas Development Council, "the academic community has not helped governments overcome their limitations with regard to measuring short-term sociopolitical change, which is at the heart of measuring progress on worker rights. Most 'indicators' are ill-defined and hard to apply, especially with regard to such intangibles as freedom of association and labor participation in decision processes" (Tucker et al. 1988:25). The Overseas Development Council had itself proved the point two years earlier when it offered a positive assessment of the first three years of CBI experience. It praised the outcomes of "negotiated agreements with 20 countries, seven of which had serious worker rights abuses." The council cited Haiti in Duvalier's last years as its most notable success (1986:3)!

It is hoped that the chapters ahead will stimulate more precise scholarly work on the impact of trade conditionality for improving labor-rights observance. We foresee at least four areas of empirical difficulty in testing the effects of GSP trade requirements in Central America and the Caribbean. They include:

1. assessing the manner in which the sanction threat is delivered;
2. determining the incorporation of specific labor standards in national legislation and evaluating the enforcement of such standards;
3. measuring the actual improvement of labor conditions;
4. testing whether or not other variables besides trade conditions might better explain the change in labor conditions rights' improvement.

Threat Delivery

The manner in which the threat of GSP sanctions is presented can have a varying effect on government and private-sector responses. If a labor union or human-rights group takes the action alone, businessmen may regard it as a small annoyance; if the AFL-CIO and the U.S. Embassy back the petition, they may regard it more seriously. If local labor unions unite in support, they may view the petition as especially threatening, but the degree of reaction remains a question.

If a petition is accepted, over time there will be an accumulation of documents and sentiments regarding petition review. But how will such sentiments evolve? To measure the intensity of petition activity, we have developed the following scale. It measures both the number of times a petition has been filed and the intensity of discussion that it generates. The scale is meant to be cumulative, so that if a specific situation misses any element, it would receive an appropriately lower rank.

1. Simple filing
2. Filing with support by international labor groups
3. Filing with extensive support of local labor
4. Accepted for review by USTR
5. Reviewed with major publicity
6. Given one extension of review
7. Given multiple extensions
8. Denied trade preferences

We expect that, commensurate with a petition's rank, the reaction of local government leaders and the business community would have a differentiating effect on the success of GSP in influencing legislative proposals and implementation.

Incorporation of Labor Standards and Enforcement

One of the first areas addressed by petitioners is the legal rights which unions enjoy in a specific country. The study will probe whether or not GSP provisions influenced the content or passage of labor laws. We propose to examine national legislation to determine when it incorporated the rights specified in the five areas listed above. Constitutional provisions or administrative decrees may state certain rights, but they may not yet be elaborated in specific legal regulations.

In many Latin countries, the recognition of appropriate labor standards can be a very different phenomenon from the actual enforcement of such standards, which is much weaker. One reason for the lack of academic scrutiny has been the inconsistent application of apparently agreed upon policies. In reviewing the evolution of the ILO and labor-rights principles, Charnovitz (1987:580) found "little linkage . . . between the various milestones . . . as if different generations have been returning independently to the same important ideas." Since many countries do not fully abide by the ILO conventions on labor statistics, compliance is also difficult to verify objectively. Nevertheless, national studies and press accounts do cite violations and describe conditions—for example, of slave and child labor (see Accolla et al. 1993). An index of free-dom of association can sometimes be derived from unionization rates and the number of viable private- and public-sector union registrations, strike occurrences, and publicized work protests and actions as well as by documented reports of anti-trade-union violence. Freedom to bargain can be assessed by the annual numbers of contracts, the number of firings arbitrated by the labor ministries, and by court records. Working conditions can be verified through reports on minimum-wage standards and compliance, work accidents, and health and safety violations as well as through studies on gender-based income and wage gaps. All these measures together may provide an indication of whether a nation's leadership is truly serious about achieving respect for rights.

Over and above the quantitative data, using case citations from the ICF-TU,[31] Collier and Collier (1991), Compa (1993, Compa (1996), Greenfield and Maram (1987), Phillipps (1991), Southhall (1988), Spalding (1977), Stahler-Sholk (1995), and other national research, our study will also appraise the functioning of national labor legislation in Central American and Caribbean countries. It also will test these findings with local trade unionists and social scientists.

Improved Labor Conditions

If labor standards have a positive effect, then the results also should manifest themselves in improved labor conditions (the dependent variable). If all key factors could be considered, such improvements could be measured with fair accuracy. Data could include such indicators as the economically active population, unemployment and underemployment rates, real sectoral wages, hours worked per week, absenteeism, average length of job tenure, health coverage, pension (indemnization), and other measures from the UN Development Index that affect all workers.[32] This study hopes to encourage such an ambitious undertaking. First, many contradictions of such data must be reconciled and fully understood. For example, the number of court actions on labor issues could increase because of greater institutional effectiveness, but they could also decrease because employers are in greater legal compliance. The more qualitative approach of this study hopes to refine conditions for better interpretation of these quantitative indicators.

Other Potential Factors

The final and most difficult areas will be determining the impact of other influences on labor rights: As pointed out in chapter 2, the countries in question might arguably have developed and enforced improved standards via market mechanisms without the threat of trade sanctions. Neo-classical economists argue that these improvements are not the result of labor-standards conditionality but are rather the normal outcome of competitive employers seeking a more qualified (and therefore better paid) workforce. To account for this, we will keep in mind four ancillary causes that could independently influence labor standards of these countries. These include: (1) improved economic conditions; (2) more open political conditions; (3) private-sector flexibility (whether from self-enlightenment or consumer pressure); and (4) union strength.

1. Economic development can be indicated by: investment rate; GNP growth; per-capita GNP; capital-to-labor ratio; percentage in metal/mechanic industry; labor-productivity efficiency; and trade expansion in manufactured goods and non-traditional exports. We will cite these in the context of economic improvements for most of the population.

2. Political forces may be assessed by: political studies assessing internal control; tax and utility rates; relative importance of U.S. trade; amount of U.S. aid; local U.S. embassy support for the current government; and government cooperation with official U.S. hemispheric objectives. We will examine some of these elements in the post-regional-war period.

3. Private-sector flexibility can be examined by: employer participation in tripartite bodies (ILO); their views on temporary contracts and rules for dismissal; lengths of job tenure and employee turnover; and their cooperation with voluntary codes of conduct and monitoring procedures.

4. Union strength will be shown by: the unionization rate (versus the employer-solidarity association rate); number and duration of strikes and days lost through strike action; inter-union cooperation (joint efforts by labor centrals); extent of participation in bipartite and tripartite activities; and the de-

gree of international support through the ICFTU, ILO, and so on (for example, union actions as described in Humphrey 1982 and Keck 1992 for Brazil).

Thus, the success of labor-rights provisions in achieving actual code enforcement has an objective basis. At this point, qualitative indicators may be most important, but quantitative measures can determine increased union recognitions, reductions in non-cause firings, collective-bargaining agreements, improved wages, and a general lessening in management-labor violence.

Intervening variables that also could affect these results include evolutionary monetary improvements that precede improved standards and labor-code reforms; political forces such as cooperation of or with the U.S. Embassy; employer attitudes and actions regarding flexible contracts and codes, which may enhance organizational or cultural influences on rights observance; and union strength, including coordinated pressure from both national and international bodies that may act as a social force independent of labor-rights provisions in influencing standards. Other aspects, such as emigration and immigration, can also affect labor-pool availability and salary levels. Extensive NGO projects and repatriated earnings may stimulate or serve to reduce labor activities. Sorting through all these factors makes an exact determination of labor-rights effectiveness a formidable objective.

CHAPTER 4

The Record of GSP Petitions in Latin America

What, then, has been the actual affect of the GSP process on Latin American countries? Has the petition process brought improvements in labor rights to the region? If so, have the improvements been lasting, or simply window-dressing to conform to U.S. pressure? To the extent that they have been genuine, would market factors have brought a more significant advance for larger numbers of people? Have certain groups benefited to the detriment of others?

Following the methodology outlined in the last chapter, we propose to answer these questions by examining how the GSP petition process has affected specific national labor policies in Central America and the Caribbean over the past ten years. Since 1985, the International Labor Rights Fund (ILRF), the AFL-CIO, and other groups have been filing petitions to eliminate the trade preferences granted to certain nations.[1] Table 4.1 presents the listing of filed petitions for Latin America as a whole.

Our focus in this chapter is on the economic and labor conditions that existed before the introduction of the GSP petitions, both for Latin America and for those Central American nations that we have selected for scrutiny. We will review the evolving tradition of labor rights in Latin and Central America and their disruption by the "lost decade" of the 1980s. We will describe the AFL-CIO's efforts in Chile and Paraguay, the first petitions centering on Latin American countries aside from Nicaragua. Then, in the chapters that follow, we will examine the impact of petitions on Central American and Caribbean countries in more detail.

Background: Labor Standards in Latin America

Latin American industrial workers won many protections in the 1920s and 1930s, ahead of their co-workers in the U.S. (see Spalding 1977; Collier and Collier 1979; Bergquist 1986; E. Epstein 1989; Plant:1994:85f). The right to strike, as well as fixed hours, required vacations, and mandated wages, came

Table 4.1. Latin American countries where petitions have been filed and whether they were accepted for review by USTR, 1986–97

Nation	Date	Filing labor group	USTR action
Chile	1986	AFL	Rejected
	1987	AFL	Accepted. Nation expelled in 1987, then readmitted.
Columbia	1990	AM+	Rejected
	1993	ILRF	Rejected
	1995	AFL, ILRF, AW	Rejected
Costa Rica	1993	AFL	Accepted. Withdrawn after promised code improvements.
Dominican Rep.	1989	AM	Accepted
	1990	AM	Taking steps
	1991	AM	Rejected
	1993	AFL	Accepted. Withdrawn in 1994 after free-zone enforcement.
El Salvador	1987	AM	Rejected
	1988	AM	Rejected
	1989	AM+	Rejected
	1990	AM++, AFL	Accepted, pended
	1991	AFL	Pended
	1992	ILRF++, AFL	Pended
	1993	AFL	Pended. Removed from review in 1994 after code reform.
Guatemala	1986	AFL	Accepted
	1987	AFL	Rejected
	1988	ILRF	Rejected
	1989	UE	Rejected
	1990	UE+	Rejected
	1991	ILRF+, AFL	Rejected
	1992	ILRF+, AFL	Accepted
	1993	ILRF+, AFL	Pended
	1995	ILRF+, AFL	Pended. Removed from review in 1997.
Haiti	1987	AFL	Rejected
	1988	AFL, ILRF	Accepted
	1989	AFL	Accepted
	1992	AFL+	Rejected
	1993	AFL	Accepted without hearings
Honduras	1991	NYLC	Rejected
	1995	AFL	Withdrawn after agreement
Nicaragua	1985	AFL	Accepted. Nation expelled in 1987.
Mexico	1991	UE+	Rejected
	1993	ILRF	Rejected
	1994	ILRF	Rejected
Panama	1991	AFL	Accepted
	1992	AFL	Pended
	1993	AFL	Petition not renewed after promised improvements in code
Paraguay	1985	AFL	Accepted
	1987	AFL	Accepted. Nation expelled in 1987, readmitted in 1991.
	1993	AFL	Accepted. Withdrawn after promised code improvements.
Peru	1992	AFL	Accepted
	1993	AFL	Accepted

Note: No GSP petitions were reviewed in 1994. + = additional filer; ++ = additional filers.

early to the continent. Borrowing from the French Waldeck Rousseau legislation of 1884, Latin American law encouraged union recognition, equitable wage determination, and dispute resolution. Hemisphere nations committed themselves to other basic labor standards in the peace accords that they signed following World War II. Hispanic countries ranked highest in the developing world in their endorsement of ILO conventions.[2]

However, in Latin America, unlike the U.S., it was the state, not collective negotiations, that often guaranteed employment, salaries, and labor organization. Governments passed labor regulations as a social-control device to minimize disruption and solidify ruling-party authority over working-class loyalty. When unions held elections or approved budgets, states would send representatives to monitor party compliance.

Academicians dispute the precise nature of state control. According to Spalding's analysis (1977) and Collier and Collier's remarkable historical examination (1991), it was worker struggles that originally forced governments to address employee concerns, although invariably the same governments deftly maneuvered legislation to favor specific unions that they could count on for political support.[3] Others stress that in the protectionist context of the 1950s, state affirmation of labor standards, for example in Argentina, became a quid pro quo for union support of import-substitution industrialization policies (Banuri and Amadeao 1992). Having a guaranteed stake in the nation's earnings marked a shift from the Collier and Collier world of union struggle and control to a relationship of exchange.

A related question was who the unions represented. Until the 1960s, labor-rights coverage in many countries was restricted to less than a quarter of the workforce (Banuri and Amadeao 1991). Agriculture and small industries usually were not included; and when they were, most employers skirted requirements by replacing permanent workers with temporary ones (see Tolkman 1992). This same trend would be repeated in the 1990s (see Portes 1990 and chapter 2 in this volume). In the 1960s, union coverage became broader, often encompassing agricultural workers as well as workers in developing industries. However, in the 1970s and 1980s, as Latin economies shifted to export-led industrialization dependent on international trade, states reinterpreted protective labor codes to hem in union demands. Protesting agricultural and industrial workers filled streets and highways in an outpouring more congruent with the Collier and Collier analysis. Nevertheless, trade unions faced growing repression during these two decades of authoritarian rule. In actions parallel to Singapore and South Korea, resurrected military governments invoked state power to restrict labor activity even as they honored previously passed protections for benefits and wages (O'Donnell et al. 1986). At best, activists quietly maintained their union affiliations.

Labor Conditions in Central America

Union protections did not arrive as early to Central America and the Spanish Caribbean as they did elsewhere in Latin America, and they did not contain the same assurances of enforcement.[4] Central American unions were not as enamored of state power as a vehicle for assuring their rights, and Central American parties or governments were less likely to extend rights to unions as a mechanism for solidifying state control (see Goodman et al. 1990). Despite a weaker tradition of union-party alliances, Central American and Dominican workers did win legal rights in the 1940s and 1950s. But the authoritarian governments that dominated the region in the 1960s often found little use for unions or labor legislation.

This is not to deny instances of union-state alliances. The Dominican Republic under Trujillo (1930–61), and to a lesser extent Panama under Torrijos (1968–78), paralleled the Argentine approach. Like Perón, Trujillo was an early advocate of an import-substitution policy through which government enterprises eventually employed 75 percent of the nation's salaried workers. He also backed laws regulating child labor and the eight-hour day. Then, in the 1940s, Trujillo set up his own Confederación de Trabajadores Dominicanos, appointing local leaders while targeting opposition and Marxist activists for elimination. Workers realized improved wages but few guarantees of freedom via Trujillo's labor legislation. The 1951 code, which drew from legislation in Mexico and Venezuela, regulated "the rights and obligations of management and labor." It allowed employers to break contracts without cause and forbade public-sector and general strikes. On the protective side, its elaborate provisions for union registration prohibited dismissal for union involvement and permitted company-related job actions.

Panama offered another example of labor rights brokered through state control. A social security law passed in 1943 eventually offered retirement, disability, medical, and worker compensation to substantial numbers. The first labor code in 1947, though "pro-employer," did include maternity protections. Price and rent controls arrived in 1950 and minimum-wage scales in 1959. When Torrijos assumed power in 1969, he supported various trade unions, set up a Labor Ministry, and implemented a new labor code in 1972. The code guaranteed job stability after two years' employment, collective bargaining, union dues, and flexibility in declaring strikes. The Panamanian constitution also specified equal pay for equal work without gender distinction. It mandated twelve weeks' maternity leave. Torrijos consulted with unions about other policies, cultivating them to maintain state control (see Phillipps 1991; Greene 1984).

In a less effective effort to court labor, Nicaraguan president Anastasio

Table 4.2. Date of first labor code, by CBI country

Costa Rica	1943
Dominican Republic	1951
El Salvador	1963
Guatemala	1947
Honduras	1959
Nicaragua	1945
Panama	1947

Somoza promised legal reforms and recognition to woo cooperation of social-ist unions in the 1940s. He promoted a labor code in 1945, based on Mexican law, which replaced collective bargaining with state intervention (Stahler-Sholk 1987:551). However, after World War II, Somoza reverted to union re-pression and appointed government loyalists to head the socialist unions.

Costa Rica, Guatemala, El Salvador, and Honduras offer clearer examples of the union-state separation. This is true despite a Costa Rican church/com-munist party alliance that formed the basis for its social security legislation in 1941 (see Booth 1987:219–21). The Chilean-influenced 1943 labor code speci-fied the right to organize, to bargain, and to be paid a minimum wage. It eliminated prohibitions on the right to strike, and it created a system of labor courts to arbitrate and resolve disputes. Nevertheless, state-union divisions remained.

Guatemala's labor code, passed in 1947 during its "revolutionary period" (1944–54), reflected Costa Rica's. It offered urban and several campesino groups the right to organize (rural workers won full rights in 1948). The code allowed political involvement. While most unions supported the govern-ment, the Confederación General de Trabajadores de Guatemala, which in-cluded nearly half of the workforce, successfully prevented the code from becoming a mechanism of state control. For example, unions disregarded any clauses that restricted strike action (see López Larrave 1979; Navas Alvarez 1979).

Sustained union demands in El Salvador won a short-lived right to strike and the formation of the Ministries of Labor and Social Welfare in 1946. The Constitution of 1950 provided for the right to form unions, pay equity, weekly rest, annual paid vacations, protections for women, and indemnization for unjust firing. It reaffirmed the legitimacy of strikes. A 1972 code reform sought the "betterment of the living conditions of workers." Despite another state commitment in the labor code of 1963, unions still struggled to make these principles a reality and to obtain the right to form federations (Menjívar Larín 1985:104f).

Table 4.3. Ratification of ILO basic conventions, by CBI country and date

	Convention 87 (Right to associate)	Convention 98 (Right to bargain)	Convention 105 (Slave labor)	Convention 26 (Min.-wage legislation)
Costa Rica	1960	1960	1959	1972
Dominican Republic	1956	1953	1958	1956
El Salvador	—	—	1958	—[a]
Guatemala	1952	1952	1959	1961
Honduras	1956	1956	1958	—
Nicaragua	1967	1967	1967	1934
Panama	1966	1966	1966	1970

Source: ILO.

[a] El Salvador passed C131 regulating minimum salaries in 1994.

The clearest example of conflict-won rights emanated from Honduras. Trade-union recognition grew out of a lengthy banana strike by United Fruit Co. banana workers in 1954. After the workers gained the nation's first collective contract, the government felt compelled to decree legal recognition to all trade unions, including their right to bargain and strike. These rights were promulgated in the 1959 labor code, which drew its principles from the Colombian labor code of 1951 (Cordova 1996; Posas 1980).

Thus, despite exceptions, much labor legislation in the region evolved out of direct worker action, not political largesse. By 1950, as indicated in table 4.2, four of the seven countries had achieved a basic code guaranteeing their rights, and by 1960, six of the seven had done so.

These countries had also adopted most of the basic ILO conventions on labor rights discussed in chapter 2.[5] Between 1950 and 1960, all countries of the region ratified ILO convention 87 on the right of association, except El Salvador and Nicaragua (Nicaragua followed in 1967). The same pattern held true for convention 98, except for Panama, which ratified in 1966 (see table 4.3).

It is notable that, as of 1997, Panama and Guatemala had ratified more ILO conventions than any other Latin nation except Cuba—seventy and sixty-six, respectively. They were followed by Nicaragua, with fifty-eight, and Costa Rica, with forty-six. The Dominican Republic had passed twenty-eight and Honduras twenty-one. El Salvador had been least active in backing ILO instruments, having ratified twenty—until 1995 only six, and most of these following the Peace Accords signed in 1993 (see chapter 7).

Nevertheless, despite these national acknowledgements, labor rights remained very tenuous, whether offered by the state as in the Dominican Republic and Panama or won by worker struggles against jealous and powerful oligarchies as elsewhere. Most nations experienced an erosion of these rights during the 1950s and 1960s. In Costa Rica, union division and fragmentation jeopardized implementation of worker accomplishments. By 1970, unions had only managed to sign four contracts. After the 1954 coup against President Arbenz of Guatemala, the military government amended the labor code to make union political involvement illegal. The Guatemalan law restricted rural organizing, eliminated the right of state workers to unionize, and raised the workweek from forty-five to forty-eight hours. It voided petitions to form unions when any petitioners were fired and virtually rendered legal strikes impossible.[6] The state refused to enforce most of the beneficial provisions of the 1947 code that remained (see also Levenson-Estrada 1994 and Monzán Fernández 1975 for effects of market integration).

Following the Lemus dictatorship (1956–60) in El Salvador, leftist unions gained a new labor-court system and a labor code in 1963. An extensive general strike in 1967 won implementation of the right to strike. However, while article 47 of the 1983 constitution enjoined government interference in worker organizing, it still prohibited campesino and public-sector unions. To reinforce the point, the state promulgated a series of decrees that further inhibited the unionization of public employees while freezing wages and curtailing wage negotiations.

In Latin America as a whole, as in Central America and the Caribbean, it was the economic backsliding of the 1980s that especially weakened political resolve and the legal mechanisms for protecting labor rights.

Latin American Economic Changes in the 1980s

During the 1980s, Latin American nations experienced a dramatic recession which had severe impact on labor conditions. Per-capita GDP fell by about 9 percent over the decade. To cover debt and investment costs, funds flowed out of the region, usually to the U.S. Prices rose by more than 1,000 percent. Real wages dropped by 15 percent for industrial workers and by more than 25 percent for agricultural workers.

At first, conditions seemed hopeless. Then in the second half of the decade they began to improve as unemployment levels dropped. Nevertheless, the new employment came primarily to the informal and service sectors. As the ILO director-general reported, large private enterprises had reduced their share of non-agricultural employment from 44 percent to 32 percent of the total over the decade, and public-sector employment also decreased. The informal sector, constituted by the self-employed and domestic service, rose from 25 percent to 31 percent of the workforce, and small entrepreneurs jumped from 15 percent to 22 percent (ILO 1992a). Informal-sector (and small-industry) workers traditionally received low pay and enjoyed virtually no benefits. One study showed that they lost even more than other workers in the 1980s, suffering an income decline of 42 percent (PREALC 1991).

Unemployment in Latin America is more consequential than in the U.S. also because employees have little protective coverage. Those let go by formal-sector businesses are often absorbed by the informal sector. For fired workers, this means their choice for survival is to become self-employed, to work part time, or to work for below-minimum wages. Thus a better measure of unemployment in Latin America is the amount of underemployment or sub-employment (both "open sub-employment"—working less than forty-seven hours a week—and "hidden sub-employment"—receiving less than the minimum wage). During the decade, sub-employment also rose. So even if unemployment stabilized in Latin America as it did in the U.S. during the last half of the 1980s, the quality of employment declined at the same time (see Tardanico and Menjívar 1997). Over the decade as a whole, the poverty level of the population increased from 41 to 44 percent.

In the dialectical interplay between global and local economic changes, labor rights are sacrificed. Formal-sector workers "have traditionally formed the core of trade unionism in Latin America," but this system has been undermined by the "spread of precarious employment: short term contracts, jobs not protected by laws governing minimum wage, social security and working conditions; and homework and subcontracting" (ILO 1992a). Such "precarious workers" were often paid 50 percent less than permanent workers covered by labor protections. Columbia, Panama, Peru, and other countries changed their labor laws during this period, with the "effect of facilitating dismissals, reducing the cost to employers . . . and broadening the scope of precarious employment contracts" (Plant 1994:88).

These changes were difficult for workers. They also belied neo-liberal predictions about the positive benefits of the market. Despite economic improvement between 1985 and 1991, the region's real minimum wages and industrial wages declined. Table 4.7 shows that Latin America's drop in minimum wages from 86.4 to 65 percent of 1980 wages was even greater than in the first half of the decade. During the last half the 1980s, although GDP, adjusted for inflation, increased by 18 percent, real industrial wages also dropped by 17 percent. The only quasi-accurate forecast related to unemployment, which fell in proportion to the increase in GDP. This did not hold true for sub-employment.

Neo-liberal warnings about the contravening effects of labor legislation did not prove correct either. Despite Latin America's labor protection laws, the labor market itself remained remarkably flexible (Plant 1994:89; see Cordova 1984 for a contrary view). Standards did not prevent a fall in wages or a shift to a non-unionized work force. Actually, since the mid-1980s, Latin

American governments had sought to reduce their regulatory role over labor matters, allowing conditions for unions and unionized workers to deteriorate further. Because of economic pressures for readjustment, states had also removed broad social protections from great numbers of people, including coverage for pensions and health. In the late 1980s and early 1990s, civilian rule returned to much of Latin America, and with it came a growing interest in regional trade integration and tariff reduction (see Sanderson 1992; Tussie 1993; Lustig and Braga 1994; Hansen-Kuhn 1997). However, despite improved economic conditions in the decade's second half, working people of the "lost decade" remained mired in a menial status (see Infante 1991). Improved market conditions even appeared to inhibit "natural" worker gains.

Economic Conditions in Central America and the Caribbean

In the Caribbean Basin, the lost decade of the 1980s had especially severe consequences for labor rights. Like other economies of Latin America, island and isthmus nations exhibited significant deceleration during the first half of the 1980s but showed some improvement in the second half. However, partly because of the wars that engulfed the region, Central America suffered an even worse economic decline in the first half of the 1980s than did the rest of Latin America, and it did not experience a *substantial* economic upturn until the 1990s. The destruction of productive capacity and the displacement of populations prevented rapid resumption of normal output and trade. Each year between 1981 and 1986, nearly every country endured a drop in per-capita domestic product and a jump in external debt. Inflation expanded and personal incomes dropped.

The Central American peace accords, signed in 1986, marked the beginnings of recovery. The wars dwindled gradually, so it took time for these countries to reestablish full economic and political stability. In addition, during the late 1980s, the international prices of the area's traditional exports, and the quota allocations guaranteeing their sale, fell even lower.

Behind this story lies the region's shift from traditional to non-traditional exports and the consequent impact on workforce conditions. Countries experienced a loss in the values of their traditional exports, reaffirming a trend that had been building for some decades. Seasonal workers were thus forced to seek other employment. Many countries also expanded non-traditional exports to exploit new markets. Unlike the import-substitution policies that held sway elsewhere in Latin America during the 1950s through the 1970s, the promotion of non-traditional exports came without labor-union participation or legislated worker protections. As governments and business adopted neoliberal approaches in the 1990s, newly hired employees faced conditions similar to those in the informal sector—virtually no worker rights at all.

Loss of Export Values in Central America

During most of the twentieth century, Central America's economy primarily depended on such "traditional" exports as coffee and bananas. In the 1950s, in response to international financial interests, many landholders also diversified into sugar, cotton, and beef (Bulmer-Thomas 1987:150f). Since then, these five products have formed the basis of Central America's income from abroad: at least two-thirds of it before 1968; about 60 percent between 1969 and 1979; and close to half since then.[7]

Central America saw both its exports and imports advance as a percentage of GNP through 1977, but then decline because of downturns in the world economy. The region became "more vulnerable to variations in the costs of raw materials (petroleum, fertilizers, pesticides), interest rates, and insurance and transport costs" (Sanz 1989). Sizable fluctuations in its terms of trade caused the region to become a net exporter of capital.

Take coffee for example. As the most important Central American export, for decades it averaged between 30 and 40 percent of the region's export income. Central America had also traditionally sold 30 to 45 percent of its coffee through quotas determined by the International Coffee Organization (ICO), which earned its participants as much as 50 percent above world market prices. However, the ICO ended quota allocations in July 1989, anticipating that lower prices would increase demand. This did not happen, partly because corporate processors did not pass on their savings and partly because consumers turned to other beverages. Yet worldwide coffee production increased, and supplies mounted. By 1992, coffee reserves reached 113 million sacks, sufficient to sustain eighteen-months' demand. This further dampened prices, bringing a dramatic loss from $1.45 to $1.07/lb. between 1985 to 1989 and down to $0.70/lb. by 1992—a fall of more than 50 percent. Urged by Guatemala and other Central American nations, Brazil began to champion the reimposition of quotas (CAR, March 20, 1992), but this did not recover the lost income. Price swings persisted, up in 1993–94, down in 1995–96, and up again in 1997–98.

What happened with coffee also occurred to a less extent with bananas, sugar, and beef. Price swings were less pronounced, but in some countries, export quotas fell. Partly because of problems with pesticides, cotton output suffered substantially between 1985 and 1986. Exports dropped by half to $35 million. Beef exports plummeted even further, from a high of $41.6 million in 1979 to $4 million in 1986, although they subsequently recovered.

CBI and the Rise of Non-Traditional Exports

In the face of potential decline in traditional markets, as in the past, coffee and other exporters began searching for alternative ways to invest their assets.[8] A

few investors were influenced by various USAID-funded non-traditional export promotion programs. Then, as indicated in the introduction, in 1983
the Presidential Bipartisan Commission on Central America (Kissinger) promoted the Caribbean Basin Initiative, which offered duty-free treatment to
many Central American and Caribbean imports (see appendix). CBI contained a host of economic measures designed to encourage the export of "non-
traditional," products to the U.S.—fruits, vegetables, seafood, flowers, and
seasonings, but also manufactured products like apparel and footwear.

To support this change, USAID offered each country a variety of financial
incentives and retooled export-promotion programs. It advised regional
governments to broaden their tariff reductions and welcome even more foreign investment. To accomplish this, USAID provided balance-of-payments
support to governments that "would take action toward a better legal and
regulatory environment for private-sector activity. . . . USAID also created
trade and investment promotion organizations, encouraged development
of export-processing zones, and provided support for assembly operations"
(USITC 1994). USAID's joint project with the Department of Commerce, the
Latin American / Caribbean Business Development Center, even sought out
potential U.S. investors and their factories. The Overseas Private Investment
Corporation (OPIC) and the Export Import Bank (Eximbank) guaranteed financing and insurance. How could a U.S. company turn them down?

Yet neither CBI, nor the Caribbean Basin Economic Recovery Act (CBERA),
was an overnight success. At first, the U.S. also insisted on protectionist tariffs,
quotas and non-tariff barriers for many products (see Harr 1990). By the end
of 1984, only 14 percent of Central America's $1.7 billion in exports to the U.S.
were under CBI (Gill 1985). Even after ten years of functioning, CBI's business
output results were not as dramatic as policy makers had expected. Despite
$16 billion from USAID over twelve years, the region did not even surpass its
own $10 billion export level in 1980 until in 1992 (see appendix). During most
years, the value of Caribbean Basin exports to the U.S. *dropped,* primarily because of declining petroleum prices.[9] "Unilateral trade preferences . . . were
expected to assure faster growth of CBERA country exports to the United
States than the growth of U.S. exports to CBERA countries. In fact, the opposite happened," admitted the U.S. International Trade Commission. "The
United States . . . maintained its surplus. . . . In 1993, the U.S. surplus
amounted to $1.8 billion. In addition, the Caribbean share in U.S. imports
from the world actually declined" (USITC 1994).

It was a dramatic admission, and it did not even address non-economic
drawbacks to the shift from traditional to non-traditional production, such
as the loss of autonomy and the damage to ecological and cultural practices

Table 4.4. U.S. imports for consumption from CBI countries, by subregion and country, select years, 1984–93 (per 1,000 dollars, U.S. customs value)

	1984	1986	1988	1990	1992	1993
Non-oil-producing countries						
Central America						
Belize	42,843	50,181	52,049	43,978	58,510	48,984
Costa Rica	468,633	646,508	777,797	1,006,474	1,402,042	1,542,098
El Salvador	381,391	371,761	282,584	237,538	383,245	481,342
Guatemala	446,267	614,708	436,979	790,900	1,072,697	1,178,094
Honduras	393,769	430,906	439,504	486,330	780,638	914,380
Nicaragua[a]	—[b]	—[b]	—[b]	15,254	68,609	124,543
Panama[c]	311,627	352,206	256,046	226,555	218,232	233,131
Subtotal	2,044,530	2,466,270	2,244,959	2,807,029	3,983,973	4,522,572
Central Caribbean						
Dominican Republic	994,427	1,058,927	1,425,371	1,725,430	2,366,509	2,667,202
Haiti	377,413	368,369	382,466	339,177	107,170	154,335
Jamaica	396,949	297,891	440,934	563,723	593,361	710,260
Subtotal	1,768,789	1,725,187	2,248,771	2,628,330	3,067,040	3,531,797
Total	3,813,319	4,191,457	4,493,730	5,435,359	7,051,013	8,054,369
Grand total[d]	8,649,235	6,064,745	6,061,054	7,525,208	9,425,616	10,094,033

Source: USITC 1994.

[a]Nicaragua was designated a beneficiary country effective November 8, 1990.

[b]Not applicable.

[c]Panama lost its designated beneficiary status effective April 9, 1988, and was reinstated in March 1990.

[d] Includes Eastern Caribbean region.

(AVANSCO 1994; Berger 1992; Thrupp 1995; Weinberg 1991). Nevertheless, USITC concluded that "CBERA had a positive impact" that helped "cushion the effects of declining world-market prices of the region's traditional, resource-based exports." It had encouraged diversification "into more profitable, nontraditional manufactured and agricultural products," making Caribbean countries "more resilient and internationally competitive."

For the nations in our study, table 4.4 indicates the rise in exports to the U.S. from Central American and the Central Caribbean nations between 1984 and 1993, the first ten years of the CBI program.[10] Exports more than doubled from Costa Rica, Guatemala, Honduras, and the Dominican Republic.[11]

The changing economies in Central America (and the Caribbean) also had a dramatic effect on the nature of the workforce and, in turn, the observance of worker rights. As in Latin America as a whole, the informal sector and service industry expanded as workers in agriculture declined (see Menjívar and Pérez Sáinz 1989). The industrial sector retained its workforce proportion, but it only did so because of accelerated maquila production.

Non-traditional Agricultural Exports

During the 1980s, under the guidance of CBERA and various USAID export-promotion schemes, Central American producers replanted their lands in broccoli, cauliflower, melons, raspberries, cardamom, sesame, and flowers. For example, the export of roses from Guatemala to the U.S. jumped from $1.2 million in 1986 to $3.4 million in 1991. Melons and peas rose to above $8 million each; other vegetables reached $20 million. Twenty-five percent of the value of consumable legal Guatemalan imports to the U.S. entered under GSP/CBI protection.[12] (Another group of non-traditional exports—cocaine, poppy, and marijuana plants—grossed more than $200 million in 1991.)

However, the growth of non-traditional agricultural exports carried significant costs in land lost to local production—forcing the purchase of more traditional crops from abroad. As farms reassigned resources, traditional crop workers and tenants were forced to comply. While certain mid-sized landowners and cooperatives did well producing non-traditional agricultural exports, many small farmers remained in debt because original contract promises were not honored. The move jeopardized the reservoir of knowledge accumulated for generations that had provided relative self-sufficiency even in the midst of wrenching civil wars.

Historically, agricultural workers had enjoyed fewer legal protections than other workers; but with the shifts of land from traditional to non-traditional production, businesses no longer even provided permanent laborers with basic guarantees of family housing and limited health and educational benefits.[13] Increasingly, rural workers sought employment in more urbanized areas, creating a fresh labor force attractive to outside investors.

Industrial Exports

In local terms, the realignment caused by the decline in traditional exports was most visibly evident in the proliferation of garment assembly operations,[14] even though the sustained nature of such investment remains uncertain. In the mid-1980s, the Central American and Caribbean governments wooed foreign investment by suspending duties for export investors on incoming machinery, equipment, and semi-finished goods. They also stepped up their promotion of industrial free zones or EPZs. As mentioned in the introduction, President Reagan modified CBERA in 1986 with a Special Access Program that brought a crucial shift in apparel employment to Central American and Caribbean nations. The CBERA agreement had not originally included such products because they were already part of the global "Multifiber Arrangement" trade agreement. Since the agreement already reduced tariffs, the Special Access Program increased national quotas beyond those stated in the Multifiber Arrangement.[15] Costa Rica, the Dominican Republic, Guate-

Table 4.5. U.S. apparel and footwear imports from CBI countries, select years, 1984–93 (per 1,000 dollars, U.S. customs value)

	1984	1986	1988	1990	1992	1993
Textiles and apparel	511,656	818,038	1,488,812	2,006,348	2,995,699	3,633,130
Footwear	10,005	10,618	39,255	35,806	45,884	42,000
Footwear uppers, of leather	71,488	116,656	121,305	151,764	199,773	—

Source: USITC 1994.

mala, Haiti, Jamaica, and Panama each eventually negotiated new "guaranteed access levels" with the U.S. directly. By 1989, 84 percent of 1989–90 Caribbean Basin apparel and textile exports qualified (U.S. Department of Commerce 1990a).

According to USITC, there was a "growing use of production sharing by U.S. companies with Caribbean facilities as a response to intensified global competition." Between 1985 and 1990, the number of maquila factories in Guatemala alone jumped from 41 to 220, with a workforce of 50,000. These plants added $53.7 million to the value of Guatemalan exports in 1990 and $86.8 million in 1991, the third most valuable export after coffee and sugar.[16] The region's apparel exports to the U.S., valued at $510 million in 1984, rose by seven times that amount to $3.6 billion by 1993. As the USITC admitted, "The rapid increase of apparel shipments to the U.S. market made Caribbean countries collectively the fastest growing U.S. supplier in 1989–93," followed by Mexico and China (USITC 1994).

While apparel and textiles were the most notable exports responsible for this shift, many other types of manufacturing jobs were also created, including in footwear, medical and surgical instruments, electrical instruments, sporting goods, and jewelry.[17] So even though overall industrial production in Central America slowed (in Guatemala, it dropped by 3.5 percent in 1988 [U.S. Department of Commerce 1990a:2]), non-traditional sectors dramatically increased. Again in Guatemala, they jumped from 13.3 percent of export income in 1986 to 37.4 in 1991, exceeding the value of coffee exports, while traditionals fell from 74.3 to 58.2 percent.[18] By 1993, manufactures accounted for 59 percent of U.S. imports from CBERA countries, up from a mere 18.2 percent in 1984.

However, there were downsides to maquila expansion as well. Maquilas rarely used local suppliers.[19] Since most Central American countries permitted unrestricted profit repatriation, for reasons of stability and exchange, even Guatemalan investors preferred to keep their deposits in U.S. banks. As a result, "at least 25% of the foreign exchange generated by the maquila industry" never entered the country.[20]

The industrial sector largely remained stagnant except for the rapid expansion of maquila workers. At first, the workforce in Central American and Caribbean maquilas was largely female, young, and unmarried, in an industrial workforce that otherwise was 75 percent male. This paralleled maquila hiring elsewhere (Sklair 1993; Kammel 1990; Flamm and Grunwald 1985). According to Fernandez-Kelly (1983) and Tiano (1990), women took on such jobs not because they wanted to, but because they were forced to do so by economic circumstance. In Aníbal González's survey of sixty Guatemalan maquila factories (1989), 70 percent of the workers were women, 65 percent of these unmarried. Turnover rate was high—as much as 10 to 30 percent a month (Petersen 1992). Governments often protected maquila zones from union organizing and overlooked enforcement of minimum-wage and minimum-hours requirements. During the 1990s, as jobs elsewhere declined, maquilas hired a greater percentage of male workers.

Indirectly, CBERA enticements also had an impact on employment in the service sector, including government employment, which suffered such a major reduction during the 1980s. The proportion of state-related jobs declined from 20 to 12 percent of the workforce due to economic restructuring and the privatization of state enterprises. Inspired by neo-liberalism, regional governments cut positions even further in the mid-1990s. While often legally prevented from striking, many workers in these jobs had solid wage and benefits advantages and were a potent force in demanding government observance of national labor laws. By 1996, the service sector was primarily constituted by workers in commerce, transport, and financial activities. The sector included many self-employed who received no specified labor protections.

Thus, as the workforce became more fragmented over the decade, governments facing neo-liberal pressures became more forthright in demanding labor concessions. They grew lax in carrying out the labor codes achieved several decades earlier, and at times facilely decreed labor law suspensions. In addition, despite some economic improvements to Central American and Caribbean economies in the late 1980s, workers, especially those in unprotected jobs, were again asked to bear the brunt of price hikes and job erosion. In some countries, repression directed at trade unions accelerated to new levels.

Overall Economic Benefits

The combination of USAID strategies, government efforts, and international pressure did bring the region some economic stability during last half of the decade, though it was less than that achieved by Latin America as a whole. Capital flight was reduced, and international indebtedness did not markedly increase. Beginning in 1987, GDP grew by 3 percent or more each year, and inflation remained under control (see table 4.8 for specific countries). The states attempted to improve infrastructure and services for foreign capital. Public-sector expenditures grew after the Central American Peace Accords in 1986. However, the business sector grew apprehensive, and reinvestment remained slow. Import values stayed above exports, and international lenders called for spending reductions. At decade's end, most governments were forced to devise additional "structural adjustments" that included further currency devaluations, reduced tariffs, fewer price controls, and freer interest rates. Inflation often shot up.

Given the economic improvements that began during the last half of the 1980s and increased in the 1990s, however, neo-liberal predictions would have anticipated an improvement in wages and employment. The following three tables proves the opposite. Table 4.6 compares urban unemployment rates of four Central American nations to that of Latin America overall. Three of the four (all but Costa Rica) experienced a great rise in unemployment in the latter part of the 1980s. All but Panama and El Salvador showed some recovery in the 1990s. Minimum wages fell between 1980 and 1991, significantly so for Guatemala (see table 4.7).

Table 4.8 shows that between 1987 and 1995, employment did increase by 30 to 40 percent in tandem with GDP (less so in Costa Rica and Guatemala, more so in El Salvador, Honduras, and Panama). However, rather than their predicted increase, wages declined in all countries except Honduras. These trends are also summarized by the correlations presented in table 4.9. Rises in GDP and employment demonstrate a very high correlation in all countries (.81 to .93) and a relatively high negative association with unemployment (-.59 to -.82). However, GDP improvement shows virtually no link to better wages in Guatemala, El Salvador, or Panama, and is *negatively* associated in Costa Rica and the Dominican! Contrary to neo-liberal principles, as GDP improves, there is no commensurate increase in wages, either as naturally occurring or as politically enforced. This reaffirms the views of Caribbean Basin workers that additional intervention is required to assure basic rights, even though the annual GDP growth for most countries under study here had approached 4 percent by 1997.

Beginnings of GSP Petitions

The transformations of labor conditions and assaults on labor protections discussed above provided the context for GSP action favoring trade sanctions. Nevertheless, at the outset, it was repressive anti-union action in Chile and Paraguay that prompted the AFL-CIO's first petitions in Latin America. The federation also could have requested USTR to review Argentina and Brazil, although as pointed out in chapter 3, fear of retaliation prevented GSP threats

Table 4.6. Urban unemployment rates in Central American nations, 1984–95

	1984	1985	1986	1987	1988	1989	1990	1991	1992	1993	1994	1995
Latin America	10.0	10.1	9.2	8.3	8.5	8.0	8.1	7.8	—	—	—	—
Costa Rica	6.6	6.7	6.7	5.9	6.3	3.7	5.4	6.0	4.2	4.4	4.5	5.7
El Salvador	—	8.5	8.3	8.3	9.4	8.4	10.0	8.0	8.5	10.0	17.0	16.8
Guatemala	9.1	12.0	14.0	11.4	8.3	6.2	6.4	6.7	6.1	5.5	6.1	6.3
Honduras	10.7	11.7	12.1	11.4	8.7	7.2	6.9	8.5	6.4	7.5	—	5.9
Nicaragua	—	20.9	—	24.4	26.0	—	—	11.1	13.6	16.2	20.0	—
Panama	12.4	15.7	12.7	14.1	21.1	20.4	20.0	16.1	13.6	12.4	17.7	17.7

Source: 1984–91 data from PRELAC, no. 369; 1992–95 data estimated from ILO Statistical Yearbook.

Table 4.7. Minimum-wage index, Latin America and four CBI countries, 1980–91

	1980	1981	1982	1983	1984	1985	1986	1987	1988	1989	1990	1991
Latin America	100.0	96.9	94.2	91.8	89.7	86.4	84.7	85.2	91.2	74.1	67.0	65.0
Costa Rica	100.0	90.4	85.8	99.3	104.4	112.2	118.6	118.1	115.0	119.7	120.8	115.0
Guatemala	100.0	120.9	120.7	115.3	111.4	94.0	68.6	61.1	75.9	68.1	48.2	38.9
Honduras	100.0	106.2	106.3	98.2	93.3	90.7	86.9	84.8	81.2	73.9	80.6	73.3
Panama	100.0	93.2	89.4	102.1	101.3	100.8	100.8	99.8	99.5	99.6	99.0	97.5

Source: PRELAC, no. 369, based on household surveys and official data.

Table 4.8. GDP growth, employment growth, and wage improvements, by CBI country, 1984–95 (1987 = 100)

	1984	1985	1986	1987	1988	1989	1990	1991	1992	1993	1994	1995
Costa Rica												
GDP	99.12	94.5	95.5	100.0	103.5	109.3	113.3	115.8	124.8	132.8	138.8	142.4
Employment	109.1	110.5	107.5	100.0	103.0	106.9	110.2	109.0	113.0	118.8	123.2	126.5
Wages	89.3	81.9	85.5	100.0	102.8	100.6	100.9	107.3	108.7	98.5	94.7	n/a
Dominican Republic												
GDP	102.7	96.9	93.0	100.0	100.7	113.5	108.1	109.1	117.6	121.1	125.9	129.0
Employment	n/a	n/a	n/a	100.0	100.0	97.6	n/a	n/a	n/a	n/a	n/a	n/a
Wages	99.9	90.9	86.8	100.0	98.9	95.2	95.5	80.8	77.3	73.4	78.0	86.0
El Salvador												
GDP	99.5	100.0	97.6	100.0	101.8	102.7	107.7	111.4	119.8	128.2	135.5	144.9
Employment	n/a	n/a	n/a	100.0	108.5	119.6	134.0	134.8	135.3	139.7	148.2	149.9
Wages	252.6	170.8	127.5	100.0	115.7	127.0	141.1	135.7	134.5	136.1	n/a	n/a
Guatemala												
GDP	100.6	99.9	96.6	100.0	103.9	108.0	111.3	115.4	121.0	125.7	130.7	134.6
Employment	112.4	107.0	102.7	100.0	114.8	116.1	115.7	115.9	117.2	121.2	122.3	n/a
Wages	125.2	116.2	92.5	100.0	94.3	90.3	110.2	115.9	103.3	96.6	98.0	n/a
Honduras												
GDP	95.7	99.0	94.4	100.0	104.9	108.9	108.9	112.3	118.6	126.3	124.1	129.0
Employment	96.4	100.3	97.9	100.0	104.2	107.3	93.3	115.0	128.8	132.2	135.7	139.0
Wages	98.4	97.4	98.4	100.0	102.7	103.0	107.6	103.8	107.7	n/a	n/a	n/a
Nicaragua												
GDP	104.3	102.0	100.7	100.0	88.35	87.2	87.2	86.5	87.9	87.3	88.9	92.7
Employment	n/a	n/a	n/a	100.0	n/a	n/a	82.8	70.5	68.8	n/a	n/a	n/a
Panama												
GDP	95.4	96.7	97.6	100.0	84.4	84.0	87.9	96.3	104.5	110.2	115.4	119.4
Employment	109.5	107.6	105.1	100.0	96.5	101.2	103.7	106.2	115.2	120.2	122.9	n/a
Wages	101.4	100.7	100.9	100.0	101.0	101.8	90.7	87.5	92.1	n/a	n/a	n/a

Source: GDP computed from World Bank Development Indicators (1997); employment and wage data computed from ILO Statistical Yearbook of Labour Statistics and (for Guatemala) Ministry of Labor statistics.

Table 4.9. GDP, employment, urban unemployment, and real-wage growth, Pearson R correlations, by CBI country, 1984–94

	GDP/employment correlation	GDP/unemployment correlation	GDP/real wage correlation
Costa Rica	.81	-.72	-.48
Dominican Republic	n/a	n/a	-.66
El Salvador	.87	.72	-.17
Guatemala	.85	-.82	.11
Honduras	.93	-.81	.90
Panama	.88	-.59	-.23

Source: Tables 4.6 and 4.8.

against larger countries. In the early 1990s, petitioners also filed on Peru, Columbia, and Mexico, but USTR accepted none of their requests for review.

Chile

In 1931 Chile became the first Latin nation to pass a labor code legalizing unions and providing benefits and labor courts. However, code passage occurred in the face of union objections that it increased state control; the government retained authority to approve unions, and labor inspectors could attend meetings and held power over contract disputes. Nevertheless, most unions made an effort to gain legal status. Numbers consistently increased until 1947 and revived again in the 1950s following a "communist purge" (Loveman 1987:134f). Thus, Chile's 1931 labor code became a model for other governments to follow.

During Allende's Popular Unity government in 1970, labor representatives held three ministerial positions, and by 1973 trade unions represented 40 percent of the workforce. However, the Pinochet regime of terror that followed the overthrow of Allende's Popular Unity in 1973 virtually eliminated all trade-union rights. Many union leaders were killed. As it promoted free-market economic approaches, the military decreed its own brand of labor legislation. It destroyed previous barriers to arbitrary firing, removed protections for employee-association involvement, and interfered with job actions. Because of international pressure, the state slightly modified the labor code, but it still reinforced existing prohibitions on much union behavior. The government controlled the activities, the numerical strength, and the affiliation of the unions and allowed juridical intervention in internal union matters.

Because of a petition from the AFL-CIO, USTR included Chile in its first GSP worker rights review in 1986. The petition addressed Chile's restrictive legislation and its abusive practices. The government denied that its code needlessly restricted union action, since "unions often contributed to unrest, and did not represent members, much less Chilean labor as a whole." It complained that Chile was being singled out for special treatment since unions had more rights in Chile than in many countries (see Dorman 1989:14). USTR allowed the government additional time to establish that it was taking steps toward labor protections.

"The first real test of GSP was Chile," said one State Department observer, explaining that President Reagan favored its free-market policies despite its labor abuses. "But the administration had also grown tired of Chile. Pinochet had insulted the Assistant Secretary when he visited, and the State Department was angry." In addition, although it slightly lowered the number of employees required to form a union, the Pinochet government responded by embedding past union restrictions in the new 1987 labor code. At that point USTR had had enough and removed Chile's $87 million worth of duty-free exports from GSP.

The trade sanctions brought early results, and the Chilean government quickly got the message. According to Hernol Flores, secretary general of Chile's Democratic Workers Central, "the suspension of some Chilean products from the GSP . . . was without doubt a strong signal to the dictatorship and its business allies, which . . . were forced to lessen the severity of their abuses and to begin to recognize the injustices of the labor law." Flores also thought it helped establish U.S. credibility among Chilean workers (AFL-CIO *Bulletin*, Jan. 1989).

Even more, the petition bolstered many other efforts by U.S. policy makers to alter Chile's human-rights policy. Those efforts included public statements by the U.S. president and other officials, financial sanctions, and efforts at isolation (Dorman 1989:14). All were elements successfully encouraging the regime to hold a plebiscite on returning to democratic institutions.

When Chile finally agreed to adopt further labor-code reforms, GSP exclusion was lifted. The nation passed a reformed code in 1994 (see Epstein 1997). As AIFLD's former organizing director David Jessup explained, "there was a long delay because of additional disputes over property rights, and there are still some problems in the labor code.[21] Central government service units are restricted from joining unions. Labor is using the proposed NAFTA access to pressure the government to change the law to conform with ILO standards, but business is raising objections."[22]

Paraguay

Surprisingly, Paraguay achieved an early labor code during the brief rule of Colonel Rafael Franco in 1936–37. Although the code significantly restricted union activity, the law established a strong Department of Labor which registered 130 unions. Under the lengthy dictatorship of General Alfredo Stroessner from 1954 to 1989, Paraguay only permitted labor membership in its government-controlled Confederación Paraguaya de Trabajadores, marshalling police to crush independent efforts. In 1981, AIFLD helped create an alternative Movimiento Independiente de Trabajadores, which by 1985 included the outlawed journalists union and other union dissidents supported by both AIFLD and the Christian Democrats.

In 1987, USTR suspended Paraguay's GSP privileges. AIFLD's 1988 special report, *Worker Rights in Paraguay,* argued for permanent suspension, and the AFL-CIO continued to file petitions. In 1989, Stroessner was overthrown, replaced by General Andrés Rodriquez, who appeared more open to labor. AIFLD unions regrouped under the Confederación de Trabajadores (CUT). However, by June 1990 the AFL-CIO had documented twenty-three cases of worker firings for union activity. Both CUT and the AFL-CIO reaffirmed the need for Paraguay's suspension from GSP.

Yet after another change in government, U.S. president Bush restored Paraguay's GSP privileges in February 1991, "over our objection," as David Jessup noted. "The old labor code was still in force. There were promises but no actions." Worker firings increased.

The CUT turned to politics. Its candidate Carlos Filizzola won as mayor of Asunción in May 1991, with strong union support, defeating the government candidate. When the government jailed CUT's general secretary Victor Baez, a former AIFLD graduate, in September 1991, the AFL-CIO obtained his release by threatening to petition for GSP suspension again. Then, in March 1993, the Labor Ministry abruptly decreed new union elections, suspending incumbent leaders and bringing all trade-union actions to a standstill. Businesses abrogated contracts and fired several thousand workers. The government also halted its labor-code reform process, as Jessup described: "In 1993 what we said would happen did happen. The president vetoed code reforms approved by the ILO and passed by the Congress." An AFL-CIO petition was accepted for review in 1993. "AIFLD Director Doherty met with President Juan Carlos Wasmosy in the presidential palace, and right on the spot got him to call in the Labor Minister who immediately agreed to support passage of the bill. It passed."

The AFL-CIO withdrew the petition after Paraguay finally ratified the reformed code. "But the labor code is not being effectively enforced," added Jessup, "and so we are doing another petition to enforce the new law."

In the early 1990s, other petitions were filed in Latin America by the AFL-CIO on Peru, by the federation and ILRF on Columbia, and by the latter on Mexico. None gained USTR review; however, the agency did accept a petition on Haiti.

Peru

Peru has enjoyed a history of strong labor unions. Between 1936 and 1982, nearly 4,800 unions were established. Numbers declined during the economic crisis of the 1970s but grew dramatically in the 1980s, especially among state workers (Bollinger 1987b:607). In 1991, the ILO chided Peru that in regard to convention 98, wage restrictions should only be imposed in exceptional circumstances, and should normally be determined by collective bargaining.

The AFL-CIO filed a petition on Peru in 1992 because of restrictions on worker rights under the Fujimori government.[23] Refusing review in 1992, USTR accepted the federation's 1993 petition, which cited threats to the trade-union movement "by a massive and premeditated attack intended to destroy it . . . laws which annul traditional worker rights . . . and gravely restrict union activities" (*Bulletin,* July–Aug. 1993). According to Jessup, the "petition was accepted because Fujimori's decrees were in opposition to ILO standards. However, the unions there did not have much specific information to support this, being unaccustomed to the review process. We were unable to back up the petition. The government argued that the decrees were not enforced, that no one was suffering. Since we couldn't collect enough detailed information, the USTR review found the country was 'taking steps.'

"It shows you the political aspects of the process," continued Jessup. "In El Salvador, we produced tons of information, and USTR stuck to the letter of the law when it denied the petition. In Peru it was the opposite; they wanted the empirical evidence before they would accept violations."

Nevertheless, the threat of petition review influenced Peru to incorporate ILO convention 1 on hours of work into national legislation. In 1991, it established the right of workers to be compensated for unwarranted dismissal, but it did not set up any insurance scheme to accomplish this, as required by ILO convention 44. In 1995, it promised to amend the 1992 Industrial Relations Act to reduce from a hundred to fifty the number of workers required to form a union above the enterprise level, to ease trade-union reporting obligations, and to change other restrictions. However, contrary to convention 87, it banned trade unions from political activity and restricted strikes to "defense of occupational rights and interests." Individuals in their probationary period did not have the right to union membership. Under the Fujimori government, workers continued to lose considerable protections (NACLA 1996). In 1992, Peru also embarked on a new system of private pension plans, but it was underwritten by a 10 percent levy on worker wages, not a contribution from employers. The ILO questioned how secure such coverage would be (ILO 1995a).

Columbia

Labor rights in Columbia were codified after 1930 when the Liberal party supported unionization efforts as a party-building tactic. In 1934, legislation enabled formation of the "first modern central" (Pedraja Toman 1987:182).

In Columbia, violence against trade unionists has been endemic. Between 1986 and 1990, its largest labor confederation (CUT) saw a thousand of its members assassinated. ILRF's petition influenced the 1990 labor code reform. However, ILRF then discovered that the "reform" permitted short-term contracts that made access to free association and collective bargaining more difficult.[24] It also cited persistent health problems among workers in the flower industry, and incessant foot dragging by the nation's justice system in investigating the murders of labor leaders, so it refiled (*Worker Rights News,* Summer 1993). The AFL-CIO had less success. Since its affiliated unions were "in the middle of negotiations and hopeful of winning new concessions," the federation failed to persuade them that the petition would provide additional leverage.

Columbia was nevertheless sufficiently worried about its reputation that in 1993 it adopted a new Social Security Act that gradually covered the entire population, including agricultural workers. In 1994, it restricted the requirement of a pregnancy test for obtaining employment to occupations of "high risk." It reduced other discriminatory requirements for public service. However, as the ILO pointed out (1995a) regarding convention 29, it still allowed private contracts for use of prison labor at half the minimum wage; regarding convention 87, it required authorities to be present at union general assemblies that took strike or arbitration votes, and gave the government other internal controls.[25]

Regarding convention 97, Columbia granted full trade-union privileges to all trade-union leaders, including those in the public sector. However, public employees were still prevented from negotiating collective-bargaining agreements, and anti-terrorist legislation was still applied to workers on strike.[26] Murders directed against CUT unionists remained unabated (another 500 between 1991 and 1995, a significant percentage perpetrated by state agents).[27] Union organizers were often fired, and the government permitted an illegal use of "collective pacts" and individual contracts to prevent unions, especially in the textile assembly plants around Antioquia and Santander. In 1995, the AFL-CIO again petitioned USTR to inaugurate an official review for these reasons, but it refused to do so.

Mexico

The conditions of labor rights and union development in Mexico, and the detrimental effect of a longtime union-state alliance between the Confederación de Trabajadores de Mexico (CMT) and the Partido Revolucionario Institucional, has been well analyzed by Cockcroft (1995), LaBotz (1995), and others. In 1992, without CMT support, but with encouragement from independent unions, ILRF filed, protesting Mexico's passage of a more restrictive labor policy to attract foreign investment. It noted violations of the right of association, such as at the Ford-Cuautitlan plant. Further challenges to Mexican labor practices have been pursued under the NAFTA side agreement (see Compa 1996; Cook et al. 1997). The ILO has recognized progressive features in Mexico's labor laws, but it has criticized the nation's failure to bring the Federal Act on State Employers into conformity with ILO convention 87. It urged allowance of more than one union in an institution, the right of state workers to leave the official union (now prohibited) and removal of rules inhibiting trade-union pluralism (ILO 1995). In late 1997, the government begrudgingly allowed the National Union of Workers to organize in certain areas. It also recognized the Authentic Labor Front's right to establish the first independent maquila union on Mexico's side of the border—the Han Young/Hundai auto plant. However, Hundai management continued its resistance.

Haiti

Although not properly of Latin America, Haiti was part of USTR's regional scrutiny of labor-rights practice. During the 1980s, Haiti became the fourth-largest exporter of apparel to the U.S. in the hemisphere, while real wages fell more than 60 percent. AIFLD set up a union-support office in Port-au-Prince in 1986. In 1987, firebombs destroyed the Workers Federation of Trade Unions office. In 1988 and 1989 the AFL-CIO cited Haiti for its repressive labor code (a vestige of the Duvalier era, which gave the government significant control over unions and limited strikes to twenty-fours hours in duration). After finally agreeing to review Haiti in 1991, USTR quickly certified the country as "taking steps." The AFL-CIO was especially incensed when USTR rejected its 1992 petition, "allowing export to the U.S. of certain goods made by exploited workers in U.S. owned firms" (*Bulletin*, Oct. 1992). It also decried the violence that caused the Confederation Generale Independante des Travailleurs Haitiens confederation to lose nearly half of its membership and forced teachers union members into hiding. The AFL-CIO again petitioned USTR in 1993, quoting the U.S. State Department finding of "widespread repression and violence against trade-union activities . . . arrests, beatings, and banning of meetings." It specified the severe beatings of officers of the Confederation Generale de Travailleurs and the lack of unions in EPZs where U.S. firms operated (*Bulletin,* July–Aug. 1993). USTR again agreed to review Haiti's violations. In Fall 1994 the returned Aristide government began to change conditions, but subsequent IMF demands and investment programs have encouraged further worker abuses (see NLC 1995).

Evaluation of Petition Impact

From these brief summaries, it is clear that GSP has been influential in bringing certain changes such as the passage of labor legislation to specific Latin nations. It is less clear that trade sanctions are responsible for achieving labor rights in actual practice, as the AFL-CIO implied when it emphasized that code implementation remained a major focus (*Bulletin,* Dec. 1993). Did the same pattern hold true for El Salvador, Guatemala, the Dominican Republic, Costa Rica, and Panama? If so, could improvement have come about simply from market forces? We can answer this more precisely after we examine each country more intensively in the chapters ahead.

Part 2

Case Studies

CHAPTER 5

Labor Petitions in El Salvador
A Weak Labor Code

The GSP petition to review labor abuses in El Salvador marked the first intensive effort by U.S. unions and human-rights groups to employ trade sanctions as a remedy. Americas Watch coordinated the early filings, generating substantial U.S. congressional support. At the outset, the petition process was hampered by El Salvador's civil war between government forces and the Frente Faribundo Martí Para la Liberación Nacional (FMLN). The contending forces stimulated divisions within the Salvadoran and U.S. labor movements: AIFLD and the AFL-CIO initially opposed the petitions filed by Americas Watch, and then ILRF in 1987–89. As the civil war (and larger cold war) waned and El Salvador's rightist government disregarded even the labor moderates, the federation had a change of heart and became the lead petitioner. As the internal war abated, the unions also became more unified in their demands. Only at this point did the El Salvador elite showed a willingness to discuss labor issues publicly. Thus, external and local pressure forced El Salvador's Congress to address comprehensively the nation's conflicting labor laws: rights guaranteed by the country's constitution, its labor code, its civil service, legislation to regulate free zones, and fresh demands that it ratify basic ILO conventions. In 1993, the Salvadoran National Assembly finally reformed its labor code, but the story of the code's passage and later implementation reveals many of the weaknesses of the GSP approach.

El Salvador's Labor History and Economy

El Salvador was one of the last nations in Central America to recognize labor rights. Although it had been a founding member of the ILO in 1919, El Salvador left the organization in 1939 and did not return until 1948, thereby avoiding the ratification of key conventions on the right to organize and negotiate.

Official skepticism toward labor coalesced in the late 1920s following successful mobilizations by the Partido Comunista de El Salvador. The Martínez
dictatorship from 1930 to 1944 prohibited unionization. The state reaffirmed
this policy after the noted Indian uprising and massacre of 1932. Persistent demands for union rights won passage of limited labor legislation in 1946, including a short-lived right to strike, and the creation of a Ministry of Labor and
Social Welfare. By the following year, however, unions were forced underground (Bollinger 1987a:311). The constitution of 1950 provided for the right to
form unions, equality of salary, weekly rest and annual paid vacations, protections for women, indemnization for unjust firing, and even the legitimacy of
strikes, but the lack of an implementing code prevented workers from accessing
these principles or forming federations (Menjívar Larín 1985:104f).[1] Following
the Lemus dictatorship from 1956 to 1960, leftist unions gained a new labor-
court system and, in 1963, a labor code and labor ministry.[2] A huge general
strike in 1967 won back the right to strike. In 1972 the labor code was amended
to reduce this right once again.[3] Nevertheless, strikes increased during the 1970s
as "hard times provoked a burst of peasant and worker organizing. . . . The
government responded by turning a blind eye to death squads, with close ties
to the military. . . . By the fall of 1980, the military and their death squads had
killed more than 10,000 people," many trade unionists among them (Armstrong
et al. 1987:5f).

To control persistent unrest, in 1982 the government formed an under-
funded, hand-picked tripartite commission to study and revise the labor
code, which remained stalled for the next eight years. Even though article 47
of the new 1983 constitution prohibited the government from interfering in
worker organizing, it still was not legal to form campesino and public-sector
unions.[4] Between 1980 and 1983 the reign of terror against trade unionists and
other activists accelerated. Many were killed. Some, like Lydia and Marta Alicia, fled the country (testimonies in Carter et al. 1989:43f).

In response, progressive U.S. union leaders and rank-and-file members
formed the National Labor Committee in Support of Democracy and Human
Rights in El Salvador (NLC) in 1981 (see chapter 3). In the years that followed,
the NLC sent a series of delegations to the country to document and publicize
the atrocities (see NLC 1983, 1985, 1988). Despite the election of the AFL-CIO–
backed Napoleon Duarte and the Christian Democrats in 1984, union repression and death squad activities expanded as the war progressed. Along with
worsening economic conditions, El Salvador's trade-union membership fell
from a reported 78,194 in 1983, to 72,668 by 1987.[5]

Socioeconomic Conditions and Labor Reactions

El Salvador entered the 1980s with its economy weakened by the armed conflict between the government, the right-wing Alianza Republicana Nacionalista (ARENA) party, and FMLN guerilla forces. Horrendous bloodshed flowed from labor, religious, and campesino activists (Armstrong and Shenk 1982; Berryman 1984, 1995; Landau 1995; New America Press 1989). As if the resulting cries for justice were not sufficient, from 1979 to 1982 the country also suffered a 30 percent decline in prices for its major exports, exacerbating a shortage of foreign exchange, international investment, and industrial output. Over the same four years, economic output dropped by 25 percent and government revenues declined.

The election of Christian Democrat Napoleon Duarte in 1984 brought a huge influx of U.S. aid. Although atrocities persisted, by 1987–88, U.S. foreign assistance, along with repatriated capital from Salvadoran émigrés fleeing to the U.S., conveyed a measure of economic growth.[6] However, the government also implemented economic measures that reduced credit and increased utility rates. Coffee export earnings continued to fall, so in their place the state promoted "non-traditional" apparel and electronics production, as described in chapter 3. Inflation rates remained high as the war moved into its last phase, although wages, which had declined so precipitously, did improve (see tables 4.8 and 6.1).

In mid-1989, the neo-liberal, ARENA-backed Cristiani administration took power. Cristiani's structural-adjustment policies won an additional inflow of aid, temporarily lowering the rates of poverty and unemployment. Yet ARENA's neo-liberal reforms did not alleviate the underlying disparities that polarized unions and employers, as renewed labor conflicts drew the attention of human-rights advocates in the U.S.

First Petitions

In its 1987 petition to GSP, Americas Watch presented forty-three instances of labor-rights abuses, including unjust arrests and torture.[7] When USTR did not accept the Americas Watch petition, fourteen congresspersons demanded an explanation. USTR answered that it was appropriate for the El Salvador armed forces to arrest, interrogate, and imprison trade unionists whom the U.S. Department of State considered opponents of the Duarte government. USTR repeatedly referred to one labor confederation, the Unión Nacional de Trabajadores Salvadoreños (UNTS), as a "'pro-FMLN' though legal union."[8]

In its 1988 petition, Americas Watch, joined by the International Labor Rights Fund (ILRF), cited fresh instances of abuse: the killing of twelve union organizers and five disappearances at the hands of El Salvador security forces, and the arrest of trade unionists and accusation of FMLN collaboration for simple engagement in trade-union activity. In addition, although the 1983 constitution outlined certain rights, it restricted organizing, bargaining, and striking. In any case, enabling legislation did not assure the rights that were constitutionally guaranteed. For example, agricultural workers, who constituted 50 percent of the workforce, routinely had no written contracts, could not form unions, and could not strike. The procedures for strikes in the rest of the private sector were also labyrinthine, and public unions were barred from strikes entirely.[9]

USTR again rejected the Americas Watch petition. AIFLD even issued a report criticizing the human-rights organization's investigations.[10] According to AIFLD, the Salvadoran Unión National Obereo-Cambesina (UNOC) had asked the AFL-CIO not to file a GSP petition because President Duarte's policies represented an improvement over the former regime. Because of AFL-CIO opposition, it is doubtful that the petition had a measurable effect on the Salvadoran government. Nevertheless, U.S. congressional reaction was vehement. Following the USTR refusal, a hundred members of the U.S. Congress asked for an official probe into the nation's labor-rights abuses.

With such backing, the 1989 Americas Watch petition, joined by two other groups, cited twenty-eight new incidents, including ARDE death squad actions, the capturing of members of the STITAS textile union who were engaged in union activities and charging them with subversive association, arrests and disappearances of Asociación Nacional de Trabajadores Agropecuarios (ANTA) and Asociación Nacional Campesina (ANC) members, military intervention in a union action at the Ministry of Public Works, harassment and bombings at the Federación Sindical de Trabajadores Salvadoreños (FENASTRAS, one of El Salvador's most militant federations), a military raid on the UNTS headquarters, death threats against Asociación Salvadoreña de Trabajadores de Telecomunicaciones (ASTTEL) leaders, the disappearance of a member of the Sindicato de Trabajadores del Instituto Salvadoreño del Seguro Social (STISSS), and the jailing of employees affiliated with Ministry of Agriculture.[11]

Facing congressional scrutiny, this time USTR expanded its explanation for rejection: "petitioners had not appropriately related the twenty-eight incidents to the five statutory worker rights criteria delineated in the U.S. Trade Act. In addition, The U.S. Embassy disputed that ARDE actually existed or that STITAS members were beaten." The Izalco textile firm, home of one STITAS-related union, was forced to close because of financial difficulties and "attempted acts of terrorism during a demonstration to support the FMLN's peace proposal." ANTA was possibly involved in violence since a search of one ANTA member's vehicle "uncovered several sharpened stakes and nail-studded wooden clubs." Two of the disappeared had ties to an informer for the FMLN. USTR quoted one union leader's description of the military intervention at the Ministry of Public Works as "typical of what happens on most picket lines when authorities announce that striking workers are involved in an 'illegal activity' and ordered to stop."[12]

But in fact these unabashedly lame explanations signaled a change of heart among USAID and embassy personnel within El Salvador. Despite promises made before coming to power in 1989, the far-right ARENA party had failed to carry out reforms, solidifying a previously divided labor movement. Even the AFL-CIO considered filing a petition that year (*Bulletin*, Nov. 1991). According to one State Department observer, "The ICFTU and ORIT were pressuring AIFLD to reverse its position on the Salvadoran conflict. With all the rank and file opposition at home, supporting El Salvador's government had become a big debate within the AFL-CIO itself. So suddenly AIFLD Director Doherty flip-flopped, and adopted a different game plan. He even contacted leftist politician Hugo Ungo to discuss strategy."[13]

Petition Acceptance

By 1990, eight other groups had joined Americas Watch in filing petitions, including FENASTRAS.[14] Petitioners charged that El Salvador had consistently failed to follow ILO conventions regarding freedom of association and collective bargaining. The country did not respect independent unions or create a climate free of violence by reinstating workers unfairly dismissed, respecting union premises, allowing organizations of agricultural workers, or opening judicial inquiries on labor violations.

In June 1990, the AFL-CIO finally submitted its own petition, citing the U.S. State Department's human-rights report on EPZs[15] and specific acts of terrorism: Since Duarte's electoral defeat by ARENA in 1989, employer retaliation had increased dramatically. The ARENA victory was seen as a green light to proceed with illegal firings. Political intervention in union affairs had worsened. ARENA leader D'Aubuisson proceeded to break up U.S.-inspired agricultural cooperatives in violation of freedom of association. The country's labor laws made union registrations difficult, and the federation believed the courts and the Labor Ministry were generally antipathetic toward unions.[16]

This time, USTR accepted the petitions. However, it painstakingly (and painfully) responded to the AFL-CIO's charges of union harassment, government attacks, and weak legal structures. All agreed there were fewer human-rights violations in 1990 than previously.[17] D'Aubuisson's "visits to co-ops" stopped after UNOC complained directly to the president in 1989. While Civil Defense Forces had interfered in several co-op meetings and police had intervened in textile and telephone union actions, there were mitigating rationales.

The minister of labor helped negotiate a textile severance agreement. Telephone company management, while beefing up security against FMLN attacks, was still negotiating with ASTTEL.[18]

USTR said the alleged weakness in El Salvador labor laws was most difficult to verify. Decree 483 had restored the right of association for employees of autonomous agencies, and decree 538 permitted public unions. Agricultural workers could organize but admittedly were denied the right to bargain. While legal "inconsistencies result in significant delays," campesino and public-sector employee groups acted much like a union in practice. The labor minister acknowledged the lack of protection from unjust firings but was seeking remedies through a reformed labor code and negotiated remuneration or reinstatement. Ultimately, USTR admitted that the constitution and the labor code diverged on the right to strike and that strike procedures were cumbersome.[19]

In statistical terms, the petition pressure may have begun some changes in the Labor Ministry (see chapter 6). However, USTR found there was a great need to reconcile El Salvador's various laws on labor rights. For example, even the government admitted that only one EPZ was subject to labor laws, and in that one, there was no record of unions attempting to organize! USTR looked for assistance from a tripartite socioeconomic commission established after the April 1990 government-FMLN agreement to renew peace talks, but it realized that momentum toward reforming the Salvadoran labor code had dissipated in 1990, and the commission would not reconvene until after the March 1991 election. Thus, USTR decided to keep El Salvador under review to gather more information about its compliance.[20]

However, the AFL-CIO and other petitioners were unimpressed by any claimed "progress." Rather than experiencing freedom of association, the unions had been forced to file an additional 750 unjust dismissal cases from May 1990 to September 1991. The State Department admitted that El Salvador's laws violated GSP standards because agricultural workers and the nine public-employee unions had no right to strike. The ARENA administration had not legally recognized a single union. Instead, in 1990, it fired 1,600 union workers at the Ministry of Agriculture; it also sent troops to break up another ASTTEL strike and barred workers from other work sites. Cristiani made statements equating union organizations in general and ASTTEL in particular with the FMLN. The army surrounded members of the Treasury Ministry employees association tear-gassed a supportive union federation demonstration (by the Federación de Asociaciones y Sindicatos Independientes de El Salvador [FEASIES]), suppressed a Maidenform protest, locked out the Sindicato de Trabajadores de Cafe, and militarized several coffee plants. The administration shut down the Government Housing Institute, putting 850 unionized workers out in the streets, and it fired fifteen workers at Salvamex, as the secretary general received death threats for citing government involvement in bomb attacks. The armed forces issued communiqués against UNTS, the Asociación Nacional de Educadores Salvadoreños, and a FENASTRAS-affiliated construction union. They bombed the Usulutan offices and killed leader Miguel Angel Martínez.

In June 1991, the AFL-CIO (and other groups) repeated their charges, citing the fresh threats and assassinations of unionists (*Bulletin*, Nov. 1991). The ICFTU annual survey of violations of trade-union rights reported eighteen activists killed from January 1990 to March 1991. A hundred and fifty unionists were held behind bars. The National Labor Committee listed forty-five members of the Coffee Industry Union killed, three disappeared, many imprisoned, an ANTA organizer abducted; Asociación Nacional de Trabajadores de Obreros Publicos workers assassinated; and the killing of three and injuring of two in the earlier bombing of FENASTRAS headquarters (NLC 1991).

USTR again decided to hold the country in abeyance by pending the review with the hope that the peace process and changes in labor code would bring El Salvador into compliance.[21]

The Peace Accords

In January 1992, the FMLN and the government of El Salvador signed the historic peace accords bringing to an end the decade-old civil war. The accords created a "Social Forum" to address the nation's socioeconomic inequalities and labor rights. The economy was improving: In 1991 and 1992, El Salvador's GDP increased despite a drop in coffee earnings (table 4.8). The government introduced a value-added tax to reduce the deficit, augmenting inflation. Investor confidence improved, but despite minimum wage increases in 1991 and 1992, income fell behind the jump in prices. Growth remained dependant on family remittances and foreign aid since imports doubled exports in value. Thus, even after the war ended, achievements inspired by neo-liberalism depended in part on U.S. government intervention and also control over labor. Death threats and murders of trade unionists persisted, and wholesale firings in the EPZs increased. Even the U.S. State Department repeatedly reported violations of worker rights. So, despite the peace accords, the AFL-CIO refiled a GSP petition in July 1992. The ILRF, which had co-filed every year since 1988, supported the AFL-CIO petition, stating that this time a simple extension of review would send the wrong message.[22] ARENA reacted by introducing a bill that made any backing of a GSP petition a treasonous offense!

USTR cited three positive developments during this period: the peace accords, the reduction in threats, and the commitment to pass a labor code. Petitioners rebutted that rights were jeopardized in all five areas defined by the ILO: In terms of association, grave violations documented by the ICFTU, ILO, the archbishop's human-rights office, and Amnesty International; a series of labor-related murders; and huge protests.[23] Regarding bargaining, the Ministry of Labor acknowledged that collective agreements were unenforceable, even in the public sector (such as when FENASTRAS-affiliated public employees were denied wage increases). Rules on child labor and minimum wages were disregarded (El Salvador workers could only purchase 30 to 46 percent of required basic goods and services).[24] In operational terms, the labor code did not reflect El Salvador's own commitments in the 1983 constitution.[25] Thus the positive changes remained illusory.

In its review of the 1992 petition, the GSP Subcommittee found violence had been significantly reduced. Several murders had been the result of personal disputes. It admitted concern over the use of child labor, the firings of union officials before protective credentials had been issued, and the blocking of unions in two export zones (in one, the government claimed the need to secure a nearby air force base)!

The GSP pressure for labor reform in El Salvador motivated the U.S. government to create several labor-management improvement programs. In 1991 it funded the Fundación Obrero Empresarial Salvadoreña (FOES), with a hefty annual budget of more than $3 million—nearly twice the expenditures of the entire Salvadoran Labor Ministry. FOES was to be administered through AIFLD "as a trust fund of $10 million to the Salvadoran government to generate local currency of 80 million," explained FOES/USAID liaison Sonia Caceres. Its objective was to promote good relations between labor and management via social and economic project loans, grants, and technical assistance. It was overseen by a representative eighteen-member board that named a president (see chapter 6). "People were skeptical at first, but we thought the plan would work based on our experience in the U.S."[26]

In 1993, USAID likewise funded a major study of the Salvadoran Labor Ministry. The study identified many of the problems noted by the petitioners—for example, "the long and complicated administrative process for registering and recognizing unions" that would "commonly take up to 12 months," jeopardizing the legal protection for organizers. It also noted that "the practice of collective bargaining is limited," and laws "that accord protection to trade union leaders and workers are not regularly enforced." It found the ministry itself to be one of the "weakest and least funded agencies within the Government. . . . The MOL's insufficient capacity to enforce labor laws and regulations have contributed to an environment in which there have been historically poor relations between labor and management, weak enforcement of wage and hour laws, and in which workers are forced to endure poor working conditions while not being accorded internationally sanctioned worker rights." In specific administrative terms, it referred to the MOL's "lack of political support," the business community's skepticism, and labor's claim that it does not defend their rights. It offered a series of recommendations to correct these perceptions (see Shepard et al. 1994 and chapter 6).

GSP pressure was also a factor motivating the government of El Salvador to replace the Labor Ministry's technical training program for Salvadoran workers with an autonomous, tripartite Instituto Salvadoreño de Formación Profesional in June 1993.[27]

However, the principal issue remaining was reform of El Salvador's labor code, "which is not even consistent with the Salvadoran constitution." The assessment helped convince USTR to continue its review.

Forum Wrestles with the Labor Code

One portentous El Salvador peace accord was the agreement to form an Economic and Social Forum. Conceived as a process to mutually address national conditions, it convened in September 1992 to address the nation's major economic problems. In February 1993, forum representatives from government, business, and labor agreed to a "Declaration of Principles" for revising the labor code. The government also raised minimum wages by about 20 percent in urban areas and 30 percent in rural areas (table 6.1). However, the AFL-CIO insisted that the draft code fell "far short of ILO standards" in the five areas and refiled its petition in 1993 for ending GSP privileges. UNOC members believed the "review process is essential for any real improvement in worker rights" (*Bulletin,* Apr. 1993).

The government replied that via the Declaration of Principles, the forum would soon present the new code to the National Assembly. For its part, the assembly ratified six and agreed to review additional ILO conventions.[28] The government claimed some of its current labor laws were more advanced than those in the U.S. (for example, requiring a day of rest, and leave policies). It charged that, since there were reasonable justifications for most specific conflicts, the petitions were only designed to enhance the influence of various labor organizations (such as the AFL-CIO, the International Union of Electrical Workers, the United Food and Commercial Workers, the Massachusetts Labor Committee, FENASTRAS, and the Labor Coalition on Central America).[29] However, government officials also claimed that passage of the other basic ILO conventions would be unconstitutional. The unions suggested that the ILO be invited to examine this question.

In July 1993, the USTR subcommittee determined that although the government had not yet enacted a labor code, a good faith effort was underway to address the problem: The forum's "Social Pact" in February could not substitute for a labor code, but it represented a credible step toward consensus. Both sides had agreed to consensual changes by September 30. To allow for a satisfactory resolution, USTR recommended a half-year review extension until September (effectively December) 30, 1993.[30]

In late September, the ILO mission arrived. It included Dr. Arturo Bronstein, who drafted suggestions that leaders from the unions, business, and government discussed. They reached an agreement (see below). In November, El Salvador government representatives appeared before USTR and promised to send the ILO proposal to the National Assembly without modification. However, when the revised code arrived, many of the suggested revisions had been weakened. USTR once again extended its review, waiting for the National Assembly to ratify the new amendments to labor code.[31]

Analysis of GSP Impact on Forum and Code

Perceptions of the role that the GSP process played in El Salvador's labor reform reveals the strategy's limitations in a country known for labor violence, which persisted despite the peace accords. A first issue is how the code became the focus of the Social and Economic Forum; a second is how GSP affected the objectives of both business and labor within the forum; a third is how business outmaneuvered labor with broken commitments; a fourth is the final contents of the code itself.

Code as Topic of the Forum

"The Social and Economic Forum gave the unions a true opportunity," stated Mark Anner, Norwegian representative to El Salvador unions. "The accords had created a broad agenda for the forum, including economic development, court reform, and code development. At the same time, the UN observation mission arrived. Then came the threat of GSP."[32]

"At first, the labor code was number 4 or 5 on the agenda," recalled Mike Donovan of AIFLD. "Business was very reluctant to deal with it. It was not the peace accords, but their fear of losing GSP benefits that caused them to give it top priority."[33]

AIFLD itself played its part. "The AFL-CIO sought a role in the peace process, and AIFLD Director Bill Doherty wanted to be part of it through the forum," said one State Department official. "He saw an opportunity to place himself in the middle of the process. He said to the unions, 'so you have a problem. Well, I can help you solve it. . . .' Then he came back to the U.S. government and said, 'our brothers have asked us to support their request, and we have to honor that.' This placed him in a position to offer something to both sides."[34]

But union acceptance of a code was not automatic. They first wanted to discuss passage of the basic ILO conventions, which El Salvador had refused to ratify, and other assurances of employment and respect for the population as a whole. As Anner explained, "There was tremendous debate within the unions on how to use the opportunity." ILRF attorney Benjamin Davis described how "tensions rose as the February deadline for USTR's decision on El Salvador's GSP benefits approached. The ARENA party and business leaders launched a systematic campaign of denunciation . . . [even introducing] a bill to make expressions of support for suspension of El Salvador's GSP privileges a crime of treason."[35]

"We were pushing the case with USTR," emphasized Donovan. "El Salvador was under review. The new government said, 'give us time.' Just at that moment, the renewal time arrived. The labor movement here was clamoring due to massive firings, and the AFL-CIO's position was that there had to be some movement in the labor code. When they turned up the heat, USTR was meeting in Washington."[36]

The State Department desk officer in charge at the time, Simon Henshaw, agreed that "all of this would not have happened without GSP pressure. In Washington, they need to grab hold of something physical to show progress in conformity with 'taking steps.' In this case it was rewriting the labor code. We explained this to the Salvadoran government and business community and they understood it."[37]

"So suddenly," said Donovan, "the private sector here said, 'Wait! We have to first discuss the labor code.' When the unions said, 'we have an agenda to follow,' the government and private sector accused the unions of blocking GSP benefits. It put them between a rock and a hard place."

Business leader Juan Hector Vidal, executive director of El Salvador's more progressive private-sector Asociación Nacional de la Empresa Privada (ANEP), disagreed: "We did not talk about the labor code because of GSP. Our discussions occurred in relation to our own process from the accords and within the forum. We didn't agree on many points, but we were in agreement that labor rights are fundamental human rights; they depend on worldwide rules of the ILO, not from the U.S."[38]

Whatever the reason, "the Agreement of Principles signed on February 17, 1993, temporarily resolved this political crisis. In exchange for the unions dropping their demand for immediate economic measures, the government and private sector agreed to discuss ratification of the ILO conventions before negotiating reform of the Labor Code. The unions muted their calls to cut off GSP benefits, and the government ceased its campaign against union leaders" (Davis 1995). For Mark Anner, "It was hair-raising because, how can you negotiate over issues of basic rights? But they finally decided, 'we'll agree not to push the labor rights violations if the government agrees to negotiate in the forum.'"[39] For both labor and business, the decision had major consequences. Whether intended or not, in searching for something to grab hold of, code reform became the bellwether of petition effectiveness.

GSP and Objectives

Labor unions acknowledged that "the Declaration of Principles was made possible by . . . denunciations about the violations of labor rights in El Salvador, and a situation perceived as causing suspension of GSP benefits" (*Informe Laboral* 1994:41). The declaration itself gave emphasis to ILO conventions regarding freedom to organize and bargain, to regulate hours for women and children, night work, the agricultural sector, and so on. However, despite this commitment, as discussions approached the self-imposed April 30 deadline, the government backtracked.

"At first the mood was deeply responsive, attempting to remove the distress of war," explained FEASIES leader Roger Gutiérrez. "But soon all we were doing was confronting and fighting; there was no real consensus. One would expect the government, at least, to 'appear' to be accommodating; but instead it took the position of the business leaders. We had a good agenda to discuss, but it was cut out in the end."[40]

"The Forum ratified improvements that would reflect ILO Convention 87 (on the right to organize)," explained the chief labor negotiating attorney José Antonio Candray. "We proposed that the law would express what El Salvador had already ratified: we were not asking anything more than this. But certain business and government officials reacted by saying this was unconstitutional—it was so broad as to include state workers, the police and even the army. But in fact our constitution does not contain limits."[41]

"In some ways the unions also sold themselves short," reflected Mark Anner. "The government very cleverly said they would 'agree to review' the union proposal of ILO convention inclusions, so the unions believed there would be a certain good faith negotiation."[42]

Unions again compromised to meet this second impasse. They suggested that ILO representatives be invited to examine the constitutional issues of the debated conventions, and at the end of July all sides signed a second "Document for the Development and Operation of Fulfilling the Agreement of Principles and Compromises."

Outflanked

The ILO delegation arrived in the middle of a series of strikes in the public sector, exacerbated by the government's failure to honor negotiated commitments.[43] The public works minister backed away from an agreement negotiated with help from the forum's tripartite commission (Davis 1995:fn210). After his investigation, the ILO's Dr. Bronstein proposed forty-nine modifications in the current labor code. On October 18, the forum set up a Tripartite Commission to redraft what was acceptable. It worked furiously since the private sector had decreed it would not participate after November 10 because of the upcoming elections. In addition, USTR was holding another round of hearings in Washington. "So we put all other elements of the ILO Convention texts into the code with help from the ILO," stated Candray.[44]

For Henshaw, who soon would become U.S. labor attaché to El Salvador, "without doubt, the labor code was rewritten due to GSP pressure. In fact, during the negotiations, the unions agreed to forty-one of the forty-nine articles, leaving only eight outstanding. Officially, the union position was that it did not agree to any unless all were accepted. But this was something they always said. In fact, they did accept forty-one. For its part, the private sector threatened to withdraw, saying it did not want to participate and allow the agreement to become an election issue. So they both were playing politics. Yet in fact, they did take the forty-one in agreement and submitted it to Bronstein. He made minor changes to reconcile contradictions, and approved it."[45]

However, says Anner, "While they accepted some ILO issues (for example, no. 107, since there are few indigenous in this country) the private sector said 'no' to conventions 87 and 98 on the freedom to organize and bargain. The government then convinced the unions to publish the list of what had been agreed upon. At first the unions refused, but the government said they would then go back to discuss the other two conventions, and this caught the unions off guard. When the list was finally published, the government said, 'but we have agreed to most of the points; so we are being reasonable. What is your complaint?'"[46]

Miguel Ramírez, former leader of FENASTRAS, acknowledged that "the Tripartite Commission had very important potential. It was supposed to involve unions, government, and industry. But in reality, the state was really industry, not an objective third party. So it camouflaged the agrarian question and skirted through other key issues. GSP pressure brought some benefits, but new problems emerged."[47]

Once they came to Washington for the hearings, the unions said if the government would pass the code as agreed, they would be satisfied. "At the hearing, the minister of labor declared the reforms would be ratified and had the backing of the president," emphasized labor attorney Candray. "Arthur Bronstein from the ILO said likewise. When the minister and his representatives returned to El Salvador, they denied they had ever made such a commitment. This began a huge debate in the forum. Finally, the government unilaterally offered a new packet of reforms. It contained the right of [minimum] salary, certain rights for women and children etc., but not the right of association."[48]

"The government would quote Bronstein's assessment that it was one of the most advanced codes in Latin America," explained Carlos Hurtado of the Confederación de Trabajadores Democraticos (CTD). "But the reforms that we had agreed upon were ultimately not included. It was a manipulation by the private sector."[49]

According to union negotiator Roger Gutiérrez of FEASIES, "The forum was an alternative, but soon it became very politicized and didn't advance. It obtained only a few reforms. We invited the International Labor Organization, but the private sector and government didn't agree. After its promises, the government removed the ILO commitments and passed the code on its own to avoid debate. It claimed to be under time pressure. The business class had no clear vision, but was not in favor of the people, that was obvious. So they passed the code—it was OK as a base from which to begin. But the forum closed without really bringing any benefit, so we lost a lot of hope."[50]

"The [ARENA] government's proposal represents a major retreat from the consensus-building process of the forum and significantly weakens the labor-rights provisions of the ILO proposal. It unilaterally effects changes that were never discussed," concluded Davis (1995). "The code has really been a mixed bag—for the labor movement," commented Anner. "It is not a big step forward. It has more bad than good. Bronstein was technically competent but politically conservative. He improved certain organizational properties but did not bother with compliance. When the government passed a watered-down version, he said, 'OK.'"[51]

Code Contents

According to business leader Juan Hector Vidal, president of ANEP, "The labor code here was a product of discussions in the forum. After one and a half years, the National Assembly ratified it. It was a most important achievement, and in the opinion of the ILO, we created one of the most advanced labor codes in Latin America. It has made work smoother for workers; it is easier to form unions now because the number of workers required is less."[52] Simon Henshaw also spoke of Bronstein's assurance that "there were no significant changes in the final version." He listed the achievements noted in table 5.1.[53]

Labor's Deep Disappointment

Nevertheless, all El Salvador's major labor organizations (UNOC, UNTS, and FENASTRAS) condemned the government's bill. They said it marked a significant retreat from proposals publicly accepted by the labor minister at the USTR hearings. For Carlos Ochoa of UNTS, "The new labor code reflects the bad intentions of neo-liberalism. It was designed to divide unions." For

Table 5.1. Listed improvements in the 1994 El Salvador labor code

1. Extends labor rights to everyone, including those working for small businesses (article 209).
2. Requires thirty-five members to form a union. Submission of names brings automatic registrations in thirty days if the labor minister does not object.
3. Legalizes agricultural unions.
4. Regulates the registration process by requiring immediate job protection to members for one year when list is simultaneously submitted to employer and labor ministry.
5. Promotes contract negotiations by fining no-show employers and/or advancing strike authorization procedures.
6. Guarantees the right to strike if conciliation fails (article 221). Workers may ask for police protection and employers must pay wages (if approved by a majority in secret vote, or 30 percent if they allow others to work). Strikers must inform the Labor Ministry and wait four days. Employers may not fire any workers or hire substitutes (articles 537, 554). Public workers and essential service workers may not strike.

Miguel Ramírez, "The resulting code is 20 percent in favor of the workers and 80 percent in favor of employers and the state." Unionists listed seven elements missing in the code (table 5.2). In the words of ILRF attorney Benjamin Davis, the "new code contains substantive defects that fail to provide adequate protection for workers."

The unions acknowledged some positive accomplishments in the code. According to Mark Anner: "They did reduce the number of unions required to form a federation from ten to five, probably hoping this would create more divisions. However, if the government does not respond to a request for union or federation organization in thirty days, it is automatically considered legal. Miguel Ramírez was able to use this with success in creating FESTRAES." Roger Gutiérrez appreciated this benefit in organizing at the University of El Salvador and in the maquilas.

Carlos Hurtado believed "the right to form a union with thirty-five people is a good benefit; for example, with a factory of a thousand, it was almost impossible to sign more than half of the workers as formerly required, especially with a repressive boss. Several new unions have now been able to form in the countryside and in the informal sector as a result."

Despite its failure to ratify certain key ILO conventions, code negotiations did stimulate the passage of six conventions in December 1993 and thirteen more in 1994. However, only two of these (C. 142 on rural organization and C. 144 on tripartite consultations) could be invoked to protect the right to organize and negotiate.[54]

Table 5.2. Listed lacunae in the 1994 El Salvador labor code

1. Excludes the public sector. While associations are permitted, negotiations are not required.
2. Requires complicated approvals for agricultural unions, virtually excluding them. Articles 264–67, which created procedures for establishing regulations, were not implemented (UNOC 1994).
3. Allows employers to set up small unions to undermine larger ones in the same place (done in telecommunications).
4. Mandates mediation with no fixed time limits that render a "legal" strike very difficult to achieve (both labor and regular courts can declare strikes illegal; only two legal strikes have occurred in the nation's history).
5. Does not require rehiring of unjustly fired workers. Even protected union leaders who require a thirty-day intervention can encounter a silent labor minister, forcing lengthy court procedures (CTCA 1996).
6. Does not protect discrimination against workers who must meet family responsibilities.
7. Leaves legally ambiguous the protections for minor children and nursing mothers.
8. Eliminates union assemblies and executive boards at the department level.[a]
9. Only protects six union executive committee members or organizers for six months following a recognition demand.
10. Creates "mixed-enterprise unions" for small business situations, which remain ill-defined and subject to abuse.[b]

[a]See letter from Ben Davis to Joe Damond, GSP, May 9, 1994. Articles 221–23 eliminated the current code, thereby removing protected executive boards from fourteen geographical departments, leaving only national structures.

[b]Under article 209, section A 14, what constitutes a *vecinos* (neighboring plant) union could be interpreted as an entire free zone, but the practice risks violating ILO intentions. See letter from Ben Davis to Joe Damond, GSP, May 9, 1994.

In summary, the code had brought a reduction in the state's intervention in the right to strike (since strikes did not require prior administrative authorization), a reduction in the minimum number required to form a union, legalization in the right to unionize for rural workers, but also the atomization of unions by allowing minority unions to sign collective contracts and the weakening of the contractual capacity of federations and confederations.

CENTRA explained the outcome as "a fruit of the pressure of the North American administration. The possible exclusion of El Salvador from GSP was applied to reform the labor code and win approval of various ILO conventions. We can affirm that the businessmen complied with the demands of the U.S., facilitating the creation of union organizations at the company level but weakening the trade union structure, creating union divisions and moving collective negotiation primarily into the company ambit. There is no longer any mechanism to fortify negotiations at the federation level" (Arriola 1995:58).

As Benjamin Davis indicated, the real loss was the possible milieu of trust and how this would affect implementation of any code: "The labor representatives always knew that the agreement would only be worth what the government was willing to enforce. They also understood that they wouldn't get the right to strike, even if they could do so in practice. Yet with the forum's 'window of opportunity,' they really thought they had a commitment from the government to talk with them. However, by their actions, the government made it clear it was going to pursue its own interpretation." This reversal fed the bitterness.[55]

CHAPTER 6

Structural Implications of
GSP Pressure in El Salvador

How one hears the story of GSP pressure and labor-code passage in El Salvador depends on where one is located in the social structure: Businessmen
understand it as a necessary compromise; labor leaders experience a rejection
of hope; U.S. policy makers interpret it as an important beginning at labor-
management dialogue. Which perspective has most validity can be tested
against labor conditions since the code's passage.

By the mid-1990s, El Salvador's labor picture had refocused from commonplace murder to abrupt layoffs of trade-union activists. The peace accords
ushered in a fresh emphasis on democratic process, which shifted the "resistance strategy" of unions and popular organizations. The ARENA party's
neo-liberal program, fortified by the election of Calderon Sol in 1994, reinforced union fears over privatization of state enterprises. At the same time,
international publicity centered on worker abuses in El Salvador's maquila
sector. State and private-sector institutions designed to handle labor-management difficulties—more official Labor Ministry interventions, court decisions,
and tripartite consultations—faltered in face of these developments. Had the
Social and Economic Forum kept to its original agenda, it could have avoided
certain impasses, but the forum had disbanded with the code's passage. Although El Salvador's economy averaged a real growth above 5 percent from
1993 to 1997, its labor-management relations and code enforcement stagnated.

Code Enforcement

The impasse over enforcement received increasing attention after the labor
code's passage in March 1994. Having praised the code, U.S. labor attaché
Henshaw admitted that "enforcement is another matter. The workers have
little redress. There must be various forms of pressure. As we use GSP to

nudge the country forward, the next step will be better application of the labor code."[1]

By 1995, ILRF attorney Benjamin Davis cited ARENA's poor record of implementation in addition to its unilateral action on the code (see chapter 5). Since November 1993, ARENA had taken no measures to resolve the many continuing labor disputes, to improve union access to the EPZs, or to end the illegal practice of year-to-year labor contracts. ILRF also reported a wave of violence directed against union or FMLN candidates in negotiations over new labor laws and also dismissals of union members attempting to organize and bargain.[2] Davis likewise described widespread violations of minimum-wage laws (1995:8). The ILO also verified "many instances of anti-union discrimination that . . . reflect shortcomings in the legal system" and "a lack of information on judicial investigations into trade union murders, assaults, disappearances (Vida Soría 1993).

Maquila Conditions: The Gabo and Mandarin Cases

Anti-union discrimination especially characterized the maquila sector, whose 1995 exports had grown to represent 22.5 percent of the nation's net export value, compared to less than 15 percent ten years before.[3] Apparel income came within 5 percent of earnings from traditional exports, despite the 1993 termination of USAID support to El Salvador's free zones. But while the expansion brought employment for many, it was not without drawbacks for workers as the well-publicized mistreatment at Gabo and GAP/Mandarin illustrated.

In the horrible health coverage scandal at Gabo Industries in March 1995 (see chapter 1), management denied permission for an employee to see a doctor; when it finally relented, the hospital would not treat her because the company had not paid up on her social security, even though it had deducted payments from her check. A few hours later, the woman died. Her sister workers wept at the news, but their sorrow turned to anger when Gabo's managers prohibited them from attending the funeral. Eighteen women went anyway, and all were fired.

Backed by FEASIES, workers blocked the entrance to the San Marcos free zone where Gabo was located. "Since the minister of labor does not address labor violations, it's up to the local people to resolve the situation," explained labor leader Roger Gutiérrez.[4]

The action caused Salvadoran business leader Juan Hector Vidal, president of ANEP, to strongly object that "the unions have gotten out of hand." Yet the Gabo case motivated Vidal to promote a policy that free zones "must create private clinics" and have "a representative of the Ministry of Labor and a union spokesperson in each zone to handle conflicts and prevent bribery."[5]

As Vidal and private-sector leaders issued proclamations, employees at other maquilas demanded code compliance. In Fall 1994, for example, the workers at the Taiwanese firm Mandarin International, San Marcos Free Zone, formed the Sindicato de Empleadas y Trabajadores de Mandarin Internacional (SETMI), a union affiliated with the CTD. At the time, Mandarin was an important producer of GAP clothing, whose contracts constituted nearly 80 percent of its output.[6] Complaining that their salary was below minimum and they had to work more hours than they had agreed, the workers made a number of attempts in 1994 and 1995 to gain management compliance with the labor code.[7] In late June, they had reached a saturation point: some workers barricaded the San Marcos zone entrance while others ceased work inside the factory and blocked the managers from leaving. CTD and ministry representatives were unable to diffuse the protest until the director of the national police threatened eviction.

The following day, Mandarin fired approximately 300 workers. It threatened a complete shutdown if union actions did not halt, claiming huge economic losses. In weary frustration, many union members accepted indemnization, but eighty-six would only sign if their pay included the work time they had devoted to union business (*fuero sindical*).

Juan Hector Vidal believed the ill effects of the Mandarin firings could have been avoided. Their occupation went so far as to detain management overnight. In a nearby zone takeover, workers briefly sequestered a former president of ANEP, and Korean businessmen threatened to leave the country. "They take over these factories without a lot of prior discussion. We can prevent disasters when we know about things ahead of time, but we cannot agree with factory takeovers. A strike should be the last resort, not the first."[8]

But even U.S. officials questioned whether discussion would solve "the problems in the Korean and Taiwanese plants, which are due to their not following Salvador labor laws. The Salvadoran business class blames Koreans but may be doing the same thing. This is why the union took over the Mandarin plant recently."[9] Nevertheless, GAP sent its own investigative team to El Salvador. It joined forces with the ministers of labor and economy and a legislative commission to assure the public that no violations of worker rights had occurred at Mandarin.

An ad hoc Salvadoran labor and human-rights group quickly formed to contact GAP: "We thought it would be good for us to take the lead for a change, since the women were more vulnerable."[10] Speaking at a labor forum in Denver, Colorado, CTD head Amanda Villatoro also publicly condemned the Mandarin firings. The U.S.-based NLC joined to demand that GAP investigate further. Shortly thereafter, Judith Viera, the teenage worker from Mandarin (see chapter 1), began a NLC-sponsored North American tour focusing on the GAP's responsibilities. In their contracting plants, young uneducated workers were producing shirts with the motto "Back to School," a theme picked up by *Women's Wear Daily* and the U.S. media.[11] As the pressure grew, GAP finally replied that Mandarin did violate their code, and it determined to "suspend orders until the government of El Salvador could guarantee the company's respect for labor rights."

Salvador's president and minister of the interior wildly blamed the ad hoc committee for putting 500 people out of work. They characterized the foreigners who signed as "part of a conspiracy to save U.S. jobs. Salvadorans who signed did not deserve to be Salvadorans."[12] But, in fact, the committee and the NLC opposed a GAP withdrawal. Instead, NLC sought to persuade GAP to adopt a code governing its procurement operations, which would be verified by an outside monitor. A series of December leaflettings at GAP outlets in the U.S. convinced the company to agree to a code and to gradually restore orders (and jobs) at Mandarin.

However, GAP's contracted workers in El Salvador were not properly informed about the U.S. campaign.[13] At the same time, the local management responded that it "would rather close than give the jobs back, no matter what they signed in New York." So when the union leaders were scheduled to return to work in December 1995, they all received death threats.

The threats prompted another visit from GAP representatives, a new resolution, and subsequent negotiations with spokespersons from Mandarin International (Taiwan) and the Apparel Consortium Charter Group from Hong Kong.[14] They finally agreed that the workers would get their jobs back when production increased.[15] GAP viewed the agreement as a success and invited the ad hoc committee to serve as monitor. It proved to be a marvelous example of employing consumer pressure to affect labor rights (see chapter 2).

The agreement at Mandarin gradually influenced Gabo and other maquilas. In March 1996, Gabo suspended without pay some 500 workers, 90 percent of them women, claiming insufficient raw material or contracts. FEASIES textile-sector head Nelson González immediately petitioned a judge to investigate, while women's coordinator Arma Bustillo created a program to "instruct youth aged 18 to 23 in ways to organize and plan work-condition improvements." Arma's committee also addressed common problems such as "ways families can prevent delinquency by obtaining access to education and sports." It set up a Saturday literacy program to help women to read.

This inclusive approach paid off as the women placed their demands before Gabo management. In July 1996, Gabo signed a new accord and rehired most workers. "The company's new general director exhibited a better atti-

tude toward code compliance. Although he promised there would be no re-
criminations, when he asked about the 128 unionists, some feared reprisals
and sought indemnization."[16]

General Labor Conditions

Outside pressure was required to improve conditions at Gabo and Mandarin,
as Piore predicted new sweatshops would need (see chapter 2). Improvements did not stem from a better economy or the application of El Salvador's
labor code. Conditions for most Salvadoran workers who lacked such leverage remained below legal standard in hours, wages, health benefits, and freedom to organize and bargain. Virtually no sanctions existed for noncompliance regarding EPZ regulations. Rolando Arévalo and Joaquin Arriola found
these conditions prevalent in their ILO-sponsored study of maquila conditions throughout Central America (Arévalo and Arriola 1995). So did CEN-
TRA researchers Marisol Ruiz and Gilberto García, who surveyed sixty-eight
workers of minor age employed in nine Korean- and Taiwanese-owned
maquila plants in El Salvador (Ruiz and García 1996).

Hours

Most workers received the minimum base salary of 504 colons for two
weeks, but did not receive payment for extra work, extra hours, or for "the
seventh day of rest" as the code required. Pay should have reached at least 525
colons. Workdays averaged between nine and thirteen hours, with ten the
average. That amounted to fifty-nine hours a week (versus six hours legal
maximum for minors). A total of 71 percent of those interviewed also said they
had to regularly meet certain production goals within those hours, and 41
percent of minors illegally worked during evening hours (Ruiz and García
1996:60). Salvadoran workers in all economic sectors work above legal limits.
Men work an hour more than the weekly maximum, and women work two
hours more. In the smaller maquilas, days of nine to ten hours and weeks of
fifty-five to sixty hours are frequent.[17]

Wages

Many Salvadoran workers receive below-minimum wages. Even the minimum standard did not meet living costs, which is contrary to Salvadoran
law.[18] The nominally tripartite Superior Council for Minimum Salary has constitutional responsibility for setting base wages. In practice the business sector
determines the increases unless a particular government intervenes to improve its chances for reelection. The council employs a "basic food basket" as
its only objective cost indicator, which does not account for expenses such
as rent and transportation.[19] Partly for this reason, between 1980 and 1993

Table 6.1. Minimum adult agricultural and industrial/service wages, El Salvador, 1984–94 (colones per day)

	1984	1985	1986	1987	1988	1989	1990	1991	1992	1993	1994
Agriculture[a]	5.20	5.20	8.00	8.00	10.00	10.00	11.50	13.00	13.00	15.00	17.00
Industrial/service	13.00	13.00	15.00	15.00	18.00	18.00	21.00	23.50	27.00	31.00	35.00

[a]Rates for temporary coffee, sugar and cotton workers are somewhat higher. Colon-dollar conversion rate increased from 2.5:1 in 1984 to 7:1 in 1994.
Source: Ministerio de Trabajo y Previsión Social, *Estadísticas de Trabajo.*

both the minimal and overall wages exhibited a dramatic decline (see table 4.8).[20]

Between 1993 and 1995, salaries finally rose an average of 8.7 percent (note nominal increases in table 6.1). Unlike elsewhere in the region, Salvadoran wages appeared to increase. commensurate with GDP (table 4.8), although some researchers challenge this.[21] CENTRA investigators also discovered no relationship between increasing profits *and* salary improvements. Wage costs represented only about 20 percent of production expenses. Workers received only a third of the value their work added to products. Contrary to neo-liberal predictions, "workers are poorer now than before ARENA arrived in the executive office," concluded Arriola (1995:46).

Benefits

Health conditions in the maquila mirrored the experiences of workers at Gabo and Mandarin. Ninety-four of the workers surveyed complained about air dust affecting their breathing. Of the 18 percent who had became pregnant, a third received paid time off, but two-thirds were terminated. While all maquila workers had social security payments deducted, only 29 percent had received required documentation, and 24 percent had been denied permission to leave work to see a doctor (Ruiz and García 1996:61).

Many workers complained about the lack of social security coverage. Table 6.2 presents the workers covered by the Salvadoran Institute for Social Security (ISSS). The percentage of the economically active population receiving

Table 6.2. Workers covered under social security, El Salvador, 1990–95

	1990	1991	1992	1993	1994	1995
Total	230,357	252,789	283,095	320,911	357,071	384,129
% active population	13.05	14.06	15.12	17.78	19.42	20.51
% formally employed	46.59	47.17	48.76	53.62	46.47	44.44

Source: Ministerio de Trabajo y Previsión Social, *Estadísticas de Trabajo.*

Table 6.3. Work accidents, by economic activity, El Salvador, 1987–95

	1987	1988	1989	1990	1991	1992	1993	1994	1995
Total	10,193	12,301	10,922	11,801	11,947	14,056	16,652	19,034	19,251
% annual increase	—	20.7	-11.2	8.1	1.2	17.7	18.5	14.3	1.1
industrial	4,752	5,747	5,170	5,921	5,816	6,677	7,979	8,374	8,367
% annual increase	—	20.9	-10.0	14.5	-1.8	14.8	19.5	5.0	-0.1

Source: Ministerio de Trabajo y Previsión Social, *Estadísticas de Trabajo.*

coverage increased from 13 to 20.5 percent between 1990 and 1995, a number that compares with other estimates.[22] At the same time, work and industrial accidents (treated by ISSS doctors) have nearly doubled between 1987 and 1995 (table 6.3). But this leaves many unprotected. In some sectors, workers are not aware of their legal right to coverage, and many go untreated. Especially in the maquila, "people who don't have any influence may be fired if they have an accident. Half the employers take the workers' money, but do not report their workers to the Labor Ministry or send the funds to ISSS," stated a UNTS representative. "This is what we are struggling for in our pacts, to give our workers the same priority and influence as those who can afford private health and pension services."[23]

Rights to Organize and Bargain

The desire to organize arises from work conditions. Despite reform of the new labor code in early 1994, El Salvador's maquila workers still reflect the experiences at Gabo and Mandarin. Without outside pressure, there is no significant reduction in mistreatment. In the Ruiz and García survey, 71 percent of the garment assemblers had been systematically abused, either verbally or physically. A total of 87 percent said they worked under conditions of general repression, often stemming from demands to meet production goals, and 94 percent agreed that there was no freedom of organization.

Some sought unionization as a result. More than half (56 percent) expressed positive views toward unions and spoke of the need to defend the rights of workers. Only 12 percent held negative opinions. The positive vote matched that of those who had not been offered individual contracts, as the law required. Many of those who did sign were asked to leave spaces blank (to facilitate an arbitrary dismissal). Although none were aware of the labor-rights rules under international trade, such as GSP or CBI, 18 percent had been previously fired for participating in union organizing efforts (Ruiz and García 1996:58, 63f).

"In the decade of conflict," reported another CENTRA study, "union activity nearly disappeared altogether due to the persecution of the leadership."

The number of organized companies dropped from more than 500 to a little more than a hundred. In the 1990s, while violence remains (for example, there were three executions in 1993), "union activity is repressed by employers who use more elaborate and sophisticated mechanisms. . . . Upon discovering that there is a union movement . . . the employer immediately fires the union backers. . . . The majority of firings occur without payment of indemnization."[24]

"When workers present the Labor Minister with documentation for constituting a new union, or legalizing an executive committee, the employers . . . normally fire the union organizers or pressure them to renounce, threatening that if they do not, they will be fired or they will close the company."[25]

"When a union attempts to register its leadership, the business owners file a preventive court action, alleging whatever they think might affect the election's outcome." Although neither the labor code, nor any other law makes any provision for such actions, they still often result in canceling the unionization attempt, leaving its leadership vulnerable to being fired (see court discussion below). Some owners follow with a submission of their own list of "union" leaders, or they create a parallel organization, such as a solidarista association (see chapter 11, on Costa Rica.)[26]

Unionists were routinely blacklisted via a computerized data bank shared by maquila owners. "The sector has gone after unions in a big way," emphasized Mark Anner. "Every organizing effort has meant a substantial number fired. The 1993 findings that for every 300 workers unionized, 1,000 were fired, remains true in 1996. Among 200 factories with 800 to 1,000 workers or more, five have unions, and they are largely symbolic. Not one of them has obtained the signatures from 51 percent of the workforce required to negotiate a contract."[27]

Between 1990 and 1993, unionization rates declined throughout the country. In 1993, for example, eight unions filed for recognition with the Labor Ministry, but only three received it—and they did so because of possible GSP suspension (*Informe Laboral* 1994:9).[28] Unions covered 11.17 percent of employees, but they only reached workers in 1.8 percent of all firms registered with ISSS and 3.8 percent of those in industry. The unionization rate was highest by far in construction (60.66 percent of 80,824 workers).[29] It covered 17.51 percent of the 308,682 workers in manufacturing.

Table 6.4 demonstrates that despite the overall decline in the unionized percent of the workforce, union membership and numbers rebounded in 1993–95, to more than 100,000 in nearly 120 organizations, bolstered by the construction unions. This signifies that the movement remains a viable one. However, unions did not engage in extensive bargaining. While workers with current and expiring contracts had been able to hold follow-up negotiations, employers successfully excluded any discussion about hour limitations and

Table 6.4. Number of unions and affiliates, El Salvador, 1987–95

	1987	1988	1989	1990	1991	1992	1993	1994	1995
Unions	98	99	103	96	99	101	103	113	119
Affiliates	72,668	70,815	72,769	71,224	60,960	55,697	74,274	118,000	102,555

Source: Ministerio de Trabajo y Previsión Social, *Estadísticas de Trabajo*.

bonificaciones,[30] not to mention lesser issues such as reimbursement of travel expenses, health and safety committees, professional training, or promotion. At best, some contracts make provisions for small company loans for workers' emergencies, medical care, maternity leave, and so on (*Informe Laboral* 1994).

Unions and Privatization

Outside the maquila sector, the largest fear about union organizing since the passage of the labor code was privatization (see chapter 1). El Salvador's public workers experienced additional job reductions "nailed by both privatization and job reduction." In 1996, as the private sector sponsored an intensive television campaign with the slogan, "privatization equals modernization and improvement of services," some "15,000 jobs were eliminated using the rationale of efficiency, including several hundred in Treasury which could not be privatized in any case. These strong unions received a hard blow."[31] Yet for the unions, the real issue was the government's failure to discuss alternative proposals. Privatization in itself would not be a violation of labor rights if they were able to maintain their union, negotiate how the change affected their working conditions, and have confidence that their agreements would be enforced.

Thus, El Salvador's overall working conditions in hours, wages, benefits, and bargaining rights remained hostage to code enforcement. We now turn to those institutional mechanisms responsible for enforcing the code: the Labor Ministry, the courts, and tripartite collaboration.

Ministry of Labor and the Courts

El Salvador's minister of labor is responsible for encouraging cooperation between business and labor, for worker training and health inspections, for assuring industry compliance with labor laws, for pre-court settlement of individual disputes and collective conflicts, and for producing labor statistics.[32] All of this would be a grand responsibility for a large organization. Yet as of the mid-1990s, it listed 450 workers, 300 less than it had in 1989. The ministry is by far the *smallest* of all federal agencies, receiving only .21 percent of the national budget.[33]

Table 6.5. Collective contracts and worker coverage, El Salvador, 1991–94

	1991	1992	1993	1994
Total contracts	298	342	326	308
Industrial	58	64	60	49
Construction	196	246	229	229
Total workers	61,471	66,542	92,862	78,541
Industrial workers	15,450	20,512	24,648	16,543

Source: Ministerio de Trabajo y Previsión Social, *Estadísticas de Trabajo.*

U.S. policy makers are not enthusiastic about the "Cinderella Ministry's" potential. A USAID-sponsored study characterized it as weak. Its staff receives "low salaries, has very low morale, and antiquated equipment."[34] "It is not seen as important," verified Mauricio Herrera, a USAID official with previous labor responsibilities. "Former minister Sifontes was viewed as very passive. However, the new minister, Eduardo Tomasino, who used to be president of the National Council of the Judiciary, has achieved a different dynamic."[35]

USAID and the U.S. Labor Department also rate ministry procedures as cumbersome. "Provoked by trade concerns, USAID advocated a labor-management cooperative plan, but to our knowledge no specific reforms have emerged. It they don't push for its use, there is little we can do. We did set up a few little grants, but they don't even have enough funds to pay for their rent."[36]

Unions hold mixed views toward Labor Ministry operations. Construction unions, which obtained the highest number of dispute settlements, were positive.[37] The CTD's Hurtado said that some ministers "hadn't understood changes of the labor code." Minister Sifontes could "speak knowledgeably about the problems of workers. We feel more comfortable going in and discussing things with him." But "the maquila sector was the same as before, and we see complicity." "The labor minister doesn't have the ability to fulfill the law," asserted Carlos Ochoa of the UNTS. "In all sectors, the ministry denies or delays union organizations."[38]

Ministry Facilitation of Union Activities

Despite ministry reorganization in 1996, the evidence supports union assessments. It has provided little assistance with contract negotiations since 1992. Total contracts dropped from 342 to 308 in 1994, and industrial contracts fell to forty-nine. Between 1993 and 1994, the number of covered workers also declined (table 6.5). Despite ILO prohibitions, the ministry has also permitted at least twenty-five employer-sponsored solidarista associations, many of which undermine unions (*Informe Laboral* 1994:9).

Table 6.6. Workers covered by labor inspections, El Salvador, 1986–90

Date	1986	1987	1988	1989	1990
Workers	225,903	297,474	262,626	255,482	184,497

Source: Ministerio de Trabajo y Previsión Social, Estadísticas de Trabajo.

Labor Inspections

But perhaps the most important test of the Labor Ministry's role in code and contract enforcement is the labor inspection system. In 1993, the ministry effectively had thirty-one inspectors working in five offices throughout the country: twenty-four in San Salvador; three in Santa Ana, two in San Miguel, and one each in Sonsonate and Usulután. In addition, five persons worked in the agricultural section.[39] The reorganization in 1996 allocated additional labor inspectors for the maquilas. "They gradually removed the old, corrupt inspectors," noted USAID's Sonia Caceres. When Minister Eduardo Tomasino arrived in 1996, he "reduced the current number of inspectors from forty to sixteen, and then to four! He was to hire ninety by 1997 and set up three regional offices to solve labor problems more quickly, but funding remained an issue."[40]

The mid-1990s decline in inspectorate staff significantly reduced inspections, both routine visitations and complaint investigations. Tables 6.6 and 6.7 indicate a drop in worker coverage from a high of 297,474 in 1987 to only 53,997 in 1995. Inspections fell from 54,062 in 1990 to 7,946. Another reason for the drop in 1995 may have been USAID's questioning of the numbers (if the higher numbers were divided by the number of available inspectors, it would mean more than 1,000 inspections per inspector, an almost impossible accomplishment!). In addition, very few inspections were conducted in the agricultural sector because of the limited transport.[41]

Related to inspections is the processing of labor disputes: "Inspectors do not have their own desks and are forced to share one table that is too small to accommodate all of them simultaneously. There is no copying machine. Pens

Table 6.7. Labor inspections, workers covered, and fines paid (in colones), El Salvador, 1991–95

	1991	1992	1993	1994	1995
Inspections	54,062	22,102	24,260	18,055	7,946
Workers covered	169,423	118,116	159,177	125,637	53,997
Fines paid	16,000	30,200	15,450	33,500	309,800

Source: Ministerio de Trabajo y Previsión Social, Estadísticas de Trabajo.

Table 6.8. Individual labor disputes and ministry resolutions, El Salvador, 1987–95

	1987	1988	1989	1990	1991	1992	1993	1994	1995
Total disputes	1,246	1,429	1,948	2,162	2,069	1,885	1,831	3,333	3,392
Resolved	738	729	1,059	1,175	1,148	942	956	1,465	1,651
% resolved	59	51	54	54	56	50	52	44	49
Abandoned	83	214	234	235	226	282	296	752	632

Source: Ministerio de Trabajo y Previsión Social, *Estadísticas de Trabajo.*

and paper are not always available." In one visit, USAID found eighty terminated workers standing in line waiting for inspectors to calculate their back wages on tiny calculators. It did credit inspectors for handling all such disputes the same day (Shepard et al. 1994).

The director general of labor inspection reported that 90 percent of dispute inspections were resolved in favor of employees (Shepard et al. 1994:35). Yet, as table 6.8 shows, the ministry has consistently resolved only about half of the individual disputes brought before it, most of which involved firings.[42] Although it did adjust to an increase in disputes in 1994 and 1995, it decided less than half in favor of the worker. Its ability to conciliate firings declined from 55 percent to 47.5 percent between 1991 and 1995, and its success in resolving disputes from women workers dropped from 58.8 percent to 45.2 percent (see table 6.9), necessitating a referral to the courts.

There was ample justification for reorganization of El Salvador's labor-inspection and disputes-resolution system. USAID representative Ricardo Muniz described one typical inspection in which personal influence superceded professional process. A maquila sewing machine worker had been fired for attending a sick child. "The employer stated that they had not terminated her but had replaced her for a week with another person. . . . The employee was present during the entire discussion—a practice that I considered usual. The inspector supervisor convinced the employer to put her back to work. No

Table 6.9. Ministry-adjudicated firings and resolutions, by sector and gender, El Salvador, 1991–95

	1991	1992	1993	1994	1995
Total firings	1,998	1,810	1,661	3,129	3,262
% resolved	55.0	48.6	49.9	44.4	47.5
Manufacturing	705	681	619	1,260	1,211
% resolved	57.8	47.0	50.4	42.5	44.7
Women	704	667	572	1,198	1,248
% resolved	58.8	52.8	46.2	47.5	45.2

Source: Ministerio de Trabajo y Previsión Social, *Estadísticas de Trabajo.*

information was gathered on the firm during the initial conference and it appeared that the employer knew the supervisor from prior inspections; no interviews [were] conducted of employees or records checked. There was some negotiation prior to the reinstatement and a report was prepared upon return to the office" (Shepard et al. 1994:37).

USAID's criticisms of such informal practices were not cultural bias that favored "professional and North American" record keeping. El Salvador provided no publications to employers, employees, or the public with information on worker rights, "formal training or in-house educational programs for inspectors. Requirements concerning record-keeping are not well explained. Corruption is rife in the inspection service. . . . It is not uncommon for inspectors to take small gifts from employers . . . to sometimes make blatant requests for cash for quashing a complaint and not enforcing workers' rights. One source in the inspection service estimated that a payoff is made in one of every three inspections" (Shepard et al. 1994:9). Since there were no history cards or other records kept, there were no penalties to deter repeat violators. In 1991, the ministry fined seven businesses (four in manufacturing) for a total of 16,000 colones ($1,818); in 1992, the total reached $2,580. By 1995, the ministry claimed to increase fines tenfold as part of its reform (table 6.7).

Finally, the ministry resolved no more than a third of the collective-labor disputes brought before it (table 6.12). A Friedrich Ebert Foundation report suggests an even lower degree of resolution.[43]

Between 1994 and 1996, USAID assisted the Labor Ministry with at least $150,000 for training new inspectors in mediation and conciliation. Presenters from the U.S. Federal Mediation Commission and the National Safety Council explained the ministry reorganization.[44] By 1997, needed implementing funds had not materialized.

Courts

Workers likewise face obstacles when their individual or collective disputes become designated as "complaints" and are referred to the labor courts. For individual cases, the employee must hire his or her own lawyer or go to the procurator general to have a lawyer assigned. Few can afford to do so, since both workers and employers know that most fines will be less than payment of back wages.

During the years of conflict between 1987 and 1991, the courts showed a gradually declining ability to settle individual complaints from 74.5 percent in 1987 to 62.2 percent in 1992, the year following the peace accords. Since then, however, court resolutions have gradually increased to 69.6 percent, although less than half are worker friendly.[45] The percentage of *judgements resolved* in favor of workers, which had averaged below 60, improved to 67.8 in 1995 (see table 6.10).

Table 6.10. Individual work complaints and favorable court resolutions, El Salvador, 1987–95

	1987	1988	1989	1990	1991	1992	1993	1994	1995
No. of complaints	1,147	1,249	1,649	1,461	1,266	1,156	1,398	1,706	2,001
No. of resolutions	855	903	1,186	1,016	906	719	944	1,176	1393
% resolved	74.5	72.3	71.9	69.5	71.6	62.2	67.5	68.9	69.6
No. favorable to workers	506	544	588	675	541	417	520	707	944
% of complaints	44.1	43.6	35.7	46.2	42.7	36.1	37.2	41.4	47.2
% of resolutions	59.2	60.2	49.6	66.4	59.7	58.0	55.1	60.1	67.8

Source: Ministerio de Trabajo y Previsión Social, Estadísticas de Trabajo.

Nevertheless, most individual complaints refer to unjust firings (compare totals in tables 6.10 and 6.11). One measure of the settlement of job-termination complaints is the payment of "indemnization" as required by law. Only between 25 and 30 percent of the indemnization cases have resulted in judgments favorable to the workers (see table 6.11). Until 1995, women represented about a third of the complaints and received a proportionate share of the awards. In 1995, perhaps due to attention to maquila conditions, they constituted half of the indemnization requests and had 57 percent of their cases favorably resolved.

When the courts do act on individual cases, companies still retaliate. In 1996, after one company received a judgment to pay a union leader who was dismissed while organizing, it claimed a temporary closing, stored the equipment, and dismissed the workers, encouraging others to do the same (CTCA 1996).

One final test of its effectiveness is the court's ability to handle collective-labor disputes brought by unions and other worker groups. Prominent collective complaints center around nonpayment of salaries, or the filing of a *pliego de petitiones* (list of specific grievances). Non-fulfillment of contract provisions

Table 6.11. Indemnization cases and court judgments, by gender, El Salvador, 1991–95

	1991	1992	1993	1994	1995
No. of worker cases	1,265	1,148	1,386	1,701	1,985
% by women	34.9	33.6	38.6	37.2	49.1
No. of judgments	362	287	369	493	604
% favorable to workers	28.6	25.0	26.6	29.0	30.4
Total awards (colones)	1,933,131	2,425,426	2,580,422	3,393,582	5,700,707
% to women	34.4	39.1	43.6	26.2	57.2

Source: Ministerio de Trabajo y Previsión Social, Estadísticas de Trabajo.

Table 6.12. Collective-labor disputes and resolutions, El Salvador, 1987–95

	1987	1988	1989	1990	1991	1992	1993	1994	1995
Total	25	36	31	20	26	47	36	12	42
Resolved	9	9	11	7	10	5	—	—	—

Source: Ministerio de Trabajo y Previsión Social, *Estadísticas de Trabajo.*

and worker firings constitute other reasons for action. Some of these actions result in strikes (see procedure above). As table 6.12 shows, the labor courts resolve less than a third of collective disputes they receive. In such conflicts, the courts usually issue judgments against the workers (for example, all ten in 1993).

Despite the commitments made in the peace accords and by the National Assembly for an independent court system, the UN Truth Commission (1993:246) subsequently found politics to penetrate all elements of the judiciary. Labor leader Miguel Ramírez pointed to the insufficiency of "four labor tribunals for 1,800,000 workers . . . much corruption and lots of payments." "We bring to court strong evidence, but they are bribed just like tax and customs officials," agreed Carlos Ochoa. "There is very little activity regarding the maquilas," repeated Ramírez. As of 1995, only one judgment had been issued—the case of Mandarin." Ramírez put partial blame on the "lack of coercive power to order reinstatements; the courts can require payment of indemnization, but it is another rule which they can't enforce."[46]

"USAID has an administration of justice program to help all courts here, but AID funds have been drastically cut. The labor courts really don't function here to enforce anything," admitted labor attaché Henshaw.[47]

Tripartite Efforts in El Salvador: The Consejo

In the wake of disappointment following modification of the labor code in 1994, virtually no national union–private sector exchange took place for more than a year. In part, this was due to ARENA's electoral victory. Despite challenged ballots in many areas, the vote brought defeat to most of the union leaders who had served in the 1992–94 assembly.

Due to persistent labor unrest, in March 1995, the Labor Ministry urged the formation of a Consejo Superior de Trabajo (top work council) as another effort at tripartite consultation. A synopsis of its failure suggests that another approach may be required to mediate El Salvador's hardened class divisions.

In theory, the forty-eight-member Consejo was designed to be tripartite, with eight representative entities from business, eight from key government ministries, and eight from the unions, each of whom had a delegate and suppliant. Officially, the Consejo was to meet twice a year, but if a major issue arose, representatives from any of the sectors could convene a meeting. As its first order of business, it was scheduled to review the proposed "organic law" for Labor Ministry reform.

From the outset, the unions were very skeptical. They had opposed the elimination of the Social Forum, which had a more democratic structure. In the Consejo, five of the eight union representatives were government-controlled, such as FESINCONSTRANS, the construction union. Labor attorney José Candray and the CTD's Hurtado believed the government would "work out its deals, leaving independent unions divided."[48] Even AIFLD agreed that "it was a mistake to replace the Forum with this group, since most of its unions take ARENA's line and criticize us and U.S. unions for destabilizing the country."[49]

Despite their controlled nature, with backing by Hurtado and others, the unions elected Roger Gutiérrez of FEASIES as one of the two labor vice presidents of the Consejo. Gutiérrez challenged government claims about stopping "the poor treatment and sub-minimal compliance with the health requirements. So many social accomplishments have been broken; families have disintegrated, but the state is not responding. We are going backwards." Gutiérrez vowed that the Labor Ministry had "to pursue a fresh strategy. We are approaching other workers who face the same conditions as at Gabo. We have also invited other businessmen: Korean capital, U.S. capital and others with differing views to discuss our differences together in the Consejo."[50]

Consejo backer Juan Hector Vidal of ANEP, who claimed a solid relationship with Gutiérrez, stressed the development of mutual confidence "through the Consejo, with representatives from the three sectors [to] . . . address issues and avoid corruption."[51]

Nevertheless, the Consejo did not go anywhere. The unions suggested an agenda originally proposed in the Social Forum, but the business and government representatives refused to accept it. "We did not have norms or internal rules that could help us to proceed," explained Edito Genovez, a suppliant from UNTS. "For example, we needed a majority to take action. When we had meetings, the unions would all show up, but only two or three came from the government, so we had to cancel the function."[52]

In practice, the Consejo proved inoperative in face of the incendiary maquila and public-sector conflicts of 1995–96. When it did meet, business representatives appeared ignorant about of the legal aspects of labor-reform proposals. Although originally scheduled to discuss the Labor Ministry reform law, it only did so perfunctorily after a six-month delay, and then mainly due to pressures from ILO advisors—a further testimony to its inefficiency (Arriola 1995:60).

Residual polarization from the Consejo's failure greeted the USTR delegation in November 1995: "The country was agitated by tremendous vitupera-
tion in the press, even though there was no pending GSP petition. The union
situation in the maquilas was a disaster, with vicious press attacks on the GSP
delegation." Several union officials sympathetic to ARENA circulated anti-
U.S. slogans on Consejo stationery opposing the campaign to convince GAP
to accept outside monitors of its production contracts in El Salvador and elsewhere (see above). In a twist of irony, one FMLN congressional delegate had
to intervene to defend AIFLD's David Jessup! Nevertheless, reported U.S.
State Department representative Gary Maymarduk, after GAP's agreement
and subsequent negotiations, "the settlement at Mandarin sent a signal to the
entire Salvadoran business community."[53]

It is unclear what message business representatives heard, since both they
and the government still exploited union divisions to prevent the Consejo
from functioning. "When we request an extraordinary session to address a
specific complaint, the Ministry of Labor is then supposed to summon the
others, but only six or seven respond to the ministry's call," affirmed Edito
Genovez of UNTS. "The law stipulates that all decrees must first come before
the Consejo so we can determine their usefulness and validity. But despite our
request, the current proposal on labor ministry reform never went through
our hands. The Consejo was really set up for international propaganda and
public consumption. Tripartism hasn't functioned in El Salvador."[54]

USAID and even the business sector acknowledged the Consejo's failure.[55] By mid-1996, the vice president of the Cámara de Comercia e Industria
de El Salvador, Luis Cardenal, "recognized" that the Consejo could not
prioritize its themes for discussion. The unions could not decide who had
rights of representation, but the government abandoned the table to resolve
emergencies, and the private sector had been preoccupied with the economic situation.[56] Oscar Ortiz, an FMLN deputy and a member of the Legislative Labor Commission, lamented that the Consejo had reached a phase of
entrapment.

Consejo labor vice president Roger Gutiérrez put primary blame "on the
government and the minister of labor more than the private sector, since the
minister would not even exert the power to get the other ministers (or anyone)
to attend the meetings. The government avoided labor issues, except as they
pertained to international opinion. The private sector also talks of an alliance,
but does not offer any concrete proposals, or even implement what we already have in place."[57]

Thus, the post-code effort at tripartism failed in El Salvador. In July 1996,
with a considerable fanfare, the private sector's ANEP issued "El Manifiesto
Salvadoreño" in the hopes of combining an overall economic strategy with

some acknowledgment of labor issues. "Cheap employment is no longer synonymous with competition," it acknowledged. "The stability of the country depends on the permanent alliance between employers and employees. . . . Both should creatively resolve their differences peacefully, understanding their complementary role." But the document could not avoid quipping that "inflexible labor markets are the worst enemies of employment" (ANEP 1996:25–26). "By rejecting various views on flexibility and privatization at the outset, the proposal contradicted any creative alliance," concluded Roger Gutiérrez.

USAID and the Improvement of Labor Relations in El Salvador

To support mutual understandings between labor and management, USAID offered the Labor Ministry further training and technical support in 1994–96. It "lauded" the 1996 "organic law" modernizing the ministry and the plan to hire thirty new inspectors, but cautioned that the government would have to fund the ministry's new budget request.[58] USAID also devoted considerable resources to the FOES project as mentioned in chapter 5.

According to Herrera, "FOES received its inspiration from a Central American Scholarship Program which brought ten management and ten labor representatives from both sides of El Salvador's civil war to Washington in 1994. They visited different models of employee/owner cooperation: a university, an aluminum company and a Virginia post office. During their workshop sessions, participants emotionally called one another 'killers,' etc., but calmed down as they studied U.S. foreign relations brokered by the House and Senate. Upon return, they formed an advisory committee . . . so FOES became part of the 'reconciliation process.'" FOES also reflected USAID's finding that the Ministry of Labor had been bypassed due to a "lack of respect and trust. . . . Disputes are dealt with either by the parties directly or by the labor courts" (Shepard et al. 1994). So FOES attempted to broaden the knowledge about methods for resolving disputes among the ministry, the private sector, and labor unions. In one concrete achievement, "on their own initiative, a trade union participant and a representative of ANEP talked to both sides preparing for a sugar mill strike, and settled the conflict."[59]

By the end of 1994, FOES had distributed 11,200,000 colones or 14 percent of its projected budget into fifty-one loans, thirty-five grants, and fifty-three programs in technical assistance, benefiting more than 75,000 families. In 1995 it sponsored a series of panels on globalization, privatization, and negotiation, and it made a presentation to the Consejo. However, by the end of its four-year program from 1992 to 1996, Herrera concluded that despite its "very good relationship with the Ministry of Labor, the FOES project has not been successful. Its objectives were very difficult to begin with, and it had a lot of problems getting antagonistic groups together, besides the internal problems it faced. It took a long time to get programs implemented, and its funding had to be cut to 45 million colones (still $5.2 million) as a result."[60]

In another admission of project inadequacy, USAID eliminated labor (and labor projects) from specific funding during its 1996–2002 regional program cycle.

Evaluating GSP and El Salvador

The story of GSP petitions in El Salvador and the aftermath of petition withdrawal in 1994 reveals the limitations of trade conditionality in achieving labor reforms. The story portrays a government and a private sector that squirmed past genuine reforms—a quintessential example of policy subversion and broken commitments that thwarted petition objectives at nearly every turn. Given the country's improved economic situation in the 1990s, this was especially surprising: Within a neo-classical framework, El Salvador ought to have illustrated how expected labor improvements follow free-market advances (see chapters 2 and 12). To a very limited extent, wages may have improved, but worker freedoms did not improve.

What did happen was a debate about attitude. El Salvador's business community believed that "there were some benefits from GSP pressure," as Juan Hector Vidal acknowledged. "Both employers and workers respect the law more. We have subscribed to fourteen conventions of the ILO, and have passed the labor code (through our own process as noted). We have more mutual confidence now, and we know each other much better." Vidal explained the anomalies: "In the U.S., you had 200 years to build a democracy. We have only been at it since 1992. You must remember that we had a long period of war. Now we seek social harmony. As employers we have an interest in peace."

"We are not opposed to regional laws," stressed Vidal. "We ourselves are struggling with the proper principles to deal with trade questions. We do not favor rapid changes in tariffs, since this could cause drastic changes in employment. We want confidence of the unions. We know we must work together, even independently of the government, to construct a national project, not a NAFTA, but a project that can benefit from the investment and services the world has to offer."[61]

Indeed, as a result of GSP pressure, U.S. labor attaché Simon Henshaw found "a real change in the business community's attitude despite the problems in the maquila: Before the war, they wouldn't sit down with unions, saying 'we won't let commies into our plant!' By 1995, they became much more moderate in their tone toward labor. They don't like it, but will deal with unions in a professional manner." But Vidal tempered his vision with his lingering problem: "Our workers are still under the influence of Marxist thinkers like Herbert Marcuse. We don't believe in the struggle of classes, but that philosophy has affected them. We need to have an alliance between the two sectors, like the Japanese model."

This last remark may exemplify why the unions have remained so skeptical of employer intent. "In our country, industry has sought protection of the state so that manufacturing can flourish," commented Gilberto Ernesto García Dueñas, labor researcher with CENTRA. "But now with regionalization this places the state in a difficult spot. President Calderon Sol announces we have to compete on an international level to improve our quality to compete with international companies. So business here is trying to improve production to reduce costs. But rather than invest in technology, they are seeking to lower labor costs. So after twenty years of a state-protected obsolete path toward industrialization with outdated machines, they have now adopted the USA model in textiles; they have reduced personnel by half to achieve a lower price."

"Attitudes have not changed in the private sector," emphasized Mark Anner, who had become head of an independent maquila-monitoring commission. "Instead, they are now saying, 'El Salvador must reduce the rigidity of its labor market and acquire more flexibility.' What do they mean, flexibility? When 200 are waiting for jobs after twenty are fired? They seek to cut benefits, to remove the law on severance pay, to make 'El Salvador less like Europe, more like Chile.' So we are left with only 5 percent of the workforce with proper trade unions, and a minimum wage of $130 a month (1,050 colones). Even that often goes unpaid in the maquilas."[62] The comment reflects Arriola's assessment that "the lack of the government's political will to facilitate the exercise of free unions [and] the strongly anti-union culture of the Salvadoran business community is closely linked to the dominant model of accumulation in the country" (1995:31). "From a company viewpoint, what is important is the economy of the country," concluded Carlos Ochoa. "They do not publicize what impact it has on the people. They say globalization helps all, but they pay below minimum salary. What they take from El Salvador does not help the workers."[63]

What does this imply for the GSP process? "I don't see any improvement after lifting of the review," Anner lamented. "Unions had always been confused on how best to use GSP strategically. And with the divisive impact of post-accord economics and politics, broken unions and confederations (including FENASTRAS, the CTD, and even AIFLD) were in no condition to mobilize another effort."[64] Some success had come from direct corporate action in the maquila sector. But from the policy perspective, while GSP had stimulated a shakeup at the Labor Ministry, hundreds of union–private sector meetings, and millions of colones pumped by USAID into the country, it had not demonstrated *significant* improvement in private-sector attitudes toward labor rights.

Perhaps the GSP process at least set the stage for more positive future outcomes. After the election of new AFL-CIO leadership in 1995, and a restructuring of its international division, AIFLD was replaced by the American Center for International Labor Solidarity (ACILS). In 1997 Benjamin Davis took over the Mexican/Central American section and progressive activist Rhett Doumitt was appointed to supervise a substantial project on labor rights in El Salvador.

CHAPTER 7

The Guatemalan Case: Reluctant Compromise

"Guatemala does not exist," exclaims Roger Graetz, the protagonist in Francisco Goldman's bittersweet novel, *The Long Night of the White Chickens.* The beauty of its land and people, half or more indigenous, and the tragedy of its pain and death cancel each other out. In roughly parallel fashion, GSP petitions have helped cancel the nation's worst labor abuses. As one UN-SITRAGUA leader stated, "They have not had much positive effect, but without them, things would be much worse." The story of GSP's ambivalence in Guatemala contrasts a business sector more sophisticated than in El Salvador with labor unions sometimes cowed by persistent violence. It traces the differing objectives of USTR, which finally began to implement U.S. law on labor rights, and the U.S. State Department, which emphasized "larger" political objectives.[1]

The GSP process began in Guatemala in 1986, just as the country officially changed from a military to a civilian government (still under the army's heavy hand). The nation remained under GSP scrutiny for eleven years.[2] We can roughly divide the nation's GSP experience into four phases: early filings, 1986–90; U.S. policy convergence, 1991–92; labor-code passage, 1992–93; U.S. policy fluctuations, 1993–97. Results brought a stronger labor code than El Salvador's and more improvements in private-sector attitudes and minimum-wage standards. However, they achieved little in labor-rights implementation.

Early Filings, 1986–90

GSP petitions were first introduced to Guatemala in response to its decade of violence (see Black et al. 1984; Jonas 1991; Trudeau 1993). Guatemala's notorious repression of trade unions came to be symbolized by the murder of eight Coca-Cola workers who attempted to form a union in the late 1970s and by the abduction of twenty-one officials of the Confederación Nacional de Trabajadores (CNT) in 1980 (Albizúrez 1988; Frundt 1987b; Levenson-Estrada 1994). During the years of heaviest repression under the presidencies of generals Lucas García and Riós Montt, virtually all unions went underground. In the mid-1980s, they began to reemerge (Frundt 1987a; Goldston 1989). The major confederations of the post-annihilation period included UNSITRAGUA, which grew out of the Coca-Cola mobilization; the Christian Democratic CGTG; and CUSG, backed by AIFLD but somewhat independent of its domination.[3]

Military suppression helped sustain underlying economic inequalities. At a macro level, however, the Guatemalan economy had remained among the most robust in the region, and its currency retained parity with the dollar until about 1980. Then, as it faced the economic crisis described in chapter 4, Guatemalan generals remained aloof. Despite a persistent drop in the GDP, declining exports, and a rapidly increasing debt burden, military officials took few corrective measures until 1984. Then, without public consultation, they suddenly imposed a currency devaluation and halted real wage increases.[4] But their dedication to violence frightened investors.

The flight of assets helped persuade the army to nominally surrender political control in 1986. Newly elected President Venicio Cerezo improved infrastructure, public-sector expenditures, and services for foreign capital. Employers reacted conservatively, holding labor costs low while criticizing Cerezo for inflationary spending. The Christian Democratic president invited CUSG's secretary general, Juan Francisco Alfaro, to become minister of labor. In exchange, Alfaro requested commitments on price controls and labor reforms. When these were not forthcoming, Alfaro refused the post. CUSG cooperated with the AFL-CIO to petition GSP for a review of Guatemala's trade privileges.[5] While denial of trade benefits would not affect non-exporting sectors or textiles since they were covered by the Multifiber Agreement (see the introduction and chapter 3), it would reduce income in sugar and cattle, both dominated by wealthy Guatemalan families that could affect national labor policy.

USTR accepted the AFL-CIO request but quickly found that Guatemala's new democratic government had "really limited human rights abuses" and was "taking steps" toward protecting labor rights.[6] In 1987, USTR refused to even consider a second AFL-CIO petition.

Petitions Cite Abuses in Five Labor Rights Areas

Labor abuses mounted, however. Although the GDP grew by 3 percent or more each year in the late 1980s, international lenders demanded spending reductions since import values remained above exports. In November 1989, the government put into effect a "structural adjustment" package that included another currency devaluation, reduced tariffs, reduced price controls, and freed interest rates. Workers bore the brunt: inflation shot up to about 75 percent in 1990—the highest in memory. By 1991, minimum-wage standards had dropped precipitously to 38.9 percent of their 1980 buying power. Even worse was the overt repression against labor organizing.

Between 1988 and 1990, such violence motivated other U.S. labor groups, coordinated by the International Labor Rights Fund (ILRF), to seek GSP scrutiny.[7] They argued that Guatemala had violated all five areas of labor rights.

1. The Guatemalan government had flagrantly disregarded ILO convention 87 on freedom of association via physical abuses, military action, and labor code restrictions. Cerezo's first two years had witnessed eight more unionists disappeared, dozens threatened, eleven teachers and six labor activists assassinated, including another worker from Coca-Cola.[8] The government had routinely stalled the applications of more than 160 unions.[9]

2. It had violated the right to organize or bargain. Government workers did not effectively have the right to unionize.[10] Unions participating in politics were threatened with dissolution.[11] By requiring a two-thirds vote of all workers, not just union members, the labor code severely limited strikes.[12] Generally, the code contained no requirements to reinstate unjustly fired workers or to bargain in good faith. More than ten code articles interfered with freedom of association, and more than eight jeopardized the right to organize and bargain collectively.[13]

Code violations happened without consequence. Since employers "routinely fail to appear" at judicial hearings, proceedings could drag on for years, such as they did with the U.S.-owned Inexport, which disregarded court orders to rehire workers arbitrarily fired (see below), and other companies that promoted employer "solidarity associations" in place of unions.

3. Slave labor was permitted. Army-mandated civil patrols routinely performed unpaid physical labor—carrying firewood, clearing roads, cutting paths to towers, building homes for army generals.[14]

4. Ten thousand children were allowed to work illegally, picking nearly a third of Guatemalan coffee. Schools were not easily accessible, and 90 percent of indigenous children remained illiterate.[15]

5. Working conditions remained unacceptable. The norm of $2.00 a day minimum wage was insufficient to obtain basic necessities. Eighty-five percent of Guatemalan families did not earn enough income to meet basic needs, and 72 percent lived in extreme poverty.

The wage increase in 1988, the first adjustment in ten years, still left workers far behind the cost of living.[16] Work often extended beyond the eight-hour day and a forty-four-hour workweek with no extra pay.[17]

Worker health and safety remained in jeopardy because of unguarded machinery, poor lighting and ventilation, and inadequate protective equipment (no goggles, gloves, or helmets). Factory employees often worked in cramped spaces, under hot glaring lights, breathing in dust and fibers. Workers applying pesticides wore no protective clothing. Nearly a third of coffee workers went barefoot and barehanded while spraying Aldicarb, Methylparathyon, Paraquat, Methamidiphos, and Tamaron. DDT in farmworker women's breast milk amounted to more than 6.7 times the amount of DDT permitted in cow's milk.[18]

USTR Remains Unpersuaded

For three years running, USTR labeled these "accusations . . . specious and/or false." For example, it found no demonstration that forty-three incidents of violence that petitioners cited were "labor related."[19] It described a military intervention against a strike by 50,000 plantation workers as police who quelled "outside elements . . . provoking vandalism." It categorized other cases as "personal . . . appropriately handled by the courts."[20]

USTR also explained away problematic articles in the labor code that inhibited freedom of association.[21] The hated counterinsurgent civil-patrol arrangement did "not violate worker rights, for there is no evidence that those on patrol are asked to do more than just patrol."[22] Child labor was needed "to sustain the family's existence."[23] The subcommittee could not verify specific allegations on work accidents, pesticide poisonings, and urban/rural death rates. It reported "unprecedented dialogue" on raising minimum wages.[24]

Nevertheless, even though the early petitions did not bring USTR review, they pressured the government to incorporate labor principles in EPZ rules[25] and to speed labor-code reform. The Cerezo administration invited an ILO advisor to examine legislative discrepancies. The Guatemalan Congress took "a big step," in USTR's view, by moving "what had been simply ILO proposals into the congressional labor committee."[26] However, management feared "that a new Code would be tilted in the unions' favor, while unionists look on the proposed reforms as giving management even more of an upper hand." All "were unanimous that the labor law . . . is doomed to failure."[27]

U.S. Policy Convergence, 1990–1992

Despite the USTR and Guatemalan government "stonewall" of any change in labor rights, political and economic transformations drew increasing attention to petitioner objectives. Following the regional Esquipulas Accords in 1987, the government began reluctant negotiations with the Guatemalan National Revolutionary Unity (URNG) guerilla forces, seeking to end the hemisphere's longest civil war. As discussions dragged on, the civil sectors, in which trade unions played a key role, cited their own inequitable treatment in face of intransigent government structures. The Christian Democrats offered a cautionary response. Although dilatory on union recognitions, Labor Minister Rolando Maldonado ushered through congressional ratification of twenty-three ILO conventions. This compared with two ratifications in the previous twenty years.

Under Cerezo, Guatemala's economy had begun to grow, thanks to better prices from its traditional coffee exports and its non-traditional exports. Clothing shipments to the U.S. jumped from 15 million in 1985 to 227 million in 1990 (U.S. Department of Commerce 1990b). The assertively neo-liberal administration of Jorge Serrano, which ruled from 1990 to 1993, substantially reduced inflation and interest rates, improved reserves, and promoted business expansion.[28] Benefits accrued to the non-traditional export sector in compliance with USAID strategy.[29] Yet as Serrano reduced government activity and investment by 7 percent, he especially neglected rural areas, and social stability did not improve.[30] The shift from food production forced the population into urban areas (see also Terrell 1984) just as the maquila sector accelerated its hiring and exploitation of young women. When such women attempted to organize unions, they were thwarted at every turn (González 1990; Petersen 1992; Ramírez 1994; Chinchilla and Hamilton 1994; MacLeod 1994; ILO 1995b).

GSP pressure brought certain government actions. Vice Labor Minister Aura Bolaños, spouse of noted analyst and current Vice Foreign Minister Gabriel Aguilar Peralta, sponsored maquila reforms and protections for women and children. Labor Minister Mario Solorzano, head of the Partido Socialista Democrático, touted a "Social Pact" between business and labor. Hoping to optimize wage- and labor-law compliance, some unions participated, but they soon became disillusioned by pervasive government-business violations.[31]

U.S./GLEP Wins Embassy Backing for Petition

U.S. backing for Guatemalan labor unions increased after 1990. Joining the petition effort came U.S./GLEP, which had mobilized support for workers at specific plants since 1987 (Hogness 1989; Coats 1991, 1993; Compa 1993; Frundt 1996). In 1991, U.S./GLEP publicized a union organizing attempt at Camisas Modernas, a subsidiary of the "world's largest shirtmaker," Phillips-Van Heusen (PVH). The PVH effort channeled protests to USTR and to the apparel company. Contacted by U.S./GLEP and the Latin (Central) American Working Group (LAWG), ten U.S. senators and more than ninety representatives urged USTR to review the Guatemalan charges.

Perhaps the pressure helped bring more competent labor attachés to the U.S. Embassy, and the straightforward, if conservative, U.S. ambassador Thomas Strook. In 1991, at the attaché's urging, Ambassador Strook hosted a reception for the ILRF/GLEP delegation and key business and government representatives, sending a clear message: broken promises to address rights abuses must cease. The diplomat confided at the end of the evening that he would oppose the GSP filing, but if things did not improve he would remain neutral in 1992 (which he did).[32]

Representatives from Guatemala's Comité Coordinador de Asociaciones Agrícolas, Comerciales, Industriales y Financieras (CACIF) promised to intervene immediately to address abusive employers such as U.S.-owned Inexport. They were "worried about the petition" and debated how "to clean up their act."[33] When the ILRF/GLEP returned in 1992, the government quickly announced 167 union authorizations. CACIF representatives *condemned* "any abuse that might exist" and repeated their commitment that "the Labor Code and Constitution should be respected, and CACIF will back it up."[34] "Just the demand that we be removed from GSP means less capital investment, and workers will have less opportunity for competitive places to work," stated one representative. "The private sector is convinced it is not a good policy to work people 12 to 15 hours a day. They won't be efficient tomorrow. Good labor relations is helpful to business. . . . We will ask that any [maquila] violators be expelled from the country."[35] Since none of CACIF's previous commitments had been honored, however, their repeated phrases did not impress the delegation.

Petition Cites Violations in Five Areas

In 1991 and 1992 many groups joined ILRF/GLEP as petitioners,[36] bolstered by a more limited petition from the AFL-CIO. In 1992, ILRF/GLEP confronted USTR's epistemological difficulties with seven years of accumulated evidence. They challenged the trade body's dismissal of the linkage between trade-union activity and many incidents of assassinations, disappearances, kidnappings, assaults, and threats, using the excuse that "violence is common in Guatemala."[37] They questioned USTR's acceptance of legislative proposals as substitutes for labor-code reform and of code reform in place of code implementation. Violations in each of the five categories of rights remained overwhelming.

1. The right of association was nearly impossible because of killings, threats, and abuse of trade unionists documented in the State Department's *Human Rights Reports,* ILO findings on abuses, case reviews of UN expert Christian Tomuschat, and the delegation's own compilation of assaults, kidnappings, and death threats. The government had truly abandoned labor-code reform.[38]

2. The petitioners also questioned code implementation. One example was the minister of labor's claim to have registered 167 unions when actual recognition only totaled nineteen.[39] President Serrano had effectively canceled the labor minister's new authority to approve union applications and to reduce the background checks of union committeemen, exemplified by the delayed recognition of the union at Phillips-Van Heusen.[40] At the same time the president had significantly liberalized procedures for approving business investments.[41] Even the U.S. State Department admitted that the low percentage of organized workers was affected by "stringent requirements . . . to obtain legal status."[42]

A crucial USTR test of the right to organize and bargain was "whether the Government was making progress to ameliorate the recognized inadequate enforcement and adjudication of Guatemalan labor laws." Petitioners argued that there had been no progress aside from declarations of good intentions. In one typical case, Inexport, a U.S.-owned maquila company, had fired 200 workers for attempting to form a union, and Guatemalan courts had decreed the firings illegal. For more than a year, thirty-five of these workers occupied the street in front of the plant, but the government refused to take any follow-up action. Workers from twelve other plantations and factories recounted similar experiences.[43] Seven national unions detailed juridical difficulties.[44]

The petitions repeated earlier charges about forced and child labor. Unpaid civil patrols constructed infrastructure projects. Maquilas locked doors to enforce overtime.[45] Petitioners demanded stronger measures to assure that children were not exploited in the industrial sector.

Although the government raised minimum-wage standards in 1992 (for the first time since 1988), the petition cited the minister of labor's non-enforcement. Half of the nation's plantations were not paying the minimum, and women were paid 30 to 50 percent of what men received.[46] Hours regulations remained unacknowledged. In a precedent, the courts did fine two Korean managers for violating worker rights, but only for $45.00. Health and safety abuses continued unabated. Despite a Ministry of Public Health plan for safety, the government had taken no action to improve data, training, inspections, or penalties.

Early Petition Responses

The 1991 and 1992 petitions again elicited further governmental and business promises. By mid-June 1991 the Congress granted proposed labor-code reforms a first reading (three readings are required before passage). The state dutifully swore that it would honor labor guarantees, via its constitution, its current labor code, and ILO convention 87.[47] Admitting that the labor minister faced implementation difficulties attributable to scarce resources, and employer non-cooperation, President Serrano offered to decentralize and bolster labor inspections.

After USTR rejected the 1991 petition, action ceased, however. CACIF's president was "worried that some of the modifications . . . to the Labor Code are taking on a slanted direction." He then persuaded the Constitutional Court to suspend a new pension law. He criticized an ILO agreement that obligated workplaces to have doctors, clinics, and day care centers. Application of health rules languished.[48]

The ministry also did not accelerate union recognitions as promised.[49] Labor courts remained ineffective as a forum for appeal. When the government persuaded Labor Minister Solorzano to include an electricity rate increase in his advocated Social Pact, unions bolted. The nation's human-rights ombudsman lambasted the labor inspector for not strictly enforcing wage, hours, and safety rules at maquila companies or taking immediate actions to end abuses, a failing the labor minister publicly acknowledged.[50] By April 1992, not one of 712 stores surveyed had complied with wage requirements, although some had forced employees to state they had done so. Facing petition renewal in 1992, the Serrano administration again promised speedy remedies.[51]

"The Government of Guatemala undertook a rush of activity to dissuade the USTR from accepting it for review . . . a hurried visit to Washington by several vice-ministers and members of the Guatemalan Congress," noted Pharis Harvey, director of ILRF. "However, it did not include any serious efforts to resolve outstanding labor conflicts or undertake labor law reform. In fact, a peaceful occupation in the central square by workers and their families who represented dozens of labor disputes which the legal system had failed to resolve were ousted in the dead of night without court order on June 21, just as the government's delegation was heading for Washington, an action which was condemned by the Catholic Church, the Supreme Court of Justice, and many others."[52]

In Washington, the government argued the "greater dangers to workers of GSP cut-off." President Serrano claimed to seek "lasting peace . . . with a strong commitment to improving the standard of living amongst the working class." Since only one third of the country's three million workers "have employment in the formal sector," conditions would be worse if Guatemala lost growth in non-traditional exports, which are responsible for more than 80,000 jobs. It would "adversely impact" economies in both the U.S. and Guatemala. The government insisted that this time it *was* taking strong measures to assure worker rights. It had made "all efforts to provide the Ministry of Labor with tools . . . to guarantee the respect for labor." Taking advantage of USAID funds, it had increased the ministry's budget "for the first time in twenty years" to augment the number of inspectors and establish tripartite mechanisms to deal with disputes. Violence could "only be addressed through institution building, such as through the Judicial Branch" (which just received 100 million quetzals via another USAID program).[53]

USTR Grants Review

After seven years of rejections, USTR finally agreed to review Guatemala's GSP benefits. Suddenly the Guatemalan business community faced the potential loss of more than $200 million annual duty-free exports to the U.S. The ILRF/GLEP mobilization had caught the national elite off guard.[54] Up to this point they had responded with superficial changes—and even those were supported by a hefty infusion of U.S. government funds. Their preference was exposed when the Congress, at President Serrano's urging, repealed a labor-backed pension law.[55]

GSP enhanced business awareness, but the sector only took labor issues seriously when the loss of benefits appeared possible. As Labor Minister Solorzano acknowledged, the petition offered receptive officials an impetus to act:[56] To prevent petition acceptance, in early July 1992, the Labor Ministry held lengthy negotiations with Inexport. It convinced the company to rehire twenty-seven of the workers it had fired three years earlier. After languishing for months on the president's desk, the PVH labor-union application received approval. By September, the Labor Committee of the Guatemalan Congress had proposed a draft labor-code reform "in response to the U.S. investigation of GSP status."[57]

At USTR review hearings in Washington in October, ten major Guatemalan federations and confederations articulated a common position in support of GSP review. Besides the annulled pension law, it cited the forceful removal of families, the failure to pay minimum wages, massive firings, threats and abuse, and violations of ILO conventions ratified by the country.[58] In ILRF's view, progress had been "directly and proportionately in response . . . to a review of the country's GSP status." The only real gains, for two unions well-known in the U.S., "smacks more of a tactical retreat by the anti-labor union forces." While the government did not deny that abuses continued, it pleaded poverty—that the country could not afford to enforce labor laws, otherwise foreign investment would go elsewhere. The ILRF responded that when the government was "sufficiently stimulated, it can act decisively" and that "reforms are all possible within the . . . constraints of Guatemala's economic situation."[59]

Labor Code Reform, 1992–1993

The GSP stimulant finally brought decisive congressional action in November 1992, when it ratified a new labor code—the first major revision in forty-five years. The code's thirty-two articles simplified union registrations, increased fines, and strengthened court procedures. It required compliance data on Labor Ministry enforcement regarding minimum wages and gender equality. Other major provisions are listed in table 7.1. "This code reform was important," emphasized Rigoberto Dueñas, organizing director of the CGTG. "Given the composition of the Congress, the prevalent philosophy, and the situation of company influence, this was what we could get. Even at that, the code would not have passed without external pressure. For example, the minister of labor proposed six changes, and we offered twenty-eight. We were able to get in nearly twenty of our proposals only because of GSP."

For Dueñas, a key reform was article 108. "Before, workers would be fired verbally. When they would complain to the ministry, the employer would deny they had been fired. He would then turn around and fire them for not having shown up to work. Other code articles prevented workers from being fired arbitrarily, or for participating in unions."[60] Women leaders also praised the code's provisions. UNICEF said Guatemala was the only country in the world that had fulfilled all goals of its Declaration of Innocents promoting breast feeding.

However, other unionists were less positive about code reforms. Its reinstatement requirement remained weak. It retained strict government supervision of trade-union activities and other practices at variance with ILO convention 87.[61] As non-enforcement and attacks prevailed over the next several months, campesino union leaders found "no improvements in the recognition of the basic rights in the agricultural sector." A U.S. Women Trade Union Delegation verified enduring sexual discrimination and abuse.[62] The government had not funded the three courts it promised to create. As USTR deliberated, U.S./GLEP insisted that Guatemala's alleged "taking steps" through changes in the labor code, etc. were not in and of themselves evidence of actual improvement of worker rights.[63]

Rather than address these issues, the Guatemalan government grew defensive. It employed three U.S. based law firms to file briefs on its behalf with USTR, none of which addressed labor-code compliance. In fact, President

Table 7.1. Key provisions of the 1993 Guatemalan labor code

1. Twenty workers may form a union, with freedom guaranteed (as in constitutional article 10Q).
2. Worker dismissals must be in writing (article 108). Unjustly fired workers must be rehired in twenty-four hours (article 380).
3. A union may bargain with assent of 25 percent of workforce, and demands approved by two-thirds vote in a general assembly (articles 221 and 222). Employers must be notified in forty-eight hours via the Labor Ministry.
4. Maternity leaves and nursing facilities for working women are mandated.[a]
5. If contract violations occur, a union can file a "collective conflict" in labor court, which if granted, forbids the violations and sanctions reprisals.
6. A conciliation and arbitration commission constituted by a judge, and labor and employer delegate must be convened in twelve hours to address collective conflicts. Commissions will be set up throughout the country. If no agreement is reached, a strike is possible.
7. Strikes are permitted (constitutional article 104). Workers must have exhausted conciliation (article 241), but are then protected.[b] Articles 116 and 243 prevent strikes by transport, hospitals, agricultural workers during harvest and industries that the president deems essential to prevent grave damage to national economy.

[a]Article 137 also prohibits physical labor the last three months of pregnancy and the termination of pregnant or nursing women (who have the right to enter late and leave early to feed their children). It forbids discrimination in employee advertising, including between single or married applicants.
[b]The judge forms a Conciliation Tribunal. If no agreement in 3 days, workers can vote to strike. If a two-thirds vote (and the judge declares the strike legal) they can strike within twenty days. They can also petition that the strike be ruled "just"—the fault of the employer, in which case they must be paid.

Serrano risked contravening ILO conventions in February 1993 by prohibiting strikes in the public sector.

Citing the "impact of GSP exclusion," Labor Minister Solorzano attempted to mollify tensions by holding tripartite discussions. Four centrals and CACIF reached a six-point agreement on March 8 to establish several tripartite commissions to resolve problems, work within labor laws, and urge the Supreme Court to nominate new judges quickly. The government would hire forty-three new labor inspectors.[64] Yet, as abuses persisted, all major labor organizations quickly demanded an extension of GSP review until December 1993.[65]

Coup and Its Aftermath

One of the most dramatic examples of GSP power happened in late Spring. Guatemalan president Jorge Serrano Elias, frustrated with his inability to win legislative backing for several government restructuring proposals, suddenly declared a state of emergency, assumed quasi-dictatorial powers, and disbanded Congress. For nearly two weeks, the military verged on supporting him. However, the nation's potential loss of trade privileges proved to be an ultimate restraint. Largely because they feared such sanctions, private-sector leaders rejected Serrano's bid and accepted former human-rights procurator Ramiro de León Carpio as president. Serrano fled to Panama, and the nation returned to constitutional rule.[66] CACIF's Juan Sánchez explained to the U.S. Trade Subcommittee that Guatemalan exports to the U.S. were "worth more than $1 billion annually." With the inauguration of de León Carpio, the business sector had "promoted statutory changes . . . for a rapid integration into the global economy . . . [i.e.] legislation to improve employer-worker relations."[67]

Despite Ramiro de León's positive reputation, GSP petitioners mobilized substantial public support for a six-month extension of review. In July 1993, USTR decided to "provide the Government of Guatemala an opportunity to make concrete progress in affording worker rights." While it recognized the training of new labor inspectors and the competitive selection of judges as positive, USTR warned that "*enforcement* of labor laws will be of particular importance" such as addressing anti-unionism in the EPZs and payment of minimum wages to farmworkers.[68]

Labor Ministry and Tripartism

The de León Carpio government articulated labor rights as a basic element of its policy.[69] Although less politically experienced than Solorzano, Minister Gladys Morfin brought more competent administration to the Labor Ministry. She expressed concern over undocumented workers in Mexico,[70] supported equal employment for the handicapped, and assured public workers of the right to strike, withdrawing an earlier decree.[71] With USAID funds, the ministry trained new labor inspectors[72] and produced pamphlets on the rights of children.[73] Less successfully, it attempted health and safety commissions in each worksite[74] and a bipartite commission to deal with disputes with the public sector.[75] However, as time grew near for Guatemala to present its own case to USTR, the ministry again chose image over substance. Convening a "tripartite . . . follow-up and advancement to the tripartite accord signed on March 8," it invited the unions to comment on GSP.[76]

UNSITRAGUA spoke for most confederations. It lauded Guatemala as "part of the group of nations able to show that a strong economy makes a strong democracy." But "the violation of labor rights remains constant." Free association "often appears blocked . . . by the intolerance of many business owners" and delays "in administrative institutions and labor courts." UNSITRAGUA credited progress in labor-code reforms, yet a high number of union applications "have taken more than a year." The greatest barrier was *impunity* in the labor courts—"corruption, the capricious application of work laws, and . . . delayed juridical procedures." Cases were "abandoned by workers because of the impossibility of waiting for a definite resolution."

UNSITRAGUA understood that deep institutional "deformities and deeply rooted viciousness will not be resolved in the short term." However, it challenged "payment of salaries below legal minimum . . . punishing workers for exercising their right of free unionization, illegal, massive firings . . . threats of death against union leaders, owner disobedience of the laws." It criticized business advocacy of "solidarity associations," whose "fundamental object" was to "prevent" or "destroy" unions. While welcoming the Tripartite Commission, it nevertheless respectfully solicited extension of GSP review.[77]

Once again, rather than addressing the unions' penetrating objections, the government submitted to USTR a whitewashed "Tripartite" report on the state's record. In place of the unions' discussion of a six-year decline in the standard of living, it described how non-traditional exports had increased productive activities and income. Even though it had not issued a single fine for violations of child labor, sub-minimum wages, or health and safety violations, it cited "more effective enforcement of the reforms to the Labor Code." Both the government and CACIF touted the "formation of a tripartite task force to solve problems," as they dismissed the union proposal for reform.[78] Their failure was a damning indictment of their commitment to real tripartism and efforts to remove the deeply rooted system of impunity.

Another USTR Hearing Reveals Two Positions

Behind the government's palliated "Tripartite Report" was the Guatemalan elite's persistent unwillingness to address labor rights. As President de León Carpio attempted to remove corrupt and incompetent judges, the courts retaliated by withholding funds for handling labor cases. The head of CACIF labeled U.S./GLEP director Stephen Coats an enemy of Guatemala.[79]

At USTR hearings in Fall 1993, corporate witnesses denied intimidating unions.[80] Textile official Willi Kaltschmitt was "excited and encouraged" over how the private sector had "worked hand in hand" with government and labor to bring about "worker rights protection." To confront "the AFL-CIO's principal concern [of] the political turmoil and instability of our government," business had played a key role "in the installation of the new administration." Since "GSP has been instrumental in developing Guatemala's integration into the global economy" and importing products from the U.S., Kaltschmitt urged removal of USTR review.[81]

Nevertheless, USTR again extended review for six months. It finally realized that Kaltschmitt and others had missed the point. The petitioners' chief concern was repression—"serious, systematic violations" with "no measurable progress."[82] "While some individuals" had "expressed a sincere commitment, even an eagerness, to rectify matters . . . most employers feel free to disregard with impunity all laws," added Coats. "If CACIF wants to maintain its trade benefits, adherence to labor law . . . would be a more effective response." Otherwise, "suspension would be the logical demand."[83]

In September 1994, ten local unions again requested of USTR "that Guatemala be kept under review."[84] Between November 1994 and mid-1995, the state and petitioners disputed the factual evidence verifying the right of association. The de León Carpio administration claimed to legalize more unions and reduce the number of steps needed for approval. ILRF countered that less than two-thirds of the approvals were for bona fide unions, and most others had been waiting more than a year.[85] Some approvals like that at Pepsi-Cola, had been marred by management's "massive anti-union campaign combining . . . tactics employed by union-busting consultants in the U.S." Retaliation was the norm. Only six out of more than 300 maquila factories had managed to form a union, and at only one was there a semblance of bargaining.[86]

Proper functioning of the Labor Ministry, the courts, and labor-code enforcement became the test for the right of association. The government pointed to an increased Ministry of Labor budget, with staff and salary enhancements, equipment purchases, and "a training program funded by AID."[87] The ministry tripled the number of official routine inspections and increased maquila investigations.[88] To ILRF/GLEP, the inspectors did not have the equipment necessary to do the job. When the government pointed to a lengthy but peacefully resolved public-workers strike in 1994, U.S./GLEP responded that the settlement required U.S. Embassy mediation by since the government had still not created a permanent dispute-resolving mechanism.

The government cited a new labor court in addition to those already in service. The petitioners questioned the boast, since the government admitted three new courts were not yet operating because of lack of funds. In addition, the government had not acted to suspend a single export license, something it could do outside the juridical process.[89]

Petitioners also challenged other government assertions. While the ministry had hired several monitors of child labor, "how many cases had been investigated, and with what results?" Children's-rights advocates also reported death threats, concluding that the state had done very little to confront the exploitation of 10,000 urban and many more rural children.

Also, minimum wages were not honored, despite 1990 regulations. There were egregious levels of workplace hazards and many injuries from lack of training, insecticide poisonings, and gastrointestinal infections due to a lack of potable water.[90] While government proponents thought USTR should acknowledge progress, petitioners found few genuine results.

Ebbs and Flows of U.S. Trade/Rights Policy, 1994–1997

In March 1994, via the State Department, USTR informed Guatemala that progress on worker rights could best be measured by evidence of improved code enforcement of the right of association, including reduced violence; organizing and bargaining; the rehiring of those unjustly fired; and payment of minimum wages.[91] Also, USAID stepped up its projects to decentralize Labor Ministry offices and increase labor inspections. However, when Guatemala's trade status came up for renewal, the new U.S. ambassador Marilyn McAfee announced that the review would be lifted without further conditions. Privately, embassy spokespersons explained that President de León Carpio deserved their full support as forces on the right threatened to derail the renewed peace negotiations with the URNG. Their actions sent a confusing message to Guatemalan leaders.

Realizing the dilemma, U.S./GLEP and LAWG rallied sixty-five members of the U.S. Congress to demand that USTR sustain its review, if not deny entirely Guatemala's duty-free sugar trade. Local trade unionists applauded the move: "Although it had revised its labor code, Guatemala had not implemented a single enforcement order in two years." At the same time, the Guatemalan archbishop's Human Rights Office revealed a plan against trade unionists that involved the army (see also Harbury 1997).

Under pressure from the U.S. State Department on the one hand and the U.S. public on the other, USTR offered a compromise "to show that improved enforcement is occurring in practice." Acts of violence had not abated, resulting "in a climate in which the exercise of freedom of association and other worker rights is made more difficult."[92]

Three-Month Extension: The Coffee Agreement

The three months brought some results: In July 1994, ANACAFE, the association representing the largest Guatemalan coffee growers, signed an agreement with two conservative campesino unions raising the minimum wage from 11.20 to 15.70 quetzals a day, including benefits.[93] While this represented a more than 30 percent increase, several other federations were critical that it did not cover basic needs. Rigoberto Dueñas was part of the negotiating team: "We started out requesting 27 quetzals, as well as labor-rights clauses, funding for schools of labor formation, etc., but they were very resistant. Then we pointed to the maquilas, where production had been cut because of potential trade sanctions, and said, 'this could also affect you.' They listened, and we got seven days' vacation, along with the 15.70 increase." ANACAFE also committed itself to a social action program and the construction and maintenance of nineteen health clinics.[94]

While GSP pressure was a feature in the ANACAFE accord, as U.S./GLEP noted, only 20 percent of the plantations complied. Those complying raised production quotas in violation of the agreement and only awarded increases to the "head of a family." ANACAFE did nothing about most of its members, who still refused to pay the old minimum and persisted in preventing unions from organizing.[95] Meanwhile, an increasing number of campesinos like Juan José at La Exacta Ranch (see chapter 1) risked their lives occupying fincas to protest non-payment of the *old* minimum-wage standard.

UNSITRAGUA leader Sergio Guzman hoped the three-month extension would reveal "the campaign to pull apart the trade-union movement. La Exacta is a perfect example. Because one of our lawyers helped them, the president, CACIF, etc., accused UNSITRAGUA of being terrorists. What persists here is a deepening anti-trade union attitude of confrontation, that tries to undermine labor laws and contravene ILO principles. They simply cannot permit workers to negotiate, to have rights and a decent job which doesn't require working seven days a week. The courts have ordered the La Exacta workers to be reinstated, and their salaries paid, with no consequence."

Another Extension?

In late August 1994, during the same period as the La Exacta killings, a special visiting USTR delegation found frustrated and fearful labor leaders facing a private sector emboldened by the congressional victory of former president Gen. Ríos Montt, and his Frente Republicano Guatemalteco. With U.S./GLEP support, Guatemalan unionists sent Exacta leader Juan José to Washington to convince USTR to postpone again any lifting of its review. As LAWG rallied U.S. congressional support, nine labor centrals reaffirmed their request for an additional six-month GSP review. They recounted the backlog of union applications, problems with labor inspections, lack of prosecution of violence against other trade unionists like those at La Exacta, continued paralysis in the courts, the absence of fines for violations of child-labor and minimum-wage standards, impunity for business that failed to participate in tribunals, lack of progress in health and safety, and illegal extensions of working hours.[96] CUSG's Juan Francisco Alfaro urged that "USTR distinguish between what the government says, what the companies say, and what is the actual fulfillment of the law." He demanded attention to the legal process, inspections, and private-sector compliance.[97] The major centrals followed up with a five-point plan of verification.[98]

A Victory with Salaries

USTR warnings brought one key change. In November 1994, after prolonged closed-door negotiations, the National Salary Commission recommended a raise in all wages to equal or surpass those in the ANACAFE agreement. While not sufficient to cover living costs, "GSP helped us achieve a double success," exclaimed Reynoldo González, the commission's labor representative. "For the first time, the business sector sent people with more experience and influence on salary matters. And, most importantly, they agreed to reexamine the standards every year rather than periodically as in the past."[99] In 1995, the government agreed on a 10 percent increase, which matched inflation.[100]

Yovany Gómez and a USTR Ultimatum

In Guatemalan fashion, however, one step forward again required a step back. In February 1995 an ILO mission arrived to investigate complaints. A month later, as the government deliberated their response,[101] workers at the RCA Industries' maquila finally thought they had obtained management recognition for their union and overdue pay. Then the company abruptly closed its doors. Workers occupied the plant in protest, demanding back salaries at the very least. Shortly thereafter, the murdered body of Yovany Gómez, the finance secretary of RCA's incipient union, was tossed into a nearby ravine. While the police and U.S. embassy treated the incident as a personal vendetta, the workers understood the first death at a maquila plant as a warning against organizing.

U.S./GLEP demanded an immediate investigation of Gómez' killing and other recent violence against unionists. Without progress, GSP benefits should be withdrawn in steps: first a suspension of sugar, then beef, then a total cancellation.[102] According to one U.S./GLEP spokesperson, "This is a real test of Guatemala's political will to investigate."

But there was no investigation, and the level of violence against activists did not abate. In the maquila sector, wages had substantially improved over 1993 levels, but there were no effective unions or in-plant organizing campaigns. U.S./GLEP then called for reimposition of sugar tariffs: While small in economic impact, it would send a political message.[103]

In November 1995, USTR made the unprecedented move of inviting UNITE, ILRF, and U.S./GLEP to participate as observers in its delegation to Central America (see chapter 4). The Guatemalan meetings were tense. UNITE's labor delegate, Alan Howard, charged the U.S. Embassy to "do the same for La Exacta, and Yovany Gómez as you demanded of the Devine investigations." U.S. ambassador McAfee agreed that responses to date had been unacceptable. Delegation chief Jon Rosenbaum demanded that Guatemalan institutions take strong measures to eliminate impunity. His blunt message, "You have six months," caught the government, the business sector, and the U.S. ambassador off guard. Changes had not been "sufficient to show real progress. The review can't go on forever."[104] CACIF, also taken aback, later admitted it had "handled things badly."[105]

Arzú Takes Over

Changes were in the atmosphere. In 1996, the newly elected and politically astute government of the Partido de Avanzado Nacional (PAN), headed by Alvaro Arzú, reduced human-rights abuses (see Dosal 1995). With a signed peace agreement on the horizon, the Arzú administration vastly lowered Guatemala's chances of a GSP suspension, giving its business-community backers little to fear.[106] So instead of addressing union rights and impunity, Labor Minister Arnoldo Ortiz Moscoso espoused a stronger neo-liberal regimen: labor flexibility and further privatization of state enterprises (see chapter 2 and Forster 1996).

The ILO, with European encouragement, inaugurated several projects "for Strengthening and Modernizing Labor Union Organizations of the Central American Isthmus." With local ILO office support, Guatemalan unions drafted a list of recommendations for court reform. They received no response.[107] Although Arzú granted the Tripartite Commission (TPC) full legal status, it devoted most of its deliberations to "what labor will say on Commission trips to Geneva or Washington." The local ILO office even had to file suit to prevent the labor minister from personally appointing the TPC labor delegates.[108]

Labor Minister Moscoso soon involved himself directly in the approval of collective pacts. He ordered municipal organizations not to negotiate improvements better than what was guaranteed in the law, effectively eliminating the freedom and power of the negotiation process.[109] Then, besides announcing plans to privatize public works, telecommunications, and electricity, the government proposed to end the public-sector workers' right to strike, a move that would diminish the overall strength of unions in the country.

The Attack on Reynoldo González

In late February, unknown assailants threatened Reynoldo González, general secretary of the bank workers union. González had received threats since Fall 1993, after he appeared for the GSP hearings in Washington. These continued as he organized union cooperation with GSP investigations. González interpreted his appointment to the Salary Commission as a "government

strategy to dissuade" him from GSP work. As the state threatened to undermine unions more, from July 1995 to February 1996 Reynoldo sought to form
an all-central union alliance. All this "made it easier for them to take me out of
the picture."

In late 1995, a threatening visitor asked Reynoldo "where to send flowers
for your funeral." Then, on February 27, men dressed as security personnel
attempted to kidnap Reynoldo's secretary just outside bank federation offices. For the next two weeks, Reynoldo González was followed. "Armed men
in a pick-up truck reportedly visited his neighborhood asking for his where-
abouts." Finally, on March 14, 1996, González went into exile accompanied
by Alan Howard of UNITE and other religious and human-rights supporters
(U.S./GLEP, May 1996). U.S./GLEP made the Guatemalan government's investigation and prosecution of Reynoldo's case "a critical factor" in evaluating progress on GSP compliance.[110]

USTR Benchmarks

In April, after consultation with petitioners, USTR provided the Guatemalan
government with a list of benchmarks it would consider in determining
progress on worker rights.[111] They included progress on ending impunity,
guarantees that changes to the labor code met internationally accepted standards, reduction in the backlog of labor cases pending before the courts, and
increased fines for violators. Despite its advances in peace negotiations, the
Arzú administration was put on notice that labor issues also deserved high
profile.

In May, after much delay, the TPC established a subordinate body to deal
with disputes in the maquila sector prior to involvement by the courts.[112] The
Arzú government put into effect a long-standing law that provided for the
denial of export licenses to worker-rights violators in the maquila sector.[113]
The Labor Ministry also created its "Supervision and Services Unit for Companies Dedicated to Maquiladora Activities" to conduct periodic visits, offer
assistance, improve communications, and establish a data bank. The government's human-rights commission quickly reported on thirteen abuse cases
that petitioners had demanded be investigated.[114]

González permanently returned to Guatemala in September 1996 after
evaluating conditions.[115] However, other events challenged governmental
progress. Despite great opposition and questionable legality, the government
ratified the law preventing public-sector workers from striking.[116] For UN-
SITRAGUA's Sergio Guzman, "the anti-strike law is nothing more than an
effort to achieve 'flexibility,' not just in opposition to the right to strike, but
also in opposition to the right to unionize. Just as unions are seen as an ob-

stacle, on a world level, businessmen are questioning them in Guatemala. The case of Reynoldo is an example of what can happen, but even in ordinary life of workers, we face an ideological war."[117]

After months of quiet help from the International Textile Federation, workers at PVH obtained the required number of members to demand negotiations. However, Camisas Modernas' managers argued that the numbers were insufficient. Even though the Labor Inspectorate ultimately verified the list, Minister Moscoso refused to rule on the requirement and referred the matter to the courts where it would be lost forever.[118]

A U.S./GLEP delegation called for direct pressure on PVH. It also encountered strong trade union criticism of the TPC for not intervening. TPC's credibility had already been severely damaged when it refused to discuss the anti-strike bill. Guatemalan unions thought TPC was simply created for "international export." Petitioners asked USTR to require real progress on its own benchmarks before lifting review.[119] In October 1996, PVH became the main stumbling block to lifting GSP review, as the U.S. Labor Department soon informed Guatemalan ambassador Peter Lamport.

The December Peace Accords

In December 1996, the Arzú government finally signed the expected peace accords with the Guatemalan URNG, ending at last the longest civil war in the hemisphere. Hundreds of thousands thronged the streets in joyous celebration, many labor activists among them. The accords brought to a legal end a series of atrocious human-rights violations, including conscripted military labor and overt racism against indigenous people. They created a new role for police and military. However, they did not promise prosecution of past abuses. Except for a vague commitment to labor negotiations, they did little to address socioeconomic issues (see LaRue 1996).

Off the GSP List

Americas Watch publicized its appraisal of the PVH status in March 1997. The organization strongly criticized the Guatemalan Labor Ministry's abdication of responsibility.[120] As a result, PVH finally agreed to negotiate with the women leading its local union, and the government promised cooperation.

In May 1997, USTR removed Guatemala from five-year probationary status under GSP review. The trade body lauded Guatemala's progress in reducing intimidation against workers, increasing labor inspectors, setting up the Tripartite Commission, and establishing a method to withdraw the export licenses of offending producers. In USTR official Jon Rosenbaum's view, "The rule of law has improved. There remained cases of impunity. Not all benchmarks were followed, but they were our benchmarks, not theirs. In our judgment, we had to decide where to put our chips. We had done what we could by then, and the Guatemalans rightfully knew they would not be undercut after the accords."[121]

Nevertheless, from the petitioner's perspective, political considerations took precedence over labor rights. Intended as a gesture of respect for Guatemala's signing of the peace accords, the lifting coincided with President Clinton's participation in a regional conference on "free trade" attended by Central American presidents. So USTR was forced to disregard Guatemala's non-compliance with most of the benchmarks the trade agency had set for the government in April 1996. As U.S./GLEP reported, "The TPC has not been able to settle a single labor dispute. . . . The only export license suspended has been at a factory (Inexport) that had already ceased operations, the newly promised labor courts have not been opened while the backlog of pending cases is larger now than when the probation began, and more labor inspectors can't improve respect for basic rights if the inspectors aren't given the funds to conduct inspections. . . . The most significant step on labor law taken by the current government has been to ram through a bill last year sharply restricting the right of public workers to strike" (U.S./GLEP 1997). The PVH case had required extraordinary measures to resolve. Many other workers still faced abuses.[122] While the Arzú government had reduced violence, "no one is behind bars for acts of violence against trade unionists, and virtually no investigative work is being conducted."[123] In fact, the government had proposed fresh labor code "reforms" that would substantially undercut article 380, which required reinstatement of workers fired without just cause, and other worker protections.

However, for the very first time, USTR threatened to initiate its own review should there be any steps backward.[124] In June 1997, it sent a follow-up delegation to underscore this intent. USTR threatened to reopen review when police attacked the locked-out banana workers in April 1998 (see chapter 1). U.S./GLEP recognized that despite being undercut by the U.S. State Department, the trade agency had handled the case "with integrity" (U.S./GLEP 1997). In June 1998, IRLF and U.S./GLEP petitioned USTR to reopen review of Guatemala's labor practices. The AFL-CIO filed a similar request.

Summary

The lengthy GSP process in Guatemala achieved more substantial improvements in labor conditions than it did in El Salvador. Guatemalan unions became fully engaged in each of the four phases of petition activity outlined above, much more so than they did in El Salvador. Despite conflicting messages sent by the U.S. government, cooperation between Guatemalan and

U.S. unions remained focused. Such collaboration first convinced the U.S. Embassy of the importance of labor rights, and in turn it pressured USTR to conduct a more objective appraisal. One outcome was labor-code reform, which the business sector thought would be sufficient. While code design had less labor involvement than in El Salvador, the GSP process had more, and this promised a more equitable transformation.

By mid-decade, however, the local U.S. Embassy and USTR had reversed positions on the importance of labor-rights compliance. U.S. State Department communications clearly showed that should Guatemala sign the peace accords, GSP review would cease. Thus, without the five years of unflinching pressure (from 1992 to 1997), the review would have ended much sooner. The embassy and the Guatemalan business community continued to believe that political changes would be sufficient. U.S./GLEP, ILRF, and LAWG beat back their enduring efforts to lift trade-agency scrutiny. USTR credited U.S./GLEP for employing the GSP worker-rights conditionality more effectively than anyone else. The lengthy review won major increases in minimum wages, recognition of maquiladora unions, and two new labor courts.

To be fully effective, however, GSP also had to address the structural barriers to labor embedded in an elite-dominated organizational and legal system. Inroads in these areas for Guatemala are appraised in the following chapter.

CHAPTER 8

Structural Residues of the Guatemalan Case: An Analysis

GSP brought improvements in labor rights to Guatemala. Its pressure was a deciding feature in the country's passage of a stronger labor code. In turn, that reform gave rise to new unions, improved women's rights, and increased fines on recalcitrant employers. In addition GSP measures promised regularized hikes in minimum wages and were at least partly responsible for the business community's decision to reject reversion to dictatorial rule in mid-1993. Trade-sanction pressure also stimulated U.S.-funded programs designed to improve the Guatemalan Labor Ministry. Union recognitions came at the Pepsi franchise in Guatemala City, the Coca-Cola plant in Puerto Barrios, and ten maquila plants including Phillips-Van Heusen. Under threat of losing trade privileges, the ministry stepped up enforcement action at North American–owned Inexport. Business concern over GSP helped propel its endorsement of the 1996 peace accords.

Nevertheless, as chapter 7 indicated, the enduring nature of labor improvements remained an issue. From the viewpoint of Guatemalan workers and GSP petitioners, very little had changed beyond the reduction in overt physical violence.[1] Labor groups experienced persistent delays in union registrations, inadequate labor inspections, and very limited bargaining. Virtually no employers had been cited for violations. The courts hardly operated. Working conditions remained painfully difficult, with below-minimum wages and disregard of health and safety regulations as the norm.

Confronted with these charges, businesspersons and government leaders invariably touted the positive changes and emphasized the unrealistic demands of GSP petitioners. To analyze that reality, to probe the structural and cultural barriers and incentives to change, we will examine four key institutions in more depth: the Ministry of Labor, which governs the right to organize and bargain; the labor courts; wages and working conditions; and the Tripartite Commission created in compliance with ILO recommendations.

Table 8.1. Budget for the Ministry of Labor, Guatemala, 1993–97 (millions of quetzals)

	1993	1994	1995	1996	1997
Budget	16	29	32	36	40

Source: Ministerio de Trabajo y Previsión Social, *Boletin de Estadísticas de Trabajo.*

Some question GSP-induced modifications as simply testing the extent to which the regulations of one nation can be absorbed by another, smaller nation with a different culture. However, we will concentrate here on changes originally advocated by the local labor unions themselves.

Labor Ministry

The Guatemalan Labor Ministry encompasses the director general (and labor minister), whose function is to normalize labor relations and assure compliance with salaries and contracts; the inspector general, who responds to worker complaints and visits workplaces to determine compliance; and the director of social benefits, who assures social security payments, and so on (Rodríguez 1994). Each division absorbs about a third of the ministry's total budget. The government augmented ministry funding from 16 to 29 million quetzals between 1993 and 1994 as GSP petitions became more probative (table 8.1). It now represents 3 percent of the government's budget—quite a small amount, but much heftier than in El Salvador.

Also, the ministry improved efficiency, "reducing the work force from 764 in 1994 to 500 in 1995. Many left because of the low salaries," explained Rodin González, head of the Statistical Unit. "We consolidated our empty positions and proportionately improved pay by 25 percent. We moved our best people to the central office, but also augmented the numbers at the regional levels."[2]

GSP pressure contributed to the creation of USAID's reform program and other changes. We will examine the consequent improvement in the ministry's processing of union applications and contracts, its handling of inspections, alleviation of child labor, and its all-around performance as a government institution.

USAID Projects

In the mid-1990s, USAID contributed about $3.3 million to the Labor Ministry to aid its decentralization, staff training, and dissemination of labor rights (see table 8.2). While the programs helped professionalize ministry personnel, they did not sufficiently address basic barriers to enforcement such as the

Table 8.2. USAID funds for labor improvements, Guatemala, 1993–97

1. $500,000 local-currency funds to decentralize labor inspector functions (expended in 1993–4)
2. $328,215 for mediator training and tripartite seminars
3. $500,000 (of $795,000) for six projects at the Ministry of Labor for:
   a. staff-management technical training
   b. training in safety and health
   c. translation and dissemination (including by radio) of the labor code in Mayan languages[a]
   d. manual for labor inspectors
   e. expedition of certain juridical procedures
   f. new negotiating techniques (win-win bargaining)[b]
4. $1 million local currency funds (allocated in 1996–7) "for modernization, decentralization, deconcentration and regionalization, as well as assistance on child workers, women workers, and labor inspectors."[b]
5. $1.06 million in special funding for health and safety monitoring and labor rights competencies (allocated in 1996–97)

Source: Estimated from U.S. Embassy reports. Estimations are complicated since the Ministry of Labor did not use all allocated funds in earlier years and they would be rolled over into later year allocations. For other USAID allocations see Escoto and Marroquín (1992).

[a]See Peace Accord on Indigenous Rights. USAID has actively supported public-information campaigns on labor rights in four Mayan languages, "a sensitive issue at some fincas." Randall Peterson, USAID, interview with author, June 1996.

[b]"In win-win bargaining, a firm needs to invest in its own resources, and to pay competitive wages based on the gains that competition achieves." Randall Peterson, USAID, interview with author, June 1996.

paucity of phones or vehicles for inspectors or weak legal clout that failed to gain employer respect.

Francisco Rivera, who first headed the projects and then became vice minister of labor under de León Carpio, insisted that "that the ideas and design of these programs has been our own, and there were no requirements put on us."[3] Despite USAID's attempt to respect local priorities, however, it obtained little labor advice in program design.[4] When the first project reached the implementation stage, Rivera formed "a professional staff familiar with the context of globalization, labor markets, and benefits in consultation with the Bank for Interamerican Development and the ILO," which was "much better in comparison to the past."[5]

In March 1993, the ministry put into effect its salary increases, designed to reduce corruption. It purchased seventeen rural vehicles and twelve motorcycles for monitoring. By November, it had opened four regional offices to simplify inspections. USAID believed that the new labor minister, Gladys Morfin, "would have made some of these changes without our influence. For example she succeeded in getting labor inspectors out to the departments whereas the former minister never did although he claimed the idea. She also has brought old inspectors back to the capital where they can be watched more closely to control for corruption." This admittedly created conflicts between the minister and the inspectors in 1994–95.[6]

The ministry's budget included U.S. $400,000 in local-currency funds in 1996 and $600,000 in 1997, with additional special-funding projects from USAID and OAS, UNICEF, the ILO, the Spanish government and others. For example, USAID designated $460,000 for such projects in 1996 and $600,000 in 1997, to continue health and safety monitoring and to improve competencies in human rights and labor rights. "The projects emerged as related to GSP," assured USAID's Peterson.[7] To determine the permanency of their impact, we will consider the ministry's processing of union applications and contracts and the functioning of labor inspections.

Union Recognitions and Agreements

A primary task of the Labor Ministry's General Directorate is the processing of union applications. Table 8.3 suggests the numbers of unions the directorate has recognized, starting with a jump between 1985 and 1986 after the filing of the first Guatemalan GSP petition. Until 1995, annual recognitions ranged between forty-one and sixty-seven, except for 1991, when they dropped to twenty-seven, probably because of the "go slow" approach of Serrano Elias's first year in office. Registrations increased under the regime of de León Carpio from 1993 to 1995.

Nevertheless, as noted in chapter 7, Guatemalan trade unionists and GSP petitioners disputed the numbers of bona fide union recognitions. Of the sixty-one unions allegedly approved by de León Carpio for example, two-

Table 8.3. New unions registered, Guatemala, 1985–95

Year	No.
1985	8
1986	22
1987	41
1988	65
1989	43
1990	60
1991	27
1992	48
1993	54
1994	67
1995	83

Source: Ministerio de Trabajo, Oficina de Estadisticas del Trabajo.

Table 8.4. Unions, federations, and confederations, by type, Guatemala, 1990–95

	1990	1992	1993	1994	1995	New unions (1990–95)
Total	859	892	945	995	1,037	178
Industrial	144	145	148	154	180	36
Agricultural	462	477	504	528	557	95
Company	488	521	547	564	586	8
Independent	300	317	344	366	377	77
Public	—	—	—	162	178	n/a

Source: Ministerio de Trabajo, *Boletin de Estadísticas*. Entries may be categorized under several types but are only counted once for determining the total. Deregistered unions may account for some of the differences with table 8.3.

thirds were peasant cooperatives that presented no major threat to business; at least ten more had been rendered ineffective by intimidations, failure to negotiate, and factory closings. Petitioners cited seventy-seven unions that had been waiting more than a year for recognition.[8] CUSG's Juan Francisco Alfaro denied "the government's claim that *tramites* [red tape] has been reduced."[9]

Ministry of Labor data tends to verify the petitioner profile of union recognitions. Of new unions, federations, and confederations recognized between 1990 and 1995, 53.4 percent (95 of 178) were agricultural unions, often similar to co-ops. While more than half (98) were company-related, only 20 percent (36) were industrial unions (see table 8.4).[10]

The government has been much slower to recognize industrial unions than unions of other varieties, lending credibility to the barriers to such unions claimed by the petitioners.[11] Ministry administrators also lack knowledge of application procedures (CTCA 1996). However, in 1996 the ministry issued agreement 143, designed to expedite *tramites* so it could recognize a union in twenty days. "It is a good indication of the result of GSP pressure," reported ILO representative Thelma del Cid.[12]

The ministry has also facilitated a much smaller number of functioning bargaining agreements. Under the 1992 code, a union gaining 25 percent of all employees has the legal right to negotiate (if there are two unions, it is the first reaching 25 percent). As table 8.5 shows, collective agreements in effect have averaged just under thirty between 1985 and 1994. The number rose from fourteen to twenty from 1985 to 1987, increased to forty-one in 1989, dropped back to the twenties under Serrano, and rose to thirty-four in 1994. Of the thirty-four contracts in effect, eight were in the industrial sector, eight in agriculture, nine in service, and seven in government. One contract was approved in apparel—Arrow Shirt's Textilos Modernos, which produces for the domestic market.[13] However, virtually no employers came to the table to negotiate with any of the new unions recognized in 1994 or 1995. PVH workers negoti-

Table 8.5. Bargaining agreements in effect, Guatemala, 1989–94

Year	No.
1985	14
1986	17
1987	20
1988	24
1989	41
1990	32
1991	24
1992	26
1993	21
1994	34

Source: Ministerio de Trabajo, *Boletin de Estadísticas.*

ated a contract in 1996, one of two current accords in the maquila sector.

Guatemalan unionists say that once a *pacto collectivo* is negotiated, the labor authorities prolong review well beyond the twenty-four-day limit, in some cases up to five months (CTCA 1996). Under the Arzú government in 1996, contracts also risked ministry veto of wage increases, contrary to law (see chapter 7). This caused Juan Francisco Alfaro to "question the government's commitment to the negotiation process." Its intervention "undermines the bargaining power of workers [who now must] regularly negotiate with the minister at the same time we negotiate with employers."[14]

Very much linked to union registrations and negotiations is the ministry's willingness to protect the workers involved from being fired. While it could invoke article 308 and insist on twenty-four-hour reinstatement, the ministry usually refers termination cases to the labor courts (see below). Despite difficulties with registrations and negotiations, union-affiliated workers did increase by 12.7 percent between 1990 and 1995. The percent of affiliated women rose by 15.6 percent (table 8.6), although they still constituted only 9.4 percent of union membership.

Table 8.6. Union members and women union members, Guatemala, 1990–95

	Total	Women	% total
1990	78,602	7,183	9.1
1992	82,100	7,011	8.5
1993	84,617	7,364	8.7
1994	86,752	7,851	9.0
1995	88,567	8,300	9.4
% increase	12.7	15.6	

Source: Ministerio de Trabajo, *Boletin de Estadísticas.*

Enhancing Inspections

A second area of potential GSP impact has been Guatemala's labor-inspection system, which comprises six separate functions:[15]

1. consultations: phone calls or personal visits to address questions from both employers and workers;
2. on-site visits to check health and safety conditions, work documents, and proper salary payments;
3. conciliations: to interpose firings and renunciations in a non-threatening atmosphere;
4. mediations: to respond to denouncements, including unresolved pact violations, plant closings, and strikes or potential strikes;
5. special investigations, as with the firings of minor workers or pregnant women, in which case the inspector can bring the matter directly before the court;
6. sanctions: follow-up interventions when company owners do not take advantage of conciliations. Inspector "solicitations" inform them they will be fined 250 quetzals. "In 60 to 70 percent of the cases the owners do come. Otherwise, we go to the courts to obtain the actual penalty, as we did forty-five times or so in 1996."[16] Inspectors are otherwise not involved in court proceedings.

While any inspector can carry out the first four functions, most have their specializations. Sanctions require special training for writing up an "act" specifying the "denuncia" and submitting it to the tribunal as a "juicio de falta" (called a *juicio punitivo*). The ministry submits between 200 and 300 such juicios a year, requesting a total of 5,000,000 quetzals.[17]

In compliance with the USAID projects, the government promised to provide the general inspector of labor with needed materials and equipment. In 1993, the ministry hired twenty-three new administrative workers and forty-four new inspectors (bringing the total to 108), "devoted to improve the monitoring and enforcement of labor regulations in the countryside through a regionalization program."[18] The ministry "demanded more formal requirements for hiring, such as five years of law school." Commensurately, it "improved their salaries from 750 quetzals to 1,500 quetzals a month." "Inspectors had been used to a system of bribery that extended back to the beginning of the century," emphasized Vice Minister Rivera. "We expected that this reorganization would help control corruption."[19] But Assistant Labor Inspector Carlos Moran compared this to "2,500 quetzals for inspectors in the public ministry. Out of this, our inspectors must pay their own bus transportation to and from factories, and they often pay the fares for workers who come here to resolve problems. The minister of finance allocates few funds for buying gasoline for our vehicles, none during the month of June 1996, for example; and we had to pay out of our own pockets." Moran explained that the ministry had no system for expense vouchers since keeping track of several quetzals per person would not be worth the bureaucratic complication; nevertheless, "while corruption has been substantially reduced, the expense problem has prevented its eradication. This is not to justify it, but corruption has a root in necessity."[20]

USAID training programs were not designed to remedy corruption. What they did help inspectors master included labor-code changes and enforcement, rules of compliance demanded by international trade agreements like GSP, and safety and hygiene regulations. "The inspectors were very interested in comparisons between U.S. and Guatemalan standards," noted Delaney. Groups "used cases to discuss various interpretations of the labor code."[21] USAID also paid for a manual for inspectors and judges (see Puga 1995). Roberto Cruz Minerva, the general labor inspector between 1993 and 1996, believed USAID funding provoked by GSP pressure had helped "improve inspections a great deal . . . with a fresh philosophy. We have many more consultations with companies and unions."[22]

Yet skepticism remained about the benefits of USAID's "considerable funding. They think this is a good project," stated Assistant Inspector General of Labor Carlos Moran, "but in practice, it is like buying equipment for a hospital without asking the people what they need; they justify their expenses, but the equipment often sits there unused, and goes into disrepair.

"They waste a lot of money holding seminars, but we have not really been able to talk over the issues. We know the theory; what we need is the practice. Legal training is not the same as competence in administration." For example, their manual, while "well constructed, did not offer specific cases for application; and was not published in sufficient quantity for each inspector to have one. They have offered good points on safety and health issues. But the presenters never really visit our work sites outside the capital to see what we need. A consultant speaks to officials occasionally, but there is no monitoring system to check results."

Although USAID had distributed $500,000 to purchase typewriters, office supplies, and vehicles, Inspector General Moran had "never seen the equipment here—it gets lost en route to the inspector's office. What we really need are vehicles, a telefax in each office, and inspectors who can function in each department. Right now we have nine vehicles overall for about ninety inspectors: five in the capital and four in the departments. Only four offices have telephones, and only three (Quetzaltenango, Coban, and here) have a computer. In the Peten, the inspector can't go anywhere without a vehicle."[23]

Table 8.7. Cases/actions handled by the Ministry of Labor, Guatemala, 1989–95

	1989	1990	1991	1992	1993	1994	1995
Cases	13,678	13,484	14,127	14,296	14,826	15,877	13,779
Conciliations	4,739	2,402	2,884	2,992	6,090	5,759	7,215
Denunciations	8,939	11,082	11,243	11,304	8,736	10,118	6,564
Off. inspections	—	—	—	—	802	967	656
Juicios punitivos	—	298	—	—	213	394	410

Source: Ministerio de Trabajo, Boletín de Estadísticas.
Note: According to Vice Ministers of Labor Rivera and Carmen Lopez de Cáceres, the figures in 1993 and 1994 were "more carefully compiled" since the previous administration inflated the numbers. But as USAID's Peterson cautioned, "accuracy may not be the point," since "if you have increased awareness, labor cases go up; but also employers may be meeting the law more, thus reducing cases. About 20 different factors could influence the outcome." AIFLD's Jessup challenges the figures as measuring intermediate steps, not outcomes. Author interviews.

The Record of Inspections

One measure of Moran's critique of USAID-supported restructuring and training is labor-inspector performance. Cases and conciliations presented in table 8.7 encompass complaint investigations,[24] routine investigations, and punitive actions.[25] Despite variations in the way the ministry has recorded information, the inspectors appear to have handled an increasing number of cases between 1989 and 1994 (with some drop-off in 1995). (They also claim to have tripled the number of official routine inspections and to increase maquila investigations.)[26] They achieved conciliations nearly 20 percent of the time. Between 1989 and 1994 they doubled the amounts awarded to fired workers to a total of 1.8 million quetzals, but awards averaged less than 45 percent of the claims (see table 8.8).[27] The government also said it had tripled

Table 8.8. Funds at stake in labor conflicts, Guatemala, 1989–94 (thousands of quetzals)

	Total	Awarded to those fired	% awarded
1989	1,712.0	926.0	54.0
1990	1,428.6	742.3	52.0
1991	3,037.4	1,514.8	49.9
1992	2,702.2	1,316.3	48.7
1993	3,544.0	1,661.4	46.9
1994	6,418.1	1,833.0	28.6

Source: Ministerio de Trabajo, Boletín de Estadísticas. "The high total in 1994 was due to a 2 to 3 million quetzal settlement at a particular finca." Rodin, director of statistics, Ministry of Labor, interview with author, June 1996.

the monetary demands presented for noncompliance with labor laws. However, claims and awards do not necessarily translate into amounts paid. The general inspector only issued punitive judgments 2 percent of the time.

Benefits to the inspection process were also less evident to ILRF/GLEP, which verified that the inspectors did not have the equipment or supplies necessary to do their jobs (see above and chapter 7). By May 1994, more than a year into the USAID-funded program, their only office in the capital was a large room with several desks and no phones or file cabinets. Two of the four regional offices were not functioning, ostensibly because of lack of funds. Inspectors found it difficult to call ahead to schedule appointments. Sixteen of twenty donated vehicles had not appeared.

This made it difficult for inspectors to call union leaders when they visited a factory so that the union could present the reasons they believed the company was not complying with the law. "Right now, the inspectors are our worst enemy," complained Juan Francisco Alfaro. "When we present complaints, they meet with the employer, then lift the act establishing the *emplazamiento*. If we go to court, the judge cites the inspector's lifting of the act, and we lose."[28] Despite their higher salaries and increased numbers, Sergio Guzman of UNSITRAGUA felt that inspector corruption persisted after 1993. He suggested that workers always be present during inspector meetings with management to reduce the chance for bribery.[29]

Ministry restructuring did not work well in the interior. "Budget shortfalls prevented government funding for gas or equipment," acknowledged US AID, which could not directly pay for these items.[30] The government's failed support resulted in wasted effort: In one routine investigation of twelve maquilas, inspectors went to four incorrect addresses and failed to answer questions about several others.[31] The non-investigation or prosecution of alleged violence against trade unionists at La Exacta, Phillips-Van Heusen, Chinook, Coca-Cola, and Marisa, cited by U.S./GLEP (see chapter 7), was at least partly due to lack of funds.

It was only because of considerable international pressure in 1998 that labor inspectors traveled to the conflicted banana-growing areas in Spring 1998. While the ministry achieved some success at professionalization, despite their touted training, inspectors faced a complex reality. No matter how "professional" they behaved, they realized how the power structure operated: They would have meager backup and risked personal danger if they individually went out on a limb to criticize a member of an important Guatemalan family.

Child Labor

In Guatemala, two million children work. While many labor in family enterprises in the countryside, many more are exploited outside the family structure. In urban areas, the abuse is rampant. The Labor Ministry defined its "main duty to give advice on labor rights to the parents . . . that working hours will not interfere with school hours." It also gave "orientation . . . to the employers." After GSP raised the issue directly, the ministry became more proactive. In 1992, the government created the National Commission for the Underage Worker, with representatives from the private and unionized sectors and from NGOs. Two social workers conducted inspections and the general inspector warned employers. With the support of UNICEF, the ministry published materials on child rights. It established a program to register underage workers with an ID that provided access to free health and recreation services.[32]

With USAID funding, the Labor Ministry also undertook "a program to help children prepare for work and understand the laws regarding education and work of minors. We are trying to get this message to the pueblos that children should study, thereby increasing their capacity to work in the future."[33]

Yet the message reached few maquilas, which consistently hired girls in their early teens to work twelve- to fourteen-hour days (see chapter 1). Although the ministry tried "to make sure young women receive the levels of education the law requires, and that both businessmen and themselves are aware of the advantages of trained employees," many were afraid to register their problems. Unions rated the effort vastly insufficient for the number of exploited children (see chapter 7).[34] When a *Wall Street Journal* reporter asked contractors for J.C. Penney Co. about monitoring rules for underage workers, they admitted that Penney buyers "don't really check." All Penney is "interested in is production time and quality, a high-quality garment, fast delivery, and cheap sewing charges," replied one manager. Worker rights were not a concern (Ortega 1995). Contractors agreed that no companies really monitored the workweek hours of kids; it was too difficult to keep separate records.[35]

Actually, the ministry registered only 2,887 underage workers in 1992, 2,637 in 1993, and 2,931 in 1994—less than .0015 percent of working children (see also LaRue 1996 on the OAS case against child labor in Guatemala). Although a 1996 U.S. Labor Department study found that most overseas apparel operations were making progress in reducing the number of working children, in Guatemala it discovered "efforts to evade the prohibitions, and that children continued to work for small subcontractors" (quoted in Meyers 1996). Attention to the difficulties faced by children motivated the Congress to pass the Code on Children and Youth in 1996, but debates in Spring 1998 postponed passage of implementing legislation.

Overall Ministry Assessment

The ministry began a more active role in 1988 under the Christian Democrats, when both Catalina Soberanis and Rolando Maldonado moved the government toward conformity with ILO policy (see chapter 7). In the Serrano administration, Labor Minister Mario Solorzano cultivated an open-door policy toward unions. His successor, Gladys Morfin, while less welcoming, set up a more efficient inspection system. The Arzú government's first labor minister, Arnoldo Ortiz Moscoso, was forced out in January 1997 because of his failure to win the lifting of GSP review. His successor has maintained a lower profile, while still carrying out neo-liberal reforms.

The Labor Ministry has had its critics within the Procurator of Human Rights Office and the Office of the President. According to one spokesperson, "The ministry does not have the capacity for timely reactions. For example, it did little to help resolve the public employees' strike that stretched from January through April 1994.[36] There is also corruption. Because of USAID support, the number of inspectors has grown. But 100 or 500 or 1,000 inspectors will not be sufficient, until they change the system of payoffs." The spokesperson thinks that "GSP really had no effect except to get USAID to spend money on training and hiring inspectors. The U.S. creates conditions, and then is forced to create a program, in this case to correct problems within the maquila, which it hasn't done."[37]

Ministry officials disagreed. While the programs had increased the ministry's workload, Roberto Cruz Minerva, inspector general between 1993 and 1996, thought that GSP had "improved the attitudes of business here, despite great violations in the maquila sector."[38]

Labor Minister Solorzano and other ministry officials remained circumspect. "GSP pressure has had both positive and negative effects on our programs and labor-rights compliance," noted Vice Minister Rivera. "In comparison with the past, we are much better at improving the capabilities of union leaders."[39] "Some labor ministers are better at this than others," acknowledged one leader of Guatemala's telephone workers.[40] Byron Morales of UNSITRAGUA found "the effectiveness of GSP pressure hard to measure. It brought superficial modifications at the Labor Ministry." But the modifications have gone deeper. Before GSP, the ministry had been regarded as the bottom rung among cabinet posts, a window dressing to placate union leaders and to buffer unrest. "However, the Labor Ministry found new dignity when the GSP process made the government more observant of worker rights," commented former U.S. labor attaché Donald Knight. "Before, it had been filled by some political hack, with all decisions made by the president, the CACIF, and the military. But now, the Ministry of Labor has become a key player in social and economic decision making."[41]

As chapter 7 indicated, the development of the ministry under the Arzú administration did not portend improvements. Unionists found conferences unsatisfactory. With declining U.S. aid, the government was unlikely to improve the ministry's funding.[42] "The Labor Ministry really does not have much power," explained John Cushing, U.S. labor attaché from 1995 to 1997. "It can cite people for not complying with the law and force them to court, but the courts have considerable backlog on handling cases."[43]

The ministry could act within its current limitations, just as it has in sanctioning uncooperative employers: "It is without coercive power. For years, this has been a rationale for inaction," stated UNSITRAGUA's Morales. "The Labor Ministry should take a political and moral stance that it will pursue company violations that it describes very concretely. In this way, GSP can help the ministry reclaim its role in resolving conflicts." In July 1994, UNSITRAGUA backed up its proposal by occupying Labor Ministry offices. Leader Sergio Guzman demanded "something no legal rule can accomplish—political will. Once the political problem is solved, we can address the incompetence and corruption."[44]

Guatemalan Courts

A second crucial area of petitioner concern has been the paralysis of the Guatemalan courts. Despite having received many *juicios punitivos* from the general labor inspector, by 1997 the courts had not issued one sentence on labor-rights violations since the isolated judgment against two Korean managers in 1993; they had not imposed a single fine for abusing child labor or minimum-wage standards; and they had not cited a single business for failing to attend tribunal hearings. When a high-profile case came before the court, the judge would often resign in fear.[45]

Although the labor-code reform had called for "rapid reinstatement of those dismissed," petitioners found "not a single instance of enforcement." Penalty orders remained "subject to review by the courts, an appeal process described by Guatemalan trade unionists as 'a graveyard,' a 'swamp of corruption' and a 'Bermuda triangle.'"[46] Even in 1997, a USTR official described the piled-up boxes in court offices as "a morass in which everything comes in and nothing goes out."[47]

Part of the difficulty was the complexity of court procedures. After workers file a *denuncia* and the inspector general determines its validity through a *procedimiento*, a case is sent to the tribunal according to its category:

    1. *Punitivos* are alleged employer violations of the law (for example, failure to attend a hearing).

2. *Collectivos* regard union recognitions and contract negotiations.

3. *Incidentes* are individual cases resulting from difficulties related to negotiations; they could deal with any contractual violation affecting an individual's rights, but they usually refer to firing and reinstallation of union activists. Instead of honoring the twenty-four-hour reinstatement rule, court procedures easily drag on for twenty-four months.[48] "If a case is finally heard, it may result in a sentence and fine," cautioned union leader Reynoldo González. "But this may or may not be paid. Workers find the entire process inaccessible."[49]

As suggested in chapter 7, the 1992 labor code mandated the creation of additional labor courts that would handle the collective cases (and their *incidentes*). In 1994, the government established the sixth and seventh courts for this purpose. Table 8.9 lists the individual, collective, and punitive cases handled by these two courts. While the number of collective cases in the courts increased from twenty-seven to 550 between 1993 and 1994, only two or three were resolved.[50] "They created the sixth court due to GSP pressure, but what has it gained us?" asked Reynoldo González in frustration. The leader had filed three motions between November 1993 and July 1994 "demanding resolution of the now 360 collective conflicts, 1,700 related *incidentes* [cases of workers affected] and 500 fines levied for *punitivos* [infractions]. The judge knows they are violating all the laws, but even the Supreme Court disregards the problem."[51]

By December 1994, the sixth court had cleared none of its 467 punitive cases and only one of its (by then) 478 collective cases. It did issue findings for about 20 percent of the 5,024 *incidentes,* and it returned 30 percent to the Ministry of Labor because they lacked proper form and data.[52] By the court's own admission, this left half of its individual cases unresolved. These delays compounded the backlog since all union cases were now channeled through the sixth and seventh courts.

Table 8.9. Collective cases handled by Guatemalan labor courts, 1993–95

	1993	1994	1995
Collective cases	27	550	165
(no. resolved)	1	1	0
Punitive cases	25	556	631
(no. resolved)	2	0	0
Related individual claims	904	5,024	1,000 (est.)
(no. resolved)	62	1,005	50 (est.)

Source: U.S./GLEP.

González' dilemma revealed contending fissures within the court system that the unions jointly identified in their recommendations to the president of the Supreme Court of Justice in January 1996, regarding:[53]

1. notifications and procedural difficulties;
2. sentencing and tracking the "resolution" of cases;
3. the new tribunals of reconciliation and conciliation;
4. the number of new courts required under the labor code;
5. proper funding of the courts that are functioning;
6. politics and the pattern of court influence.

Notifications and Procedural Difficulties

Employers render the processing of cases more difficult by capricious petitions to modify or nullify proceedings and/or to file penal charges against workers. Courts allow this but do not allow oral arguments from workers. Parties are often not personally notified about hearings, or they may be appraised of a hearing on Friday afternoon, requiring a response by Saturday, thereby reducing their right to obtain proper counsel. To delay the legal process, workers may be required to meet preliminary requisites not stated in procedures.

Tracking Sentencing and Case Resolutions

Courts often do not complete the sentencing process, thereby placing workers in jeopardy. They fail to inform workers of precautionary measures they might take to guarantee compliance with court findings. After recognizing an *emplazamiento* (see above), they fail to order reinstatements, "leaving the worker with no protection to exercise his/her rights." They do not issue an *impulsode oficio* to ensure that sentences are executed. Finally, they do not apply legal sanctions, including fines that "would benefit the court system" as well as society.

Finally, it is very laborious to ascertain court decisions. The sixth court's claim to resolve 20 percent of its individual cases is difficult to verify because of the way court records are maintained. Each year, the courts dispose of hundreds of individual cases and many punitive cases. In 1994, the third labor court, regarded as most efficient, processed an estimated 300 of the 500 cases filed. Most were small complaints about individual contract violations. Yet there remained no reliable, independent way to determine their outcome.[54] Labor advocates state that no fines have ever been paid, a claim undisputed by the government.[55]

New Courts Required

To assure unions in various parts of the country access to legal procedures, the 1992 labor code specified that tribunals for handling collective complaints would be set up in each region (presumably, each of the nation's twenty-two departments). "Prior to the new code reform, we had five labor courts in the capital," noted labor leader Juan Francisco Alfaro, "but regional judges also had the capacity to handle 'collective' as well as individual cases. Then, because of GSP pressure, we got a sixth judge, and finally, a seventh. In fact, the law specifies that there is to be permanent judge in each area, not just a national judge. On paper, there are 50 percent more judges, yet five are prevented from handling collective cases."

The two courts empowered to handle collective cases were located in the capital, but "who is going to travel from San Marcos or Puerto Barrios?" asked the judge of the first court.[56] "No workers are going to come here for the six to eight months it takes to process these cases," agreed sixth court assessor Cesar Avila. "They have to eat. We are also dealing with political conflicts and regional issues that we are not in a position to understand. It is a grand error to centralize all work here. In my view, we are unable to function."[57]

"This tribunal was created because of international pressure [through GSP]. But because the Supreme Court created only one judge to consider collective conflicts and complaints against specific employers for the whole country, we are saying that it is unconstitutional," explained the knowledgeable secretary of the sixth court.[58]

Tribunals

Article 294 of the labor code also specified that Tribunals of Reconciliation and Arbitration should be attached to each regional labor court. They would involve a representative from labor and another from business appointed by their appropriate bodies and presided over by a judge. In practice, the requirement proved cumbersome. It did not differentiate the compensation for the judge and tribunal members or any enforcement mechanism that could be applied to non-participants. "We have twenty-two departments with labor judges," explained the judge of the sixth court, Raul Alfredo Pimentel. "Now we have to select an additional forty-four permanent tribunal delegates for all departments that are paid the same as the judges. Internal problems in the constitutional court are preventing the funding to support these delegates. They don't even want to pay our salaries. Never in my fourteen years on the court have I seen anything like it—they say, 'well maybe your check will arrive, in a couple of days.' We also get paid less than judges in other Central American countries [an estimated $1,500 a month]."[59] Others have shared Judge Pimentel's frustration. In the first three months of its existence (March through May 1994), the sixth court went through three judges. By July, it had convened a tribunal four times but still lacked a budget to support full investigations.

"In addition," said Pimentel, "the employers don't accept the invitation to serve." Court secretary Brenda Alvarez had "issued requests to private-sector representatives, but 95 percent do not show up."[60] "Although the Conciliation and Arbitration Commissions are not being paid, the worker representatives still come, yet the employers use this as a reason for not participating," noted Reynoldo González. "Since all cases must go through the Tribunals of Reconciliation and Arbitration, which now exists only in the city, we are worse off than before," concluded Juan Francisco Alfaro.[61]

Non-functioning tribunals jeopardized all collective bargaining. Following USTR's mission in 1995, the government explored other methods of salary allocations that would enable the tribunals to begin.[62] In Fall 1997 it finally publicized a specific regional plan for creating additional tribunals, but by mid-1998 none had been convened. In a few cases judges attempted arbitrations on their own.[63]

Court Funding

The lack of funding also undermined current court operations. "Our telephone is not direct, and does not always work," noted court secretary Brenda Alvarez. "Some of our representatives have no desks. We must take buses to serve notifications. Besides this, we have no computers, which would facilitate preparing the cases, since much of what we type is repetitive."

"We work very hard here," exclaimed court assistant Avila. "We stayed until 5 or 6 P.M. every night to process 500 *incidentes* from the police alone." "Refusing to equip the court just keeps things in the hands of the bosses," added González. "Deals are cut between employers and judges to avoid decisions."[64]

The president's office explained that since "the courts are independent, autonomous institutions, the president is prevented by the constitution from telling them how to use their funds." However, unions believe that the president could cite the courts for non-functioning and budget allocations would quickly improve.

Politics and the Pattern of Court Influence

Although there has been limited progress in some areas, most observers and participants see the Guatemalan courts as an intransigent system almost impossible to comprehend. While a lack of money remains a key issue, the courts have received considerable external funding without exhibiting change. In 1990, Harvard University refused to renew its supervision of a USAID-funded project on juridical reform.[65] Despite political changes in the mid-1990s, the Americas Watch appraisal still holds—a judiciary "crippled by a combination of sloth, corruption, and perhaps most decisive, fear of the consequences should it seek to touch the military's impunity" (1990:74). Even USAID, which had scheduled planning funds for training court personnel in 1994, decided not to put money into the courts in 1995 since "the court system is nearly impossible as a dispute settlement mechanism and we don't have the money to address it."[66] In 1996, they were willing to fund criminal-investigations training and gave some attention to "the awareness, flexibility and efficiency" of judges.[67]

Part of the courts' imperviousness is the structure of appointments. As one spokesperson admitted, "The Congress does appoint new court leadership, but this only happens at the top levels. It does not affect the entrenched levels of corruption below. You have to remember that the president must serve many groups and interests, and some of them are very powerful."[68]

Yet President of the Supreme Court Lic. Donaldo Peláez held judges accountable: "They don't deal directly with difficult cases, but keep saying they 'have to do other things.' Collective cases are even easier than individual cases, but it depends too much on the personality of the judge to resolve them."[69]

More than personality is the judges' reliance on personal connections to alter the outcome of proceedings. Invariably this means a settlement in favor of those with capital and power. The alleged payoff that a Coca-Cola franchisee made to the bench in Puerto Barrios, cited by Rodolfo Robles, is typical (see chapter 1). "The judges often collaborate with the employers, not the workers," commented attorney Mynor Andrio of CIEP.[70] Like labor inspectors, judges know that over the long term, their interests are best protected by decisions conserving the status quo. "Remember that judges are the only ones who can force owners to pay fines, and they can take years to make such a judgment," added Assistant General Inspector of Labor Carlos Moran.[71]

Court personnel also realize that they are caught in a web of politics, such as the vendetta that occurred in 1995 between the Supreme Court and President de León Carpio, which stalemated labor-court funding. Within this context, the judiciary has limited power. Judge Pimentel favored judges being "chosen for their competence in labor experience. The separation of ordinary from collective cases allows more opportunity to study the cases." However, even Judge Pimentel was unhappy with outside probing. He told his staff "not to cooperate," and, if necessary, "to provide the wrong information."[72]

However, Supreme Court president Peláez placed primary blame for corruption and procedural delays on the court unions, which "regularly protect the incompetent work of their colleagues. Union leaders won't cooperate in helping us end bribery. They promise us one thing in the morning, but then file an *amparo* against us in the afternoon."

"There may be some corrupt workers," retorted CUSG's Lic. Alfaro. "Yet we, who have more cases than any other confederation, have never been requested for a bribe. In November 1995 we offered to help the court secretary address the difficulties of specific workers, but have heard nothing."[73]

Solutions

"Losing GSP benefits would not be sufficient to get fast change in the Guatemalan judicial system, although the GSP threat might push things along," acknowledged former U.S. labor attaché Don Knight. "There must be fundamental changes. President de León Carpio came in with the best of intentions, but encountered all the problems facing Serrano. The government was broke. There were sharp divisions among the three branches. This left the president standing by himself against a corrupt congress and court system. Even before the new labor courts, judges could only handle half their caseload. You can't expect revolutionary changes in dispute settlement."[74]

Nevertheless, GSP pressure could gain adoption of certain solutions that unions advocated in January 1996: proper notifications, clear sentencing, and improved supervision. It also could enable labor courts to function in "several of the nation's ten economic zones," as court secretary Brenda Alvarez suggested, or let labor-court judges address collective cases in major municipalities like Quetzaltenango. Local justices also could be empowered to handle collective cases valued above the current 3,000 quetzal limit.[75]

Court reform also means increasing penalties. Otherwise, as Carmen Lopez de Cáceres warns, "Companies will simply not comply. Their violations earn them three times as much as any fine they would have to pay." The ministry attempted redistributing functions to "improve punishment: For example, demanding that a certain business must pay minimum wage by a specific date" along with "a court request for automatic penalty for non-compliance," but the tribunals must follow up.[76] Reform also must resolve who controls the *fiscales*, police and ultimate enforcers of court judgments.

The period from 1998 to 2000 will be the test. "We hope with the signing of peace, the courts will change," exhorted businessperson Carlos Arias, who attributed past defects "to the war environment. The Arzú government will inaugurate genuine reform." The high number of unresolved cases has been "a problem with all of our courts on all issues, not just labor issues, because of a culture of delay in enforcing any aspect of the law in Guatemala. It is in the private sector's interest to reverse this practice."[77]

Table 8.10. Daily rural and urban base minimum-wage standards, in quetzals and dollars, Guatemala, 1980–98

	Agriculture	Non-agriculture	Dollars
1980–86	3.20	3.80	1.16–1.40
1988	4.50	5.40	1.67–2.00
1990	11.40	11.40	2.49
1993	11.40	11.60	2.02–05
1995	14.50	16.00	2.51–77
1996	15.95	17.60	2.65–93
1998	17.86	19.71	2.83–3.13

Note: Non-agricultural wages represent an average of the minimums of construction, commerce, industry, etc. Required benefits add another 10 percent. The dollar amounts do not account for inflation (see table 4.8).

Others were prepared for more dramatic approaches: USAID was "searching for alternative ways to resolve labor problems, because the courts are ineffective."[78] Enrique Alvarez, formerly of CIEP, advocated "direct worker pressure." He, Alfaro, and others also sought to change the code, constitution, and other laws to make implementation more certain but details less specific. They agreed with Carlos Arias that the peace accord agreement and, by implication, the multi-sectoral Commission on Strengthening of the Justice System could make this easier.[79]

Working Conditions: Wages

While GSP pressure had a mitigated impact on Guatemalan political and legal institutions, it had a noticeable effect on the nation's "wage fixing machinery" (see chapter 7). Guatemala's minimum-wage standards rose by 10 percent at the end of 1995, in turn positively influencing real wages.

Increases were long overdue. Table 8.10 lists the enhancement in minimum wages, and table 8.11 portrays the increase in real wages over a ten-year period (from 1985 to 1994). For agricultural workers and all IGSS affiliates, there had been little improvement. Industrial workers experienced a large drop in buying power, especially between 1985 and 1990.

Thus, despite predictions of neo-liberal economists (see chapter 2), Guatemalan wages did not rise in conjunction with GDP alone.[80] On the other hand, GSP pressure helped achieve real wage stability in both voluntary agreements and government determinations.

Voluntary Accords

In mid-1994, GSP played a part in the private sector's agreement to raise wages by 25 percent on the coffee fincas (see chapter 7). The more militant unions like CONIC and UNSITRAGUA objected, since "given current living

Table 8.11. Average real monthly salary index, by activity, Guatemala, 1985–94 (1983 = 100)

	Total	Agriculture	Industry	Public-sector
1985	112.34	58.51	182.03	101.51
1986	103.57	56.14	166.81	96.03
1987	113.55	58.60	170.20	117.58
1988	117.87	58.17	167.04	129.00
1989	115.02	58.51	165.63	127.29
1990	83.03	42.95	112.79	82.76
1991	95.47	51.63	125.09	85.97
1992	105.95	62.69	130.03	106.54
1993	115.17	65.23	131.59	112.34
1994	116.84	65.42	132.05	107.68

Source: Ministerio de Trabajo, *Boletín de Estadísticas* (IGSS affiliates only).

costs, there should be no minimum below 25 quetzals. They also manipulated it to happen before the discussion of socioeconomic problems in the Civil Assembly and the National Salary Commission."[81] Labor attaché Donald Knight acknowledged that the agreement did not cover basic living costs. However, "It occurred between the private-sector unions without government involvement. Both thought they would get something different from what they ended up with, but what is important is that they did it themselves."[82]

Government Machinery

The government followed the coffee accord with general wage increases at the end of 1994 and 1995, recommended by the National Salary Commission. Equally important, the government agreed to make annual commission review a permanent feature that included participation of key business leaders. Wage increases involved a four-step process:

1. Each of seven commissions carries out a study.[83]
2. The National Salary Commission, made up of six (two labor) representatives, digests all the particular commission reports and submits recommendations to the Labor Ministry.
3. The Labor Minister, after inviting comments from the IMF, IGSS, the Bank of Guatemala, etc., submits her/his recommendations.
4. The President signs the recommendations into a law that is promulgated as the new minimum wage.

Before the 1994 agreement, there had only been seven previous revisions over thirty years. "Employer representatives hardly ever came to commission deliberations, but the union representatives always did," explained commission head Sra. Sagastume. "When the former showed up at the national level, they usually resisted any proposed changes. They used their non-participation as an excuse, saying they needed to consult further, etc." For Sra. Sagastume, GSP helped generate more objective cost-of-living data.[84]

Implementation

While the threat of GSP sanctions brought an administrative victory, it had much less clout in obtaining minimum compliance. GSP petitioners cited the continued *non-payment* of the minimum in rural areas documented by CONIC and CIEP.[85] CIEP attorney Mynor Andrio decried the "5 quetzals received by most campesinos. In the North, some patrons provide the workers with a little land on which to grow subsistence crops, and use this as a reason to pay them as little as 3 quetzals a day. They also ask for free labor, such as having the workers patrol their property without pay." Donald Knight also admitted that "in terms of enforcement, the vast bulk of coffee growers won't pay the increase due to strong opposition within the ANACAFE organization."[86]

In practice, Guatemalan employers tend to view the minimum wage as a "maximum"; though prohibited, they also pay differential wages to men and women.[87] Although CACIF's Carlos Arias only believed "a few outlying cases" violated the law, even with "a war going on in coffee areas," Assistant Labor Inspector Moran found that "in the Verapaz coffee fincas in 1996, 80 to 90 percent of the owners were paying their employees 4 to 5 quetzals a day, a third of the minimum." However, when Moran returned in the second phase of the project, he "found that non-compliance with wage payments had dropped to 20 percent."[88]

Other Working Conditions

Guatemala's record in improving other working conditions is spotty. To protect field workers, the government regulated pesticides in 1990, but it lacked a "registration or inspection system for accidents, pesticide dangers, etc."[89] The 1992 labor code, section 148(a) specified regulations governing unhealthy or dangerous jobs that prohibited the employment of women and young workers. It did not bring weight loads in conformity with IGSS recommendations (see ILO 1995a:C127). IGSS assigned only fourteen inspectors to monitor workplace conditions outside Guatemala City. As Petersen chronicled, eight departments had no inspectors (1992:67–68). In follow-up, GSP petitioners found egregious levels of workplace hazards, injuries, and insecticide poisonings that they attributed to the lack of employee training. They traced gastrointestinal infections to contaminated food and water supplies.[90]

Table 8.12. Number of accidents related to work and per 100 workers, Guatemala, 1985–94

	No. of accidents	Per 100 workers
1985	81,495	12.9
1986	86,500	13.1
1987	91,327	13.4
1988	96,082	12.3
1989	98,982	12.5
1990	93,991	12.0
1991	91,753	11.6
1992	78,213	9.8
1993	86,331	10.5
1994	71,463	8.6

Source: IGSS (only for workers covered by the State Health Benefits Plan).

Nevertheless, reported accidents that remained at a constant level per hundred workers through 1991 have begun to drop, as table 8.12 indicates. Most accidents are in agriculture (57 percent in 1993 but only 7 percent in industry). The percentage of workers receiving Social Security coverage has dropped slightly since 1986. In 1987–88 there was an increase of nearly 100,000, perhaps because of the incoming Christian Democratic government's emphasis on health policy. However, coverage declined under the Serrano administration in 1990. In 1997, the government inaugurated a more restrictive health care program that required co-payment.

As noted in chapter 7, for a brief period the government sought mandated health and safety committees in each business, but this pursuit was quickly dismantled by the private sector, which "carries out its own health surveillance."[91]

IGSS pension coverage has gradually risen from 19,000 in 1987 to 35,000 in 1993, still a very small proportion of Guatemalan workers (other plans in effect reach a minimal number). "In the countryside they often provide no health services or social security," notes Mynor Andrio. "Employers are to deduct 4 percent of their paycheck (and contribute an additional 10 percent of salary above their paycheck)." Many times this does not happen, as in Cobon, where "a number of retirees (at age seventy-two) suddenly discovered that their employers had not kept up payments. Legally, they could have retired at age sixty, although the pension would have been smaller. But in fact, they got nothing."[92]

Tripartism

A fourth area of GSP impact revolves around the establishment of a tripartite approach to problem solving that includes labor, government, and business, as the ILO has advocated for many years (see chapter 2). Theoretically the approach should appeal to the "corporatist" or paternalistic tradition of Latin nations, which seeks to include all involved sectors in major decisions (see Wiarda and Kline 1985). Nevertheless, in Guatemala consultation is more the consequence of vociferous demands than of cultural inclusion. In the Cerezo period, the Labor Ministry invited representatives from the three sectors to discuss common issues, but it virtually ignored the independent unions. Under Jorge Serrano Elias, Labor Minister Solorzano made tripartism a key administrative component, culminating with a major agreement in March 1993; but, as shown in chapter 7, Solorzano was not permitted to honor his commitments or respect union recommendations. Lic. Gladys Morfin, the next labor minister, attempted to reinforce Solorzano's initiatives, offering USAID-backed courses "to each of the three affected sectors, stemming from the agreement in March 1993." The sessions covered collective bargaining, productivity (using statistics to measure output), and interest-based negotiations. CACIF remained "reluctant." Members refused "to show data to anyone." In one course, UNSITRAGUA was the only participant.[93]

In the mid-1990s, tripartism became USAID's measure of GSP compliance. The agency bestowed funds directly to the private sector to improve their labor relations activities, for example "to help train managers at Pepsi and Bandegua in negotiations; to raise consciousness in the Gremial for Non-Traditional Exports on the importance of labor issues, international labor laws, minimum wages; to do labor training for CAIM, a group of businesses."[94]

Yet, by mid-1995, USAID acknowledged that while "we often take a tripartite approach, tripartism at the national level never worked."[95] "Tripartism was an idea of Mario Solorzano," a presidential spokesperson explained. "We have not pursued it." However, Vice Labor Minister Rivera, who authored the tripartite submission to USTR in September 1993, claimed to "take a tripartite approach to dealing with CACIF, FENESEP, CUSG, CGTG, CTC, UNSITRAGUA," which involved about ten meetings in 1994–95. They dealt with such issues as "the Commissions on Minors and Labor Training." However, by 1996, Rivera, who had returned to USAID, had a change of heart. Tripartite training "did not work well. Participation was low so we put the dollars elsewhere."[96] However, soon after the installation of the Arzú government in 1996, the Congress passed the ILO Tripartite Convention, no. 144, and declared the TPC official. Labor Minister Ortiz made the "big move" for tripartism after USTR's visit, explained USAID's Randall Peterson. "He hoped to bring a united front from both the unions and the private sector to Washington to inform USTR. But then he advocated the anti-strike law, and the unions walked out!"[97] The mistake also caused members of CACIF to boycott discussion of the anti-strike law in the Tripartite Commission.

Yet for local ILO project head Thelma del Cid, tripartism in Guatemala had stepped beyond being the political strategy it was under Solorzano. Unions ought to "take advantage of this new commitment to challenge recent government actions such as the anti-strike law and civil/municipal service 'flexibility'; and to protect the right to organize and negotiate." They also could employ the tripartite process to reduce jealousies that emerge among labor leaders.[98]

GSP Influence on Tripartism

Official U.S. personnel in Guatemala agreed that GSP had a "positive impact" on awareness of "labor inequalities always known to the workers, but not to the business community." "People were blown away by the labor violations, and GSP helped show that the government was incapable of investigating," explained USAID's Randall Peterson.[99] For labor attaché Donald Knight, the elite "paternalistically viewed labor as something to be exploited and thrown away. The strong threat of benefits cutoff helped refocus their attention! A majority still wish that the military would enforce whatever they want to do, but a growing minority realize this era has passed."

Nevertheless, U.S. representatives also insisted that market forces were at least as important as GSP influence in creating attitude shifts among Guatemalan businessmen. Knight believed "a minority has already been improving labor standards to become more competitive." He cited the sugar industry, where "producers understood that their market loss in the mid-late 1980s was partially due to low output per worker. They initiated changes to increase production. They no longer wanted entire families with their chickens and dogs. The workers would not work as hard, would take off more days, and would return to the highlands to plant their milpa. And the company didn't want to maintain entire housing areas. So, they just accepted men and boys for whom they provided barracks, protein-enriched food, and better pay. They tell me that this has increased sugar production per worker from one ton to seven tons a day."[100]

U.S. labor attaché John Cushing (1994–97) was even more emphatic that what improves worker rights is not external pressure but market forces. "Despite the large supply of labor in the maquila, when competition improves they will pay more to get better workers. Maquilas are folding up that don't have good training programs or treat their workers well because they don't produce as good a product."[101]

For USAID's Randall Peterson as well, "The most important link for labor rights is in the competition of the market and the need for economic growth; improved relations will come from improved production, as employers seek better quality. Companies are wasting their investment if customers have to make use of warranties and return goods. Customer relations will demand a workforce that is trained and capable, and this will improve labor rights.

"With global competition, the private sector is also seeking a stronger state. People who had preferred to spend funds on their own security guards now desire to play in the world game, and they need an effective court and police. They must pay the cost of services or they will lose customers, for example to protect tourism, investors, etc. They must honor international property agreements. The World Bank also believes that the government is not devoting enough funds to health or social investment. But the market will assure that labor gets their fair share of growth."[102]

More progressive members of the Guatemalan business sector also adopted this dual approach. Maquila spokesperson Carlos Arias stressed that GSP pressure "did have an effect. We changed the labor code. The private sector played a key role, as did the ILO principles. If the ILO, which was created in 1919 to prevent unfair competition, is still going, there is no reason why we don't accept it as a fact of life. We understand that there must be ethics in the world market and laws which one must abide by, among them labor rights."

"We also approach things on a tripartite or bipartite basis with unions. We agree with the unions that retraining can make their members more productive and competitive in the world market. They will make better wages—not equal to those in the U.S., but with higher sales, every day better. On an informal basis, we have seen tensions here calmed down substantially.

"However, we are moving beyond the time that the U.S. grants us programs like GSP to help our economy get started. The programs are really grants, and logically have conditions, among which are labor rights. Yet whether or not there are labor-rights conditions is really not relevant. There are already laws on the national level to do this. Such laws shouldn't be in trade. We will do it ourselves. We will enforce convention 87 for free unionization in compliance with the rest of the world. But we can't expect aid in our life any more. We need trade, to sell and buy, to look for an open market."[103]

Arias's compatriots agreed: "CACIF wishes to take a proactive position regarding unions. We are committed to follow ILO convention 144, and work together in a Tripartite Commission. We are also using this mechanism to evaluate the political conditions of the country, to examine the evidence on taxes and other issues. We had tried this four years earlier, but we couldn't implement it as well under the former governments." CACIF members would pursue their past promise to set up a special bipartite subcommission that would investigate labor disputes in the maquila. It is hoped that it would avoid prolonged court battles that never satisfy anyone.[104]

Arias remained concerned that "the future is not too bright for the maquila that has lost is position in exports to the U.S. Cooperation between unions and management will enable us to compete responsibly. The primary reason for shutdown is *bad image*. When you have to fight against constant attacks and negative information, it affects investors and customers. That brings low sales. You can cope with a union if you have enough financial resources, but if you are marginal, you have to close. It makes it so difficult for the plants to keep up with demand; it is simply easier to move the plant. It only takes seven weeks to restart one."[105]

Nevertheless, Guatemalan unionists were less sanguine about the market's ability to improve their conditions and more appreciative of GSP pressure. In response to the rationalization of sugar production and the displacement of families, they were reminded about the difficulties faced by Rigoberta Menchú. She picked coffee as a child so the family could be near her father on a neighboring sugar plantation. She recounted how the finca owners refused her small brother medical aid and banished her mother for taking time to bury him (Menchú 1984). Now, finca owners can banish entire families without the stigma, but with similar effects on migrant workers (see also Oglesby 1997 on sugar-industry rationalization).

While the market conveys some benefits, controls are essential. Sergio Guzman cited the agreement on employee rights, which UNSITRAGUA reached with the Korean maquila owners in 1996. "GSP was important in this respect, as well as the ILO meetings in Geneva. GSP can focus criticisms and mobilize U.S. pressure. The Korean government is taking action, but in fact, many illegal conditions remain. We have lost many unions in the maquilas. We have denounced GSP violations. Guatemala is one of the worst cases of worker abuse, and now with the new anti-strike law it has deteriorated further."[106] One example was the business tendency to blame improvements for the nation's alleged loss of maquila plants in 1995–97. Actually, the value of Guatemalan apparel exports has risen and its job numbers have remained stable.[107]

Unions also were skeptical of business commitment to tripartism. In 1995, AIFLD's Michael Donovan attended the same two-day meeting as CACIF representatives. "Never once did any of the business participants use the word 'union.' The anti-communist attitude still exists."[108] For Juan Francisco Alfaro, the big problem with tripartism was "the actual honoring of an accord. "When we sign a *convenio* or pact, the employers say all is well, but in fact little is well. Union liberty is often jeopardized. Potential leaders are fired for

trumped-up reasons. They have the same attitude toward collective negotiations. They make sure there are only a minimum number of union members so
they will not have to negotiate."[109]

The common view is that the Arzú government officially set up the Tripartite Commission for international consumption. Labor Minister Ortiz also
used it as a "dumping ground" for conflicts he did not wish to handle (such as
Pepsi). Despite CACIF's commitments, between January 1996 and January
1998 the commission did not resolve a single case. "They only worry when
they are up for evaluation," cautioned Thelma del Cid. "They are not desirous
of any permanent structure; what we need is constant pressure by way of the
Procuradoria [Human Rights Office] and unions etc. to improve ways of conducting negotiations etc. that are very difficult. We also need foreign pressure
to monitor implementation."[110]

Summary

This chapter has probed the structural impact of GSP outlined in chapter 7 on
Guatemalan institutions dealing with labor: the ministry, the courts, wage
mechanisms, and the tripartite system. The pressure evoked a more professional and well-regarded Labor Ministry. Union registrations and the investigation of complaints increased, albeit helped by GSP-stimulated funds from
USAID. The newly created labor courts, bottlenecked by legal snafus and lack
of funding, would not budge in processing cases. The unintended mistakes
in their creation benefited elite interests and fed into traditional patterns of
power.

GSP pressure did influence a more secure wage-review system. The 1995
coffee agreement, though widely disregarded, did raise agricultural wages,
and the National Salary Commission accomplished an annual cost-of-living
assessment. CACIF members testified to an attitude shift among the nation's
private sector, although "tripartism" as such has yet to establish itself as a
bona fide decision-making body. However, the GSP process failed to catalyze
genuine structural change, as petitioners continued to point out. The government was persuaded to prevent violence in the 1998 lockout of banana workers but not to enforce local labor-law compliance. The business community,
while anxious to avoid losing trade benefits, remained reluctant to back a
thorough membership transformation.

On the other hand, one also can assess what the market might bring to
these same institutions. The Guatemalan case has hardly shown that general
business competition improves conditions. Despite optimistic views from
USAID and the U.S. Embassy, the dramatic rise in maquila, fruit, and veg-
etable shipments along with coffee exports between 1988 and 1993 brought
few changes in labor standards. While the nation's mainstay coffee, sugar, and

banana producers may be modernizing, there is little evidence of any wide-ranging rural-family benefits. In lieu of GSP, paltry data show that maquila assemblers would have otherwise substantially raised wages or improved conditions for their workers. The trends were quite the opposite.

In a general assessment, within the context of necessary vigilance in a highly repressive state, conjointly with ILRF, the AFL-CIO, and other groups, U.S./GLEP's strategic utilization of the labor-rights petition in Guatemala yielded more substantial accomplishments than in El Salvador. As David Jessup noted, "We started this process in 1985. In the early nineties we filed again, and due to the pressure we did reform the labor code that made it better for union leaders. But the code was never fully implemented. Only a continued offensive has made it work."[111]

CHAPTER 9

GSP and Labor Changes in Honduras

The GSP process in Honduras was much more limited in scope than it was in El Salvador and Guatemala. At first, it focused less on structural conditions than on specific labor abuses that coincided with the presence of U.S.-funded contra forces in the mid-1980s. Ever since the banana strikes of 1954, Honduras had been known as "the best unionized country in Central America." In the early 1990s, unions reportedly held 40 percent of the urban and 20 percent of the rural workforce and played a key role in national affairs.[1] Nevertheless, working conditions deteriorated in Honduras, especially following state privatization efforts after 1989. Only 30 percent of the population held full-time employment. Seventy percent earned less than $60.00 a month. It remained the hemisphere's poorest country after Haiti. As workers protested declining conditions, military and government officials took a hard-line position. They easily involved themselves in union affairs and at times killed trade unionists without compunction. A GSP petition filed by the New York Labor Committee in 1991 stimulated national and international attention, forcing some reduction in violence. However, the rapidly expanding maquila sector brought more rights abuses. In 1993, the AFL-CIO filed its own petition, which ultimately led to an enforcement agreement between the state and USTR. The Honduran case offers another model of trade-sanction effectiveness.

Labor Rights Traditions in Honduras

Historically, Honduras lagged behind Guatemala in recognizing labor rights (see chapter 4). Early in the twentieth century, workers organized mutual-aid societies, and the national legislature passed a Sunday closing law in 1921. Strikes won specific local gains for railway and banana workers in the 1920s, but in 1933 the government crushed a large strike to reign in "communist influence." Labor freedoms did not reemerge until 1954—ironically, the year they disappeared in Guatemala following the invasion of CIA-backed forces from Honduras. To deepen the irony, Honduran unions blossomed from a lengthy strike by United Fruit Co. banana workers, who won the nation's first collective contract. President Juan Manuel Galvez, a former United Fruit attorney, was forced to grant legal recognition to trade unions and the right to bargain and strike. Social security coverage came soon thereafter.

In 1959, during the reform period of Liberal party leader Ramón Villeda Morales, Honduras promulgated its first labor code that the government dutifully monitored (Pearson 1987). Key provisions, listed in table 9.1, also strengthened the Labor Ministry's power. In addition, the Labor Ministry could force violators to compensate trade unions and could impose other administrative fines.[2] Anticipating similar action in other countries, the Ministry of Economy and Commerce could invoke investment law article 6 to suspend temporarily "certificates of investment" for companies not comply-

Table 9.1. Key provisions of the 1959 Honduran labor code

1. Unions can organize with thirty members (art. 517). Organizers are protected from being fired without cause—i.e., as authorized previously by a labor judge.
2. Those employing violence and threats to deny the right to free-trade unions can be fined 50 to 10,000 lempiras, imposed by the Labor Ministry (art. 469).
3. Two or more employees may request negotiations (art. 54), but demands require approval by a majority of the union (art. 465).[a]
4. No reprisals are allowed against employees who exercise their labor-code and constitutional rights (art. 10).
5. Firings and prejudicial treatment because of trade-union participation are prohibited, as well as acts that weaken or restrict other labor rights or offend worker dignity (art. 96).
6. Workers have the right to strike, under strict and complicated Ministry supervision (art. 551). Two-thirds of the workers have to vote in favor.[b] Employers may not enter new contracts or complete work during strikes (art. 573); however, the minister can declare strikes illegal and dissolve the union, and workers can then be fired (art. 571).
7. The Labor Inspectorate has the power to penalize contract violations (art. 83).

[a]The union must furnish certification of the general assembly vote, of its approved negotiators, and its application for a labor inspector to present demands. Employers have to receive the request, which they often try to avoid. If contract violations occur, the ministry could intervene, but since 1959 the ministry has not published the rules for doing so.
[b]Article 555 also requires the ministry first to resolve disputes in essential services and government. Strikes can occur only after direct negotiation, mediation, conciliation, and arbitration. Workers then must inform employers by writing of their intention, demands, and cited portion of article 551, six days prior to action, with a copy to the ministry's Conciliation and Arbitration Board. Employers must respond within forty-eight hours. After eight days, the ministry can create a three-member commission to propose a settlement formula. Workers can accept or reject via the above procedure, and reengage the strike for another eight days.

ing with the "Labor and Social Security" law. The Labor Ministry was less attentive to smaller rural unions until protests from peasant organizations won additional agrarian-reform laws in the 1970s. However, the government did not raise minimum wages for agricultural workers above 5 lempiras ($2.50/day).

In 1978, the government opened the first EPZ in Puerto Cortés in 1978. Four years later it enforced the constitutional guarantee of seventh day–thirteen month pay, bringing a 25 percent wage increase to all workers. This did not dissuade a union organizing drive in Puerto Cortés. Over the next several years, workers successfully negotiated contracts with seven multinational clothing companies that secured "stable labor-management relations." However, the government permitted privately held EPZs. As the maquila sector expanded, resistant employers built barriers to any further collective bargaining.[3] In the late 1970s through the early 1980s, the Honduran military remained somewhat restrained in its treatment of labor (see Peckenham and Street 1985). Most unions did not align themselves with the National or Liberal center-right parties, although at times they supported specific administrations. Laws allowed public-sector workers to form associations, although not to federate. Persecuted Guatemalan unionists often fled to Honduras for safe haven.

Economic Difficulties

During the first half of the 1980s, Honduras's largely agricultural economy had remained stagnant because of low export prices for its raw materials, increased import costs for petroleum, credit shortages, and higher rates of interest. Inflation rose in the mid-1980s, enhanced by an infusion of U.S. funds for anti-contra operations (see Shepherd 1988). These funds aided Honduras' GDP to rebound to nearly 5 percent a year in 1987–89, but their withdrawal contributed to the substantial drop in 1990 (see table 4.8). The crisis motivated the government to carry out "liberalized reforms": lower tariffs, reduced expenditures, and privatization of state enterprises. While not suffering the same loss as in Guatemala, by the end of the decade, both minimum wages and industrial wages had declined to less than three-quarters of their 1980 values (see also table 4.8). Although urban unemployment lessened from 12 percent in 1986 to nearly 7 percent in 1992, total unemployment increased to 15 percent and underemployment to 43 percent. Like Guatemala, Honduras reached an exceedingly high rate of poverty—70 percent of its population. For those who had jobs, it remained a substantial hurdle to meet living costs.

Nevertheless, monetary conditions exacerbated employer resistance to organized labor. Before the economic downturn in the early 1980s, unions had been much more active. They had negotiated more than 260 contracts. Work stoppages and strikes averaged about eighty-five per year, nearly half "over improper dismissals." In 1982, companies issued seventy-nine requests for work suspensions affecting 17,100 workers (U.S. Department of Labor 1984). By 1989, with less labor militancy, company suspension requests dropped to nineteen, affecting only 952 employees (FLT 90-65:5). Strikes dropped in half to thirty-seven, mostly among health workers in the public sector.

Growing repression was an aspect in this trend, ominously signaled by the elimination of a major teacher's union in the mid-1980s[4] and attacks against the Consejo Nacional de Trabajadores de Campo (CNTC; Benjamin 1987). Then, as the GNP began falling in late 1989,[5] newly elected president Callejas, at the urging of USAID, slashed state expenditures by privatizing state enterprises and firing 7,000 public employees.[6] He put into effect the Structural Economic Law, devaluing the lempira from 2 to 5.50 per dollar. This raised inflation by 60 percent and basic services by more than 100 percent.

In Fall 1989 the major unions formed a united labor front and a common "Platform for Struggle to Democratize Honduras," staging three successive demonstrations against the government's economic reform. The Platform for Struggle brought together the main labor federations of Honduras.[7] They demanded wage increases tied to inflation, an end to the large-scale firings of government workers, cessation of state intervention in the internal affairs of union organizations, land reform, the release of political prisoners, an increase in spending on health and education, labor-code reform, and respect of labor rights. Rather than respectfully treating it as an expression of popular frustration, government and corporate officials unleashed a fury of anti-union violence. Both rural and urban industrial unions were fair game. A military colonel directed a troop attack that killed members of the AIFLD-affiliated Asociación Nacional de Campesinos Hondureños (ANACH). Any union leader involved in labor actions or strikes received death threats.

For example, the Health Ministry hired military goons to assassinate Brulio Caneles López, the local president of the Sindicato de Trabajadores de Medicina, Hygenica y Similares (SITRAMEDHYS) and union activist Manuel García, who had been leading a month-long strike. After a Honduran soldier testified that officials paid three assassins $390 to kill López, SITRAMEDHYS leaders insisted on an investigation. They were accused of defaming the state, and the army occupied all public hospitals. Administrators fired two members of the union's national executive board and another local president and fined or transferred dozens of strike activists. The government placed other union members under surveillance. The Health Ministry proposed legislation that labeled union actions as "acts of terrorism." The Committee in Defense of

Human Rights in Honduras concluded that SITRAMEDHYS leaders had been systematically "harassed, threatened, dismissed, persecuted, prosecuted." (NLC 1991:32).

Not to stop there, the Honduran brewery fired 300 members of the Sindicato de Trabajadores de Bebidas y Similares (STIBYS) for a day-long sympathy strike in concert with the Sindicato de Trabajadores de la Empresa Nacional de Energia Eléctrica to protest raises in electricity rates. They tortured STIBYS's leader Liliana Esperanza López, cutting off her breathing with a "capuche." The government illegally fired other labor leaders without repercussion.[8] In 1990 alone, government agents had assassinated five union and peasant leaders and illegally detained 357 others, whom they frequently tortured during interrogation (NLC 1991).

The Platform for Struggle and the ensuing violence became the basis for a petition to USTR filed by the New York Labor Committee, a regional representation of unions affiliated with the National Labor Committee for Democracy and Human Rights in Central America (NLC; see also chapter 4 in this volume). The New York Committee conducted its own investigation. While Francisco Guerrero, secretary general of CTH, had not heard much about filing such petitions under GSP, he informed the AFL-CIO of his support: "The Honduran labor movement feels isolated internationally, yet it is precisely such pressure from outside the country that is needed to move the Callejas government" (NLC 1991:34).

Petition Filing

The New York Labor Committee's petition described a pattern of labor-rights violations over the past decade.[9] The petition described the killings and torture of rural trade unionists laying claim to their own land or unoccupied land. The government had not carried out one single investigation to punish the guilty.[10] Industrial unions had been equally affected. According to one leader from FITH, it was impossible to enter industrial free zones to organize: They were met with "threats, beatings, firings, and plant closings," and those fired were "immediately blacklisted." The state also refused to investigate when maquila factories closed and reopened to avoid unionization.[11] The petition also cited the interference of *solidarista* associations, which had grown to cover 10,000 workers even though they were not officially recognized by the government (see chapter 11).

The above actions threatened the freedom to associate and to bargain. Regarding the latter, the New York Labor Committee petition recounted the 1990 murders of Francisco Bonilla, a leader of the Sindicato de Trabajadores del Instituto Hondureño de Seguridad Social, who had been in the middle of bitterly contested contract negotiations, and of Ramón Briceño, a bank worker just leaving Bonilla's wake. The continuing intimidation of the Sindicato de Trabajadores de la Tela railroad company (SITRATERCO) Chiquita banana workers also prevented bargaining. When the union went on strike in 1989, Chiquita filed an unfair-labor-practice suit and demanded dissolution of the union, a three-year suspension of the union executive board, and $1 million in indemnity. It fired fifteen union activists the following year. The workers struck again. After enduring forty-two days, the company summoned the military. They entered shooting, destroying union phones and property and wounding two unionists. Rather than investigate, the government called the strike illegal and threatened to imprison union leaders and eliminate the union.

The New York Labor Committee petition further showed how the nation's decade of inflation had brought deteriorating working conditions with no increase in minimum wages until late 1989. Even at that, companies routinely disregarded rules for hours and wages. One company ran shifts for 12 hours a day, paying $20.00 for a seventy-two-hour work week.[12] They bypassed health regulations such as the proper application of pesticides like the fungicide Dithane. Sixty percent of the banana workers had suffered headaches, nose bleeds, and fainting spells.[13]

USTR and Embassy Answers

The U.S. Embassy appeared surprised by the New York Labor Committee's allegations. The embassy believed that labor unions enjoyed a privileged position in Honduras. In 1989, three key confederation leaders had won seats in the national legislature, and one became a vice president. Unions remained more a part of national culture than in other Central American countries. Politicians routinely sought union support since they usually reflected "the political views of the general population" (FLT 94-05:5). The embassy thought the recent killings and attacks against trade unionists were "not necessarily related to labor rights." For example, a presidential-appointed military commission traced the Bonilla and Briceño killings to student activities and intra-union disputes. While the four murders of trade unionists during 1990 "remained unsolved," the U.S. State Department acknowledged that having military officers "appointed to command positions in the police forces . . . limited" their work on human rights. It also cited "press reports that the military or police may have been involved" with the campesino unions, and that an anti-terrorist law was commonly used to evict campesino squatters (FLT 91-55:6). Even President Callejas admitted that the ANACH co-op members had been massacred on their own property, by persons illegally dressed in military uniforms. But these were "isolated incidents."

Mass firings, on the other hand, should be understood within their economic context. Layoffs were inevitable, as the Callejas government stressed export competitiveness and the privatization of "inefficient" state enterprises, which the embassy applauded. The president was also under pressure to lay off those in government jobs "customarily awarded to supporters of the winning political party," bringing charges of involvement in internal union affairs. If anything, the embassy thought the Honduran government had been overly sensitive to labor concerns! It described how former president Azcona had agreed to pay back wage following an eighty-one-day walkout of teachers pension fund employees in 1989, thereby encouraging "further walkouts by using public monies to pay wages lost during the strikes" (FLT 90-65:4). (The embassy raised no objections when President Callejas decreed that the Chiquita company could hire outside workers during a 1990 strike and ordered the army and police to guard the banana farms [FLT 91-55:5].) The President consulted regularly with labor unions on labor issues and resolved disputes personally, counseled the embassy. While it acknowledged several conflicts over poor working conditions at Asian-owned factories in the Puerto Cortés Free Zone, the Labor Ministry was monitoring the situation. (In 1989 the Labor Ministry had mediated 13,510 individual labor disputes, higher than in Guatemala.) In addition, fifteen assembly plants had trade unions. The government also promised to ban the offending *solidarista* associations. The embassy concluded that "despite high levels of inflation, which significantly reduced workers' buying power, the Callejas administration managed to maintain social tranquility" (FLT 94-5:5). In July 1991, after tripartite negotiations, the government even increased the minimum daily wage by 21.8 percent (to between $1.25 and $2.45 per day).

USTR rejected the New York Labor Committee petition, believing that Honduras had taken sufficient steps to protect labor rights.

Petition Impact

While it did not have the impact it would have had with AFL-CIO backing, the 1991 GSP petition nevertheless generated discussions among Honduran government officials, U.S. Embassy staff, and the nation's unions about trade-based labor rights. Although killings abated, intimidation of trade unionists persisted, and the petition set the stage for future federation action.

For its part, the government reneged on carrying out its ban on *solidarista* associations. It summoned the 105th Army Brigade to quell striking miners in 1991. Even though the Honduran economy rebounded in 1992 because of improved export earnings, the benefits to wage holders dwindled as they faced an unofficial inflation of 20 percent.[14] In 1992 and 1993, it strengthened property protections, precipitating campesino land takeovers and a banana workers strike protesting withdrawal of plantations from banana production. As unemployment rose above 15 percent, tripartite negotiations motivated the government to up the minimum wage by 13.7 percent in June 1992 and

14.4 percent in May 1993. To furnish affordable housing, the state initiated a Social Housing Fund, but the fund primarily depended on worker contributions.

Mushrooming Maquilas

To counter unemployment, the Callejas administration's strategy was to encourage foreign investment for export. Shipments to the U.S. had doubled to $88 million between 1987 and 1989, a rate twice that of El Salvador, and now Honduras could compete with Guatemala. A new Export Processing Industrial Zones Law likened maquilas to public services, protecting them from possible strikes![15] Over the next three years, it would quadruple export shipments.[16] By early 1994, it would establish six EPZs, holding forty-one companies that employed 15,070 workers, and another eleven industrial processing zones, with 134 plants hiring 34,407.[17]

In 1990, Honduras was the region's only country that had registered collective-bargaining contracts in the maquila sector. However, the Honduran Foreign Ministry assured Korean maquila owners that if they located in the EPZs, the labor code would not be strictly enforced and they would not have to deal with unions.[18] The stratagem attracted business, but as employer machinations accelerated in 1991, more and more workers in the EPZs sought union affiliation.

Besides the ILO instruments that Honduras had ratified (see chapter 4), at least five articles in its 1959 labor code offered potential remedies. The first line of protection came when a labor inspector notified a company that its employees wished to form a union. However, neither this nor other provisions had teeth without enforcement, as the Callejas government was well aware and as the AFL-CIO discovered:

"In many cases, corrupt labor inspectors (some of whom end up as company personnel managers) simply give the names of the workers to the plant manager prior to formal notification, thereby allowing the company to fire them without cause. In other cases, the labor inspector goes through a ritual of attempting to deliver the formal notification, only to be turned away at the gate of the industrial park by an armed security guard after leaving the papers with the provisional list of union founders. The workers are then fired. Under the perverse interpretation of law in Honduras, the company is allowed to claim it had not been notified because it had not signed a receipt for the notification it has in its possession! The Labor Ministry then washes its hands of the matter, leaving it to the workers to go through the expense and delay of a lawsuit to gain reinstatement, which can take up to ten years. The result in practice is that most employers don't bother obtaining prior authorization before firing workers."[19]

In late 1992, after the Honduran press publicized the illegal and corrupt practices of a labor inspector, Vice Minister of Labor Armando Urtecho investigated difficulties faced by EPZ labor organizers. He met with tripartite and U.S.-government representatives, who reminded the Honduran official of possible GSP action. With Supreme Court authorization, the ministry specifically agreed to:

1. fine companies and EPZ administrators 5,000 lempiras the first time a labor inspector is denied entry;
2. impose fines of 7,500 to 11,250 lempiras for two subsequent denials;
3. close the factory for fifteen days if entry is denied a third time, with assurance that workers are paid;
4. eliminate requirements that unions in formation show names of thirty founders prior to notification of employers.[20]

President Callejas encouraged the vice minister to "take whatever measures necessary to correct all violations."

However, the ministry did virtually nothing. It stood by over the next year as at least five corporate officials refused to admit labor inspectors. In one example among many, in late January 1993, a plant guard at Wan Chang Industria turned away a labor inspector who came with the list of potential unionists. On a second attempt, no company official could be found to accept notification. On February 3, the company fired thirty-five of the listed workers.[21]

Despite the government's promised remedies, it imposed no fines and closed no factories. Most workers lost their jobs permanently, and companies successfully destroyed all unionization efforts. When challenged, the Callejas administration shifted blame, arguing that it had no authority to order reinstatement of illegally fired workers, since that required a court judgment. Union leaders responded that the executive invoke *via judicia ejecutiva,* or executive judicial review, which would permit reinstatement of illegally fired workers within twenty-four hours.[22] It also could carry out its promised fines or suspend operating or export licenses.

Conditions Exacerbate

The Honduran workers understood that their own action, not the Labor Ministry's, had to be the primary source of change. When four workers were fired for union organizing at the Continental Industrial Park in February 1993, 5,000 co-workers occupied the premises and closed eight factories. Five days later, workers shut down five plants at Galaxy Industrial Park for similar reasons. Then, in June 1993, after the firing of six pregnant women in the Puerto Cortés Park, 6,000 workers from six companies marched onto the highway and demanded restoration, claiming what the U.S. Embassy admitted was "a clear violation of the Honduran Labor Code" (FLT 95-7:5). When activists were fired for union organizing in the Choloma Industrial Park in November, 5,000 more walked out. Workers demanded that the Labor Ministry respond to their needs. Its regional offices were not enforcing the code. The ministry was at best indifferent and more often overtly pro-management. For example, Labor Minister Carlos Torres López' reaction to notorious firings at Paraiso Co. was to waffle between "workers and management. On the one hand, the organization of a union is a right recognized by the constitution, and on the other the closure of a company would signify losing an important source of employment."[23]

In late 1993, labor-sector discontent inspired a heavy labor vote for opposition Liberal party candidate Carlos Roberto Reina, who won 56 percent of the ballots.

Considering a Second Petition

In October 1993, the CTH asked the AFL-CIO to begin preparations for a GSP petition to review Honduran trade privileges. In January 1994, incoming Reina government officials assured a visiting AIFLD delegation that they would "take forceful action to enforce the labor code against violators."[24] The new minister of labor also proposed changes in the labor code, for "the modernization and strengthening of the State," which would reduce restrictions on the right to strike and end requirements that trade-union officers must be Honduran and that there could be only one trade union in a single enterprise (ILO 1995a:87).

However, not only did these proposed code reforms languish, but conditions in the maquilas exacerbated. Some workers, like Eber Orellana Vásquez, were happy to escape from rural oppression to gain a maquila job (see chapter 1). While some found friendly, well-ventilated factories (Rohter 1996a), many simply faced more abuse. When they did not meet production quotas, workers were "forced to hold a chair over their heads for a half-hour or hour . . . [or] stand like a statue with eyes fixed on a spot on the wall . . . [or] stand in the hot sun. Those caught chewing gum have it stuck on faces. Those who don't work fast enough are struck with a yardstick." Women face continuing sexual harassment; their medical leaves are denied; their work hours are extended to fifteen hours a day without overtime; they are given stimulants and amphetamines in order to work forty-eight hours straight. There is no rest on holidays. The companies grant vacations at whim. They fire pregnant women and hire underage children. They renew contracts annually to avoid severance.[25]

"Many plants are modern day sweatshops, where rows of teenagers work elbow to elbow twelve hours a day," reported the *Miami Herald*. "Some of the thirty-seven Korean plants are especially troublesome. . . . Only a few unions have been legally recognized, and even though the right to form unions is enshrined in the labor code, hundreds of workers have been fired for organizing. The understaffed Labor Ministry rarely investigates complaints" (Otis 1994).

In March 1994, an investigation headed by Honduran Congress member Orfilia de Mejía blamed strikes in eight factories on the dismissal of union leaders in violation of labor-code provisions. Mejía also discovered one girl who had just been hit in the face by a Korean supervisor. There was "a clock in the workplace for timing production, and if the garments were not made on time the Koreans become angry and react in that fashion."[26] The Congressional Commission cited the "incorrect calculation and awarding of maternity leave, vacation time, overtime pay, weekly pay, seventh-day pay, and benefits" and "delay and sometimes apathy of labor inspectors." It recommended a permanent Labor Ministry representative in each EPZ, an increased EPZ minimum wage, recalculated every four months according to cost of living, the Labor Ministry's constant monitoring and publicity of EPZ violations, and expulsion of foreign violators as "persona non grata."[27]

In September 1994, the National Labor Committee invited Lesley Rodriguez, the fifteen-year-old maquila worker from Galaxy Industry, to present testimony to the U.S. Senate. Lesley had been making sweaters for Liz Claiborne since she was thirteen years old. She described the painful conditions she had experienced in her sometimes eighty-hour work week for $21.50 in pay (see chapter 1). Minister of Labor Cecilio Zavala's first fear was that Rodriguez' testimony might "damage not just the government but the country." It was an isolated case of an underage worker, not an indication of massive violations. If Honduras was cited as violating rights, it could jeopardize trade "that the country needs so much in order to export."[28]

However, Lesley Rodriguez' story did inspire the owners of several Honduran maquilas (Galaxy, Mi Kwang, Dong Woo) to meet with a vice president of Liz Claiborne and representatives from the NLC and the International Ladies Garment Workers Union (ILGWU), to protect the goodwill and business of the name-brand label. The Liz Claiborne vice president put it bluntly: "If the firms did not change their labor practices and obey the law, the company could no longer buy their products." A sobered Galaxy agreed to respect the Honduran labor code, establish a day care center, reinstate the fired workers, dismiss abusive managers, and obey the hours and conditions for minors required by law.[29]

However, the contracting firms only fulfilled some of their commitments.[30] AIFLD's David Jessup concluded that "unions had been unsuccessful in the rapidly growing free zones where connivance among Asian employers had kept them out." He sought to "muster the facts" for another petition.[31]

The facts were that by May 1995, eighty-nine factories operated in twelve private EPZs; another fourteen operated in Puerto Cortés; and ninety more operated outside the zones, employing 45,000 workers. While several companies had recognized a union, none had negotiated collective-bargaining contracts, save the seven original firms in Puerto Cortés mentioned earlier. Despite promises, the Reina government perpetuated past failures by not enforcing labor protections for women, hours, overtime, minimum wage, age, health and safety, and the legal obligation to bargain when unions did manage to organize. "Thousands of women in the maquila industry are forced to work in degrading and unsafe circumstances without their fundamental rights to organize and bargain to change these conditions." When workers informed international unions and the ILO about this, business groups accused them of being "traitors to their country." The press publicized uncorroborated stories of U.S. union funding, and officials warned that 50,000 jobs would be lost if unions organized.[32]

Petition Filing

Honduran trade-union leaders agreed that the Reina administration had not honored the promises it made in January 1994. In early 1995, the unions revived their talks with U.S. labor leaders about filing a GSP petition. According to one leader, "These discussions occurred over a number of months. We developed a general understanding and were appraised of the types of problems they were facing. The unions were aware of the GSP procedures."[33]

In June 1995, the AFL-CIO petitioned USTR for a review of Honduran labor policies. Reversing the usual order of charges, it cited the nation's failure to:

1. enforce laws regarding women's rights, hours, minimum wages, minimum age, and health and safety;
2. protect workers against reprisals by employers;
3. enforce the obligation to bargain collectively and enforce collective agreements;
4. prevent company interference in worker organizations.

To support its allegations on working conditions, the petition quoted from the accounts on maquila conditions noted above, such as the report from the Honduran Congress, various journalists, and Lesley Rodriguez's testimony in the U.S. It challenged the effectiveness of Honduran labor law and the 1992 agreement for not confronting employer reprisals. "In some recent cases, illegally fired workers have been reinstated in their jobs, as required by ILO conventions," but most "reinstatements took place not because of government action, but because of outside pressure."[34]

For failure to enforce bargaining requirements, the federation reviewed the complex rules governing negotiations. It argued that most businesses ignore the labor code's bargaining requirements anyway, since the government imposes no sanctions. Even worse, most union leaders are fired before the inauguration of any formalities.[35] The only genuine penalty for refusal to talk is the strike.

A legal strike, however, required a four-step procedure that was so cumbersome it is worth describing: First, the union must convince the labor minister that the business owner has refused to bargain, so s/he can declare a termination of "direct agreement." This requires a joint statement that most employers refuse to sign. Next, it must go to great lengths to get the minister to appoint a mediator and inform the owner. The employer may create a six-month delay by appealing this decision up to the Supreme Court. Third, if the owner refuses to meet with the mediator, the labor minister must declare a "conciliation" step. By refusing to attend conciliation hearings, the employer can again delay the process several years. Finally, the labor minister can declare all steps to be exhausted and approve a legal strike. Even then, strike procedures are cumbersome (see table 9.1 and labor code article 551).

Needless to say, over a thirty-four-year period less than 10 percent of strikes in Honduras have been declared legal. The "work stoppages" chronicled above usually arise to protest illegal firings. "Workers argue that since the Labor Ministry and judicial system allow employers to violate the laws with impunity, they have no other recourse than to take direct action. . . . These bargaining sessions, often conducted in a crisis atmosphere, result . . . in *actas* . . . witnessed and signed by representatives of the Labor Ministry." Despite labor code article 83's provision for punishing contract violations, employers rarely honor such agreements. They view them as "mere ploys to end the crisis and get the workers back to work."[36]

Lastly, the petition addressed company interference in worker organizations. It pointed to the increasingly common employer practice of registering phony contracts to preclude negotiation with a bona fide union. In one instance, AAA Honduras Apparel Manufacturers broke its union agreement, fired the union leadership, then signed a *pacto* with non-union workers. Despite its illegality, the Labor Ministry recognized the *pacto* because the fired workers had accepted severance pay.

Hoping for some change in Honduran enforcement practices, USTR postponed an immediate decision on its consideration of the AFL-CIO petition to review labor conditions in Honduras.

Another Agreement

In November 1995, a USTR delegation arrived in Honduras, led by Deputy Assistant Jon Rosenbaum (see chapter 4). Invited as consultants were David Jessup of AIFLD and Alan Howard of UNITE. In meeting with leaders from all Honduran centrals, U.S. labor representatives encountered an increasingly sophisticated understanding of GSP. Trade sanctions had been a big media issue, which now featured the delegation's visit. The unions saw GSP pressure as a useful tool, although labor-movement divisions also piqued some ambivalence. Even to protect common interests, the CLAT-related CGT was leery of an alliance with U.S. unions. Some members even preferred a linkage with nationalist employers. The CTH and the FITH stood closer to one another in advocating trade-pressure tactics. Despite these differences, all the centrals offered ideas about what should be included in any list of demands for settlement. The USTR representatives accepted most of the labor group's proposals, with the exception of a stated deadline for compliance.

The U.S. Embassy, on the other hand, remained quite resistant. The officials did not show a solid grasp of labor-rights rationale or legal requirements. The ambassador and labor attaché insisted that "Honduras is trying hard" and that "GSP sanctions would do more harm than good." The USTR delegates took pains to explain the need for Honduras to defend itself against the criticisms listed in the AFL-CIO petition. They found little variance between the perceptions of embassy staff and those of the business community with whom they also held discussions. Jon Rosenbaum warned both groups that unless they implemented labor rights, U.S. trade benefits would be severed.

Despite U.S. Embassy reticence, the Honduran government realized the implications of Rosenbaum's warning. On November 15, Labor Minister Cecilio Zavala Méndez signed an 11-point agreement with USTR.[37] It concretized changes in fines and inspections, assurances of association, and other methods of enforcement such as a two-week suspension for export licenses (table 9.2). The Honduran government signed the agreement to strengthen Labor Ministry action against rights violators in exchange for a postponement of USTR's decision to review the AFL-CIO request. Deputy Director Rosenbaum gave Honduras six months to comply.

An Early Test

"We got a signed agreement," David Jessup announced elatedly in late 1995. "AIFLD effectively used the threat of GSP" to gain leverage for labor-code implementation, agreed Michael Donovan. The government immediately issued a three-month work suspension against one Korean factory for its violations. Then, in December 1995, the Hu-Ywa factory in the Puerto Cortés zone attempted to undo its union, which had been in the plant since the early 1980s. According to UNITE's Alan Howard, "Suddenly the employers decided to knock out the union there and replace it with a CGT affiliate, so we communicated directly with the labor minister, with copies to USTR. Hu-Ywa signed an agreement with the new union, but the labor minister did not accept it or the new union's legitimacy. No question, this was GSP related. But we need more

Table 9.2. Summary of the USTR/Honduras agreement on labor-rights implementation

INSPECTIONS

1. Companies will be fined 10,000 lempiras for their first denial of access (10,000 per plant in EPZs).
2. Police will escort inspectors after second denial.
3. The frequency of unannounced inspections will increase.
4. Inspectors currently identified as corrupt will be dismissed.

FREEDOM OF ASSOCIATION

5. *Via judicia ejecutiva* will be employed to reinstate illegally dismissed workers within twenty-four hours.
6. Lists of union founders will be submitted directly to Labor Ministry; sealed information will be opened by plant manager in presence of union reps.
7. Union registration procedures will be expedited to avoid firings.
8. The ministry will seek management concurrence in labor-code changes:
   a. Union with 50 percent plus one of the workforce can bargain.
   b. Strengthened protections for union organizers.

EGREGIOUS VIOLATORS

9. The Labor Ministry will develop with the Economic Ministry procedures for two-week suspensions of export licenses for multiple labor-law violators.

OTHER

10. The Ministry will seek the budget to improve inspector salaries and training, to reduce likelihood of bribery.
11. The Ministry will earmark fines on maquiladoras, etc., for compensating inspectors.

---

pressure. The company did not show at the hearing, but it did threaten to move to Nicaragua."

"The government now has six months to show compliance, and this will be the full test," said Howard.[38]

By mid-1997, well past the six months, Honduras had not yet changed its labor code. Employers still accused unions, especially the CTH, with treason for reporting abuses that brought reprisals from the U.S. The Labor Ministry retained its extraordinary powers. While violations of the old code persisted, however, there was a new spirit. The unions also stepped up organizing drives in the EPZs, especially textile unions with assistance from the International Textile Federation and UNITE. The women at Kimi achieved a satisfactory accord despite disagreements over the proper ways to conduct external monitoring (see Frundt 1998). Yet USTR found unions in remarkable agreement that GSP pressure and the signed accord in Honduras had contributed to a new era of union action.[39]

CHAPTER 10

Petitions in the Dominican Republic:
Stronger Maquila Unions

Unlike in El Salvador (results in Guatemala and Honduras were mixed), the GSP petition process in the Dominican Republic brought more effective labor-rights implementation. However, such implementation only came after considerable struggle (and luck). The country's 360,000 union members constitute only 12 percent of the labor force. Because half of this labor force is underemployed or unemployed, business owners have easily used intimidation and government complicity to avoid unions. Politicized union divisions have made this task easier.

The petition process was able to overcome some of these obstacles, but only after a protracted period of general strikes that expressed popular discontent but weakened the labor movement. After considering the evolution of labor rights in the Dominican, we will trace petition antecedents, including the larger contesting forces and the more specific treatment of Haitian workers in the Dominican sugar industry. We will see how the labor code itself underwent reform and how its implementation played out in the "battle in the free-trade zones."

Evolution of Labor Rights

While the Dominican Republic's modern labor history is sometimes dated from the divisive impact of the U.S. military occupation of 1916–24,[1] the more important influence came from Rafael Trujillo's rise to power and extensive rule from 1930 to 1961. As suggested in chapter 4, Trujillo backed legislation protecting child labor and the eight-hour day and finally pushed through a labor code in 1951. However, since Trujillo manipulated both law and labor unions to his advantage, workers gained few rights. While the code allowed the right to strike, it forbade public-sector and general strikes; while it prohibited dismissal for union involvement, it permitted employers to break contracts without cause. In principle, the dictator had inaugurated rights, but their realization had to await his assassination in 1961, when 200 new unions suddenly signed up with the secretary of labor.

Yet, after Trujillo, unions still experienced a bumpy ride. In brief parallel to the Guatemalan revolution of 1944 to 1954, many unions supported the democratic administration of Juan Bosch of the Partido Revolucionario Dominicano (PRD) before U.S. occupation of the island in 1965. The U.S. installed as boss Joaquín Balaguer, who would affect Dominican policy until nearly the end of the century (from 1966 to 1978 and from 1986 to 1996). Unions enjoyed few freedoms, even though article 11 of the 1966 constitution guaranteed their right to organize. Invoking the same provision, the state monitored maximum work hours, minimum wages, and social security. In 1972, the Balaguer administration even required certain forms of profit sharing.[2] In effect, unions came to view their primary negotiating role via the state, not contract bargaining.

Social and Economic Barriers to Implementation

Nevertheless, as state (and corporate) bureaucrats skimmed from rising sugar revenues during the mid–1970s, they shared little with the near million impoverished workers they imported from Haiti to cut the cane. The government, along with Gulf and Western, then owner of the eastern third of the country, reinvested their hefty earnings into tourism and free-trade-zone operations. They countered unionization attempts with threats and murder. As free zones expanded, Balaguer promoted a policy of trade-union repression to attract new investment (see Frundt 1980).

In 1978, with strong labor support, the more liberal PRD was finally able to defeat the long-time political patriarch. Union freedom blossomed; in two months, new affiliations jumped by 100 (Espinal 1995:69) and in two years by 350 (Murphy 1987:271). The main areas for organizing were tourism and agriculture. In agriculture, with sugar prices now in decline, the state sugar agency was closing or privatizing many mills. After scores of attempts, unions won contracts with some hotels. Public-health workers gained key victories. By 1982 in the EPZs, where 12,000 workers now assembled jewelry, shoes, electronics, and clothing, "there remained a fairly big disjuncture between free-zone labor organizing and the rest of the economy."[3] The liberal government struggled to meet union concerns by putting in price controls and raising minimum wages. Business swiftly criticized PRD linkages with labor. In 1981, it prevented congressional passage of a new labor code. It also challenged social expenditures, even though the Instituto Dominicano de Seguro Social's health coverage had dropped to 41 percent of the labor force (Ramírez 1988).

Table 10.1: Real minimum monthly wages, in pesos, Dominican Republic, 1987–95 (1987 = 100)

	1987	1988	1989	1990	1991	1992	1993	1994	1995
Wages	350	500	700	1,120	1,456	1,456	1,456	1,675	2,010
% increase	40.0	42.9	40.0	60.0	30.0	0	0	15.0	20.7
Consumer price index	100.0	144.4	210.0	334.9	515.2	538.9	567.2	614.1	671.0
Real wages	350.0	346.3	333.3	334.4	282.6	270.2	256.7	272.8	299.6

Source: Compiled from FLT and IFM reports.

Over the next five years, the PRD's inexperience and persistent divisions led to significant errors. The party chose economic policies that enhanced discordance within the labor movement and between labor and popular organizations. In 1980, when the rising cost of petroleum imports dampened the Dominican's somewhat healthy economy, the PRD pursued the IMF's technocratic and neo-liberal guidelines opposed by its labor constituency. Taxes and inflation rose dramatically as income and wages declined. While the GDP increased in fits and starts between 1985 and 1995 (table 4.8), unemployment and underemployment expanded. Poverty also touched 70 percent of the population—a new high. Rural areas suffered profoundly (Vargas-Lundius 1991). Thus, PRD actions inaugurated a fifteen-year period of chafing demonstrations and dramatic general strikes.

Prices, Wages, and Public Reactions

The strikes parallel the evolution of minimum wages in the Dominican, charted in table 10.1. Trade unions called the first strike in 1979 to oppose price increases on fuel. The strike spread to poor urban neighborhoods that experienced higher living costs. A similar strike in May 1980 reached even more groups, risking government repression, lost jobs, and pay.

This sobered the unions. They urged a stop to all negotiations with the IMF. However, when the government announced another surge of price increases during Holy Week 1984, they first stood on the sidelines while the popular movement spontaneously took to the streets for three days of "food riots." But ultimately the unions called for a general strike. The government and the leftist parties then recognized them as "spokespersons" in attempting a settlement. While the movement lacked permanent leadership however, in Roberto Cassá's view union opportunism helped undermine popular confidence in both labor and the governing PRD even though the latter resisted massive privatization. Internal divisions exacerbated as leftist political spokespersons turned to non-labor forms of organizing. National reaction polarized behind "territorial revolutionaries" on the one hand and "reformist negotiators" on the other (Cassá 1995). Labor and popular uprisings increased from 103 in

1984 to 293 in 1986 (see Espinal 1995). But even though both protests were still met by billy clubs and rifles (see Murphy 1987:272), the alternative approaches found it difficult to reconcile in a common struggle.[4] As workers in the popular movement grew disillusioned, the PRD became vulnerable to charges of clientism and corruption, and Balaguer was reelected over the incumbent party in 1986.

At first, the restored patriarch defied IMF warnings and inaugurated a large public-works program to create jobs. In Fall 1987, the government raised minimum wages from 250 to 350 pesos; by April 1988 public employees received 400. As inflation swiftly accelerated, even these raises did not cover living costs (see table 10.1). Once again, the drivers' unions poised for action against gasoline price hikes. In a display that again divided the protest movement, top unionists met with Balaguer and muted popular calls for a general strike in early 1988.[5]

The strike prevailed nonetheless. In Spring 1988, its momentum forced government, business, and labor into tripartite negotiations mediated by the Catholic church. They reached a tentative agreement on general social security coverage, higher minimum wages, labor-code revision (especially articles 69 and 78 governing freedom of association), pensions, and Christmas bonus improvements (Espinal 1995).

However, a few days later businesses raised their prices, forcing the unions to reject the agreement. Yet when momentum again mushroomed for a similar strike in June 1989, labor again refused its backing. Nevertheless, after the strike won another small increase in minimum wages, the Balaguer administration wisely meted out construction jobs, confining protests to specific localities. Popular leaders accused the unions of being insensitive to the people's deteriorating living standards. Sporadic strikes for higher wages and lower prices exploded in November 1988 and March 1989.

Labor/Popular Coordination

In mid–1989, unions and opposition parties finally awoke to their joint opportunities. Concerted action in October brought another increase in minimum wages, though only after much internal conflict. For example, in June 1989, a group of lesser-known political parties and six of the eight labor confederations successfully carried out a two-day work stoppage to decry the high inflation–low wage crisis and the failure of government services.[6] Although the labor code forbade general strikes, the Supreme Court declared it was not a strike but a protest of general conditions and therefore not illegal. Balaguer capitalized on the event, predicting that IMF-imposed austerity measures would create social and political turmoil. The government would "not hamper the country's development." He shrewdly reduced debt-service payments and announced he would pay "only within the country's means."[7]

While labor offered its strong support, it also coalesced in demanding a wage increase.[8] Other demonstrations of union militancy, such as a medical workers strike in July 1989, challenged the intolerable conditions of public hospitals, despite the law prohibiting such actions. Nevertheless, the opposition remained sufficiently divided, and U.S. backing sufficiently strong for Balaguer to squeak through another election in 1990, despite a falling GNP and rising inflation.[9]

Nevertheless, in Fall 1990 the revived labor-popular coalition forced another increase in minimum-wage standards. With contracting sugar exports, increasing foreign debt, and a declining GNP, the government was in jeopardy. On August 1, President Balaguer summoned business and labor leaders to discuss an "Economic Solidarity Pact." Most labor leaders, in no mood to attend, countered with a unified plan for price controls and improved minimum wages. Balaguer's reply was to do the opposite, lifting price ceilings on basic goods and curtailing construction projects by 15 percent.

Again, just before the inauguration of Balaguer's new term, grassroots activists and small leftist parties convened another general strike, which shut down the country for several days. When the state remained unmoved, the popular groups mobilized a second strike. Hesitant labor unions joined with fury when the Dominican Electric Company fired many workers. On September 7, the government cried uncle. The Dominican wage board increased minimum wages by 60 percent (from 780 to 1120 pesos). The Balaguer administration also signed a twenty-point pact with most of the labor confederations, committing itself to the persistent issues: modifying the labor code, increasing social security coverage, improving the supply of goods, granting labor and community representation in parastatal (state-affiliated) companies, and investigating the Electric Company conflict. Nearly all labor and popular leaders called off the strike.

Finding no action on the electric workers by mid-October, however, labor gave the government seventy-two hours to resolve the matter. A week later, with no resolution, most unions withdrew from the pact and called for strike renewal. However, when two opposition parties supported the action and demanded Balaguer's resignation, the moderate, AIFLD-related Confederación Nacional de Trabajadores Dominicanos (CNTD) and the Confederación Autonoma Sindical Clasista (CASC) eschewed participation, citing political motivation. Between November 19 and 21, the strike gained wide support, yet it failed to budge the government. Invoking an old 1966 law for the first time, Labor Secretary de Peña made good on his threat to cancel the legal status of participating unions.

Balaguer again tried his divide-and-conquer techniques. Choosing from among public employees who had supported all of the general strikes, he raised medical-employee salaries alone. He admitted that the other salaries were too small to live on, but said he needed to attack inflation first. This precipitated a series of regional strikes in March 1991. Nevertheless, surrendering to IMF initiatives, the government imposed tight monetary policies and canceled consumer subsidies for gas, flour, and sugar. It floated the peso, removed controls on interest, and inaugurated a major tax reform. It was able to obtain some debt forgiveness through the Enterprise for the Americas initiative (see appendix). These measures stabilized the GDP (7 percent growth in 1992) and brought inflation under control.

The protesting strikes for price controls and improved wages and benefits that followed revealed weakness in the opposition. "The population had grown disgusted with strikes for costing them more than they got," explained Jeffrey Hermanson, organizing director of UNITE. The violence created a lot of anti-union sentiment. People were hurt and they couldn't earn anything. In a country that is 70 percent poor, going without work for a week or even a day is a huge loss for people who need to feed their families."[10] Years of partisan, fractious battles forced both Balaguer and the unions to search for fresh methods of conflict resolution just as the nation's labor practices began to draw international attention.

First Petitions

Early notice came from church-sponsored shareholder resolutions challenging corporate treatment of Haitian cane cutters and free-zone workers (see Ledogar 1975:72f; Frundt 1980). Since the Dominican Republic had signed several ILO conventions on union rights (see chapter 3), in 1983 the ILO's Commission of Inquiry sent a "Direct Contacts Mission" to investigate the country's misuse of article 689 of the labor code, which permitted employers to break open contracts without cause. Trade unionists had complained that the clause was being used to fire employees who attempted to unionize in the free zones. The ILO also objected to the labor code's prohibition of strikes by public workers, although teachers, judges, public doctors, and sanitation workers had struck without recrimination.

The ILO also expressed concern about the treatment of Haitian workers in the Dominican sugar industry. The mission generated sufficient publicity to put the government on guard. After 1985, the government did not pursue its arrangements with Haiti to recruit or transport workers, although subcontractors still brought in truckloads. However, in 1989, Balaguer cancelled a visit by the ILO director general to inspect the 1989–90 sugar harvest. The ILO's Committee on Application of Conventions and Recommendations censured the Dominican Republic for "continued failure to implement" convention 105 prohibiting slave labor.

Americas Watch Takes Action

Because of widespread mistreatment of Haitian braceros, Americas Watch petitioned USTR in May 1989 to review the Dominican Republic's trade privileges. It documented instances of forced labor, restricted travel, child labor, and sub-minimum wages in violation of international standards. When USTR agreed to review the petition, the government denied systematic abuse of braceros. It nevertheless inaugurated discussions with the Avril government in Haiti to create a bilateral plan of migrant protection. However, no accord was reached.

Again in June 1990, Americas Watch (with AFL-CIO support) submitted another petition. USTR extended its 1989 review into 1990. The U.S. Embassy conducted on-site visits but found "no pattern of abuse, which had been greatly reduced in the last two harvests in any case" (FLT 91-41:9). Tensions remained, however, and in October, Balaguer established fresh procedures to register and regularize the immigration of Haitian workers. The registration process required employers to issue individual contracts, in both Spanish and native languages, that listed a worker's right to quit, to seek work elsewhere, or to return to his or her country.

Americas Watch applauded the 1990 presidential decree and the distribution of work contracts. However, the steps were only taken after significant outside economic pressure, and "were not sufficient." Preceding the USTR's review, "the Dominican authorities would not even admit that there was a problem in the sugar industry. If the Dominican Republic is to be persuaded to go beyond its minimal first steps, it is essential that the U.S. maintain is scrutiny . . . [and] threat of sanctions."[11]

In January 1991, the government did permit an ILO observatory mission, and a year later an Americas Watch team visited the state sugar mills, co-sponsored by the National Coalition for Haitian Refugees and Caribbean Rights. It found "evidence of continued Dominican army and State Sugar Council collaboration in forced and deceptive recruitment of Haitian workers and forced confinement of those workers on state sugar plantations." Calling for prosecution of soldiers and others who forcibly recruit sugar cane cutters, it demanded that the workers receive contracts before being recruited. Nevertheless, USTR turned down the Americas Watch 1991 petition. The U.S. commerce secretary, a friend of a prominent family that had purchased G&W's sugar holdings, opposed the petition's acceptance and rendered moot its impact.[12]

However, the ILO monitored the condition of Haitian workers: In 1994, their pay per ton had been increased from 25 to 30 pesos, which was above minimum wages but substantially below the rate of inflation. The braceros sampled could cash in their weekly payment vouchers without having to go through company or government stores. The use of child labor and restrictions on worker travel had diminished. However, the government had issued few residency permits. Latrines, water supplies, and general health conditions remained below standard. While the government had laudably appointed eighteen inspectors to examine cane cutter conditions, the ILO found no evidence of plantation visits. Labor inspectors had not located *any* instances of discrimination directed against Haitians or preferences for Dominican workers, or any usage of forced labor. Despite complaints, there was no monitoring to assure that employee union representatives were present when cane was weighed for salary payment at the Consejo de Estatal de Azúcar (CEA, the state sugar company) (ILO 1995a).[13]

Free-Zone Conditions

Because of its review of the Americas Watch petition in 1989–90, USTR was required to examine the nation's entire labor practices. Besides the braceros, the trade agency focused on employer behavior in the Dominican free zones, which had grown to twenty-three over the decade, jumping from 10,000 to 130,000 workers and 300 companies.[14] Many worked in apparel and footwear.[15] While USTR concluded that steps were still being taken to observe labor rights, it cited concerns over "the rights of workers to organize, the inclusion of the free zones, and how the labor code clears up the just cause dismissal."[16]

In contrast to a 1981 study of women in the modern industrial sector, Helen Safa found no legally recognized unions operating in the Dominican free trade zones: "Workers are fired and blacklisted with other plants if any union activity is detected." Nevertheless, in common with women from the earlier sample, 70 percent of Safa's respondents favored unionization. Hilda, an apparel worker, thought "unions could bring about many improvements such as better wages, transportation, and cafeterias for workers." Hilda believed that the most of the women were afraid: "Necessity makes law . . . and one doesn't want to run the risk of losing the bread of one's children." According to Safa, while the women are aware they need to organize, they "can be dismissed for any reason and know that there are a lot of others waiting for their jobs." Safa also cited the lack of support women receive from the Ministry of Labor. Most were unaware of the office, but when those who did know brought complaints of mistreatment and unjust dismissals, the ministry usually favored management. Eighty-six percent of those surveyed claimed not to know about the ministry. Twelve percent had presented complaints, but found, like Luz, a twenty-six-year-old garment worker, that "the Secretary of Labor does not defend one of us" (Safa 1995:109).

The National Labor Committee also listed specific cases of corporate mistreatment. Westinghouse transferred jobs from Connecticut in 1985, using USAID funds (NLC 1993:34f). "Westinghouse paid its 52 cents an hour in the Dominican Republic. It also demanded overtime, most often without overtime pay. . . . Whenever the workers at its plants in the Dominican Republic attempted to organize they were immediately fired and their names placed on a blacklist that was circulated openly among free-zone companies."[17]

In 1990, the U.S. Department of Labor sent its own investigators to the free zones, and they found serious and credible allegations of anti-union discrimination. Previously established unions now existed only on paper. Their workers had been fired and there were no current pacts in operation. Zone security guards denied entry to any labor organizers (U.S. Department of Labor 1990).

Confronted with these charges, Dominican secretary of labor de Peña promised a sixty-day day limit on any legal EPZ union application. The CNTD immediately sponsored union recognition drives at Westinghouse and Sylvania in the Itabo zone and at Undergarment Fashions in San Pedro de Macoris. The response typified worker treatment throughout the zones (see FLT 91-41:10):

1. The Westinghouse union received recognition on October 29, 1990. Two and a half weeks later, management fired half the union's original members and half of the union executive board. The union retorted with three legal actions, one for the firings, one for criminal violations of worker rights, and one for civil damages of DR$10,000,000 ($789,000). In February 1991, management dismissed most of the remaining union members.

2. The Undergarment Fashions Union won recognition on January 29, 1991. Management fired the entire executive board and most members of the union on February 19. After the union reorganized in March, the company laid off the new executive board.

3. Sylvania management recognized its union, but only after five months of a difficult drive in which Sylvania fired several labor activists.

In Spring 1991, the massive firings at Baxter, Hanes, GTE, Westinghouse, Sylvania, and Undergarment Fashions caused the AFL-CIO itself to consider petitioning USTR: "April 1990 saw a particularly disappointing determination in the USTR's certification that the government of the Dominican Republic was taking steps to afford its workers internationally recognized rights.

The AFL-CIO had presented clear and verifiable evidence that a Dominican free-trade-zone employer-association president fears no reprisals . . . [and] states openly that workers are fired for trade-union activity."[18] In early 1991, the AFL-CIO threatened to file directly, but it withdrew this possibility when the government promised action on a labor code.

The Labor Code

Reforming the labor code had also been recommended by both the ILO missions and the USTR review. In Fall 1990, Balaguer appointed a study commission. By February 1991, the draft code:

1. clarified basic principles regarding the prohibition of forced labor;
2. reconciled conflicting laws that prevented court judgments in favor of the worker;
3. reasserted the right to organize and to receive a just wage;
4. extended the decree on worker rights to Haitian braceros;
5. protected the job security of union leaders and organizers (*fuero sindical*);
6. eliminated prohibitions on political and sympathy strikes;
7. liberalized the restrictions on public-sector strikes;
8. increased the application of prison terms for violations of labor laws;
9. updated fines by tying them to minimum wage standards.

The business sector labeled the code recommendations "pro-labor." The three major (and sometimes contesting) labor confederations (CNTD, CASC, and CTU) stood unified that the code did not far go far enough.[19] To mollify opposition and push through a revised code, in March 1991 Balaguer appointed Rafael Alburquerque de Castro to replace de Peña as secretary of labor. Alburquerque was the seventh labor secretary to serve under Balaguer's second reign after 1986. An expert in labor law with experience in conflict resolution, Alburquerque had served on the Labor Reform Commission.[20]

In May, under the guidance of the new labor minister, the government issued the Law on Civil and Administrative Service (no. 14/91). It assured public servants of stability of employment; however, it expanded coverage gradually, for example not yet extending to the Labor Ministry itself. The Dominican Chamber of Deputies debated the proposed code during Spring, but congressional action remained slow.

Nevertheless, in May 1992 the AFL-CIO again threatened to file under GSP. After an intense series of business-labor negotiations mediated by the Catholic church, Congress finally passed the code. It eliminated the open-contract provision, which allowed employers to dismiss workers without notice (see

Table 10.2. Principles of the 1992 Dominican labor code reform

1. Unions can register with more than twenty workers, with automatic recognition should the government not act on a specific application.
2. Unions can negotiate at enterprise, local, regional, and national levels with assent from 51 percent of the workforce (art. 111).
3. Wage protections are extended to rural workers, including on sugar plantations (sec. 281).
4. The right to strike is broadened to "non-essential" public services (arts. 403, 404, 406). The prohibition against general and sympathy strikes is eliminated.
5. Legal strikes require assent of 51 percent of the workforce (art. 407), certification that arbitration has been attempted, notification of intent to the labor secretary, and a ten-day waiting period. Without these steps, employers can dismiss striking workers and participating unions may be decertified.[a]
6. Special labor courts are mandated to speed up dispute resolution. These contain *vocales* selected from employer/worker nominees (art. 467) who serve first as conciliators, then as arbiters (art. 480).
7. Refusal to bargain is an "unfair labor practice" (art. 333) sanctioned by a fine of seven to twelve times the bimonthly minimum wage (arts. 720, 721).

[a]The union must submit a written intent to the labor secretary that the strike concerns economic issues and conciliation has failed. The secretary notifies the employer within two days, and another eight days must elapse before the strike. Police can protect workers. But courts can order workers back to work after four days. While illegal strikes void contracts, simple procedural violations allow workers 24 hours to return to work (art. 412).

additional provisions in table 10.2). The labor code of May 1992 offered extensive improvements in worker rights. Free-zone businesspeople protested, but the AFL-CIO's "recourse to GSP procedures was an important contribution" in obtaining a pact agreed to by zone businessmen, the ILO, and labor leaders (*Bulletin*, November 1992).

In the AFL-CIO's view, however, the government failed to back up code provisions: "With participation from the ILO, we were able to get the labor code reformed," noted David Jessup, AIFLD human-rights director. "Language gave union leaders protection and restrained arbitrary firings. However, these changes were not enforced." For example, in June 1992 companies fired several hundred workers for union activity in the Santiago and Bonao EPZs. Employers claimed they were just making routine cutbacks.[21]

However, the labor secretary charged several firms with labor-code violations. ADOZONA, comprised of zone businesses, vehemently attacked the labor secretary for partiality in disputes, for providing legal advice to unions, and for attempting to destroy EPZ companies. However, Balaguer backed his secretary, and the unions remained firm, coordinating their positions and salary negotiations with the ILO. Faced with united government-labor resolve, on September 26, 1992, ADOZONA signed an accord with all labor unions.

While they accepted a six-month ban on wage increases and a thirty-month ban on strikes and lockouts, ADOZONA agreed to respect the labor code and the ILO Convention on Freedom of Association.

ADOZONA couldn't get its members' approval, unless the wage ban was extended to December 1993. The firms refused to ratify the pact, accusing the labor minister of accepting AFL-CIO payoffs to "destroy the free zones" (*Bulletin,* November 1993). They "accused unions with ties to U.S. labor groups of aiding alleged foreign conspiracies to damage or destroy export-based Dominican industries in an effort to prevent job flight from the U.S." (FLT 93-31:5). Dominican trade unions summarily rejected ADOZONA's retracting tirade.

Despite the failed accord, under the new code the revised labor-court system embarked in January 1993, just in time to witness augmented conflicts in the zones. Employers countered unionization attempts and strikes over wage increases with mass firings and intimidating blacklists. In the face of lukewarm government interference, management crushed organizing efforts at GTE, General Electric, Hanes, Baxter Health Care, and Abbott Laboratories. At Best Form, women workers were "strip-searched for the enjoyment of management. At Carter-Galvis, which produces clothing for Gitano, married women applying for a job must submit proof of sterilization" (NLC 1993:37). Workers at an American Airline data-processing subsidiary that had transferred from Oklahoma to the San Isidro free zone also lost out in their efforts to unionize.

The Second Petition

In 1993, with much support, the AFL-CIO officially filed[22] and USTR agreed to review the Dominican Republic's trade status. The federation argued that virtually all of the ninety-nine new unions registered in free zones were in name only: There were no elections or officers to conduct activities. Managers fired workers with impunity. In the La Vega and Bonao free zones, employees (many of them women) consistently described low wages, compulsory overtime without pay, children working, and reprisals for registering their complaints. Its principal reasons for filing were the government's failure to carry out the labor code and its inefficient and corrupt justice system. Even the new courts were not functioning to handle labor cases.[23] While the Labor Ministry had cited 222 companies for code violations, the courts made no effort at enforcement (for example, one court refused to admit in evidence a compilation of blacklisted workers on a company's letterhead).[24] Over a four-month period, the government had not acted on any of the forty-seven cases that the minister of labor had targeted for action, including eighteen incidents in free zones.

The petition cited as examples of court treatment:

1. union members fired for union activities who had been unable to gain reinstatement because the court did not find any protections in the law (Candelaria, Karon, Ambar);
2. cases lost because of court negligence (Industrias Rayan, So Investments, Importacions);
3. cases lost because of company pressure and bribery (FAB, On-Time Caribe);
4. delayed decisions (Bibong, H&J, Cari Flo).

Given this pattern, it was it was understandable why no unions existed among the 450 firms in the zones. Even when the court did find in the workers favor, businesses faced no consequence. Illustrative was Bibong, which fired seven union leaders in July 1992. The company abrogated a signed contract and refused to pay fines levied by the court or to rehire workers.[25]

The Dominican government responded that the petition was not based on substantial new information but rather that the new labor code was not being effectively applied. "You asked for a law, which we passed," it argued in essence. "Now you are asking for compliance, which takes time to accomplish."[26]

The AFL-CIO acknowledged that the Dominican had reformed the labor code in May 1992. However, after more than a year the government had not issued any enforcing regulations. The Ministry of Labor acted forcefully but had no enforcement power. The justice system as a whole was in a virtual state of collapse because of corruption and influence peddling.

"Does this mean new reforms are still needed to meet the requirements of GSP legislation?" asked federation spokesperson Rudy Oswald with a note of sarcasm. "Mass firings occur even when union leaders are protected. Before, the explanation was a simple denial of legal recognition. Now when they are under scrutiny, they register unions and fire leaders. Yes, it is easy to register a union, but it exists only on paper with leaders fired and members successfully intimidated." Oswald chided the government for touting unions at Westinghouse and Undergarment Fashions, whose members had all been fired, and others suffering similar repression.[27]

The government did not dispute many of the violations referenced in the AFL-CIO petition. For example, it admitted that Importación Apparel employed a blackmail list. Instead, it challenged factual issues on technical grounds, such as a union that filed its case in the wrong court or workers that allegedly failed to notify their employer that they were forming a union!

While the government claimed to work together with business and labor in a tripartite process, business stalled adoption of regulations and thwarted Ministry of Labor negotiation of any arbitration and conciliation pact in the

EPZs. Church-mediated negotiations again broke down in May 1993, when labor unions charged managers with attempting to delay implementation of the code (FLT 93-31:6).

In June 1993, the CNTD brought its complaints about violations in the free zones to President Balaguer directly. It accused the justice system of collusion and the government of indifference. The press openly acknowledged that "repression and the daily abuses of the companies in the free trade areas are known to all. They range from dismissals of the entire officialdom of unions to dismissals of pregnant women" (*El Siglo,* June 18, 1993). Workers at the Bonao zone denounced miserable working conditions and illegal firings of union activists at Bibong Apparel.

Thus, two years after the last GSP review, there still was no progress. The government said the ILO-based code required time to be applied; full implementation would take some years. It urged that the country be found "taking steps" toward this objective. To test the resolve, in November 1993 the CNTD formally requested ADOZONA action on eleven firms cited by the secretary of labor and found guilty of labor violations in court.

USTR's Response

In its investigation USTR determined that the Dominican government had recognized more than fifty EPZ unions since the adoption of its new labor code in June 1992, but fewer than five unions were still operating at the end of 1993. It appeared that their disbanding was connected to alleged anti-union behavior.

Regarding specific labor-rights conditions, while there was a better environment for the right to associate and register unions, the EPZs had experienced an erosion of the right of association. USTR cited findings by the U.S. Department of State that "none of the existing unions in the EPZs has been able to function freely in the work place." Although the 1992 code specified that workers could not be dismissed because of trade-union activities, and specific numbers of union organizers were protected from dismissals by *fuero sindical,*[28] yet "some EPZ companies have a history of discharging workers who attempt to organize unions." On the right to bargain, no union in an EPZ had succeeded in concluding a collective agreement with management (see also Payne 1993). Usually case histories showed the frequent failure of the Dominican judicial system to punish effectively labor-code violators.

The conclusions did not prevent Dominican ambassador to the U.S. Carmen Ariza from urging USTR to lift its review: The labor code, approved in May 1992, represented an historical milestone that had resulted from tripartite dialogue that included ADOZONA.[29] The government also reaffirmed the right of public employees to form associations without interference.[30]

In mid-April 1994, the AFL-CIO met with USTR about the latest findings in the State Department human-rights report. The free zones were now populated by about 160,000 Hispanic women workers laboring in 400 plants. Two-thirds of them were manufacturing apparel for U.S. markets (9,000 workers also produced Timberland shoes). Of the fifty unions formed in Dominican free zones since June 1992, "none was apparently able to function freely in the work place," due largely to employer reprisals. Neither the Dominican government nor the private sector had shown evidence of any unions functioning in free zones—such as through electing officers, engaging in activities without reprisals, or in negotiating contracts when 51 percent of the membership agreed. For the federation, the best indicator of the government's seriousness would be the existence of union contracts: none existed, and the primary reason was the government's refusal to enforce its own labor code or to apply free zone law 8-90, despite its commitments. As the government had acknowledged, ADOZONA could act on own initiative (under 8-90, article 19(f)), yet ADOZONA had taken no steps. Despite the CNTD's complaint in November 1993, eleven firms had disregarded court judgments, and the ADOZONA council had not responded. AIFLD's David Jessup finally told the Dominican ambassador, "If you don't use free zone law 8-90 to pull the export license, GSP will be withdrawn."[31]

The Bibong Case and Government Action

During these months of impasse, union supporters rallied because of court action against Bibong Apparel in the Bonao zone, where workers seeking a union had undergone flagrant violations for more than two years. Managers even resorted to extortion and bribery to force the workers to abandon their legal case. Despite their lawful obligation, ADOZONA did not intervene. This hardly surprised zone employees, since ADOZONA had done nothing to resolve the conflict at Graham Apparel in the Baní zone, where police beat, tear-gassed, and jailed the workers. The employees had carried out a brief work stoppage, protesting below-minimum-wage payments, the withholding of social security payments, and compulsory overtime. When management locked them out, they embarked on a peaceful demonstration. The AFL-CIO believed that government complicity compounded such free-zone violations.[32]

UNITE, which lent organizational and legal support, was nevertheless delighted that "in the Bonao case we got a friendly justice. We could then take the ruling back to the court and demand an embargo so that the company could not sell the machines or close the plant, as they had threatened to do."[33]

Suddenly the government began to take action. First, it cited a manager at Bibong for sexual harassment.[34] Then, on April 26, 1994, ADOZONA suspended the export license of Bibong Apparel, citing free zone law 8-90. Also, ADOZONA signed a tripartite agreement with five of six labor confederations (the CNTD signed soon after). Recognizing the new code as governing, it set up a Tripartite Oversight Commission with a detailed procedure to conduct full mediation in times of confrontation. Where there was no resolution, the commission would refer cases to ADOZONA.[35] Relations at Bibong seemed to improve. The union's secretary general, Aurelia Cruz, and three others were restored to their jobs. Because of the changes, Labor Minister Alburquerque restored the company's license on May 6, and Bibong began negotiating with the union.[36] The Tripartite Oversight Commission went into gear and won settlement of several disputes. Dom Do Sung Textile granted full pay to one worker, reinstatement to four, and 50 percent back wages to two; H.I.J., SA, agreed to make monthly arrearage payments to the Dominican Social Security system to amortize its debt. Caribbean Shoe ceased scofflawing on social security payments. Karina Fashion committed to a stable labor climate and union-dues deductions. Conditions at Graham Apparel remained under investigation, and it was cited for violations of *fuero sindical.*

What broke the impasse was a combination of GSP pressure and a progressive Dominican official. "The AFL-CIO had the advantage of working with a more open labor minister. He was of the opposing party, and was more socially oriented," explained Anthony Freeman, director of the ILO Washington office. "In the government, the ministry was viewed as the voice of social concern, and so had the advantage in improving labor rights."[37]

However, in late June, Ambassador Ariza worriedly approached USTR: once again Bibong was balking, and the minister would investigate.[38] UNITE's Hermanson noted that "the minister called the Korean ambassador. In turn, the ambassador called in Bibong's owner, saying 'write a contract you can live with.' It was our first organizing in the free zones, and very important to get started under the code, since 100 unions had just been eliminated."[39]

USTR's Follow-up

USTR responded to the AFL-CIO's 1993 petition in July 1994.[40] It principally addressed the right to association and organization in the EPZs and the violations cited above. The agency appreciated the government's Fall 1993 invitation to workers to join the review process, which "readily facilitated the recognition of labor unions." Organized labor now represented between 10 and 15 percent of the Dominican labor force.

USTR also found a willingness to enforce law 8-90, which allowed the state to suspend export-production operations for firms in zones violating labor and other laws. In April, the government temporarily withdrew the export license of an apparel firm (Bibong) that had a perilous record of anti-union activity. The suspension, revoked ten days later, resulted in marked improvement. USTR also noted that zone businesses were willing to invite labor representatives to attend council meetings, and it noted the Tripartite Oversight Commission's enforcement progress. Nevertheless, to be certain that these efforts would sustain, USTR voted to continue review for ninety days.

The monitoring period proved important. In the late summer, a Dominican government representative furnished USTR with collective agreements from Bibong Apparel and Caribbean Shoe. The Tripartite Oversight Commission had mediated disputes at Graham, SA; Phil-More Dominicana, SA; and FAB in the La Vega zone. Three more unions had formed in the EPZs,[41] and the Karina Fashions agreement would soon be finished. Dominican labor leaders hailed the agreements, and government spokespersons enthusiastically quoted press accounts that "the Dominican Republic has begun to force U.S. multinational companies, particularly those operating within the country's twenty-five free-trade zones, to allow the formation of unions."[42]

Shortly thereafter, Ambassador Ariza informed USTR that the Dominican Republic had created new laws, new courts, new rights, and new protections, particularly for those engaging in organizing activities. The new courts streamlined procedures via limited jurisdiction (established in early 1993) and implemented regulations (published on October 15, 1993); the Ministry of Labor was aggressively investigating complaints and fining violators. The government and ADOZONA were committed to vigorously enforcing law 8-90 and to take other administrative measures, including the withholding of export visas for textile and apparel shipments where free-zone companies did not honor obligations under domestic law. The Tripartite Oversight Commission, established to mediate disputes, was acting with assistance from the Catholic church. Every Dominican labor confederation had signed an agreement to use the commission, which already had achieved successful mediations and two collective-bargaining agreements.[43]

AFL-CIO Withdraws Petition

In late September 1994, the AFL-CIO's Rudy Oswald happily told USTR of the changes: The labor minister had invoked law 8-90 via ADOZONA. The ten-day suspension had changed a company's treatment of its workers. The government had pledged to both the Dominican union movement and the U.S. government that it would enforce law 8-90 in the future and allow labor representatives to attend meetings of ADOZONA to press complaints and urge actions. Oswald described remaining problems: the failures in handling other companies that illegally fired many union leaders and members in retaliation for forming unions and the slow functioning of the judicial system for workers outside the export sector. Nevertheless, reserving right to reinstate, the

AFL-CIO was withdrawing its petition.[44] "The minister of economy took that famous step of suspending an export license, which helped achieve the first collective bargaining agreement in a free zone," explained David Jessup. "Three or four other contracts have been signed, so we withdrew the petition in 1994."[45]

"We withdrew the petition because we got a contract in the plant, and it was well worth it," exclaimed Hermanson. "We could always refile. But it was so important for us to get the first contract signed as a message to all the workers, as an example to bring all the forces to bear to get one step, to create a new environment."[46]

Aftermath: Longer-Term Effectiveness

While the dramatic events of 1994 showed the short-term success of GSP pressure in the Dominican Republic, there are indications of a more lengthy success. The government took additional steps after petition withdrawal. Denisse (formerly Karina) Fashions signed a bargaining agreement in November 1994. Through mediation, Phil-More Dominicana, SA, agreed to a union. Management and workers heatedly disagreed over several firings, but when ADOZONA threatened suspension of the export permit or quota, "the company signed an agreement" to reinstate and went on to negotiate a collective agreement by December, dropping all charges against three of the four workers.[47] Government statistics listed seventy-five unions and three federations in the EPZs. During the last year, it had taken penal actions against fifty-four enterprises, sentencing fourteen.[48]

Bonahan

While these achievements were significant, for the unions they only represented a first step, a step that would only become effective in combination with on-the-ground organizing to gain negotiated contracts. By the end of 1994, "Nurses had staged a successful strike, but doctors in the public hospitals had a disastrous failure," emphasized Jeff Hermanson of UNITE. A year later, "Most of the seventy-five unions that the ministry claimed in the EPZs were not functioning; their officers were often not even working in the plants. The tripartite system and ADOZONA's enforcement mechanism still existed, but were not operative. They were created in time of crisis because of necessity. It remains a power struggle at every step."[49]

As AIFLD's Jessup admitted, "There was some backsliding in 1995. The labor minister, like labor ministers elsewhere, still had no enforcement mechanisms. Cases died in court. The business community was aware of benefit advantages under CBI, so the unions needed to become more aggressive."[50]

For UNITE, it was the Bonahan case that brought the country another step forward (see Frundt 1998). Bonahan was owned by Hanchang, a Korean company that also had other Central American investments (such as four other apparel plants in the Dominican and El Salvador). Bonahan refused to allow a union.[51] After months of seeking legal redress, the workers finally called the first legal strike in the free zones. It was no mean achievement. Guided by union head Jacobo Ramos and organizer Ignacio Hernandes, a majority voted yes in the presence of a notary. The labor minister then requested postponement, stating the company had agreed to talks. The leaders acquiesced to a day at the table, but "all they did was ask us to give up the strike, so the strike began."

The actual strike stretched over four and a half days. At 10:00 A.M. on Tuesday, November 1, 1995, the workers just stopped working. Management called in the police, accused the leaders of sabotage, and demanded that they be removed. The police then tear-gassed many workers, pushing those who fled back into the plant. Confusion abounded, but at least half of those inside refused to continue working.

On Wednesday, the leaders tried to reenter the plant but the company locked them out, so other workers inside joined them. In the plant nearby, Bibong workers stopped work for five minutes in sympathy. As solidarity strengthened, "by Saturday, the company approached us seeking settlement," said Hermanson. "'You proved your point,' they said, admitting that many of the workers supported the action. We accepted an immediate pay settlement, because we knew that when the 400 workers received checks that day for the days they missed, *they* would know that they had proved their point, and that the company would have to approve their position. It also would send a victory message throughout the zone." The company immediately began bargaining; workers completed the contract by November 30. Management agreed to take back fired workers and to grant important benefits: a 70 percent–subsidized lunchroom; transportation; 35 percent for overtime; lunch provided when working after 7:00 P.M. "This cleared the way for other agreements. Perhaps even some employers realized that it is not the end of the world to have a union in their plants."[52] The Bonahan strike conveyed a reality to labor-code reform and union recognition in the Dominican.

1. As the first legal strike, it moved the expression of worker discontent beyond an irrational explosion of tension to a planned strategy of collective bargaining. It became an important achievement for both law and social behavior.

2. Because it involved one of the largest employers in the Dominican, the success there exhibited union capabilities: "If we can organize this company, we can organize anybody," noted Hermanson. "Unlike

Bibong, it was a major transnational corporation with plants in various countries. It was a top producer of men's apparel—regarded as one of the big players worldwide. It had strong ties to the Korean Investment Association."[53] UNITE's achievement at Bonahan provided it with a solid base from which it could organize other areas.

3. GSP pressure was an important factor in its success. "We combined the treat of GSP with pressure on industry," explained Hermanson. The sourcing vice president from Jones New York, told them, 'we are going to get this settled or we are out of the country.' We also took advantage of ADOZONA's desire for trade parity with NAFTA."[54]

4. But most important, "we had the pressure from the workers themselves, most of them women. As I tell all international support committees, 'no matter how much power you have with these other techniques, if you don't have solid organization at the base, you can't realize the gains.'"[55]

In the mid-1990s, UNITE negotiated several contracts representing thousands of Dominican workers, but it was not sufficient to end the nation's labor turmoil. In 1996, a new president, Leonel Fernández of the PLD, was elected to replace the ailing Balaguer, with great hope for cleaning up corruption and addressing national needs. However, missing in the regime was "the very positive attitude of Labor Minister Albuiqueique." National laws were compatible with ILO conventions, but authorities were not disposed to promote them. Labor inspectors won jobs through patronage and often issued reports favorable to employers. The labor secretary's Mediation Division was non-functioning (CTCA 1996). As costs again rose, many Dominicans took to the streets, ending a five-year period of relative peace.

Conclusion

The petition process in the Dominican Republic substantially differs from that in El Salvador, Guatemala, and Honduras. In those nations, the focus was first to eliminate physical threats and anti-union violence. Labor-code reform and compliance became a follow-up objective. In the Dominican, the first petition arose in the environment of broad national strikes which offered no constructive method of protecting livelihoods; however, it was inspired by mistreatment of Haitian immigrant workers. The issue resonated with the U.S. public's sympathy for agricultural workers within its own borders. To the extent that attention centered on conditions in the cane fields, there was limited alleviation of child- and slave-labor conditions.

The USTR investigation and developments within the Dominican brought a change in focus. While petition pressure generated code reform, publicity of free-zone circumstances, where labor leaders were routinely fired despite the law, drew an emphasis on code implementation. During 1994, the process catalyzed a remarkable tripartite enforcement program that resulted in several functioning free-zone unions. Equally important was that it opened the space for genuine organizing. While the code itself was a victory, GSP pressure was essential for winning the Bibong and Bonahan cases in 1994 and 1995. UNITE moved from a small company, where it had strong support, and a lucky court judgement: "After our first contract in September, we got two more contracts from employers that were not such die-hard resisters, and went on from there." Such a statement illustrates how success on the political level also required pressure at economic and organizational levels: The pressure of workers remained the most important ingredient.

The Dominican standards improved by GSP pressure were primarily in the area of freedom of association and bargaining. The implementation of minimum wages, often a demand of general strikes, became more a consequence of direct union action.[56] Market forces alone generated none of the standards won by Dominican workers, despite a hefty GNP growth in the Dominican economy. Respect for standards was only achieved through organization and pressure at every step. In this sense, the Dominican example represents the most successful application of trade-based labor sanctions in obtaining labor-rights improvement.

CHAPTER 11

Regional GSP Efforts in Costa Rica, Panama, and Nicaragua

Central American labor-union supporters have also filed GSP petitions to review labor-rights conditions in Costa Rica, Panama, and Nicaragua. In the first two cases, pressure from the AFL-CIO sponsored petitions stimulated important, though reluctant improvements in labor legislation. Nicaraguan political conditions make assessment more difficult, but especially after the presidential victory of Violetta Chamorro in 1990, petition strategy complemented popular efforts at assuring labor rights.

Costa Rica

As with Honduras, the filing of a GSP petition on Costa Rica might appear surprising. With its strong democratic tradition, Costa Rica has maintained a reputation of more equitable labor relations. Along with Chile, Costa Rica has also exhibited strong economic growth and one of lowest unemployment rates in the hemisphere. The nation was the earliest Central American country to pass a labor code. In place of labor conflict, its successive political administrations have stressed employer/employee harmony. The union movement covers 15 percent of the labor force, second highest in the region next to Honduras. As of 1995, Costa Rica had registered 420 unions, with 180,000 members (FLT 95-21:3), and was especially vibrant in the public sector. Nevertheless, in Costa Rica more than anywhere else, unions must compete with employer-controlled *solidarista* associations that have now surpassed unions to enroll a claimed 20 percent of the workforce. *Solidaristas* have often done this with state encouragement by extracting the loyalty of former union members. The trend accelerated during the 1980s, precipitating labor-supported GSP resolutions in 1991 and 1993 to force relevant changes in Costa Rican labor law.[1]

Evolution of Labor Rights in Costa Rica

Costa Rica has a lengthy history of respecting certain worker groups, beginning with its recognition of miner guilds in 1830. It established laws for professional guilds in 1857, and for other mutual aid societies soon thereafter. At the turn of the century, influenced by the papal encyclical letter "Rerum Novarum," the local Catholic hierarchy supported rights for all unions. However, the government remained cool to the idea until its tacit acceptance of the right to strike in 1920. Two decades later, a church/communist party alliance helped usher in a progressive government and social security legislation (see Booth 1987:219–21). In 1943, the government passed the nation's first labor code, which guaranteed any twenty workers the right to organize. When unions held a third of all employees, bargaining was required. Even without a union, "permanent worker committees" could develop grievance procedures (employers would later misuse this clause to form *solidarista* associations that they controlled). The code also set up a system of labor courts. It granted the right to strike, but with stringent conditions.[2]

However, the 1943 code offered union activists few protections from reprisals, which only came into force after 60 percent of a company's workers signed a *pliego de peticiones,* or list of grievances. Even at that, workers were only protected until disputes were resolved. Managers routinely pressured workers to remove their names until they could undercut the 60 percent requirement and fire the "troublemakers." Three code articles permitted terminations. Article 81 listed twelve valid reasons for immediate dismissal (such as not "abiding by the responsibilities imposed by the work contract"). Should that fail, article 85 also presented the "will of employer" as justifying termination. Finally, businesses could cite article 28, which allowed immediate firing without any cause at all.

In 1949, constitutional revisions specified work hours, overtime, vacations, protections for women and minors, and compensation for being fired, somewhat modifying the labor code's restrictive measures. The civil code also prevented arbitrary dismissals in the public sector (broadly interpreted to include banking and telecommunications). Public unions grew adept at winning *laudos,* or favorable juridical decisions in contract disputes. Union fragmentation in the 1950s and 1960s jeopardized implementation of these accomplishments. By 1970, labor had achieved only four contracts. But labor reactions unified in 1978 when the government denied public employees the right to collective bargaining. Persistent barriers against the right to strike and lack of protections for union organizers caused unions and public associations to coalesce around labor-code reform in the early 1980s.

Economic Downturn

In 1980, declines in trade coupled with overly ambitious government expenditures precipitated a dramatic change in the Costa Rican economy (see tables 4.6 and 4.8). However, by 1982, the government had taken early action to stem its high inflation (81 percent), devaluing the colon by over 200 percent. In 1983, in consultation with unions and business, it shifted the cost of this adjustment to its middle sectors, not the poor (García-Huidobro 1990). One manifestation was its policy on minimum wages. Real minimum wages increased over the decade by 20 percent. Clerical wages also rose, but industrial and government wages remained flat. Urban unemployment declined from a high of nearly 10 percent in 1982 to just over 5 percent in 1990 (and to 4 percent in 1992–93), one of the lowest rates in the hemisphere.[3] During the last half of the 1980s, Costa Rica's GNP generally increased, aided by an infusion of U.S. funds to support insurgency attacks against Nicaragua.[4] Both economic and political stability seemed assured, and by 1992 foreign investment grew to nearly four times its value in 1983, especially in non-traditional exports, clothing, and sporting goods.[5] There was a commensurate decline in sub-employment. The poverty rate also dropped over the period from 35 to 27 percent.

Economists have bestowed kudos on Costa Rica for its forthright, equitable, and balanced handling of wages during the 1980s economic crisis (García Huidobro and Infante 1992). In 1986, the government revised its wage guidelines, pegging increases to biannual calculations of the consumer price index (CPI). Government-mandated wage increases, social security benefits, and medical care softened union antagonisms. Even though Costa Rica was less directly affected by the regional wars, economic conditions were anything but rosy. By removing wage questions from collective bargaining, the state weakened the unions, yet still manipulated CPI calculations to its advantage. Despite clerical wage hikes, women, who represented close to 30 percent of the workforce, felt the brunt of low salaries, little child care, and higher unemployment. The Interamerican Institute for Agricultural Cooperation estimated that in 1988, 58.5 percent of rural women workers earned less than minimum wage (FLT 90-33:5). Following the 1990 Law to Promote the Social Equality of Women, women's wages in the private sector actually fell (see Gindling and Crummett 1995; Gindling and Terrell 1995).

The Growth of Solidarismo

Begun in 1949, *solidarista* associations expanded rapidly during the 1970s and 1980s, by promising employees financial incentives in exchange for their commitment not to strike.[6] In one telling example in 1987, a *solidarista* association sponsored by the Pope John XXIII Social School successfully outflanked one of the most radical unions, the militant communist Atlantic coast banana workers. The Social School applied the law to its advantage, since a *solidarista* required only five members to gain association status. It also employed the *arreglo directo* legal mechanism to form a "permanent committee" between association and employer. Workers who joined surrendered committee independence. U.S. companies quickly switched to *solidarista* associations, while unions and most Catholic clergy criticized the device as "selling out the workers' interests."[7]

In 1989, one *solidarista* association (Tres Rios Textiles) did seek independence. When management would not approve their elected representatives, they went out on strike, also claiming that a manager was embezzling their funds. When the workers demanded free elections, the company fired 200 of them. The subsequent publicity forced other *solidarista* proponents to admit certain management abuses, and improper use of funds. In Limón (a traditional stronghold hostile to *solidarista*) in 1989, workers struck for a union "program" that raised pay, increased pensions, funded schools and health services, and ended forcible squatter evictions.

Early "Petitioning" on Worker Rights

As the *solidarista* movement grew in the 1980s, Costa Rican unions called upon international forums and ILO instruments to highlight labor-rights abuses. In 1984, unions claimed that a government-IMF agreement violated ILO conventions 87, 98, and 11 (the Right of Association in Agriculture). The proposed legislation not only promoted *solidarista* associations, it removed public-sector collective bargaining from the jurisdiction of the labor court, froze wages without discussion, and tacitly accepted worker blacklists. The ILO urged Costa Rica to respect its obligations: "A State cannot use the argument that other commitments and agreements can justify the non-application of ratified Conventions" (Plant 1994:47). But the damage had been done. Between 1981 and 1987, union contracts dropped from an annual average of forty-two to twenty-two while *solidaristas* rose from thirteen to forty-seven (CEPAS 1988). The following year, the International Confederation of Free Trade Unions (ICFTU) again complained to the ILO about union persecution and the misuse of *solidarista* associations in Costa Rica.

In response to ILO investigations, in 1989, the nation's labor unions and its government signed the "Regulation on Union Freedom" to remove restrictions on public-sector organizing and to protect union organizers from reprisals. The state promised to create a National Inspection Board that would investigate the firing of labor leaders. However, the private sector and *solidarista* associations labeled the agreement an attack on free enterprise and a boon to communist unions. So strident was their opposition that they forced the Arias government to withdraw its commitment. Nevertheless, in 1990, the ILO Committee on Freedom of Association determined that the decline of trade unions in Costa Rica was linked to *Solidarismo,* which could engage in profitable financial schemes while unions could not. It also reaffirmed that workers were threatened with termination if they did not leave unions and join *solidaristas.*

However, the *Solidarismo* movement persisted in opposing legislation that would allow unions to compete with their own credit associations. While skilful public-sector unions still won favorable *laudos* in court and prevented wholesale dismissals during government privatization efforts,[8] the *Solidarismo* movement expanded, and union organizing became increasingly difficult. The Labor Inspector confirmed to visiting U.S. unionists that the effort to gain new affiliates and seek contracts was foolhardy, since "there are no effective sanctions to prohibit reprisals by employers against workers for trying to form unions."[9] For example, the usual fine for labor-code infractions ranged from 20 to 1,000 colones ($.15 to $8.00), the original penalty imposed in 1943.

An illustrative example: that on the day following their triumph at receiving union recognition in 1989, workers at Aurind, SA, were all fired without any recourse. That same year, others in relatively strong unions suffered arbitrary dismissals including five from the Standard Fruit Company union, SITAGAH. Over the next two years, workers received pink slips without stated reason at Empresa Talmana, SA; Peters Corporación, SA (coffee mills); Empresa Partisand, SA (shoes); and Corporación Rojas Cortes (agriculture). Companía Bananera Agropecuaria Rio Jimenez fired twenty. Industrias Realtex, a Korean clothing company, fired all who attended a union assembly. In 1991, the Ministry of Labor surveyed twenty-eight businesses and identified 194 labor-code violations but could do little about any of them. In May, the vice minister was pained to acknowledge, "It's absolutely impossible to form a union in the private sector."[10]

The GSP Threat

In June 1991, in stronger language, the ILO asked the government to implement legislation guaranteeing union rights. It stressed that article 2 of ILO convention 98 demanded authentic independence of worker associations. In Costa Rica, management's use of *solidarista* associations for collective bargaining violated this article. Employers still intimidated workers into leaving unions.

In support, the AFL-CIO threatened to file a GSP petition to protect the right to organize, to improve the labor code, and to eliminate the special advantages given to *solidarista* associations. "The government went wild," said AIFLD director of organization David Jessup. "They pledged to ratify twelve more ILO conventions, and to protect legally the rights of the public sector unions to bargain." Costa Rican president Calderon immediately promised both the ILO and the AFL-CIO that it would bolster union protections and establish a tripartite Superior Labor Council to review Costa Rica's fifty-year-old labor code. The government guaranteed that thirty ILO conventions would be submitted to the legislature by December 1991, including a commitment to the collective bargaining for government employees. The Labor Ministry was not to recognize any direct (that is, *solidarista*) agreements in companies where unions were negotiating. The government even submitted supporting legislation to prohibit them entirely. "It was," concluded the embassy, "a clear victory for trade unionists" (FLT 92-15:7).

However, by October 1992 no victory laurels appeared. The promised legislation never made it to the Assembly. Instead, President Calderon convened a labor summit "to develop proposals on union rights and bargaining in public sector." While he again agreed to protect trade-union freedom, he took no concrete action to implement ILO conventions 87 and 98. Some found his backtracking consistent with the underside of Costa Rican resistance to trade-union action: Over a fifty-year period, only twenty-two out of 552 strikes met the necessary legal requirements to win official approval.[11]

In January 1993, the newly formed Confederación de Trabajadores de Rerum Novarum filed a grievance with the ILO about non-compliance. It then joined with AIFLD and the AFL-CIO to file a GSP resolution.[12] The federation had also consulted with the Asociación Nacional de Empleados Públicos (ANEP) and the Federación de Trabajadores de Limón in designing the request. Getting wind of the actions, in March the government finally issued a regulation prohibiting managers of *solidarista* associations from engaging in collective bargaining. The rule had minimal effect: the Labor Ministry registered an increase in direct agreements with non-unionized companies.

When the GSP petition went to USTR in June, the federation argued that Costa Rica's record was "marred by violations both in law and practice. . . . There are few collective bargaining agreements, and there are virtually no unions in the country's six free trade zones." Unionization rate of the private sector had dropped to 5 percent. The AFL-CIO petition also listed many workers fired for labor activism (*Bulletin*, July–August 1993). "Leaders are not killed as in Guatemala," said the federation, "but they are routinely fired and blacklisted, and unprotected under Costa Rican law" (*Bulletin*, October 1993). The petition reviewed extensive violations in the maquila sector documented by Costa Rica's Ministry of Labor. It also asked that new legislation narrow the definition of "public sector" and abolish articles 333 and 334 regarding criminal penalties for any workers organizing strikes. Lacking such changes, the petition called for GSP termination, with consequential tariff hikes of $327 million on Costa Rica's exports to the U.S. Products affected would include fish, flowers, seeds and plants, paper and wood products, pottery and china, and electrical and mechanical parts.

Between the petition's filing in June 1993 and USTR's acceptance of its review in October, the business sector vehemently and repeatedly denounced the filing as a violation of national sovereignty driven by protectionist impulses from abroad (FLT 93-43:4). "In Costa Rica, they went ballistic when we filed," AIFLD's Mike Donovan acknowledged. Businesspeople called trade unionists "traitors," forcing labor leaders to adopt a low profile, and let friendly congressional spokespersons represent their concerns. "They have a strange situation," Donovan explained. Since workers can easily lose their jobs, "unions are [effectively] illegal in the private sector, but bargaining is legal; they are legal in the public sector, but unions can't bargain."[13]

Government Response

However, the government finally grew serious. In June 1993, the Costa Rican legislature repealed sections 333 and 334 of the penal code that had mandated fines and jailing for striking public-sector workers (effectively eliminating work-action penalties for the bulk of the unionized workforce). After extensive internal debate, the state appointed a commission to seek ratification of ILO conventions and control of *solidarista* associations.[14] When USTR accepted the petition for review, President Calderon immediately sent a labor-reform package to the National Assembly. In parallel, the Supreme Court ruled that the guaranteed right to freely organize had existed since Costa Rica ratified ILO convention 87 in 1976!

The Assembly then approved the labor-code reforms listed in table 11.1. It also ratified certain ILO conventions. On November 8, 1993, the state and three main unions signed an agreement clarifying the implementation of the reforms.[15] The government promised that union leaders could not be fired for advocating collective actions, and in any case such termination needed a labor court's prior authorization. In another important move to balance conditions for unions and *solidarista* associations, it agreed that employers could not control or influence "permanent worker committees," and unions could manage employee funds. It also committed itself to pass additional laws securing rights for public-sector workers, empowering new labor inspectors, and ratifying thirteen additional ILO conventions. President Calderon urged a law that would require employers to fund universal severance accounts for workers, and minimized his rhetoric on privatizing state enterprises. The AFL-CIO then withdrew its petition, "reserving the right to reinstate . . . if the above expectations are not met." In December 1993, USTR terminated its review.

Table 11.1. Key 1993 labor code reforms in Costa Rica

1. Prohibits all actions that impede the free exercise of collective rights, such as an employer dismissing workers who try to organize or join a union (art. 364).
2. Equalizes at twelve the number of persons required to form either a trade union or a *solidarista* association; prohibits *solidarista* associations from bargaining, or impeding labor unions in any other manner.
3. Unions can bargain when 33 percent of the workforce agrees.
4. Tightens enforcement procedures and increases fines against employers who violate code provisions; designates the funds for improving Ministry of Labor enforcement, especially of minimum wages in EPZs.
5. Workers have the right to strike, although the process is severely cumbersome and public-sector strikes remain disallowed. Sixty percent of the workforce must vote in favor, after an unsuccessful court conciliation. The court proposes a settlement, with a twenty-day waiting period. If that does not work, it creates a Conciliation Tribunal, which effectively has sixteen more days to effect a settlement. In the meantime, employers may ask the court to declare the proposed strike illegal. Solidarity strikes are not permitted. Articles 375 and 376 deny the right to public employees, agricultural workers, transport workers, and any workers that cause grave damage to the economy.

Petition's Aftermath

Achieving a reformed labor code in Costa Rica represented an important example of GSP pressure. Such pressure may have contributed to the defections from *solidarista* associations, especially on the Atlantic coast. By 1995 however, business attitudes remained unchanged. The private sector threatened a lawsuit to prevent implementation of the November 8, 1993, government-union agreement. The Labor Ministry's lack of resources and manpower diminished its ability to enforce the new law (FLT 94-43:7). The government also had not accomplished ratifying the additional ILO conventions as promised. The labor code still included the prohibition against strikes by public employees.

According to David Jessup of AIFLD, "Costa Rica did not honor its promises," despite President Calderon's commitment "on two occasions to take all these steps. The unions asked us to withdraw the petition, and we did so. But the government didn't follow up. The Labor Minister said, 'I believe in the rule of law, but frankly, the employers are too strong.'"[16]

From the AFL-CIO's point of view, and the U.S. Embassy in Costa Rica, the opening created by subsequent change in labor code was not exploited, and business attitudes remained unmoved; contrary to the law, union activists were still routinely dismissed. "We thought we had an agreement to end the discrepancies," emphasized Michael Donovan. "But people think they can get away with a lot because of our government's waffling."[17]

Table 11.2. Actual practice of the 1993 Costa Rica labor code

---

1. Forming a private sector union is "virtually impossible." Employers take vigorous measures to prevent their workers from organizing, and activists get buffeted by contradictory juridical procedures (CTCA 1996).[a]
2. Employers can challenge union representation by substituting *arreglos directos* via a complex strategy. They also "reorganize" by transferring workers to non-union portions of the firm, and then claim that union percentage requirements not met.[b]
3. Employers often refuse to negotiate, or even to attend sessions at the Labor Ministry that already "is taking no steps . . . for gaining the right to bargain collectively" (CTCA 1996). The ministry cannot compel bargaining. Since trade unions have limited legal standing to request compliance, they then face an exceedingly slow court appeal.
4. The right to strike does not function even in the private sector (see table 11.1, no. 5). The initial conciliation often lasts many months, diminishing worker energy; strikers are often fired.

---

[a]For example, the Constitutional Court claims that union protections (*fuero sindical*) should be dealt with administratively, while the Ministry of Labor claims it can only determine facts, not sanctions, so organizers remain unprotected.

[b]Technically, employers can only sign *arreglos directos* when no union exists, and then they need agreement from 60 percent of the workforce. However, employers file with much less, since unions are then required to show 51 percent of the membership, not 33 percent. The complexity of proof and the Labor Ministry's "dubious" verification procedure often leaves the *arreglo* in place (CTCA 1996).

In 1994, Costa Rica installed a new president. The U.S. embassy labeled many union members as "enthusiastic PLN [Partido de Liberación Nacional] supporters" who "expect the (incoming) Figueres Government to view labor's agenda in a more sympathetic light" (FLT 94-43). Figueres reconstituted the tripartite Superior Labor Council to reduce tensions and increased the minimum wage by 18 percent. To maintain economic reforms, Figueres made a pact with the outgoing Calderon administration that effectively reduced labor benefits, creating a large union opposition.

The ILO Committee welcomed "the considerable progress which has been made" in Costa Rica's honoring of convention 87, the freedom to organize (ILO 1995a:C87). The revised labor code only permitted employers to fire union leaders for just cause as established by a labor court. Advocacy of collective action was not a legitimate cause. New legislation on *solidarista* associations prohibited employers from controlling "permanent worker committees" or the use of "direct accords." Unions were free to manage funds to benefit workers (ILO Committee of Experts, cited in FLT 95-21:4). The ILO also insisted on the right of unions to administer compensation funds for dismissed workers. However, only eight of the thirteen ILO conventions that the government agreed to in 1993 were submitted to the legislature, and in February 1995, even these were withdrawn and referred to the Superior Labor Council for tripartite discussions.[18] A law guaranteeing collective bargaining and the right to strike in the public sector promised by March 1994 had yet to be enacted by 1998. Costa Rica had been unable to restrict the number of services it defined as essential and to eliminate other restrictions in labor-code section 369 preventing public and agricultural strikes. Despite commitments, the Labor Ministry had also been hit with large cuts in its budget. Forces in the government and business had undermined many of the code reforms, replacing accomplishments of table 11.1 with practices of table 11.2.

In 1995–96, the segment of the private-sector workforce that was unionized dropped to nearly 2 percent (FLT 95-21:5). While some unions threatened to join the AFL-CIO in supporting a reactivated GSP petition, the public-sector unions, led by education and health workers, turned their attention to the threat of large-scale workforce reductions. By 1997, only two unions existed in the EPZs (the Union of Workers of the Paperboard and Allied Products Industry and National Association of Private Industry Workers). Verbal mistreatment, physical abuse, and sexual harassment were commonplace. Salaries remained below minimum wage, with no payment for overtime and routine violations of minimum-age and health and safety rules. Fines were absurdly low (CTCA 1996).

Such an outcome presents a sobering picture of GSP action. It invites reflection on how local class interests can reverse commitments when trade sanctions are no longer perceived as a threat. Nevertheless, the regression did not eliminate the substantial accomplishment of code reform and union-*solidarista* equalization.

Panama

Unlike cases heretofore considered, Panama already had a forceful labor code. In eliciting GSP to aid its defense, the Panama case offers a telling counterpoint to the others in this study.[19]

While Panama had achieved limited labor rights in the 1940s, these rights expanded during the 1970s, under the presidency of Omar Torrijos. Strong unions persisted into the 1980s. By early 1987, the nation's 262 unions represented 14.9 percent of the workforce and enjoyed many protections. In 1989, however, the U.S. military invaded Panama and forcefully removed General Manuel Noriega from power. It installed the business-dominated Endara government, which officially restricted labor-code enforcement to attract investment. In 1992, despite significant neo-liberal, anti-union sentiment within the U.S. Embassy, the AFL-CIO petitioned USTR to review Panama's recently imposed code restrictions. The story thereby also amply illustrates the divided positions among U.S. policy makers on the labor-standards question.

Labor Rights History

In the half-century before World War II, the Panamanian government curtailed most union activities, ostensibly to stimulate the nation's industrialization. After the war, interest in social legislation increased, and organized labor gained a voice. A Social Security law, first passed in 1943, expanded to offer medical services, worker compensation, and a generous retirement clause to nearly two-thirds of the population (62 percent). The latter took effect at age fifty-five for men and fifty for women. The Panama constitution also required equal pay without gender distinction. In 1946, women unionists supported passage of the nation's first labor code, which included maternity protections. In 1950, a joint union and barrio association protest won price and rent controls; a second in 1959 gained minimum salary scales.

When General Omar Torrijos assumed power in 1968 he supported various trade-union federations (not just the AIFLD-backed Confederation of Workers, to the chagrin of the U.S.).[20] He established a Labor Ministry, and in 1972 devised a new labor code. The code guaranteed collective bargaining, flexibility in declaring strikes, a system of union dues, and job stability after two years' employment. The Panamanian constitution added more specifications for equal pay and mandated twelve weeks maternity leave. While public sector workers could not form unions, they could create their own associations. Torrijos came to depend on unions as a barometer of the success of his policies (Greene 1984). By 1977, collective agreements had jumped from 30 to 800 (Phillipps 1987:581). But in the late 1970s and early 1980s, labor had a more difficult time. The economic downturn brought rising unemployment (to 17 percent [USAID]). The government also eliminated certain labor code protections in 1976 and 1981 (see Phillipps 1991).

Panama and Labor in the Early 1980s

Historically, Panama's economy has operated somewhat separately from the other Central American nations. The nation did not participate in regional trading agreements, in part because of its ties to the U.S. and the Canal Zone.[21] During much of the 1980s, Panama's economy experienced modest growth as it successfully used state controls over prices and export earnings.

In the early 1980s union elections in Panama were, in the words of the U.S. Department of Labor, "democratic, fair, and free from government interference." The government had institutionalized policy consultations on employment issues, "through a national commission representative of major labor organizations." In the U.S. Labor Department's judgment, the nation's constitution guaranteed the rights to bargain collectively and strike, although these rights were forbidden "for a great number of workers." Nevertheless, union pressure was forcing the reemergence of labor-relations law.[22] In 1981, Law 8a amended the labor code and restored some of the rights suspended in 1976. However, it exempted small businesses, farms, and plants processing raw materials for export from job security requirements. In addition, government employees and Colon free zone workers still did not have the right to organize or strike. In 1986, the government again amended the labor code. The legislation reaffirmed the right to organize, bargain, and strike. In conformity with the ILO standards, it guaranteed protections for women and children and minimally acceptable conditions of employment and wages. However, labor voiced suspicion about embedded incentives for industry and agribusiness. In response, the government validated seventy-four bargaining contracts, and appointed a tripartite commission to raise wages, which had not been increased in four years.

The Noriega Crisis

However, in mid-1987 the nation's political groupings polarized around the possible ouster of Defense Chief Manuel Noriega, who had accepted payments from both Colombian drug lords and the CIA. To force the issue, U.S. economic sanctions essentially shut down the banking sector, severely retarding the circulation of currency. The crisis paralyzed the state administration, which quickly cut funds allocated to social programs. This precipitated antigovernment demonstrations. Public and private employers retaliated with lockouts. Despite growing instability, Noriega remained as virtual head of state for two more years, as the GDP declined by 20 percent (FLT 91-50:3). Average real wages did not fall until 1990, but inequalities developed earlier (table 4.8). Since its currency is on parity to the dollar, Panama's minimum wage and industrial wages remained in equilibrium. Yet the country's rate of unemployment jumped to 21 percent in 1988, where it more or less remained for three years.

Consequences of U.S. Invasion

Following its invasion of Panama in December 1989 the U.S. installed a market-oriented government favorable to business interests.[23] The new administration gladly accepted a conservative state budget in agreement with World Bank and IMF recommendations. Investors returned, and Panama's economy improved. But in 1992, the nation's GNP fell, and its rate of inflation skyrocketed from virtually zero to over 100 percent. Although Panama's GDP grew by 5.9 percent in 1993, about 44 percent of the population remained below poverty. The dramatic increase in unemployment and underemployment in 1994–

Table 11.3. U.S. Embassy criticisms and labor responses concerning the Panamanian labor code

1. **Difficulty in dismissals.** Employers have to pay severance costs,[a] or provide a just cause acceptable to a labor court. For "permanent" workers who have been employed two years or more, employers *must* establish cause. If not, the employer must reemploy the party or provide a 50 percent premium over the allocated severance, and back pay.

   Employers argue that the severance is too high and court appeals can be lengthy and biased toward workers. Unions retort that the job security provisions exist in the code because there is no other protection in a milieu of high unemployment, and because otherwise union activists would be quickly fired. Contrary to the rhetoric about high penalties, workers win "unjust firing" awards in only 25 percent of the cases. At that, they usually take home less than 2 percent of their salary. What is at stake is that employers do not wish to undergo a third-party review.[b]

2. **High benefit costs.** Employers state vacation costs and health insurance coverage add another 34 percent to salary. Others calculate a lesser amount, and cite the lack of enforcement by the Ministry of Labor.[c]

3. **Workplace inflexibility.** The code governs many task assignments. Even the temporary relocation of employees requires their express consent. The unions see this as protecting members from being shifted far from the capital, etc., to undermine union leadership. On the other hand, the code allows much more flexibility than detractors care to admit. Companies can negotiate clauses reducing many of the severance and work rule restrictions (a point admitted in Gregory and Davila 1993).

4. **Compulsory arbitration,** at union or government request, but not company request. Companies must close during a legal strike, and pay workers. Unions point out that few strikes are declared legal, and loopholes exist to postpone closing, such as demanding a list of strikers.

5. **Other impediments** include high overtime costs (up to 45 percent of base) and the link between pay and productivity.[d]

---

[a]Four weeks' salary for a year, ten weeks' for two years, three additional weeks' per year up to ten years, one additional week per year after that.

[b]Sharon Phillipps, U.S. Department of Labor, interview with author, September 1995. See also Phillipps (1991:147–48), which notes that many employers interviewed repeated the same story of the frivolous worker lawsuit.

[c]The embassy, and Gregory and Davila (1993), include in benefits calculations these additional percentages of base salary: Christmas bonus, 8.3; social security, 10.75; education insurance, 1.5; work-risk insurance, 3.0; vacation, 9.0; retirement (*prima de antiguedad*), 1.9. Phillipps, who has somewhat lower figures, points out that many of these allocations predated the labor code (1991:table 9, 129). All sources agree about the lack of ministry inspections to assure benefits payments.

[d]Employers also had difficulty linking pay to productivity, since incentives had to be locked into permanent pay (unless they were negotiated through bargaining or ministerial agreement). Maquila owners found this difficult in piece work apparel production where product changes demand shifting pay scales. AIFLD's David Jessup acknowledged that the code contained generous provisions for overtime pay for government workers especially. He thought such details were "better left out of codes." Interview with author, May 1995.

95 weakened the union movement (table 4.6). Over the next two years, imposed privatization reduced public sector employment by nearly 14,000 positions. Many families were forced to seek double incomes. While the participation rate of women had increased since the 1950s, it jumped to 37 percent holding official jobs, among the highest in the region.

To make matters worse for unions, late in 1990, the government declared a national economic emergency. To attract investments and improve Panama's global competitive position, it accepted employer arguments that the 1972 labor code was still highly biased in favor of workers, despite its later amendments. So the Endara administration pushed through laws 13 and 16, "temporarily" suspending collective bargaining, and law 25 preventing reinstatement for workers unjustly fired. Law 13 offered new companies a three-year moratorium on the obligation to bargain. The law also extended current contracts for two years beyond their expiration and permitted some contract suspensions.[24] Via law 16, companies in the nation's three free zones (Isla Margarita, Ojo de Agua, Telepuerto) received a four-year holiday from collective bargaining and looser restrictions on layoffs and firings.

The laws had their intended impact. More than fifty companies invoked law 13 and refused to bargain, detrimentally affecting the lives of at least 18,000 unionists.[25] In a mass dismissal of public-sector workers in December 1990, the government invoked law 25. The ILO Freedom of Association Commission soon determined that the law "seriously compromised the ability of public-sector trade organizations to take action" and that legal procedures on dismissals "were not observed."[26] This did not deter the Supreme Court from declaring their validity or modifying union dues check-off procedures. Predictably, between 1987 and 1995, the workforce unionization rate declined from 14.9 percent to 9 percent. While the number of unions remained at about 300 through 1991, they dropped to 284 by 1993 and 257 by 1994.[27]

The labor movement raised a huge outcry at the new legislation. The government retaliated by raising the retirement age for social security.[28] Yet the U.S. Embassy chided that Laws 13, 16, and 25 did not go far enough, given Panama's high cost of benefits ("among the most generous in the world"), and its restrictions on employee dismissals, and worker controls over work shifts and task assignments. An embassy report quoted labor-code article 159 as typical, wherein "it shall be unlawful to reduce the agreed wage by any means, not even with the consent of the workers." The embassy believed such rigidity converted "labor into a fixed cost" and prevented management from responding to market conditions. It urged additional reforms, lest employers turn to "temporary workers" for the bulk of their workforce (table 11.3).[29]

Petition and Response

To Panama's trade-union leadership, the government's espousal of neo-liberal arguments and the U.S. Embassy's bickering over benefits, etc., clouded the nation's basic rejection of international labor standards. When it implemented laws 13 and 16 to suspend collective bargaining and permit the firing of more than 1,000 protesting workers, the Endara administration had directly violated ILO conventions 87 and 98.[30] Thus, in 1991, Panama's largest labor confederation, the CTRP, encouraged the AFL-CIO to petition USTR for a review. Faced with the two new Panamanian laws, which suspended workers' collective bargaining rights for up to four years, USTR could hardly refuse to reconsider Panama's beneficial trade status.

The trade agency's appraisal moved Panama to take several corrective measures in 1992, but this did not alter the law's status. USTR therefore "pended" its review. Because the Federation renewed its threat, and USTR did not terminate consideration, the Endara government suddenly engaged in "a 3-year marathon in union contracts and free zone improvements."[31]

Nevertheless, conditions within Panama deteriorated. In anticipation of Panama's full takeover of the Canal Zone in 1999, the U.S. laid off 6,000 well-paid zone employees. An Endara government plan to absorb them into the export sector did not materialize. Union protests mushroomed into many, mostly illegal strikes. Reviving the battle, the U.S. Embassy persisted in blaming "the restrictive labor code, an issue which labor, allied with protectionist oriented businessmen, has avoided confronting" (FLT 94-24:4).

Business-Government Steps

Unions and progressive businesses replied by forming the Fundación de Trabajo to offer employment services and improve relations.[32] Sufficiently embarrassed, the Endara administration restored full freedom of association and collective bargaining rights to private-sector workers in January 1993, replacing laws 13 and 16 with law 2. Immediately, unions "began renegotiating collective labor agreements that had been postponed. One hundred four . . . were successfully concluded in 1993, as compared with only 15 in 1992" (FLT 94-24:13). The government also promulgated a large minimum-wage hike (one of the largest since 1972). It reduced its monitoring of union affairs and required documents and relaxed biannual record inspections (although it did not amend the offending sections of the labor code). It also corrected a proposed civil service law, reflecting the ILO's criticism of law 25 as effectively preventing public employees from organizing and bargaining collectively. The Labor Ministry recognized fifteen new unions in 1992 and 1993. With these changes, and two of the offending laws rescinded, the AFL-CIO

Table 11.4. Key provisions of the 1995 Panamanian labor code changes

1. Forty may to form a union (one per enterprise). Petitions are recognized in fifteen days; leaders are protected for thirty days (law 44, art. 412).
2. Bargaining is encouraged. The union general assembly must approve demands, signed by each worker (art. 428). Once signed by negotiators, contracts are legally binding.
3. In-plant worker mobility is allowed.
4. Unions can employ three procedures to resolve contract disputes: ministry mediation; a more lengthy ministry interpretation of contract in which the employer is obligated to attend by a third summons (law, August 28, 1975); and a declared violation that can lead to a strike.
5. Unions may strike under article 480, after first exhausting conciliation and a twenty-day grace period (arts. 423–46).[a] Strikes among public-sector and essential service workers (broadly conceived) are excluded.

[a]Conciliation over violations cited by a union's general assembly can take more than a month. A union majority must then vote to strike and give five days' notice. Employers have three days to appeal its legality. If found illegal, workers have twenty-four hours to return.

did not refile its petition, and USTR ended its review. Unions believed they had valiantly resisted most changes to the 1972 labor code.

Renewed Attacks on the Labor Code

However, from 1993 through 1995, businessmen and U.S. Embassy personnel still denounced the labor code as a "major impediment to investment." Their criticisms and the resulting outcome shed additional light on the labor-rights debate.

Code opponents cited the difficulties in dismissing workers, high benefits costs, limitations on workplace flexibility and compulsory arbitration, among other encumbrances (see table 11.3).[33] The U.S. Embassy persisted in reiterating the neo-liberal argument that all such clauses in the labor code harmed the majority of workers. Protections and benefits aided some at the expense of many. They forced Panamanian businesses to avoid the restrictions by hiring on a contract/contingency basis or by investing in more capital-intensive equipment. The embassy cited the World Bank's assertion that without labor-code changes, foreign investors would simply overlook the country (FLT 95-17:7).

Panamanian unions believed much broader economic forces were the determinants of foreign investment, and true restrictions represented a relatively small cost to employers. Despite code protections, the government still refused union recognitions, for example in the Colon free zone and in the banking sector. Public workers also remained excluded and were denied the right to bargain and strike (section 2(2)). Yet without protective clauses, all people (not just unionists) could be subjected to modern forms of servitude.[34] The code brought benefits to a broad spectrum of workers, yet it did not jeopardize Panama's economy.[35]

The Debate in Action

When Ernesto Perez Balladares of the Partido Revolucionario Democrático was elected president in 1994, the U.S. Embassy again predicted no improvements since Balladares had courted the unions and espoused the right to strike (FLT 94-24). The Balladares government even joined the Fundación de Trabajo and passed civil-service law 9, which allowed more unions in the public sector. Yet by the following year, the embassy complimented the government for appreciating the need for structural change that would open the "highly-protected import-substitution economy . . . and reform the skewed labor code" (FLT 95-17:3).

Fearing that Balladares would turn the country into "one giant maquila," Panamanian labor re-invited discussions on code modifications. In Spring 1995, the Fundación de Trabajo, (sometimes called the Comisión Tripartita Laboral) proposed ninety reforms to the labor code that were said to be in compliance with ILO standards. They included a system of limited individual contracts, a fund to compensate workers suffering job loss, and a reduction in the penalty for unjustifiable firing.[36] The government fought very hard to add unilateral job transfers, but labor strongly resisted. In compromise, all sides agreed to accept worker mobility inside the workplace to a position of equal or improved pay if both worker and employer approved, i.e., to functional mobility but not to total mobility. Unions also inserted provisions that would enable them to organize more effectively. For example, they won a reduction in the minimum number of workers needed to form a union from fifty-one to fifteen.

As in El Salvador, the government accepted the package but turned right around and submitted legislation that modified many of the provisions. Forty-nine labor centrals objected, led by the Sindicato Unico de Trabajadores de la Construcción, the Sindicato de Trabajadores de la Bananera Chiriqui (Land Company), and the Central Auténtica de Trabajadores Independientes, all of which opposed all changes from the original agreement. When the National Assembly debated the bill in August, these militant unions led a two-day strike. Workers blocked the streets with burning rubber tires and paralyzed traffic. Police intervened with tear gas. The Assembly was forced to postpone discussion. After a tense week in which at least two people were

Table 11.5. Key points of 1996 Nicaraguan labor code

1. Thirty-five workers can form a union (more than one allowed per enterprise).
2. Unions can be dissolved for political affiliations, for issuing propaganda, for coercion in pressing grievances, or forcing affiliation.
3. Unions may negotiate when they represent a plurality and list all workers who support demands (art. 303). Workers then cannot be fired for participation (art. 324). The labor minister designates a labor judge who creates a Conciliation Committee that sets dates for negotiations in which the ministry participates (arts. 305–6).[a] The committee supervises union ratification of employer proposals (60 percent vote required). The ministry must approve the draft agreement (art. 22).
4. The Labor Ministry can fine employers for contract violations (art. 308).
5. Unions can strike with a 60 percent workforce vote (art. 222 and constitution art. 83); public-service workers and essential service workers cannot (arts. 227–28). The union must present required documents to the Labor Ministry, which sets up another Conciliation Committee, as in no. 3. Workers must be paid during legal strikes, although the committee can keep plants partially open for economic reasons. Even after approval, the ministry can rule a strike illegal on procedural grounds.[b]

[a]The unions were unsuccessful in obtaining fines for employer refusal to negotiate. However, if the employer does not appear, the committee can arrange a strike vote (art. 309).
[b]Prior to strike, unions must list all workers, supporters, demands, and three representatives. The ministry appoints a strike judge who sets up a five-member Conciliation Committee to supervise two five-day periods of negotiation. Employers can appeal results to a Superior Labor Court (CTCA 1996).

killed, dozens wounded, and 300 jailed, the Assembly scheduled a second debate. On August 12, the President offered labor representatives from the Fundación a proposal that protected many but not all union rights (table 11.4). Most unions accepted the agreement as "the best deal we could get."[37]

However, in January 1996, bowing to Taiwanese development interests on the Atlantic Coast, the Balladares government took the further step of excluding free zones from labor laws. This time, Panamanian unions and the AFL-CIO challenged the measure's legality in the courts.[38]

The role of GSP in Panama is idiosyncratic, and the usual circumstances are often reversed: In comparison with conditions faced by other Central American trade unions, Panamanian labor took a much stronger hand in influencing labor law and, to some degree, its enforcement. Because of an effective labor code, unions hold a viable negotiating position in devising policies for economic improvement. On the other hand, businesses have been more cooperative, not only in accepting a labor code, but also in honoring the bargaining process (although not necessarily the contract observance). GSP helped keep this system in place.

The trade sanction story in Panama also exposed tensions over trade policy conditions in the U.S. Contrary to USTR's counsel, and despite solid empirical evidence that code requirements do not inhibit economic development, the U.S. Embassy vociferously attacked code provisions as well as the labor movement. Embassy reports routinely disparaged unions as self-interested "neo-Keynesian . . . favoring continued paternalistic intervention" and as having "watered down to the point of relative ineffectiveness" any viable economic programs (FLT 95-17:6–8). GSP action in Panama revealed profound divisions and anti-union sentiments within the U.S. government and its unabashed efforts to promote a neo-liberal model of political administration. But, ultimately, it protected a labor code under siege.

Nicaragua

Nicaragua was the first Latin American country subjected to GSP petition and review. The intent was primarily political, not social (see chapter 4), which substantially compromised its impact. While objective assessment in Nicaragua is difficult, the interplay between outside pressure and labor-rights observance deserves scrutiny.

When the Sandinistas assumed power in Nicaragua in 1979, they rated labor rights as a primary objective. However, the U.S. government soon declared an unofficial war on Nicaragua as it created and supplied the contra forces throughout the 1980s. From mid-1985 to 1990, it also imposed a full trade embargo. The war and embargo took its toll on union autonomy and on other protective social institutions. Thus, U.S. termination of GSP trade privileges in 1987 brought little additional leverage. Following the Sandinista electoral defeat in 1989, unions mounted major protests, but neo-liberal adjustments gradually eroded worker strength and the state's commitments to labor. As pressure for trade expansion accelerated, international monitors evoked CBI/GSP labor requirements. Nicaraguan unions rejoined, inspired by their legacy in defense of labor rights.

Evolution of Labor Rights

The first U.S. military landing in Nicaragua in 1910 ushered in conservative administrations that stymied liberal reforms similar to those developing in Costa Rica. Yet workers fought against relentless abuse; many, like the striking employees of Braggman Bluff Lumber Company in 1932, joined Sandino's army. One of Anastasio Somoza García's first civil acts, following the entrapment that led to Sandino's murder, was to attack incipient labor organizations. However, as workers persisted in joining the Partido Socialista Nicaraguense (PSN) in the 1940s, Somoza promised legal reforms and recognition to woo cooperation of PSN unions. The dictator promoted a labor code in 1945, based on Mexican law, that replaced collective bargaining with state intervention (Stahler-Sholk 1987:551). With his allegiance to the business class and the U.S. solidified, Somoza reverted to union repression after World War II, appointing government loyalists to relieve PSN union leaders. The state established a social security system in 1957 and set minimum wages in 1962, but did not enforce payments. While the PSN remained important in the construction industry, less than 4 percent of the total workforce remained union members.

Sandinista Accomplishments and Errors

During the 1970s, a revolutionary impetus flourished under an increasing regime of worker abuse and a growing ambiance of discontent (see Walker 1985; Landau 1995; Paige 1997).[39] Guerilla responses began in rural Matagalpa and Segovias, but labor enthusiastically joined the movement in the 1970s as Somoza's national guard accelerated its bloody tactics and the Frente Sandinista de Liberación Nacional (FSLN) broadened its political efforts. The Sandinista victory in 1979 brought openness to labor organizing and bargaining. Union coverage jumped from 11 percent to 40 percent of the work force by 1983, and to 56 percent by 1986. The government revived forgotten provisions of the Nicaraguan constitution that guaranteed the right to organize, bargain, and strike. The Ministry of Labor became pro-active in enforcing articles of the previously ineffective labor code. Nevertheless, the state did pressure unaffiliated urban unions to join the Central Sandinista de Trabajadores (CST), founded as an organizing committee before the Sandinista victory. The army took control of certain factories and jailed resistant union leaders (O'Kane 1995:184). Over the next five years, FSLN-related unions grew to represent more than 85 percent of the country's labor organizations, and subsequent union elections became a major arena of affiliation struggle.[40] In the early 1980s, the opposition AIFLD-funded Confederación de Unificación Sindical (CUS) participated in national labor coordination efforts such as the Coordinadora Sindical de Nicaragua. However, when CUS and others joined the anti-Sandinista "Coordinadora Democrática Nicaraguense," which involved right-wing business and political representatives aligned to the contra forces, the government became more antagonistic toward non-FSLN-related unions.

While the Nicaraguan economy improved after the Sandinista victory in 1979, the U.S.-backed contra war soon exacerbated the economic crisis. A five-year period of stagnant real wages brought early disputes over wage policy. Imposing a ban on strikes between 1981 and 1984, the government argued that its redistribution measures and provision of inexpensive or free education, health care, housing should count as a "social wage." Usually it was able to mediate union disputes and achieve "voluntary labor restraint." Workers praised CST gains in food distribution and day care, and temporarily won back the right to strike during the 1984 election campaign. Independent observers credited Sandinista labor rights policy with enhancing observance in the countryside.[41]

Nevertheless, the opposition unions remained bitter, as expressed in the AFL-CIO–sponsored GSP petition filed against Nicaragua in 1985. The petition cited the government's insistence that all unions belong to one labor central as "a blatant violation of freedom from government control." It spoke of how the Sandinistas had demanded union "elections time and again until the results were to their liking. Unions which refused to affiliate . . . had their leaders arrested and jailed indefinitely, their members harassed and beaten, and their offices attacked and destroyed."[42]

In addition, in February 1985, the government's economic stabilization plan detrimentally affected wages. Seeking a realistic compromise, the National System for Organization of Labor and Salaries convened all centrals to determine workloads and wage norms for occupational groups. By increasing pay scales and canceling price supports, the government hoped to stimulate work incentives. Yet as the war expanded, inflation skyrocketed. Export earnings dropped by nearly half between 1983 and 1988, and for eight consecutive years the GNP declined. Until 1987, Nicaragua's levels of poverty and unemployment were lower than elsewhere in Central America, but in face of unprecedented levels of inflation, the economic difficulties could no longer be postponed. Official unemployment jumped to 25 percent, and salaried workers felt the brunt of accelerating prices.

GSP Petition and ILO Follow-up

Deteriorating economic conditions further polarized the Nicaraguan labor movement. Those opposing the Sandinista government included CUS, which formed the umbrella Congreso Permanente de Trabajadores (CPT) in 1987. CPT took on an overt political role.[43] Most Sandinista unions remained ardent government supporters. Even while they carried out a series of strikes and attacked specific policies, they reaffirmed their solidarity with the revolution that had repelled the odious and repressive Somoza National Guard and given them a stake in their society and workplaces.[44] Some leaders still grew fearful of becoming overly-dependent on the FSLN (O'Kane 1995:185).

By 1987, USTR had reviewed the allegations that all the unions must belong to one government confederation and that real trade-union rights and collective bargaining did not exist. It ruled that "freedom of association has been suspended in Nicaragua and that the Government of Nicaragua has sharply limited the rights of unions to organize and bargain." The trade representative removed Nicaragua from the GSP program effective March 4, 1987.[45]

That same year, the Nicaraguan government passed a new constitution. Article 87 guaranteed workers the right to organize and elect their own representatives. However, the state only allowed one union in any business location. Sandinista managers were still said to threaten workers with demotion or termination if they did not join Sandinista unions. In confrontations following imposition in 1988 of a major austerity policy that devalued currency and liberated prices, police disrupted several CPT affiliate gatherings and hauled off striking workers. Even CST leaders became worried as their FSLN backers lost managerial positions and firings increased.[46]

After complaints from both the CPT and the Consejo de Sector de Empresas Privados (COSEP) in 1989, the ILO sent an investigative mission to examine labor rights violations. It determined that abuses had occurred, but most had been corrected (for example, the Sandinistas had eliminated the one union/one workplace rule by the time the delegation arrived). It agreed that the labor code "was used to establish a system of trade union monopoly" at variance with convention 87. It also stated that Sandinista confiscation of COSEP property had been influenced by their position as employers "strongly opposed to the government," and that employers should not be bypassed in future code reforms.

Chamorro's Election and Labor's Reaction

The election of Violetta Chamorro in 1989 is often explained by the Nicaraguan people's inability to sustain a prolonged war in face of declining living standards and over-arching U.S. power (see Walker 1997). However, aided by a large infusion of U.S. funds, the CPT unions worked strenuously for the Unión Nacional Opositora (UNO) victory.[47] Sandinista unions formed the Frente Nacional de Trabajadores (FNT) to defend themselves. Through trial and error, they learned quickly; their defeat forced them to develop a resource base of their own apart from either state or party. This became the more apparent as the UNO government, with some FSLN support, reduced state expenditures and "liberalized" the economy. Seeking "optimal work conditions" for business, the government invited fresh foreign investment. For example, it eliminated any "closed shop" and decreed an end to union check-off dues which had been so essential in supporting CST activities. The labor minister resisted declaring legal strikes, and he permitted companies to have many unions. After effectively reducing wages for state employees, President Chamorro issued decree 8–90, which temporarily ended collective bargaining in the public sector and permitted unilateral dismissals. The government followed with policies forcing large layoffs in textiles and construction. Unemployment jumped to 53 percent (Stahler-Sholk 1995:88).

First in May, then in July, 1990 the FNT declared a national strike which brought the country to a standstill.[48] It protested the new government's structural adjustment approaches and demanded protective labor-code reforms, minimum-wage improvements, jobs for the unemployed, and participation in the Chamorro administration's plans to privatize state enterprises. Ironically, the CPT articulated similar goals. Since the CPT had approved UNO's economic agenda, however, CPT and FNT unions often conflicted during specific struggles. The FNT still held the majority of union affiliates, but FNT base members became increasingly disaffected, especially in health, education and the hotel industry.

FNT strikes in 1990 resulted in a National 'Concertación' that included participation of COSEP, the Union Nacional de Agricultores y Ganaderos (UNAG) and the CPT. The Chamorro administration committed itself to address wages as indexed to inflation, job security and worker participation in exchange for "social peace." Nevertheless, the government fulfilled none of these promises. Over the following six months as many as 70,000 workers lost their positions (O'Kane 1995:190). Soon the FNT realized that Chamorro was just buying time needed to weaken labor's resolve. It resisted the president's (and FSLN's) "guided adjustments" which included receiving USAID funds for "occupational reconversion." The FNT also informed the ILO that the new government was challenging its collective contracts. In its review, the ILO urged the Chamorro government to "abstain from any acts of coercion or favoritism" and "avoid any acts of discrimination based on ideological grounds" (FLT 93-10:9). Because of ILO and ICFTU criticism, the state backed down on its decision to eliminate union check-off dues and modified certain of its structural adjustments.

In March 1991, after the government's "Plan Lacayo" imposed a currency devaluation that brought high prices, the FNT won an agreement over wage hikes in exchange for a ninety-day labor truce. In July, the National Assembly created a tripartite commission to update minimum wages regularly. In August, another "Concertación" established guidelines for privatizing state enterprises whereby workers could purchase 25 percent of government-held shares. Although they objected to selling state enterprises to workers, COSEP and CPT accepted the general principles.

Battles between FNT and CPT unions and between labor and government persisted—nearly one-hundred strikes over wages, and significant conflicts surrounding enterprise privatizations. Yet as Stahler-Sholk (1995:96) points out, the FNT gradually became convinced that with privatization coming, massive strikes were counterproductive. Instead it sought to maximize worker ownership. For example, the FNT's Asociación de Trabajadores de Campo affiliate requested that certain "Areas of Work Property" be allocated to them from public agricultural enterprises. In September 1993, workers from the key centrals did collaborate in a transport strike called to oppose IMF-advocated hikes in gasoline and vehicle taxes.

Changes in the Labor Code

As a reward to Chamorro's UNO coalition, the Bush administration allowed Nicaragua to join CBI in Fall 1990, reopening preferential access to U.S. markets. As an unintended consequence, CBI requirements on labor rights complemented Nicaraguan union efforts to win improvements in their labor code. In 1991, both UNO and Sandinista parties submitted draft legislation to the National Assembly and a Labor Ministry–sponsored seminar debated provisions over worker-dismissals. The government stressed the need for flexibility and low severance pay, and the workers demanded stronger protections, so talks stalemated.

By 1994, the government had backed away from retaining *any* significant code protections. Forced into a difficult negotiation on loans from the World Bank, the minister of labor proposed to "prohibit strikes in the public sector and in services of collective interest"—however the ministry determined. The proposal gave "priority to individual contracts" over the right to bargain collectively; indeed, it committed itself to "guarantee the cancellation, suspension or termination" of any collective contracts that stood in the way! It eliminated all negotiated benefits such as vacations, health services, transportation etc.; and it guaranteed "that the worker can be freely terminated . . . to promote efficiency in the allocation of resources . . . without any difficulty whatever."[49]

ILRF associates challenged these provisions as the grossest violations of the UN Charters of Human Rights and core international labor rights, including conventions 87, 98, 105, 111, and 138, all of which Nicaragua had signed (see chapters 3 and 4). Giving the Ministry of Labor control over strikes was a classic method "by undemocratic regimes of repressing trade union activity." Asserting the primacy of individual contracts simply reinforced the unequal power individuals already have in attempting "to counterbalance the economic might of the employer. That is why they choose trade union representation. . . . Incentive pay schemes are properly a subject for collective bargaining, not for government fiat."

As ILRF argued, the government's plan to replace benefits with a temporary cash equivalent, made "workers even more vulnerable to currency devaluations, wage-restricting policies and other assaults on their living standards." The ILRF insisted that "flexibilization" and the overriding of labor contracts also would "open the door to a greatly expanded use of child and young teenage labor." Unless Nicaragua (and the World Bank) modified the code proposals, the nation could be subject to trade penalties under CBI.[50]

In the waning months of Chamorro's rule (September 1996), the Nicaraguan National Assembly overwhelmingly adopted a new labor code (table 11.5) that had been under debate for five years. Alba Palacios of the Sandinista Farmworkers Association praised the code for balancing "the interests of private enterprise with worker rights to seniority, social security, collective bargaining and indemnification if they are unjustly dismissed."[51] However, the law did not alter recent ministry practice of failing to deliver notices or send out inspectors, pleading lack of resources. On the other hand, ministry power to set deadlines and approve agreements contravened ILO principles, for example, by allowing employers to drag out negotiations for up to two years. The right to strike remained, but it required concurrence by a Labor Ministry judge after a complex administrative review. Strikes also grew rare because the Labor Ministry or strike conciliation committee could nullify them on either technical or political bases (see table 11.5). Unions still decried "a relationship of corruption and complicity between the Ministry and employers" (CTCA 1996).

Yet, labor was pleased with many aspects of the code. Combined with external pressure, debate over its provisions had brought better conditions in the textile and mining sectors.[52] However, a labor rift had complicated efforts to strengthen the code. In the 1994 Sandinista Party Congress, loyalties of the growing FNT divided in support of Daniel Ortega, who urged labor mobilization to oppose added structural adjustment; and Sergio Ramirez who advocated compromise with the UNO (see Stahler-Sholk 1996b). However, the FNT faced corruption scandals, and eleven of twenty-nine CST federations walked out. The labor division did not help either candidate. In Fall 1996 Nicaraguans voted in right-wing Arnoldo Aleman of the Liberal Alliance who defeated Sandinista leader Daniel Ortega.

Nevertheless, with ILO support, unions from two major confederations agreed to collaborate in supporting mutual struggles in the EPZs. For example, the Las Mercedes zone near the airport hosted nineteen factories, seventeen of them apparel maquilas. It employed more than 10,000 workers. More zones were scheduled for Carazo, Leon, and Masaya. The clothing and textile federation, which remained affiliated with the CST, organized in surrounding neighborhoods, identified leaders and published a newsletter. By May 1997, three more of its unions achieved legal recognition.[53] The Ministry of Labor, which condoned management's anti-union strategies, decertified two of them.[54] In October 1997, an NLC/Hard Copy investigation unearthed repeated sweatshop conditions in Nicaraguan EPZ companies producing for Wal-Mart, Kmart, and J.C. Penney.[55]

Summary

U.S. removal of Nicaragua from GSP benefits may have played a minor part in its destabilization campaign to undermine a nationalist revolution that promised improvements in citizen and worker rights. The U.S. war was the essential factor, even as the Sandinista errors also contributed. Then GSP/CBI's positive prescriptions faced equally insurmountable forces in the global economy. The pro-business requirements of the IMF, the World Bank and the Chamorro government weakened Nicaraguan unions, although GSP/CBI leverage aided their resistance. The neo-liberal Aleman administration further debilitated labor. Unemployment remained high despite union efforts to obtain fresh job programs. General coverage of social security declined, as did union membership. Nevertheless, from another point of view, GSP pressure reinforced the resilience and demands for rights of workers under the Chamorro and Aleman administrations. Even as the vestiges of war still took its toll, they pursued these demands in a more self-reliant and autonomous fashion under conditions of peace .

GSP action in Costa Rica and Panama had diverse objectives: to gain code reform and counter employer unionism (Solidarismo) in Costa Rica and to prevent dismantling of worker protections in Panama. It accomplished both goals. And strangely, what happened in Panama anticipated a similar impact in Nicaragua. The last case began as a political punishment against the Sandinistas; but at least indirectly, it also became a force to protect labor's past accomplishments. Thus, in a world increasingly dominated by neo-liberal ideology, GSP influence gained limited improvements in labor rights in all three countries.

CHAPTER 12

Workers Evaluate Trade-based Labor Strategies

Our evaluation of trade conditionality would not be complete without an appraisal by the workers affected. What is *their* view of GSP? At the plant or field level, many workers remain unaware of foreign trade requirements, as an above-cited survey of El Salvador maquila workers revealed (chapter 6). However, labor leaders and many constituents have made informed judgments about international labor sanctions.[1]

U.S. filers have learned that an effective GSP petition must engage the workers of a particular country. U.S. reviews that did not have strong union support, as in Peru and Columbia, brought weak results. In the countries we examined more intensively, the degree of petition success was generally associated with the strength of local involvement. In nations like Costa Rica and Panama, union participation was largely restricted to a single confederation that supported a petition to achieve a specific policy objective. The outcomes seemed limited. Unions in El Salvador and Guatemala, and to a less extent in Honduras and the Dominican Republic, enmeshed themselves in GSP evaluation and follow-up investigations over a longer time period. Their reactions appeared more enduring. To further test this impression, a sample of leaders representing all major sectors from El Salvador and Guatemala were asked to appraise the following aspects of GSP effectiveness on:[2]

1. the original GSP filing;
2. the impact on labor legislation and rights to organize and bargain;
3. code implementation;
4. impact on non-discrimination;
5. changes in private-sector attitudes and tripartite participation;
6. future trade-sanction efforts and regional cooperation.

While their responses often represent subjective, time-limited impressions, their perceptions remain an essential aspect of trade condition effectiveness, and just as often bridge the gap to objective reality. As Herzenberg (1996) warns, "initiatives which one country imposes over labor rights will only succeed when linked to a broad local movement of workers."

Original GSP Filing

Worker involvement in Central American and Caribbean nations happened despite misgivings and misinformation concerning the purpose of U.S. trade-union delegations coordinated by ILRF, U.S./GLEP, NLC, and the AFL-CIO. Under the guise of nationalism, business leaders strong-armed labor officials, claiming that GSP information gathering was an attempt to prevent jobs from leaving the U.S. They demanded that local labor leaders renounce their involvement. In turn, union members debated the strategic significance of filing a petition with USTR, and whether they should participate.[3] Despite the persistence of business pressure however, members from various federations and confederations eagerly offered testimonies. Vulnerable to reprisals, they recounted their struggles with magnetic heroism.

El Salvador businessmen were especially blatant in claiming that unions cooperating with the GSP process were pawns of North American interests. After several well-publicized cases of labor abuses in the maquila sector (including the woman reported in chapters 1 and 6 who died after being refused medical services because her employee had not submitted the payments deducted from her salary), Salvador's business sector sought a convenient scapegoat in "North American unions arriving to stir up trouble."

Juan Hector Vidal, executive director of ANEP, the more enlightened of that nation's private-sector organizations, typified the business attitude. He objected to "the way U.S. labor unions aligned to our unions manipulate GSP . . . we will not accept factory takeovers as an instrument of negotiation." Vidal cited U.S. labor's purported $10 million war chest "targeting Central America."

Vidal's reaction, as explained by U.S. labor attaché Simon Henshaw, was traceable to El Salvador's nationalism: "If the business class has an opportunity to blame foreigners, they will do so." But the embassy official also believed that some Salvadoran leaders were "pawns of U.S. unions pushing GSP" who sought to employ the sanctions "without really losing benefits, since that would be suicidal."[4]

Vidal and Henshaw's comments illustrate the criticisms of utilizing trade sanctions to leverage worker rights discussed in chapter 3, but El Salvador's labor leaders remained undissuaded. "They complain we are manipulated," commented Carlos Hurtado of the CTD. "Before it was by the FMLN, now it is by North American unions. They always have to have us manipulated by somebody, but say nothing about the problems here in El Salvador."

"The government and business sector claim North American union manipulation" affirmed Miguel Contreras of FESTRAES. "The truth is *they* are not complying with labor-rights standards. They demand extra hours, refuse to pay for medicine and social security benefits and mistreat pregnant women. It was the woman's death at Gabo Industries that mobilized protests from two labor federations, not manipulation by North American unions." "When the employers and leaders charge manipulation, it is our national leaders playing a game," repeated Roger Gutiérrez of FEASIES.[5]

"The recent attacks against us are due to their attempt to shift the focus. They don't want to deal with the working conditions in the maquilas—such as 50 to 60 hour straight time or 'don't come in'; the physical abuse, and firings after worker unions have achieved their *persona juridica*. The Minister of Labor doesn't act, and women in the free zones can't wait the three years for it to go through the courts. Workers can't afford attorneys to support their case. Instead, they attack us." Similar vociferous charges exploded in Costa Rica and Honduras, where they labeled organizers as "traitors to the country land."[6]

Business responses in Guatemala were less acerbic, but the message was similar. According to the local manager of J.C. Penney, local unions were "fomented by U.S. unions with impossible demands—asking for a four-day work week, free meals, etc. It is a strategy to force factories to close and save U.S. jobs."[7] Juan Francisco Alfaro retorted that it was "a lie that the U.S. unions are using this as a ploy simply to protect jobs. We both know Guatemalan factories could never pay $5.00 to $8.00 an hour. What we do want is a 'NAFTA chiquita' with GSP protections and investigations on truth in the workplace." "U.S. unions have a very positive role to play in helping us resolve our problems," noted GUATEL union's Mario Lutini.[8]

GSP Impact on Labor Legislation and Rights to Organize and Bargain

Former U.S. labor attaché to Guatemala Donald Knight thought that "GSP helped focus congressional and union attention to code reform."[9] USAID trade specialist Karen Delaney believed that "GSP was a contributing factor but not the only factor in bringing about changes. Free market forces, i.e., the drive for businesses to be competitive via a better motivated and qualified workforce, was also responsible."[10]

But union leaders emphasized that GSP pressure directly affected code ratification. Enrique Alvarez, then head of the CIEP union leadership academy, thought GSP had "brought the first changes in labor legislation in many years. It has also built bridges between Guatemalan unions and unions in the U.S." Alvarez even believed GSP pressure had encouraged "discussions for peace between the government and the guerrillas."[11] Juan Francisco Alfaro found "GSP pressure useful in helping to improve the labor code, and in set-ting up the tripartite system for ongoing consultations between business, la-bor, and government."[12]

In El Salvador, CTD general secretary Carlos Hurtado felt that GSP gave a push to the Tripartite Forum's efforts to get the labor code discussed. Carlos Luna, secretary of organization of UNTS, also saw it as "a campaign to protect our struggle against neo-liberal economic progress carried out on the backs of our workers. When we were negotiating in the Forum, first the employers did not want to accept a labor code; but because they wanted the trade benefits [which they would lose without GSP status] it got them to deal with the code." Hurtado also believed GSP helped the discussions on health benefits. "For example, they even wanted to stop making contributions to the social security system. But the government and businessmen had a greater fear about losing trade."

GSP pressure had a positive affect on addressing specific maquila viola-tions. "At first EPZs didn't allow union access, and now they do," explained Roger Gutiérrez of FEASIES. However, the union movement didn't "have the knowledge or the coordinating ability to utilize GSP more effectively."

Miguel Ramírez of FESTRAES acknowledged "minimum advances be-cause of foreign pressure. Although the code became a fait accompli without a consensus, business and labor talked about the status of labor rights for the first time. The code also provided for automatic approval of union applica-tions if the government did not respond within thirty days."[13]

Leverage with Specific Negotiations

For Rodolfo Robles, a leader of the Coca-Cola Workers and former head of IUF-Guatemala, GSP was more of a leadership tactic. "The rank and file here don't know much about GSP. They hear the private sector and the Ministry of Labor say that such pressure will cause us to lose jobs. Labor code reform has also had minimal effect."[14] However, Robles was able to use GSP leverage to gain corporate concessions: FRESA, a company with a successful chicken ex-port business, "understood the problem of having exports reduced. Thus in-directly, GSP stimulated FRESA's commitment to labor rights, not just for a small unionized group in Villa Nueva, but for the company as a whole, and the workers all know this." Robles won similar commitments from a shrimp exporter in Chuhuapan, where "the workers earn more now because of GSP pressure. The GSP threat has helped unorganized as well as organized work-ers. In agricultural areas, many companies would otherwise not give any ben-efits at all."[15]

Evoking GSP also worked for Rigoberto Dueñas of the CLAT-related CGTG, who cites it "as important for avoiding the worst, for reducing the massive firings that used to occur and for bringing about the rehirings. With employers, we have successfully argued: 'We can close off your exports to the United States unless you rehire these workers.'"[16]

Suida Alvarez of the CTD in El Salvador spoke of how unionists used GSP to cause "headaches for abusive maquila managers: When an employer hits a woman to improve the quality of her output, she now says 'it will be a bad market for you if you persist in doing this.'"[17]

"As workers, we need a lot of support in convincing the government and business to fulfill the law," stressed Mario Lutini, secretary of organizing of the GUATEL workers. "Prior to GSP pressure, there was no space for organizing. Now, after it has come, there are some possibilities due to making the pressure conditional. Private-sector attitudes also boomerang into the public sector. GSP has prevented massive, unjust firings and moderated the tendency to single out certain workers."[18]

Thus, trade union leaders generally believe that GSP pressure has been important in gaining labor-code reform and bringing employers to the table regarding specific demands. Reynoldo González, labor representative to Guatemala's National Minimum Salary Commission, also found GSP "fundamental" in winning salary improvements.[19]

Implementation

While they viewed GSP impact on legislation and leverage positively, many unionists cautioned that it had little effect on the implementation of labor laws. "GSP did affect the passage of the labor code in Guatemala, as it did in El Salvador," acknowledged USAID official Karen Delaney. "The Guatemalan government then thought GSP pressure would be lifted: 'we passed it, what more do you want.' There were a lot of bad feelings because code passage was sufficient for GSP withdrawal in El Salvador, but not here."[20]

Code implementation severely lagged in most countries, but GSP pressure was sustained in Guatemala due to the coordinated efforts of U.S. and Guatemalan unions, aided by the U.S./Guatemala Labor Education Project. CUSG's Juan Francisco Alfaro persisted in reporting the "many differences" between what the government and companies said and what the law demanded regarding labor inspections, employer compliance, and the legal process.[21] Rigoberto Dueñas cited "some accomplishments, i.e., certain businesses now provide coffee and pure water for their workers. However, near the Roosevelt highway, some maquilas only pay half salary, and half goes to the boss. To avoid unions, they close and reopen somewhere else."[22] "They continually fire their workforces to avoid accepting union petitions," reiterated Mario Lutini of GUATEL. "There is very little compliance with legal requirements, and their greatest violations are directed against women who have children to care for. What GSP has accomplished has been changed views, not compliance."[23]

CIEP attorney Mynor Andrio found no change from GSP pressure: "Yes, we have a new labor code, but it is not well applied, and has not helped the workers. The enforcement of minimum salaries comes only to city workers that are well organized, such as those in the juridical system, the banks and financial services, the labor ministry, the Procuradoria and the University of San Carlos. But for others, the labor code doesn't help: when we present papers, the process is very slow. Also, very few lawyers work for unions—a number fear to do so.[24] GSP proponent Reynoldo González also expressed "doubts that additional reviews will bring changes because they don't want the courts to function and they don't want to pay for them. The Minister of Labor has insufficient funding from the President to be effective."[25]

In El Salvador, despite unilateral passage of the labor code by the government-business coalition, businessmen still disregarded its precepts. In AIFLD's view, code implementation was "practically nonexistent. The Minister of Labor is the last man in any budget; the inspector arrives and gets bribes from the management. The pro-business government carries the baggage from the war. USAID has offered programs in industrial relations to improve the situation. ANEP received funds from the European Community to set up its own industrial relations program. So in some ways the word is out about the need for bettering relations But a lot will depend on the government and private sector's recognition that unions represent the society's workers, and seek a better life for the workers they represent." FESTRAES committeemen agreed, and joined with their old AIFLD antagonists to protest "maquila managers who still act as they wish, hiring children, beating women. We are not opposed to owners, whether from here, North America, China or Taiwan, but we want business investors that respect labor rights."

"I can't say GSP has no effect," sighed Carlos Ochoa, UNTS, "but to take advantage of it requires legal assistance, a full time attorney who works well with union leaders. We have a new project to improve inspections at the regional level. But for this to work, we first need national coverage on labor rights and more effective completion of requirements for union organizations."[26]

Impact on Nondiscrimination

One of the most controverted aspects of labor standards is their effect on the less-protected workers. In choosing targets or mobilizing support, Central American unionists are much less likely to differentiate between the formal and informal sector than their counterparts in Latin America. Most leaders

remain ideologically committed to a class-based approach. Even for pragmatic reasons, their countries cannot afford a labor aristocracy. To forge an
effective movement, they must include a broad range of popular organizations. Since the mid-1980s the *Unidad Acción Sindical y Popular* (UASP)
brought together committees seeking redress for the disappeared, widows
and refugees of violence, and unorganized campesinos protesting price hikes.
UNSITRAGUA responded to community crises, such as squatter groups that
faced eviction when the state threatened to sell railroad lands (see Frundt
1997).

Nevertheless, despite the trade law's implicit references to non-discrimination, unionists were unanimous that the GSP process has usually not conveyed beneficial changes to the more exploited social groups. "Women have
not been helped by code provisions," noted Juan Francisco Alfaro. "Sexual
abuse continues, and the 1992 code provisions for maternity leave, etc., are
disregarded." While GSP pressure stimulated a 1992 union recognition at
Camisas Modernas, the clothing maquila owned by Phillips-Van Heusen
which employed mainly women workers, it did not get the company to negotiate a contract until 1997 (although GSP action remained the motivating
force; see chapter 7).

Some women praise their new employment opportunities as offering them
a chance to escape traditional role expectations. However, a women's project
sponsored by FESTRAS found "little benefit for women, most of whom still
receive less than $1/day in factories." "Women are paid below minimum
wages. Only a few are members of a union," added GUATEL's Lutini. Sergio
Guzman agreed that "the situation of women has not improved. Only in cases
where we have registered complaints [*denunciaciones*] have we occasionally
earned some respect from the Labor Ministry. When women workers do demonstrate, they gain attention, but we have a machismo society, and they are so
few among many thousands of workers."

Adelia del Gado, head of the CIEP women's project, believed that "women
face a difficult situation, with even less attention paid to those in the countryside. Often there is only *one* salary received in the family, and it goes to the
man. Women are also not registered in the statistics for rural workers. In the
cities, 70 percent of those working in the maquila are women, but it is very
difficult for them to gain unions" (see also Green 1997).[27]

Similar conditions faced indigenous workers, despite the resurgence in
Mayan cultural expression in Guatemala and the passage of ILO convention
169 on indigenous rights in Guatemala and El Salvador (see Tuyuc 1994; Wilson 1995; CERIGUA 1997). Sergio Guzman found that indigenous people received "few benefits" despite the topic's high visibility. "However, both in-

digenous and Ladinos have awakened with new interest due to the denunciations and demands for respect. Bringing problems to light has also created
awareness among government officials that indigenous rights deserve discussion and resolution" (see also Otzoy 1996).

"Indigenous workers have faced discrimination as a different class, a
group apart," explained Lutini. "They have their own proper customs and
ways to live, especially on coffee and sugar fincas, and now they have proposed a plan for greater autonomy." Byron Morales noted "some improvement in how different sectors view the Puebla Maya, and how they have
become inserted into the society. Yet, structural racism remains a very fundamental factor, with little energy given to its solution. There is not yet a sufficiently profound debate on the links between women's and Mayan issues."
Morales hoped that USTR action could become a catalyst for this discussion.[28]

Tripartite Discussions

While unionists recognize certain benefits from GSP pressure, they have remained wary of changes in private-sector attitudes. Although southern cone
nations have more experience with the ILO principle of "tripartite" joint busi-
ness-labor-government approaches to common problems, that tradition has
been largely absent in Central America (see Palomoes and Mertens 1993).
"The tripartite system is not functioning, and we need help to implement the
law," emphasized Juan Francisco Alfaro. "The reforms resulting from GSP
pressure do not specify how this will be done. How will USTR understand
this? Employer attitudes have remained as they were before. When we meet
with the private sector, CACIF never has a proposal. Its members deny that
the abuses we cite involve any of its affiliates. They prefer to talk vaguely
about the future."

However, there were glimmers of hope: Mario Lutini thought that CACIF
had shown some "minimal changes. Between 25 and 35% of employers had
improved their outlook and treatment of workers."[29] While Robles believed
"CACIF remains unchanged, there are divisions within it, exemplified by the
more flexible style that Pepsi Cola is using with the unions compared to the
heavy-handed one of the agro-exporters." Robles himself had decided to
"take a new approach" by meeting directly with business owners. This was an
approach some unions "did not understand. It's like having a guard at a factory. The guard can have a gun, but if the gun is showing, it has a very different effect than if the gun is hidden and the guard speaks politely. Some unions
carry an open gun—i.e., they won't talk to the business leaders."[30] Robles
thought unions should make use of the tripartite approach to form commis-

sions regarding contracts with workers and employers. Otherwise, "governments try to manipulate the union representatives. We never know how the representatives are chosen, or who they are."[31]

We discussed the failure of tripartism in El Salvador (see chapter 6). Despite some signs of attitude change in the Forum when business sat down to dialogue with labor in an aura of mutual respect, AIFLD's Michael Donovan could see "no attitude shifts since then: they may be pro-worker, but they are definitely anti-labor. They take advantage as well as any foreign exploiter to pay low wages, to refuse to negotiate, to refuse to make severance payments, and they still send workers away who attempt any organizing."[32]

One important potential topic for tripartite discussion concerns government efforts to privatize areas of state-controlled activity mentioned in chapter 1 and in the subsequent cases (chapters 5–11). In response to structural adjustment requirements during the 1980s, Central American governments transferred a number of functions to the profit sector, significantly reducing the public workforce (see chapter 4). Despite such pruning, in the 1990s, neoliberal governments implemented further dramatic cuts, especially in El Salvador, Guatemala, Costa Rica, Nicaragua, and Panama. The reality and threat of further privatization created substantial anxiety among Caribbean Basin state workers, a feeling they shared with co-unionists in the U.S., Canada, and Europe. As articulated by GUATEL's Mario Lutini, "The big issue for us is privatization/de-monopolization. We know that in an age of globalization, change will come, but we believe that now is not the moment for a developing nation to privatize, cutting social services as it happens."[33]

Yet unions have been unsuccessful in their efforts to discuss this far-reaching issue with corporate and government officials. In early 1994, threats of privatization in Guatemala helped stimulate a lengthy public strike which government functionaries found unintelligible. "Many of the state-supported businesses are heavy with employees who do little," quipped one official.[34] "The Labor Ministry held forums about the need to modernize and rationalize state operations."[35] However, the public unions did not necessarily oppose privatization. Rather, they sought an opportunity to present their case on questions of efficiency and service which the forums did not allow them to do. Take for example, the telephone company, "one of the society's most profitable companies. They really only want control over the capital and the major cities," stressed Lutini. "However, we also offer help to rural areas where people pay four quetzals ($.75) a month for their telephone. What will happen to these people under privatization?"[36] In 1996, the state placed the phone company on the market, and also decreed the layoff of 2,500 employees in the public-works division. The Guatel sale remained in dispute in the late 1990s.

Private-sector unions remained "very concerned about privatization," stressed Byron Morales of UNSITRAGUA which mainly represents private and public affiliates. Private-sector unions worked through the broad UASP coalition, the Grand Alianza Sindical, then the Unión Guatemalteco de Trabajadores and the Movimiento de Trabajadores de Estado to coordinate actions. But in no instance were they able to evoke tripartite mechanisms to resolve the issues.[37] When the government forced through legislation canceling public employees' right to strike, members of CACIF "refused to discuss the issue."[38]

Labor Response to Privatization in El Salvador: A Model

According to Carlos Ochoa, of UNTS, the privatization process in El Salvador was "a plan fostered by neo-liberalism to further concentrate wealth." Without tripartite involvement, it had "become worse, treating workers criminally. We are asking for workers to be included in negotiations about privatization—the loans, proposals, and decisions regarding its various stages." Ochoa thought some businesses could be privatized without problems: hotels, movie theaters, "but those essential for the country such as energy, water, and strategic institutions are better controlled by the government than by private employers and transnational firms."[39]

Facing threats of privatization in 1995, for six months, the unions requested an audience with President Calderon but he did not respond. Labor characterized the president and businesspeople's perspective as the state washing its hands of social concerns. They invited the government to consider competing in such sectors as electricity, telephone, and water, and even in education, and social security.[40] Hearing no response from government or business, in March 1996, the unions then offered a more complete proposal "to modernize but not privatize, lest these institutions like our telephone, electrical services, social security and pensions pass into the hands of foreign companies," said Ochoa. "We engaged twenty-one congressional Deputies from the FMLN, led by Oscar Otiz, Eugenio Chicas, and Rigoberto Gutiérrez. We had a large rally in Morazan Park on June 1 that involved more than a thousand leaders. We also conducted a questionnaire (via the University of Central America) in which 75 percent of the sampled population expressed opposition to privatization. We also filed a document about the unconstitutionality of privatization." The CENTRA labor research institute held five preparatory meetings with workers at the various affected labor centrals to draft the proposal. The electrical unions urged that the state continue to generate power, and the private sector to distribute it. The health related unions offered a mixed system of coverage from both sectors. Most unions in telecommunications sought to challenge the privatization effort (see Frundt 1997). But none of these proposals underwent tripartite discussion. Elites and government leaders simply condemned them on ideological grounds.

"In March 1996, we offered a counterproposal that would protect the workers of ANTEL, and later CEL," explained Mario Vasquez, FEASIES. "The ARENA government prevented its discussion, but this forced them to buy off certain workers (with higher salaries) in an attempt to undermine our confidence and maintain divisions." Vasquez told how this had lengthened deliberations at INPEP, the pension institute, where management proposals kept us "negotiating for a year, despite the labor code's twenty-day limitation."[41]

García believed the telecommunication proposals "had a chance of passage after discussing aspects of them with ARENA."[42] However, just then ANTEL inaugurated a strike to protest privatization and living costs:

"The ANTEL strike has emerged because the market basket price of food etc. has increased, but not their salaries," stressed Ochoa. "They also faced the threat of privatization. The ANTEL strike is a test for the Minister of Labor, who has been incompetent to resolve labor problems. He issues executive orders, then folds his arms. The Procuradoria acts in a similar fashion. He has even fired workers. So we are experiencing a huge reversion from the peace accords. There is less violence, but many of the same difficulties continue."[43]

Such lack of communication and polarization of perceptions among the three major sectors do not bode well for the tripartite process in Central America or the Caribbean.

Summary: Overall Evaluation

Union leadership appraisals of the impact of GSP petitions range from positive to mixed. They reach a general consensus that while petitions have changed private-sector attitudes very little, if at all, they afforded greater space for union action. Sergio Guzman of the independent UNSITRAGUA offered this summation: "GSP pressure has not gained anything substantial or extraordinary. However, it has opened space for discussion between employers, workers, and the government. We can raise issues of unemployment and work instability. A public debate stimulates the creation of opinion among workers and the population. In some cases, change may come through legal means." Guzman cited a 1994 Ministry of Labor investigation of sixteen maquilas. "But in many way things have gotten worse with the ministry and judges. So I would say first, nothing has come from GSP directly, but second, it has opened public debate."[44]

Byron Morales of the same confederation found GSP results "hard to measure." He saw little effect on business attitudes: "There simply continues to be

noncompliance. Businessmen do not participate in discussions, Labor Ministry matters, etc. Meanwhile labor conflicts have risen, and kidnappings and
assassinations are unabated. Their object is to debilitate unions. When business owners decide to modernize their equipment, they then want to recuperate their investment in the quickest manner possible without any regard to
impact on workers." However, Morales admitted that "perhaps a small group
in the business community is concerned, and talking about solutions." While
"they really don't exert a major force, they are willing to dialogue about the
consequences of modernization, for example those who signed the 1994 accord raising wages for coffee workers. In this sense, GSP has helped the export
sector be a bit more open. Thus, in spite of what it hasn't done, our experience
with GSP has been positive. It has preoccupied the elites, and this has been
useful.[45]

"GSP did bring some results," articulated Luis Merida, former organizing
director for UNSITRAGUA. "It accelerated the *tramites* required for unions to
obtain a *persona juridica*. The Ministry of Labor also called us in more often,
and formed a Tripartite Commission to work out accords. Of course they still
tried to manipulate the law as they do in the U.S. This was especially true of
the producers of non-traditional exports, the textile factories in particular,
who are very reactionary and mistreat workers continually. GSP caught them
in contradictory positions of which we could take advantage. GSP was responsible for global attention to the La Exacta killings, and the interest from
the United Nations and the Organization of American States, which has made
a difference in helping to address the case in the courts."[46]

Yet El Salvador labor attorney José Antonio Candray remained cautious
about trade condition impact. "Undoubtedly, there are benefits; we need equitable salaries and better health, and we can say to employers, you are not
complying with the law and could lose trade advantages. But if change comes
via GSP, it is always as a reaction to pressure instead of fulfilling a political
commitment. There remains no respect for wage workers, and in practice,
women are still mistreated in stores, factories and offices. I have seen no
change in attitudes toward workers or unions in the private sector. On the
contrary, the GSP threat even impelled employers to declare a higher level of
'patriotism.'"[47]

Mark Anner, representative of the Norwegian Labor Federation in El Salvador, thought that GSP had "contributed some results, but it could have
produced much better results if the labor movement had been more strategic.
Although Amanda Villatoro, head of the CTD, understood how to use the
GSP process, there was always confusion on how to best employ it." Anner
described how the most active Salvadoran filers, FENASTRAS, and even the

CTD/AIFLD later disintegrated. FENASTRAS members even paraded in front of the U.S. Embassy to protest *against* the USTR delegation when it visited El Salvador in November 1995.[48]

Present and Future

In the mid-1990s, labor leaders in Central America and the Caribbean wrestled with various trade-conditions options. They knew the GSP program was under severe challenge in the U.S. Congress. At the same time, the governments of Central America had signed the Treaty on Central American Social Integration, which added a new dimension to their commitment to an integrated Central American system in 1991 and a further accord in October, 1993. While progress remained slow, as we saw in chapter 5, El Salvador moved to drop tariff barriers, as did Guatemala. The economics ministers from Central American nations met to develop common strategies on import-export policies. Linked with this came subsequent efforts to achieve more unified labor legislation. The region's labor ministers gathered in 1995 under USAID and Spanish auspices, to reconcile national social policies and labor codes. Trade-union leaders realized that issues of labor code harmonization and social clauses in trade agreements were complementary.

To understand worker perceptions of future trade conditions, our sample of leaders were also asked questions about the continuation of GSP, labor-code regionalization, and a trade-related social contract.

GSP

Given the record of the GSP petition process in Central America, what did workers think about its continuation? Some believed the same kind of petition process should be repeated; others advocated fresher tactics.

In Guatemala, labor attorney Mynor Andrio thought U.S. petitioners "should maintain international pressure, in spite of the lack of change. Especially in the rural areas, workers who cite human rights are threatened with death, or their crops can be destroyed. Thus there is *much fear!*"

"We realize the situation is complicated regarding GSP," explained CGTG's Rigoberto Dueñas. "We want it as a pressure point, but we want the review continued; we don't want Guatemala to lose its benefits or to be excluded from the GSP system. We favor bringing the country to the brink to gain compliance, but not going beyond this. Otherwise, 80,000 workers could lose their jobs. It would be an incredible shock. The problem is, we can only cry wolf so many times. The ideal would be to remove one or two products from the preferential list, but not all of them at once, thereby showing our intent, but not with as severe consequences."

Byron Morales concurred: "GSP should help the Labor Ministry reclaim its role. It is an opportunity for them to become more effective in resolving conflicts, i.e., inaugurating more legal reforms in 1996–2000 to give the ministry coercive power to enforce labor laws."

Sergio Guzman and others argued that "the U.S. Embassy can also play an important role rather than simply a political one. When maquila owners from a country act very irresponsibly, for example, the ambassador from that country could respond. We understand that the embassy can't dictate, but it can monitor, since businesses often enjoy permissions from embassies to operate. The U.S. Embassy has authority to act. Unfortunately, it has not done so. On three occasions, with Inexport, Agroexport, and CMT, all owned by U.S. nationals, we asked for the U.S. Embassy's help, but none was forthcoming."[49]

Usually supportive of labor concerns, former U.S. labor attaché Donald Knight raised a concern that GSP might cultivate "the belief of some union leaders that if any problem develops, they can come to the U.S. Embassy to resolve it. This can keep them from developing their own skills. While a rights violation by a certain employer should be noted in the GSP report, the workers also have to create their own mechanisms for responding."

"It is true that the government is not complying with the law, but then, what country does comply!" exclaimed Knight. "GSP can only be strategically effective as a pressure point. I can't see what we would gain by cutting off benefits. The country has opened up the political process, which would then really be hurt. The reactionaries would cry, 'this is all your fault,' and such a reaction would put the country back fifteen years.

"The unions must become more involved in politics, and change these institutions in their favor. They tend to see everything stacked against them and pass it all onto us, but they have to utilize what little space they have to get a bit more."[50]

Like Knight, Mark Anner did not dispute the importance that U.S. trade-based standards have had for mobilizing business, government and labor to face the labor rights question within a global framework. But Anner also faulted the labor movement for becoming overly dependent on international action and support, and not sufficiently relying on its own organizing and fund-raising (see Frundt 1997).

But local labor leaders had already begun a "time for new approaches," as Byron Morales put it, "talking with U.S. unions about collaborating on organizing. The new strategy of developing codes for companies to follow [as U.S./GLEP has done with Starbucks Coffee; see chapter 2] is very positive. It can serve as a mechanism for pressure and follow-up."

"The GSP strategy now requires change," articulated Luis Merida, who testified at USTR hearings in 1994. He learned "that a country can't remain under review indefinitely. USTR must either lift the review, or take away the benefits." Merida correctly predicted that it would "lift the review" which he attributed to "the pressure of commercial interests for free trade without restrictions. The U.S. is not interested in the problems of Guatemala, but in maintaining their dominant power in world commerce." But Merida favored "putting pressure on certain products under a new version of GSP," and "going directly after companies using the code approach." He cited the U.S. clothing importer GHR's Guatemalan plant (Marissa), which had kidnapped union leaders and "practically destroyed the union. GHR also has a plant in El Salvador, so the idea would be to build enormous pressure on their U.S. customers so that they accept a new approach."[51] In October 1996, this new approach moved Guatemalan unions to officially notify USTR that they would not oppose the lifting of review.[52]

The skepticism over GSP's future was shared by Salvadoran labor leaders. Carlos Hurtado, CTD, had "concerns over what will happen with CBI or the Initiative of the Americas. GSP may disappear. What is important is that some measure of pressure be included in CBI, the Initiative of the Americas, or GATT. We need investment, but with respect for the laws of El Salvador, not to violate the legal requirements. We want an economic opening, competition, yes of course to improve production. But what happens to the workers? Will their salaries improve without having to work twenty-four hours a day in a maquila?" Hurtado concluded that "there is no strategy more effective than to put pressure on company earnings and products. We can raise a grand campaign, and establish sanctions."

Miguel Ramírez believed that "if people organize, they can petition and get their rights. They need organizations in the maquila, as well as in construction, in the informal sector, in services (hotels), in the countryside." Carlos Luna from UNTS, was equally insistent on a similar mechanism since "the workers face increasing economic costs—reduction of benefits, changes of exchange rates and increases in sales taxes which also affects our production. The government here is closed to these consequences. But the unions will protest. We are setting up broader coalitions, including international groups, to encourage participation."

"Right now, our peace is a fragile one; rights really don't exist for many—with firings and denial of credit, workers here have no access to possibilities. Many are not even literate, so are easily denied social and cultural benefits, and can easily be fired. In the U.S., 85 percent have access, here 85 percent do not. If the peace can continue, we may increase those who benefit. For example, labor judges could order reinstatement or payment; if there was not payment, the government could declare an embargo of the company and its merchandise."[53]

While the commentaries reveal a sophisticated understanding of GSP potential and drawbacks, they also point to the necessity for a broader approach.

Regional Efforts at a Social Clause

Despite the concern of some that GSP has made Central American workers overly dependent on U.S. actions, they have absorbed the concept of labor rights as their own, first by their participation in recent party building efforts at the national level (in post-accord El Salvador and Guatemala), and second, in their insistence at the regional level that labor-rights language be incorporated into any area agreement on Central American trade as has been attempted in the Southern Cone (Alimonda 1994).

Regionalization of Labor Codes

In 1995, the regional ministers of labor began working with USAID to develop common understandings about their various labor laws and the relationship to regional investment.[54] They commissioned an extensive two-part study, headed by Luis Monge, former president of Costa Rica. Lic. Juan Francisco Alfaro directly attributed the effort to GSP pressure, and the consequent labor rights commitment made at the Miami Summit on the Americas in December 1994. The first part of the study dealt with general labor-management principles. The second part developed recommendations for labor code reform and "harmonization." However, prior to the study's completion, labor leaders voiced concern over USAID's intent: "In January 1995 Monge promised us he wouldn't make labor problems more difficult for the countries involved," stated CUSG's Juan Francisco Alfaro. "As one of his general principles, he suggested that national governments set up a public office paid for by state funds to offer legal assistance to workers (i.e., designated legal aid). We said yes, the principle is good, but if it functions poorly, it could do a lot of damage, e.g., if the lawyers got their orders from the government or employers. We agreed that if a specially constituted congress of labor confederations could name those serving in such an office, and could control what they try to do, we would support it."

"In another example, Monge wanted to give more power and budget to the ministries of labor because otherwise the inspectors would get their funds from the employers to overlook violations. Yet we don't need an even greater number of corrupt inspectors; rather, what we need is a complete renovation of the labor ministries. Monge also confuses the difference between unions and worker organizations. According to the codes, you only negotiate with unions."

Table 12.1. Comparative organizing and bargaining requirements in Central American and Dominican labor codes

	No. for union	No. for negotiations[a]	% of union members[a]	No. for strike	No. conciliation days[b]
Costa Rica	12	33%	51%[c]	60%	36
Dominican Republic	20	50%	—	51%	10
El Salvador	35	51%	—	51%	4
Guatemala	20	25%	67%	67%	24
Honduras	30	2	50%	51–67%	30
Nicaragua	25	no min	60%	60%	6
Panama	40	no min	50%	50%	25

Source: Computed from data provided by CTCA (1996) and country labor codes.
[a]Percent/number of workforce required to request negotiations and percent of union members who must approve pact demands.
[b]Minimum days possible. Conciliation invariably extends the waiting time for many months.
[c]Total of 51 percent must approve when employer challenges membership.

In response to the first part of the Monge study, with AIFLD's help, the Confederación de Trabajadores de Centro América (CTCA) examined the labor codes in each of seven countries (see CTCA 1996). Table 12.1 presents some of the different rules for organizing and bargaining. For example, in Honduras, Nicaragua, and Panama the union simply decides to begin negotiations, but elsewhere they must have more than 25 percent of the workforce to do so. There are also large discrepancies in how strikes are handled. "We all agree that there cannot be harmonization of the codes at this point," explained Alfaro. "For example, El Salvador has not yet ratified ILO convention 87 on freedom to organize. To date the ministers have not commented on the uniformity question.

"In reply to the second part of the study, we hope to hold them to a more consultative process. We told USAID 'you can't do a study of workers if they are not part of the project. We would like to participate in conducting part of the study, and before the final decision, we wish to make editorial suggestions.' USAID agreed. But the overall project raises the question about who influences the financing of such projects."[55]

As labor codes from the various countries are reconciled, what is at stake for the workers is a commitment that no current labor right is jeopardized.

Global versus National Interests

Labor leaders in Central America and Caribbean share the same suspicions about regional trade agreements that their U.S., European, and Southern

Cone counterparts do. They have begun to demand counteractive social clauses.

These regional accords are established to help the industrial countries, say the workers. "NAFTA has caused great disequilibrium between Mexico and the U.S. and Canada. For example, some 23,000 small producers have closed in Mexico because of GATT provisions. This negates benefits to the communities."[56] Reynoldo González reminded the private sector (CACIF) that they "stood to lose" with globalization: Pan-Bimbo from Mexico was already forcing many small bread producers out of work. "The industrial sector in Guatemala has been fractured," elaborated Sergio Guzman of UNSITRAGUA. "It wishes to remain competitive globally, yet it is not modernizing, and remains backward. Some companies know they must compete by more humane methods, but many seek to destroy any union. 'The country is in crisis,' they say, 'so we must cut back, and raise production.' Thus they decide, '*employees* have to modernize.' But what is the cost? To improve competition, they fire many workers, and move others from eight- to twelve-hour shifts. If they wish to keep their jobs, workers face more exploitation. They find it very difficult since industry will not adapt in any other manner. So most use the trade accords to excuse their anti-union actions."[57]

In El Salvador, Mark Anner found many contradictions in the private sector's support for globalization: "They invite investors from Taiwan and the U.S. Yet they under fund the Ministry of Labor and they oppose a corporate agreement on outside monitoring of labor rights [see chapter 5]. The government ought consider what it means to operate in a global context. ARENA purports to be a nationalist party, while it promotes expansion and relinquishes control. Nescafe just bought our Cafe Lista. Local gas stations, pupuserias, etc., are being swallowed by Exxon and Macdonald's. To quote one teacher at the UCA, the fourteen families will soon be replaced by the twenty-four TNCs. Meanwhile, this same right-wing patriot party opposes those who seek local independent monitoring over factories to help protect national interests and identity."[58]

To counter these trends, "unions and popular organizations must play a larger role in regional agreements," urged Enrique Alvarez. "We have exchanged delegates with each other and Mexico, searching for an understanding continent-wide forces. Everywhere, people are losing work and benefits. We need interrelations to help this. Our unions have created COCENTRA to address common concerns. Structural adjustment, while necessary, harms the poor. In Guatemala, our private sector currently pays no taxes. Government structures need to respond by improving justice, and becoming less bureaucratic."

"As the peace process progresses, and we develop a full proposal for Central America, it is important to include GSP protections in any regional accord," assured Rodolfo Robles who is participating with COCENTRA in this effort.[59]

Juan Francisco Alfaro sought "to take advantage of the peace process, but this can't happen without a more general understanding of globalization. We can't ignore the rights of workers as market integration moves forward." Alfaro was also working with CTCA, a member of the Iniciativa Civil para la Integración Centroamerica (ICIC), which also includes COCENTRA and other groups, "to demand that any regional integration includes the same protections currently under GSP."[60]

Sergio Guzman of UNSITRAGUA recommended "proposals to address regional integration, that would guarantee the minimum labor rights employees now hold in a country. Our principle is to assure the rights we have, and then improve them. To achieve this, we need to consolidate and offer one plan." Guzman helped draft a COCENTRA proposal to specifically assure "the continuation of social security benefits and economic stability."

"We are planning for market integration at the national level," insisted Byron. Morales, "not only to defend ourselves, but also to respond more globally. The peace process is a part of this." At the regional level UNSITRAGUA worked with COCENTRA to widen participation to small business owners.[61]

Salvadoran unions were also developing a position on labor rights in conjunction with COCENTRA and ICIC. "Without this, President Clinton's emphasis will only lead to short term accomplishments," insisted Roger Gutiérrez. "We hope to include the same protections that exist in the European Community." Backing CTCA and other bilateral efforts, Carlos Hurtado of the CTD warned that "the integration must include social as well as economic and political processes." Miguel Ramírez of FESTRAES would make sure that any regional agreement would not replicate the World Trade Organization "which does not include any labor regulations." International unions were mounting an effort to reverse their rejection.

"In the public sector, we know we can't face the issue of privatization alone," admitted M. Lutini, "but as a region, we can! The free market is coming, and just like countries in the Caribbean, Central American nations have to meet it head on."[62]

Conclusion

This chapter was mainly concerned with the subjective responses of regional labor leaders, largely in El Salvador and Guatemala, to the GSP petition process. Clearly, the workers reject business (and neo-liberal) arguments that the

GSP mechanism was primarily protectionist and that they were pawns of North American unions. In terms of impact, they thought the petition process had some positive effect in obtaining legislation, opening public discussion, and gaining leverage in specific negotiations. However, they were less sanguine about the effect GSP pressure had on actual enforcement, benefits to women and indigenous, the struggle over privatization or improvement in tripartite dialogue.

Union responses did not directly address the theoretical questions of labor standard effectiveness. However, they did imply that despite increasing economic investment, there was no indication of a "natural improvement" in labor conditions. Quite the contrary, they found that both foreign and domestic firms routinely disregarded current labor laws and violated basic norms of human treatment, lending credence to trade unionist demands for improved enforcement, and the supportive role played by international standard-backing solidarity.

For the future, while some leaders hoped that the GSP leverage would continue, they recognized that new tactics would be required in the face of regional trade agreements. However, they clearly demanded that the basic rights that GSP indexed must be preserved with mechanisms for adequate review. To that end, they have embarked on discussions with other Central American unions to obtain social clauses in future trade arrangements. For international supporters, they urged emphasis on company code compliance and other forms of government to government pressure. But they see fresh forms of trade regulations as essential for regional peace.

CHAPTER 13

Conclusion

Do workers benefit from labor-rights requirements in trade agreements? To address this fundamental question, we have reviewed a broad range of theoretical evidence and intensively examined national cases. We focused on labor-rights conditions within U.S. trade legislation (see chapter 3), notably the General System of Preferences (GSP) petition and review structure adopted in 1984 which other programs, such as CBI, have emulated. The evidence has affirmed our first hypotheses that in Central America and the Caribbean, labor-rights provisions have positively influenced national labor-rights legislation and enforcement. Our second hypothesis, that labor conditions have been improved, has more limited support.

Key Improvements

Trade conditions via GSP caused most nations considered to strengthen worker-rights provisions in their labor codes. The others officially committed themselves to dramatically improve specific applications of current law. Trade rules have been a factor in substantially reducing violence against workers in the region. The AFL-CIO further credited the clout of GSP withdrawal for stemming the drive to weaken worker protections and labor codes in other Latin nations. While direct corporate pressure was also a factor, GSP action also helped reduce the exploitation of child labor. Achievements of GSP in the countries under study are summarized in table 13.1.

In the positive column, GSP pressure has enabled workers to:

1. organize unions more easily;
2. receive improved service and augmented power from their ministries of labor;
3. gain increased attention to labor concerns in the media and forums of public debate;
4. increase wages and certain benefits;
5. begin to establish a more consultative tripartite system.

Table 13.1. Accomplishments of GSP review, by CBI country, 1989–97

Guatemala

1992	Reform of labor code
1993	A factor in removing threat of dictatorial rule; began reform of labor inspection system
	Settlement of several union recognitions and contract disputes
1994	Accords in coffee sector and salary commission
1996	Reduction in anti-labor violence; investigation of attack against labor leader
1997	Negotiated contract in maquila sector

El Salvador

1990	Began reconciliation of labor laws
1991	A factor in peace negotiations; began program to improve labor-management relations
1992	Limited reduction in anti-union violence
1993	Formation of Tripartite Commission; negotiation of labor-code reform provisions; enhanced labor ministry training
1994	Reform of labor code

Dominican Republic

1989–90	Improvement in recruitment and contract terms for immigrant Haitian workers; accelerated de jure (not de facto) union recognitions
1992[a]	Reform of labor code
1993–94	Enforcement of labor code recognition and bargaining provisions; intervention of employer association versus recalcitrant members
1995[a]	De facto respect for right to strike

Honduras

1995[a]	Agreement on labor code enforcement, especially in the maquilas

Costa Rica

1993[a]	Reform of penal and labor codes; removal of legal advantages for solidarista employer-employee associations

Panama

1991–92	Accelerated approval of union contracts and free-zone improvements
1993	Withdrawal of draconian labor laws;
1995[a]	Prevention of additional provisions that would dramatically weaken labor code

Nicaragua[b]

1989	Allowance of multiple unions
1994	Withdrawal of proposed draconian labor provisions
1996	Reform of labor code

[a]Via negotiated withdrawal of petition requesting review.
[b]Via related pressure while nation remained under GSP suspension.

In our comparison of national labor codes (see tables 5.2, 7.1, 9.1, 10.2, 11.2, 11.4, 11.5, and 12.1), we also consistently noted the legal right of private-sector workers to negotiate and strike. These are milestones of accomplishment that deserve widespread recognition. Trade conditions can reverse systemic patterns of abusive treatment and help reconstruct more equitable and responsive institutions.

Our study nevertheless exposed many cautions and qualifications regarding these findings. Let us first review the individual cases, then the general framework, and finally speak about lessons for the future.

Case Results

In chapter 1 we recounted experiences of the region's workers who sought dignified conditions. Employees in agriculture, industry, and services often expressed common problems: long hours, below-minimum pay, poor health and safety conditions, abusive treatment to enforce production goals. This represented the viewpoint of most workers, yet some preferred these work conditions to what they had before—hoeing stubborn crops in the countryside, selling candy on the street corner, or having no job at all. However virtually all agreed that if they attempted to organize or join a union, they faced especially opprobrious retaliation and often were fired. They had found little redress with the courts or the Ministries of Labor.

The trade sanction threat induced some changes in this picture. In the first case of El Salvador (chapter 5), the study found that by virtually all accounts, GSP pressure brought a change in the nation's labor code in 1994; nevertheless, the union-employer battle over the code substituted for genuine dialogue over the enormous socioeconomic problems left in the aftermath of the civil war. In the end, not only did the conservative government unilaterally imposed its own version of the code; the "tripartite" consultation failed to address a single fundamental issue. Chapter 6 revealed a gradual erosion of Salvadoran unions and negotiations. While the nation's Labor Ministry was completely revamped, the courts remained ineffective. With 1,000 workers fired for every 300 organized, most worker rights in the maquila sector emerged from direct pressure on corporations, not from the requirements of the GSP process.

The second case of Guatemala (chapter 7) manifested a more hopeful story. GSP action not only brought code reform in 1992, but also created an atmosphere for public debate and code implementation. Union registrations and contracts improved slightly, and higher minimum-wage standards exhibited GSP influence. Yet longer-term institutional benefits were not apparent, as the institutional examination in chapter 8 indicated. Both health care coverage and court reform remained woefully inadequate. Guatemalan labor courts functioned even less effectively than those in El Salvador. Between 1993 and 1998, virtually no sentences were issued or fines imposed. However, while maquila organizing remained exceedingly difficult, at least one union (Phillips–Van Heusen) had negotiated a contract by 1997.

Honduras (chapter 9) represented another example of mixed trade influence. Not subject to the same intense GSP campaign as El Salvador and Nicaragua, Honduran officials nevertheless claimed to learn from their neighbors' experience. After some years of unofficially blocking organizers from the nation's free-trade zones, the country finally relented in an historic 1995 agreement with USTR. Although the Labor Ministry still arbitrarily exerted power, several unions achieved contracts.

In the Dominican Republic (chapter 10), unions used GSP threats to genuinely strengthen union organizing. While they had only been minimally successful at employing the GSP process to resolve the deficient treatment of Haitian workers in the late 1980s, or to unify and propel national unions into a coherent popular political coalition in the early 1990s, GSP brought a revised labor code in 1992. By 1995, with sustained trade-sanction pressure and international union help, their own organizing skills could thrive. Free-zone workers negotiated a number of bona fide contracts to which employers remained committed.

The briefer treatments of the GSP process in Costa Rica, Panama, and Nicaragua (chapter 11) each conveyed a telling lesson. In Costa Rica, GSP pressure helped turn official government policy away from a complete embrace of the employer-sponsored "solidarity association" alternative to trade unionism. Given Costa Rica's privatization drive, it remains to be seen whether private-sector workers can take advantage of this new opening to unionize. In Panama, labor used GSP to *prevent* extensive backsliding of its reasonably strong labor code, especially in the area of job protections. Nicaragua was denied GSP benefits in 1987, purportedly for its failure to protect non-Sandinista unions. The Sandinista government remained more open to trade-union activity than others in the region. Following difficult struggles and a weakening of labor in the early 1990s, the Chamorro administration finally reached an accommodation with the unions and a new labor code. GSP's indirect impact via CBI provisions may have played some role. But the subsequent neo-liberal Aleman government further reduced union and Labor Ministry power and free-zone abuses persisted.

Just as the GSP experiences of these nations varied, so worker perceptions of the GSP process were not monolithic (chapter 12). Some reiterated the business class's anxieties about protectionism; others expressed an acute fear that if they participated in the process, they would be labeled as unpatriotic, or

worse—threatened and even killed. Generally, however, they offered a qualified but positive appraisal of GSP's success regarding legislative improvements and its "opening the debate" about labor-rights issues. A number had
also beneficially invoked GSP rules in specific negotiations.

Leaders were less enthusiastic about GSP's usefulness in gaining compliance or winning institutional change. Those interviewed did not believe the
process had brought improved benefits to women or indigenous workers or
stimulated the state to negotiate over privatization efforts. They saw little
noticeable reduction in child labor despite surveys suggesting the contrary.[1]

Most were unenthusiastic about their own labor ministries, although some
(Honduras, Nicaragua) thought the ministry held too much arbitrary power.
Most agreed that despite reforms, the ministries failed to enforce time limits
and penalties or to expedite negotiations. Yet they had been motivated to approach the ministries and the courts. Some demanded that the ministries of
labor exert a "moral force" beyond simple legal requirements or budgetary
constraints. The ministry should advocate for worker rights and offer leadership to the larger community in calling public attention to abuses. Lic. Gladys
Morfin in Guatemala and Rafael Alburquerque in the Dominican Republic,
served as models for this possibility.

While most workers bemoaned the failure of tripartite discussions, they
could conceptualize what a genuine "tripartite consultative process" might
look like. To date, they felt that none of the national elites had really understood the meaning of such a process, despite the impassioned rhetoric of business leaders like Carlos Arias of Guatemala and Juan Hector Vidal of El Salvador. Private-sector employers largely illustrated Michael Piore's rendition of
the "sweatshop" mentality (see chapter 2). They faced global competition by
cutting wages, not investing in their workforces.

Generally, our case studies demonstrated positive, negative or unchanged
patterns of both the codification and the implementation of labor rights, as
summarized in table 13.2: If we granted each of these factors equal weight,
then we would note eighteen improvements and thirteen declines, resulting
in a slight improvement overall. Within the context of a competitive world
economy and a declining state sector, this represents an advance.

The General Framework

While this study primarily focused on evidence and policy issues surrounding trade and labor-rights compliance, it also tested the sociological validity of
neo-liberal theory. The evidence decidedly challenged assumptions about the
beneficial effects of the "market" on labor conditions. Neo-classicists inaccu-
rately predicted that corporate demand for labor would automatically increase security, dignified treatment and wages.

Table 13.2. Positive and negative changes in codified and actual rights to organize and bargain, Caribbean Basin countries, 1992–97

	Costa Rica	Dominican	El Salvador	Guatemala	Honduras	Nicaragua	Panama
Agricultural workers	=	+	+	+	+	=	=
State workers	=	=	=	-	=	-	=
Union registration	=	+	+	+	=	=	=
Job protections	-	=	=	-	=	-	=
Independent federations	=	+	-	=	=	+	=
Basic rights	+	+	+	+	+	=	=
Right to strike	=	+	=	-	=	-	-
Contract approvals	-	+	-	=	+	-	=
Court functions	=	+	=	-	=	=	=

In chapter 2, we grappled with the meaning of worker rights. Despite the fascination such a discussion holds for U.S. economists and managers, there is very little acknowledgement in the literature that the International Labour Organisation (ILO) has attended the question of labor rights since its founding in 1919. By mid-century, the organization had achieved wide international agreement on the basic right to organize and bargain. It had also addressed the major concerns expressed by the workers above—prohibiting the use of slave and child labor, and requiring reasonable hours, vacations, and minimum wages. These rights were agreed to by a wide spectrum of nations, irrespective of cultural differences. By the 1980s, the ILO had added to its list of core rights the observance of health and safety regulations, non-discrimination in hiring and wages, and the protection of indigenous rights. In addition, the ILO urged each nation to form "tripartite" consultations between labor, management, and government, to address problems of mutual interest, such as national productivity, development, and labor conflicts.

Despite the ILO agreements on core worker rights, winning consensus on their assurance was another matter. We unearthed a considerable range of views over the pros and cons of market forces, union strength, corporate and consumer responsiveness, and state-imposed standards. These mechanisms overlapped. As production improved, the market might enhance labor benefits, or it might cultivate conditions ripe for labor organizing. In the latter 1990s, voluntary corporate employee codes that depended on consumer pressure were certainly market-related. Because trade sanctions involved government regulation, our case studies devoted attention to the complex interplay of market and state in ensuring worker rights.

The debate over which agency is superior for realizing rights became complicated when the topic of relations *between* countries was introduced. As chapter 3 recounted, even a number of neo-institutionalists who normally advocated government action retained reservations about employing trade conditions to redress labor concerns. They feared that protectionism would restrict the greatest asset of countries most in need of development—less expensive labor. They also thought entrenched labor aristocracies within such countries would manipulate labor rights trade provisions to prevent jobs and economic benefits from percolating throughout the larger society. We found little verification for either fear in U.S./Central American trade. Rather the labor movement remained one of the strongest advocates for extending benefits to informal sector workers and the larger society.

Building on the discussion in chapter 2, our evidence moved beyond simplistic assertions that the market always exploited working people, or that state intervention routinely retarded orderly improvements. The neoclassical proponents whom we interviewed masterfully stressed how competition required quality production, which in turn required higher wages. Investors solicited an even-handed police and an expeditious judiciary that benefited workers as well. Their fear that imposed standards forced companies to restrict benefits to an ever-decreasing privileged few, or that firms would clandestinely come to rely on informal-sector workers was not been born out in Central America or the Dominican.

What we did uncover was the large gap between real free markets that would demand free-labor transfers and endless, unpolluted resources and free competition, and the reality in which "free" simply meant a license for corporate transfers and worker repression. Our cases were well stocked with companies that had exploited their workers for lengthy time periods without loss of market share. On the other hand, worker improvements in El Salvador and elsewhere emanated much more from trade requirements than unrestricted market forces. One illustration discussed in chapters 7 and 8 was the 1994 Guatemala Anacafe coffee agreement that came at a time of accelerating coffee prices. Union negotiators had to "press the GSP threat" to get company representatives to agree to wage/benefit increases. Yet when coffee prices took a later dip, employers had no compunction about lowering wages and eliminating social programs.

The fears of neo-classical and some neo-institutional economists that labor rights would rigidify employer ability to hire and fire workers had little basis throughout Central America or the Latin Caribbean. Job and wage protections, not widely carried out in any case, rarely had detrimental effects, and usually had positive results on employee income and treatment in other sectors. While GSP petitions may have saved several hundred jobs from termination, few could argue that its net impact had forced governments or businesses to retain large numbers of workers in inefficient positions or industries.

The revived efforts at privatization that infected the leadership of many Central American governments in the mid-1990s devastated union membership and employment in the formal sector. While labor codes do offer some job security for union organizers, except in Panama, none guarantee employment for ordinary workers. The *emplazamiento,* which for a time had covered all signatories to a "list of complaints," had become undermined by countersuits and endless court delays. The record of satisfactory resolutions to job terminations (via conciliations or court proceedings) was minuscule compared with the total number of firings. In nearly every country, despite allegedly peremptory regulations, the erosion of labor unions kept up its pace.

Concluding Lessons

Finally, our investigation has explained several requirements for future effective trade sanction regimens.

1. To assure the basic rights to organize and bargain, sanctions must realistically appraise and modify national labor practice.
2. The U.S. role in trade sanctions must shift toward a more participatory regional approach.
3. Implementation demands both a functioning tripartite consultation and local organizing backed by international solidarity.

National Labor Practice

Most rights observers agree that if workers have the right to organize and bargain, they hold the most essential right of all: They can then mobilize their own organizations to demand and obtain other necessities that their socioeconomic situation requires. What our analysis of the cases revealed, however, was that despite being granted in principle, nations denied this basic right to many through a maze of legal stratagems. For example,

1. Freedom from intimidation—the guarantee of the right to life and assembly—remained a feeble right.
2. The right to organize was often forbidden to key groups such as state workers and agricultural workers and tacitly forbidden to maquila workers.
3. Worker protections from termination because of union participation had little follow-up enforcement.
4. Procedures for union registration depended on extensive reviews by ministries of labor.
5. The right to affiliate with independent federations was not assured.

6. The ability to negotiate was severely hampered by employer threats or non-participation with no enforcement from labor ministries or courts.

As we saw in chapters 3 and 4, while Latin America tended to encourage an alliance between unions, parties, and the state to achieve both political and economic objectives, this was much less true in Central America. Traditional elites manipulated and controlled workers and government institutions. When they were forced to adopt labor codes (most were in place by the 1960s), they insisted that the state play a major interventionist role in restraining union behavior. Codes also included many of the above restrictions. Still, as union movements expanded, at times workers won benefits superior to those in the U.S., for example, mandatory Sundays off with pay.

However, debt repayments and the "lost" decade of the 1980s proved enormously detrimental for Latin economies. This in turn affected organized workers, especially in industry and government. With the shift to non-traditional exports and to informal-sector production, as we noted, the strength of the union movement waned, governments stepped up their attacks on the public sector organization, and traditional elites reasserted their anti-union sentiments. National courts and labor ministries remained ensconced in traditional power alliances and obligations, despite labor-code reforms.

Code reforms in the 1990s still retained the state in a controlling role. While the right to negotiate and strike remained, they were rarely exercised in practice since business interests were able to pressure ministries of labor to delay proceedings (if they would not do so on their own). A comparison of the chief provisions of national labor codes (see tables 5.2, 7.1, 9.1, 10.2, 11.2, 11.4, 11.5, and 12.1) manifests common difficulties. Union organizers are still routinely fired without cause. Efforts to achieve a contract are often endlessly postponed. Conciliation, while laudatory, is used as a delaying tactic by labor ministers and courts to prevent final resolution of any labor issue. Similar procedures are employed to prevent legal strikes.

At the behest of power interests, courts also invoke dilatory tactics. Guatemala's experience was not entirely idiosyncratic when the Supreme Court refused to fund the Commissions of Conciliation and Arbitration created by its 1992 code reform. This provided (and still provides) the judiciary with additional excuses to defer labor proceedings. For decades in the Dominican Republic, Honduras, and other countries, tribunal decisions have been more of a reflection of power than of principle. Because of the volatile nature of "collective" cases, few judges or politicians are willing to stake their careers on reform efforts or speedy resolutions.

To remedy these conditions, constitutional rights must be reconciled via

Table 13.3. Recommended improvements in Central American and Dominican labor codes

1. Clear regulations to protect workers from unjust dismissal: guaranteed reinstatement within 24 hours with fines; prior court approval for firing union leaders.
2. Fifty percent union vote and 25 percent workforce vote required to begin negotiations; no government approval necessary.
3. Enforced rules for reasonable negotiation period (first requiring Labor Ministry intervention, then specifying an automatic right to strike).
4. Grievance clauses and resolution machinery embedded in negotiated contracts, which have legal status when completed.
5. Legal steps for resolving disputes when grievance procedures are disregarded (set time limits for Ministry and Court deliberations and imposition of fines before automatic strike authorization takes effect).
6. Streamlining of other legal procedures that minimize employer appeals (i.e., judicial power to freeze employer assets, restrict travel, and withdraw licenses).
7. Speedy conciliation steps and approvals for special types of legal strikes. Such rules ought be included in any regional trade agreement.

amending legislation to define precisely the "revoke and expedite" powers of the Ministry of Labor, to incorporate grievance procedures in negotiated contracts (to facilitate dispute resolution at the local-company level), to let strikes happen, and to have automatic enforcement for juridical decisions unhampered by endless employer appeals. These recommendations, drawn from Central American unionists (see CTCA 1996) are summarized in table 13.3.

U.S. Role

The U.S. is not responsible for these perduring difficulties of labor mistreatment and institutional malfeasance in Central America. However it does share the blame. Its supportive interventions, prolonged funding of Central American warfare, and specialized training of torturers, assassins, and reactionary leaders have contributed to the demise of national democratic institutions. The behavior of regional courts and labor ministries as well as private sector proclivities remain testimony to the U.S. military's penetration and lingering reinforcement of the class divisions we have described above. Any balanced response to labor rights must account for these long-term influences and inequities. Such writers as Aguilara Peralta (1989), Burbach and Flynn (1984), Burbach et al. (1997), Jonas (1991), Torres Rivas (1989), Walker (1997) and others have begun this discussion, a full analysis of which takes us beyond the scope of this study.

Nevertheless, we can say that, ironically, the U.S., which has been reticent to adopt ILO standards and notorious for propping up dictatorial governments that repress unions, did take the lead in advocating trade conditions, as we discussed in chapter 3. We saw how the U.S. is made up of contesting forces, and in the case of trade policy, union-rights advocates—who also favor freer trade—have had limited influence. As our case studies verified, the U.S. trade representative, the office charged with the responsibility of overseeing GSP, had been prone to political pressure before 1989, but subsequently became more evenhanded and articulate.

Nevertheless, as chapters 6 and 8 documented, GSP petitions were a major impetus behind USAID's decision to pour more than $15 million into regional labor-management programs during the mid-1990s via its Trade, Commercial, and Labor Relations Division.[2] While most funding ended by 1997, the case studies illustrated the cultural biases and complex organizational assumptions embedded in USAID's programs. One example was the agency's use of training seminars to reform national labor inspection systems. The program prompted one local-government official to exaggeratedly portray GSP's only impact as "getting USAID to spend money on training and hiring labor inspectors—the U.S. creates conditions, and then is forced to create a program to meet them." The comment reflected a common perception held by unionists and co-workers.

Not all instructional efforts at conflict resolution failed, as the cases set forth; but enhancing basic resources in inspection delivery ought to have gained more USAID attention. The agency's donation of equipment and vehicles brought more improvements to labor inspections than did its seminars, even when half the donations were purloined. Both USAID and local officials must come to terms with labor ministries where "expense accounts make no sense" yet inspectors "must pay from our own pockets to cover transport costs not only for ourselves, but sometimes for the workers."

Future USAID funding and programs will be needed to accomplish the transformations outlined above. In the longer term, the influence of the GSP program will gradually diminish as preferences themselves decline with reductions in trade barriers generally. To be effective, the U.S. must explore ways to encourage other nations on a regional level to join in advocating labor rights. Although it failed in a similar campaign with WTO and GATT in 1996, the U.S. effort involved very few developing country participants. A renewal of this would have much greater chance of success via the Summit of the Americas and the traditional hegemonic sphere of the U.S. in Central American and the Caribbean.

Tripartism and Solidarity

The future of trade and labor agreements in Central America and elsewhere also will depend a great deal on a reconfiguration of tripartite consultations. Workers are asking to be members of free-zone trade councils that supervise maquila activities. Owners are recognizing the usefulness of union contacts, but on their own terms.

In Guatemala, El Salvador, Nicaragua, and the Dominican for example, CACIF, UNEP, ADOZONA, and COSEP claim a proactive position regarding unions. CACIF is committed "to follow ILO convention 144 . . . to jointly evaluate the political conditions of the country; to study the evidence on taxes and other issues." "We want the productive sector to become more involved," said one spokesperson, who called for training to improve worker technical abilities. "How can we compete with Europe without this?"[3]

Yet while businessmen in Guatemala and elsewhere expect workers who participate with them to speak favorably about the nation's productivity goals and its overall image, they are not yet ready to listen to (much less to forgive) those who publicly condemn current and past abuses.[4] They view tripartism as a class instrument; they do not yet understand that it means listening to other points of view, which must precede any "united front." Our findings on tripartism and the reluctance of the business class to compromise on labor legislation at every step of the GSP process in virtually all the cases studied reinforces a conflict model of social behavior.[5] Bona fide tripartism is an essential ingredient for a successful regional trade and labor policy. However, it will require that business leaders appreciate the value of both labor participation and respect for labor rights as a contribution to national identity, not as an unpatriotic activity. Local businesses must cooperate with international firms linked to AIP and other groups seeking union input in outside monitoring.

Simultaneously, a regional trade accord will depend on the continuing efforts of international solidarity. The GSP process has been a vehicle for such expression. U.S. labor solidarity groups have devoted their greatest attention to El Salvador and Guatemala. As we argued in chapter 4 and proved in the case histories, the *way* in which petitions were promoted through the delegations, on-ground discussions, press action, embassy contacts, and U.S. political work was very much related to their local success. Former U.S. labor attaché Donald Knight thought U.S./GLEP's work in Guatemala had been especially important. "We didn't have such presence in El Salvador, and the review was soon lifted; in Costa Rica they also were let off the hook, despite [or perhaps because of] of the strength of *Solidarismo*."[6] But in the Dominican and Honduras, union leaders involved in an organizing campaign also took the lead in gathering GSP endorsements. Everywhere labor representatives stressed the importance of trade conditions as an element of international labor solidarity, and as a crucial component of regional trade agreements to assure the limited rights workers already enjoyed.

Solidarity and consumer-labor coalitions also publicized the companies that violated codes of employee treatment. They succeeded most effectively when they synchronized their campaigns with trade union organizing, as with PVH in Guatemala and Bonahan in the Dominican. If such strategies succeed, if labor gained a fresh militancy that resulted in widespread improvements, then state power could again become a contested arena, and trade policy a tactical manifestation. The dialectical interplay of workers uniting across borders and employing state mechanisms to confront business interests remains the most satisfactory explanatory dynamic behind local and U.S. government behavior and corporate responsiveness.

In Summary

The seven countries of the Caribbean Basin presented here are, along with Chile and Paraguay, the primary examples of effective trade conditionality. The transformation in these nations tells a different story than the improvements in labor conditions portrayed in the countries of East Asia prior to their 1997 economic crisis. No doubt we did not take into account all variables or remove all biases; but after carefully weighing a wide range of evidence, it is the overall finding of this study that trade-based labor standards applied here have avoided and even reduced protectionism, and also enhanced respect for basic worker rights in both the U.S. and the Caribbean Basin as a whole.

Our own evidence also demonstrated how these nations preserved flexibility in wages and employment security. Public debate over labor issues increased in countries that endured the GSP process. With less hostility, unions and employers held more discussions about common interests such as improving production and attracting investment. While code violations persisted, wages improved and abuses dropped in the mushrooming maquila sector, which expanded in all the seven nations considered. The informal sector, which was bloated largely by landless workers, not formal sector terminations (contrary to the predictions by some in chapter 3) also gained indirect advantages in salaries and treatment from the public attention to labor rights. Theoretically, expanding markets and increasing global awareness could have, over time, brought similar changes. However the ferocity of employer resistance and governmental justification in each of the documented cases suggests that time alone would not have conveyed equivalent change.

Therefore, GSP review has and can serve as a model for trade agreements.[7] It would, of course, require modifications to respect the sovereignty of local laws, to achieve multilateral participation, and to become functional for a regional agreement (if not for GATT, and its oversight body, the WTO).[8] Despite the disadvantages arising from its unilateral approach, it is essential to emulate the relative simplicity of its criteria and its review process, one that is open to people of all nations.

The Impact of CBI on Central American and Caribbean Nations

U.S. president Ronald Reagan proposed the Caribbean Basin Initiative to the Organization of American States in 1982 as a measure to address the Caribbean region's economic crisis, exacerbated by higher oil prices and lower export prices. He advocated a program of trade preferences, tax incentives, and financial assistance. The U.S. Congress incorporated these suggestions into the Caribbean Basin Economic Recovery Act (CBERA), which passed in mid-1983 and took effect in 1984. CBERA promoted trade as the primary method of developing the economies of Caribbean Basin nations. The act contained six points: duty-free treatment for area products (except textiles and apparel) for twelve years; investment tax incentives; aid to the private sector to take advantage of trade (through USAID, OPIC, etc.); technical assistance and training, including export marketing; coordination of developmental assistance with other countries; and special support to Puerto Rico and the Virgin Islands.

Prior to CBERA, the U.S. had granted most-favored-nation tariff status to area nations in accordance with the General Agreement on Tariffs and Trade (GATT) and other agreements. Altogether, 35.3 percent of all U.S. imports from CBERA countries had entered free of duty the year before the program went into effect, including 20.5 percent under most-favored-nation provisions and 5.9 percent under apparel provisions of the U.S. Tariff Schedule (now the Harmonized Tariff Schedule).

CBERA increased these percentages of duty-free products. However, in general terms, CBERA nations did not become major players in U.S. trade. In 1984, when CBERA was launched, CBERA countries accounted for 2.7 percent of overall U.S. imports. This ratio declined to 1.8 percent by 1993. By contrast, U.S. exports to CBERA countries, while dipping slightly in some years from the 2.8 percent recorded in 1984, stood at 2.7 percent of U.S. exports in 1993. As

Table A.1. U.S. trade with CBERA countries, 1984–93

	U.S. exports (millions of dollars)	% of world exports	U.S. imports (millions of dollars)	% of world imports	U.S. trade balance (millions of dollars)
1984	5,952.9	2.8	8,649.2	2.7	-2,696.4
1985	5,743.0	2.8	6,687.2	1.9	-944.2
1986	6,064.6	2.8	6,064.7	1.6	-0.1
1987	6,668.3	2.7	6,039.0	1.5	629.3
1988	7,421.8	2.4	6,061.1	1.4	1,360.7
1989	8,105.0	2.3	6,637.4	1.4	1,467.6
1990	9,307.1	2.5	7,525.2	1.5	1,781.9
1991	9,885.5	2.5	8,229.4	1.7	1,656.1
1992	10,901.7	2.6	9,425.6	1.8	1,476.1
1993	11,941.9	2.7	10,094.0	1.8	1,847.9

Source: USITC (1994), compiled from official statistics of the U.S. Department of Commerce.

the tenth-largest U.S. export market, the Caribbean Basin is one of the few regions with which the United States had a trade surplus.

Table A.1 shows that between 1984 and 1993, CBERA exports to the U.S. only averaged 7 billion while its imports from the U.S. averaged 8 billion (see table 4.4 for export figures from specific countries). By 1993, CBERA nations had a trade deficit of $1.8 billion.

Table A.2 presents the trade balances by various commodities. The U.S. did have a net deficit of $1.8 billion in textile products, but it made up for this with machinery, forest products, chemicals. etc.

In table A.3, the countries' percentage share of CBERA shipments to the U.S. is presented. Note that five countries—the Dominican Republic, Costa Rica, Guatemala, El Salvador, and Honduras—accounted for about four-fifths of all duty-free CBERA exports to the U.S. (The same nations are responsible for a doubling of apparel exports.)

Nevertheless, as table A.4 indicates, the Dominican Republic, Costa Rica, Guatemala, and Honduras often experienced a net trade loss in their exchanges with the U.S.

Parallel to CBI, in June 1990, President George Bush proposed the Enterprise for the Americas Initiative, which would extend similar programs to other Latin American nations. Congress was not enthusiastic about this second initiative and only implemented a few of its programs. Presidents Bush and Clinton offered some of the incentives to other nations via Executive Order.

Table A.2. U.S. exports, imports, and trade balances with CBERA-eligible countries, by principal industry sectors, 1989–93 (millions of dollars, U.S. Customs value)

	1989	1990	1991	1992	1993
Textiles and apparel					
Exports	1,205	1,258	1,570	1,946	2,294
Imports	1,836	2,064	2,622	3,379	4,097
Balance	-631	-806	-1,052	-1,433	-1,802
Footwear					
Exports	70	57	60	62	65
Imports	120	158	166	202	241
Balance	-50	-101	-106	-140	-176
Agricultural products					
Exports	1,531	1,553	1,558	1,629	1,878
Imports	2,011	2,046	1,972	2,161	2,235
Balance	-480	-493	-414	-532	-358
Forest products					
Exports	561	571	595	621	684
Imports	71	74	56	57	66
Balance	490	498	539	564	618
Energy-related products					
Exports	613	904	933	821	757
Imports	1,066	1,354	1,403	1,476	1,295
Balance	-453	-449-	471-	655-	538
Chemical products					
Exports	1,112	1,144	1,194	1,260	1,225
Imports	611	642	705	683	527
Balance	501	503	489	577	698
Machinery and transportation equipment					
Exports	1,512	1,637	1,637	2,018	2,303
Imports	90	78	75	90	100
Balance	1,422	1,559	1,562	1,928	2,203
Electronic products					
Exports	715	789	816	933	1,030
Imports	276	288	335	393	468
Balance	439	501	481	540	562
Minerals and metals					
Exports	526	491	498	541	604
Imports	412	406	383	396	373
Balance	114	86	114	145	231
Miscellaneous products					
Exports	260	903	1,025	1,071	1,102
Imports	144	415	512	589	692
Balance	116	488	513	482	410
Total					
Exports	8,105	9,307	9,886	10,902	11,942
Imports	6,637	7,525	8,229	9,426	10,094
Balance	1,468	1,782	1,656	1,476	1,848

Source: USITC 1994.

Table A.3. Percentage of U.S. imports from CBERA countries, selected years, 1984–93

	1984	1986	1988	1990	1992	1993
Dominican Republic	11	17	24	23	25	26
Costa Rica	5	11	13	13	15	15
Guatemala	5	10	7	11	11	12
Jamaica	5	5	7	7	6	7
Honduras	5	7	7	6	8	9
El Salvador	4	6	5	3	4	5
Panama	4	6	4	3	2	2
Trinidad and Tobago	16	13	12	13	9	8
Bahamas	13	7	4	7	6	3
Netherlands Antilles	23	7	7	6	6	4
Haiti	4	6	6	5	1	2
All others	4	4	4	3	5	7
Total	100	100	100	100	100	100

Source: USITC 1994.

Table A.4. Trade balance between the U.S. and CBERA countries, selected years, 1984–93 (millions of dollars, U.S. Customs value)

	1984	1986	1988	1990	1992	1993
Dominican Republic	-364	-167	-85	-105	-303	-377
Costa Rica	-51	-171	-94	-47	-84	-38
Guatemala	-76	-222	132	-47	95	89
Jamaica	92	148	300	353	321	370
Honduras	-90	-108	6	68	9	-47
El Salvador	-1	55	168	309	344	366
Panama	419	322	332	581	780	854
Trinidad and Tobago	-772	-264	-379	-578	-401	-261
Bahamas	-608	307	457	279	111	327
Netherlands Antilles	-1,416	-84	4	99	-120	110
Haiti	28	11	82	122	106	65
All others	144	174	438	748	621	390
Total	-2,696	[1]	1,361	1,782	1,476	1,848

Source: USITC 1994.

NOTES

Introduction

1. Some analysts distinguish between labor rights and labor standards (see Elmslie and Milberg 1997:70 and chapter 2 in this volume).

2. Lee and Schmidt (1996) estimate that low-skill workers in the U.S. suffer a resulting drop in income between 5 and 20 percent. They also lose benefits and suffer increased job insecurity.

3. According to USITC (1994), CBERA has safeguarded U.S. industries threatened by imports. Competitive food products had to be locally grown and could only be imported from a country with a "Stable Food Production Plan" that assures that its agricultural exports do not interfere with its domestic food supply and with land use and ownership. Sugar, beef, and other agricultural imports were additionally subject to U.S. quotas and food-safety requirements.

The value of a manufactured product had to be at least 35 percent of export sale (or 20 percent with an added 15 percent in U.S.-produced content). The 35 percent could include inputs from Puerto Rico and the Virgin Islands. However, clothing imports fell under a separate agreement (see chapter 4). For example, basin countries produced 28 percent of women's blazers sold in the U.S. during the ten-year period.

4. Dick Lynch, retired International Electrical Union worker, interviewed by the N.J. Plant Closings Committee, 1982 (author's notes).

5. Gerald Epstein (1993) argues that job transfers primarily affected certain industries (autos, textiles) but not others (insurance, metal fabrication).

Chapter 1: Caribbean Basin Workers Search for Decent Treatment

1. Juan José Antonio García, interviews with author, October 1994, March 1995.

2. Carlo Lobos, general secretary of public works, Alta Verapaz, and coordinator of thirty-six unions and popular organizations from the region, interview with author, July 1994.

3. Interview with author, July 1994.

4. FESTRAS filed an unsuccessful appeal in the Constitutional Court, claiming political interference and anti-union prejudices. However, the workers faced additional difficulties: The Puertos Barrios plant was old and had been temporarily shut down for contaminated water. INCASA, which owned the Puerto Barrios Plant, also owned

Embotelladora de Bibida de Oriente, "a much more modern plant in an anti-union Teculután, Zacapa, where managers and workers often ported arms." Rodolfo Robles, interview with author, July 1994.

5. Interview with author, July 1994.

6. Testimony, April 21, 1994, quoted in AFL-CIO, "Petition to USTR on Honduras," June 1995.

7. Interview with author, March 1995. Soida was reelected general secretary of her union in 1995.

8. Worker interviews with author, July 1994, at Gabo in the San Marcos EPZ, a compound of eighteen huge semicircular metal buildings divided by a wide road.

9. In many Central American nations, workers are obligated to receive an extra day's pay for having worked six straight days.

10. Interviews with author, March 1995.

11. Interviews with author, July 1994.

12. Interview with author, March 1995. The author verified a worker's monthly pay stubs from the Rem+B Company, SA, totaling 1,027 colons. Considering the worker's extra hours and Saturday pay recorded on the stubs, this amount registered below legal minimum salary. It even fell below the 57 cents an hour proclaimed in El Salvador's advertisement in *Bobbin,* August 1990.

13. Interview with author, 1995. Zones in El Salvador were El Progresso (2,500 workers, eight maquilas), El Pedrigal (2,000 workers, four exporters), San Marcos (7,000 workers, eleven maquilas including Mandarin), San Bartolo (9,000 workers, fifteen maquilas), and Exporsalva (a new zone with 900 workers). According to the minister of economy, as of 1995 there were 141 more maquilas outside the zones.

14. Interview with author, March 1995.

15. Interview with author, March 1995.

16. Interview with author, July 1994.

17. Interview with author, July 1996.

18. Interview with author, July 1994. Services offered in that building included seventeen clinics (ultrasound, eyes, skin, dental, heart, family), a dining room, and a pharmacy that replaced the state-supported pharmacy, which was moved to a less accessible location in the municipality.

19. Interview with author, July 1994. Union members blamed the World Bank for the privatization drive. While often a likely culprit, in this case the blame would have been better directed toward the government and the tax-phobic private sector. As the Washington-based Center for Democratic Education has indicated, the World Bank's requirement for Guatemala's reception of a $120 million structural-adjustment loan was that Guatemala increase its spending on rural health care by 15 percent (see Ruthrauff and Carlson 1997). Following this view, rather than utilize additional taxes, in 1993–94 the government may have attempted compliance by shifting its health funds out of the regional hospitals and into direct rural programs. To replace expenditures in Esquintla and elsewhere, the government then invited Fundazucar to privatize "urban" health services.

20. Interview with author, July 1994.

21. Interview with author, July 1994. In December 1993, forty-seven were fired in the Municipality of St. Maria Cabon. Sta. Maria case no. 364-4-94 received a court hearing

in January 1994, and it was sent to the sixth labor court, where as of 1997 it still remained. In December 1992, thirteen were fired by the mayor in Santa Cruz de la Paz. They were ordered reinstated in August 1993, and the government appealed on January 11, 1994. The situation is not yet resolved.

22. Lobos, interview with author, July 1994.

23. Mercedes Sotz, quoted in Reed and Brandow (1996:101).

24. Interviews with author, July 1994, March 1995.

25. Letter from Brown to Ambassador Kantor, September 9, 1995, USTR.

26. Interview with author, July 1994.

27. Interview with author, July 1994.

Chapter 2: The Debate over Methods of Achieving Labor Rights

1. Several fine studies examine the current status of employee rights in the U.S. (see Edwards 1993; Ezorsky 1987; Greenberg 1995; Lynd 1994; Westin and Salisbury 1980; Yates 1991). Edwards (1994b) offers comparative information.

2. The Committee of Experts on the Application of Conventions and Recommendations, made up of legal experts and social practitioners, provides technical appraisal of individual state compliance; the Conference Committee on the Application of Conventions and Recommendations meets annually to discuss more generalized trends; and the Committee on Freedom of Association investigates specific complaints. Countries may also decide to reject a convention that they had passed earlier, though this is difficult to do (see Myrdal 1994).

3. In 1943, the ILO lively debated the concept of fair wages and issued a report on "fair remuneration" (Charnovitz 1987:572).

4. The right to collective negotiation was reemphasized via convention 154 (1981).

5. The UN covenant included policies that encouraged full employment under conditions safeguarding fundamental political freedoms (article 6), just and favorable conditions of work including fair wages and safe and healthy working conditions, equal opportunity for promotion, rest and reasonable limitation of working hours (article 7), the right to form and join unions and to strike in conformity with local laws (article 8), social security (article 9), and protection for the economic and social exploitation of children (article 10).

6. The second convention the ILO passed, on unemployment (1919), mandated states to set up free public-employment agencies under centralized control. This was followed by the Fee-Charging Employment Agencies Convention, no. 34 (1933), and the Employment Service Convention, no. 88 (1948). During a later period, the ILO passed the Termination of Employment Convention, no. 158 (1982), to prevent job loss without a legitimate reason and to provide for adequate severance.

7. Other social security and health-related conventions include the Maintenance of Social Security Rights Convention, no. 157 (1982), which promoted an international system for social security rights; the Convention on Occupational Safety, no. 155 (1981); the Convention on Health Services, no. 161 (1985); the Convention on Working Environment, no. 148 (1977); and many others (ILO 1992a; see also Otting 1993).

8. Myrdal (1994). According to Caire (1994:311), the lower rate of ILO ratification began earlier, falling to 30 percent in 1950–55 and to 15 percent in 1965–70. However, he attributes this to the difficulty governments had translating international standards

into law and law enforcement, a difficulty that lengthened due to the increased hetero-geneity of national political situations.

9. Using social criteria, NACDC eliminated technical and administrative conven-tions and those directed at particular groups. It centered on fundamental conventions that incorporated ancillary ones (van Liemt 1989:437).

10. By 1990, the ILO had adopted 171 conventions and 178 recommendations. The conventions had received 5,500 ratifications from member states, two-thirds by devel-oping countries. Nine conventions had been ratified by more than a hundred countries:

No. 29, Forced Labour, 1930):	129 countries
No. 98, Right to Organize and Collective Bargaining, 1949:	115
No. 111, Discrimination (Employment), 1958:	111
No. 105, Abolition of Forced Labour, 1957:	109
No. 19, Equality of Treatment (Accident), 1925:	108
No. 11, Right of Association (Agriculture), 1921:	108
No. 81, Labour Inspection, 1947:	107
No. 14, Weekly Rest (Industry), 1921:	104 (ILO 1994a).

11. "Certain actions are abusive anywhere, among them: slavery, prohibitions on freedom of association or on collective bargaining, exposure of workers to unsafe or unhealthy working conditions . . . and the employment of children. . . . These are outrages against the human condition . . . [but] once these [labor relations process] conditions have been satisfied, labor standards might best be gauged in terms of *labor market outcomes*" (Fields 1990:20; emphasis in original). However, Fields never recon-ciles process and outcomes results

12. For Banuri (1990), excessive concern for job security impeded restructuring in India. The government would find itself lucky if it could exclude labor demands in areas of union tradition, but such a step risked polarizing the society.

13. In 1991, for example, the AFL-CIO began promoting "Maquiladora Standards of Conduct," which were developed through the Coalition for Justice in the Maquila-doras, made up of religious, labor, and human-rights representatives.

14. See Sonnenberg (1993); see also Osigweh (1990), Donaldson and Werhane (1995), Hallett (1989), and Martinez (1994).

15. Corporate retailer codes and tripartite commissions have historically received greater attention in Europe than in the U.S. (see Compa and Diamond 1996).

16. U.S. Department of Labor (1996) reports that thirty-six of the forty-two largest U.S. apparel companies have standards prohibiting child labor and forced labor in their U.S. and foreign operations. The department investigated six countries, including the Dominican Republic, El Salvador, Guatemala, and Honduras.

17. Lim traces other examples. The 1968 Employment and Industrial Relations Acts, which restricted the rights of organized labor, were implemented for political reasons, not simply to attract investments. Seventeen percent of the workforce remained union-ized, even though labor had no right to strike, could not bargain on retrenchment, and received below-market wages. In the early 1970s, improved exports forced an excess in labor demand; wages rose and the country even had to import substantial amounts of foreign labor. However, when exports dropped in 1979, the government mandated restrictions on foreign hiring. After 1983 there was more collective bargaining, and a bipartite National Wages Council began to function.

18. In Thailand, the government also played as much of a role as the market in improving labor standards. It augmented minimum wages after a jump in export manufacturing in 1987 and likewise inaugurated social-security protections and recognized unions (Lim 1990). See also Deyo (1993) and Bonacich et al. (1994) for a more pessimistic picture of labor conditions.

19. Piore et al. (1996) also finds problems with certain protective legislation in Mexico.

20. Langille (1994:335) cites Sen's version of the prisoner's dilemma, where the state has enough evidence to convict two prisoners only of a misdemeanor even though they have committed a felony. When the state separately offers each a reduced felony conviction, each confesses and implicates the other, which seems the rational choice even though a refusal to confess would have brought a lower sentence to both. Here, companies would face a similar choice in not knowing whether the state would enforce its laws.

21. The Fallon-Riveros study may indicate some pressure at the World Bank to shift from neo-liberal prescriptions. Another World Bank study, van Adams et al. (1992), shows the positive role of wages and employment (Plant 1994:64). However, most indicators demonstrate little change in World Bank behavior.

22. Adriana Marshall (1996) did find some linkage between job-protection practice and employer investment, but it was complicated by many partial variables.

23. Lim (1990) denies that export-led success in Singapore resulted either from labor repression or from free markets. Countries like Vietnam and Burma, which enacted labor controls without also offering the other attractions, failed. South Korea and Taiwan, which passed labor control laws for domestic stability, were forced to relax them. Lim believes state labor controls are insufficient to ensure cheap, disciplined production workers. In fact, over the long haul, wage policy did not depress wages below market, while manpower training enhanced skills.

24. In historical terms, Piore says that the introduction of mass production demanded capital intensification. The length of the run, not labor cost, then became a primary managerial focus. As mass producers outdid sweatshop producers, they accepted collective bargaining because such bargaining generated wage increases that supported demand. However, mass markets have fragmented, making it more difficult to justify large investments.

25. Blackwell (1988) believes that it is the more dynamic and productive plants in U.S. that are being replaced by low-cost sweatshop producers in developing countries.

26. In *Contested Terrain* (1979), Richard Edwards makes a similar point about reorganization over the pace of work as society moves from the put out system of greater individual control to one of enforced control. Furthermore, because EPZ mass production and sweating does not respect labor-standard observance, Portes also envisions a role for government, but one more flexible than a strict labor code (see also chapter 4 in this volume).

Chapter 3: Implementing Labor Rights Through Trade Conditions

1. While we focus on trade, in the "market of political choice" voters could influence a variety of state sanctions, such as monetary inducements, reduced aid, and changes

in tax laws to encourage better worker treatment. Some Democrats support the last strategy, but the Clinton administration has not (see Clymer 1996b:A17).

2. Again, state sanctions could be "market-driven" if the population elects officials to implement them (see Freeman 1994).

3. In this view, employment security in the globalized economy is no longer guaranteed to anyone, whether a white-collar or blue-collar worker (Potter 1994:357; see also Friedman 1994).

4. According to both Jong-il You (1990) and Lim (1990), Asian countries believe that U.S. labor standards are protectionist and paternalistic. Their application could reinforce economic nationalism. However, You admits that U.S. trade law was one reason that South Korea amended its labor laws in 1986 (see also chapter 2 in this volume). On perspectives in Latin America, see Lustig (1994).

5. Caire (1994:304) asks why concern is expressed for the trade sector, where worker conditions are frequently better than in other sectors of national economies. Why are sanctions not linked to capital flows (lending, aid)? Social dumping can also come from unfair monetary arrangements, exchange-rate differences, and so on. The current institutional framework of the international trading system is responsible for the perverse effects of unrestricted free trade, not developing countries.

6. Businesspeople such as General Electric executive Frank Doyle (1994) believe that it would be a mistake not to engage in a debate on international labor standards and trade (see chapter 2).

7. Elmslie and Milberg call these "labor standards" as distinguished from the other "core labor rights" (1997:70). In a somewhat different perspective, safety and health standards would not substantially raise average production costs, but freedom of association would do so, especially in agriculture and services (G. Engren, quoted in van Liemt 1989).

8. A "fair share" to the worker is traceable to the 1919 League of Nations Covenant and the 1927 Conference on National Trade Policies. Various commodity agreements (rubber, sugar, tin, cocoa) subsequently included social clauses to improve the standard of living of agricultural and industrial workers, although they contained no enforcement mechanism (Charnovitz 1987; see also van Liemt 1989:438; Servais 1989).

9. The U.S. is signatory to ILO conventions on hours worked and occupational health and safety, but no other basic conventions. However, like all European Union countries except Great Britain, it accepts some form of social charter.

10. In 1987 the U.S. House of Representatives passed the Trade and International Economic Reform Bill, which asked the president to "instruct the Secretary of the Treasury to enforce without delay" the 1930 law (Charnovitz 1987:31).

11. As Charnovitz (1987) notes, in 1917 the AFL was rebuffed in its efforts to restrict child-labor imports. GATT article 22 (1947) did allow nations to refuse products made by slave labor but not necessarily by other forms of forced labor. Ironically, the U.S. would soon attack "communist" governments, such as those of Indonesia, Iran, and Guatemala, that restricted and monitored child labor.

12. Alston believes that by failing to ratify many basic ILO conventions and principles contained in the UN International Covenant on Economic and Social Rights, the U.S. has retarded the development of an international consensus on labor rights.

13. Founded as a working group in 1984, the ILRF became the International Labor Rights Education and Research Fund in 1986 (the name was shortened in 1996). Its purpose was "to assure that workers in all countries labor under reasonable conditions." The ILRF *took the lead in stressing the importance of labor rights as an element of trade policy.* It convinced Congressman Donald Pease to amend the 1974 GSP trade legislation up for renewal to include labor-rights language and a review mechanism to ascertain compliance through USTR (see below).

14. The GSP Renewal Act of 1984 explicitly references the UN Universal Declaration on Human Rights (see Dorman 1989:7 and below).

15. U.S. House of Representatives (1984).

16. While the original act made a brief reference, the Caribbean Basin Economic Recovery Expansion Act of 1990 made the program permanent. It prohibited the president from designating any country as a CBI beneficiary if that country has not taken or is not taking steps to afford internationally recognized worker rights as defined under the GSP program. While this lifted CBI protections to a rank equal with GSP, including the same enforcement mechanisms, there are some differences. Country-of-origin conditions for duty exemptions are less stringent under the CBI (there are no competitive need limits). Many CBI products remain eligible for duty-free entry under either GSP or CBI, at the choice of the supplier. In 1993, some two-thirds of CBI-country exports entered the U.S. free of duty under both programs.

17. These include the Overseas Private Investment Corporation Amendment Act (1985), the Comprehensive Anti-Apartheid Act (1986); and the 1993 and 1994 foreign aid appropriations laws. Section 301 of the 1974 Trade Act was reinforced by an extended clause 301 of the Omnibus Trade and Competitiveness Act of 1988, which enabled the U.S. trade representative to take retaliatory measures against any "unfair" act that was deemed "unjustifiable," "discriminatory," or "unreasonable." The definition of an "unreasonable" act, policy, or practice was expanded to include "a persistent pattern of conduct" that violated basic worker rights (Lawyers Committee for Human Rights 1991). However, out of all these laws, the GSP legislation contains the only workable enforcement procedure.

18. The funding authorization passed by the U.S. Congress required U.S. bank participants to assess respect for labor rights as a requirement for loan approvals.

19. Technically speaking, the review and/or denial can occur at several levels within the Office of the U.S. Trade Representative, including the GSP subcommittee. Denials can occur for violations of intellectual property rights as well as worker rights.

20. Data did not include six "pended" petitions (those that were granted continuing review), four from the AFL-CIO. After review, USTR was less preferential in exonerating nations. Through 1990, the agency received seventy-six petitions worldwide, covering twenty-nine beneficiaries. It accepted twenty-four for review but only denied benefits to eight: Burma, the Central African Republic, Chile, Liberia, Nicaragua, Paraguay, Romania, and Sudan.

21. Interview with former State Department official Anthony Freeman, June 1994.

22. For example, USTR denied petitions on Guatemala in 1987–89, using such language as this: "If a requirement submitted pursuant to part 2007.0(b) [of the 1974 Trade Act as amended] does not conform to the requirement set forth . . . or sufficient infor-

mation related to subsections 502(b) or 502(c) [19 U.S.C. 2642 (b) and (c)] to warrant review, or if it . . . does not fall within criteria of suspension, [it] shall not be accepted . . . [it] again failed to provide sufficient information related to the statutory provisions." Little additional information was provided.

23. Interview with Anthony Freeman, June 1994.

24. The Lawyers Committee on Human Rights (1989) and economist Peter Dorman (1989) evaluated these criticisms. Dorman recognized the skepticism of petitioners regarding "understandings" between the State Department and foreign governments. He demonstrated USTR's ambivalence about the linkage between economic and political rights. For Dorman, key procedural issues arising under GSP included the appropriateness of USTR's discretionary review of petitions and the confidentiality of its fact-finding. All petitions should be accepted for review. Although intensive investigations should be selective, country data and decision rationales should be made public, though not necessarily the details of its deliberations. Dorman also argued for a much closer linkage between worker and human rights and urged reconciling the GSP "taking-steps" criterion with sustained pressure for labor-rights reform. He also recommended coordinating trade conditionality with other international policies.

25. November 29, 1988. While Kirkland was referring to the need for a social clause in GATT, he went on to say, "We have already urged our Government to exclude from the GSP a number of counties that . . . failed to show progress in correcting abuses of worker rights, and we shall just as actively pursue enforcement of the 1988 provisions making persistent denial of worker rights an unreasonable trade practice" (see Kirkland 1989:3).

26. Freeman, interview with author, June 1994.

27. Freeman, interview with author, June 1994.

28. According to USTR staff member David Shark, "It is also possible for interested parties to raise worker rights issues in our consideration of product specific decisions," but this has never been done. Statement before the Subcommittee on Human Rights and International Organizations, U.S. House of Representatives, June 30, 1987.

29. The GAO report identified other deficiencies and suggested appropriate remedies, parallel to Dorman (1989). It advocated flexibility for filing petitions as a timely response to specific problems (rather than being forced to comply with an annual June 1 review date).

30. Jon Rosenbaum, comment to author, December 1997.

31. Every year, the ICFTU publication *Trade Union Rights* reviews labor violations across the globe. In 1988, violators included Brazil, Chile, Columbia, El Salvador, Guatemala, Haiti, Honduras, Nicaragua, and Paraguay.

32. For example, by a composite ordinal index with weighted data from the UN Economic Commission on Latin America and the Caribbean (ECLAC) or the World Bank. Poverty rate, literacy, morbidity, life expectancy are also measured by the Interamerican Development Bank.

Chapter 4: The Record of GSP Petitions in Latin America and the Caribbean

1. For example, in 1989, Americas Watch, the Labor Campaign for Unions in El Salvador, the National STISSS Support Committee, and the Massachusetts Labor Com-

mittee all requested review of El Salvador's trade status; Human Rights Watch filed on the Dominican Republic.

2. As of 1995, nineteen developing countries had ratified more than fifty ILO conventions, including ten Latin nations: Cuba, Panama (69), Mexico, Argentina, Peru (66), Brazil, Guatemala (62), Nicaragua (58), Ecuador, and Venezuela.

3. For example, in Argentina, at first Perón exclusively provided union support to the Confederación General de Trabajadores. Only as communist unions were thwarted did he extend social protections to the general society.

4. Guatemala and El Salvador passed accident compensation laws prior to World War I, but this was unusual.

5. These nations joined the ILO in 1919; Costa Rica joined in 1920; the Dominican Republic joined in 1924.

6. Unions required twenty-one petitioners, but a single firing could void the request. Strikes could be legal when 75 percent of employees agreed, but only after eight months of unsuccessful contract negotiations. Even then, a court had to determine that the strike was also "just"—that is, that the company could satisfy union demands as proven by citing the company's books (which the union had to produce). By the mid-1970s, only one strike (INCATCU Shoe Co.) had been declared just (López Larrave 1979).

7. Based on Bulmer-Thomas (1987:316–17), who adds meat to the four other traditional exports, calculated at 1970 prices, net estimated factor cost.

8. A flexible investment strategy is not new for Central American exporters facing a variable world market. In the 1940s and 1950s they shifted to cotton and beef (see Williams 1986).

9. This was due to a significant reduction of petroleum-refining operations in Trinidad and Tobago between 1984 and 1989. U.S. imports of petroleum products shrank to 26.2 percent of their 1984 value. Bauxite prices and sugar quotas also dropped. But if petroleum products were excluded, the trend in export values would have increased over the period.

10. According to USITC (1994), "The value of U.S. imports from the Eastern Caribbean declined during the CBERA decade, probably because the region chose to depend more on tourism than on industry. By contrast, the importance of Central America and the Central Caribbean grew rapidly; the former's share of total imports increased from 24 percent to 45 percent, and the latter's share from 20 percent to 35 percent. Their growing significance is explained by U.S.-Caribbean production sharing—particularly in apparel."

11. The three leading exporters to the U.S. were the Dominican Republic, Costa Rica, and Guatemala. They were also the region's largest purchasers of U.S. exports (the Dominican Republic expanded from 11 to 19 percent, Costa Rica to 13 percent, and Guatemala to 11 percent). However, Guatemala was the only one of the three with which the U.S. had a trade surplus in 1993 (see appendix).

12. Based on data from CAR, October 11, 1991.

13. For example, in the 1990s, finca owners routinely refused to provide facilities for worker families or schools for children, although they offered better facilities to single workers (author interviews, 1994; see also Oglesby 1997).

14. There are four stages in apparel manufacture: initiation, cutting and pre-assembly, assembly, and finishing (pressing and packaging). Maquila plants handle the last two stages, for which developed work skills are less essential. Companies quickly entered production to compete for contracts.

15. The Special Access Program involved clothing and textiles assembled from fabrics formed and cut in the U.S. Duties are effectively levied only on the value added outside the U.S. (USITC 1994).

16. Export license applications rose from eight in 1984 to a cumulative total of 193, not including about eighty smaller sub-maquila contractors (Petersen 1992). This growth rate of more than 75 percent each year was typical for the region. By 1992, $350 million in full product value of garments had been exported to the U.S. The Guatemalan Export Association reported that the apparel industry as a whole had grown from an output value of $19.5 million in 1986 to $207 million in 1990, with jobs rising from 5,120 to 80,000 and companies rising to 280, including thirty Korean companies and such U.S. companies as Calvin Klein, Liz Claiborne, Perry Ellis, Levi Straus, Guess, London Fog, Wrangler, Van Heusen, and Ralph Lauren (see CAR, February 7, 1992). By 1996, Guatemala had more than 400 maquilas, employing 100,000 (see Ramírez 1994; Armbruster 1997).

17. When the U.S. Congress expanded CBERA in 1990, it conveyed a 20 percent duty reduction to previously excluded leather products (except footwear)—handbags, luggage, flat goods, work gloves, and leather wearing apparel. It added 122 product categories in 1991–92, including some athletic equipment, bandages, certain carpets, certain meats (chicken, duck, goose, and turkey), conveyor belts, headgear (headbands), jute yarns, mattresses, plastic and rubberized fabrics, sporting goods and wrist watches, plastic floor/wall/ceiling coverings, plastic plates/sheets/film, vulcanized rubber sheets/plates/strips, conveyor and transmission belts, and ink pads—virtually all Caribbean product categories and then some (USITC 1994).

18. Banco de Guatemala, "Exportation of Goods, FOB 1986–1991."

19. The demand for laundry service, button and zipper companies, and even lunch stands represented a minuscule amount of value. Most textiles are foreign in origin. Under the Multifiber Arrangement, U.S. components (that is, materials cut in U.S. mills) must comprise 65 percent or more of total declared value for maquila exports to qualify for the Harmonized Trade Schedule (HTS) programs, thereby preventing local textile development (although NAFTA reduces this requirement). Petersen (1992) believed that two-thirds of textile product volume was currently made in the U.S., one-fourth in Korea and Southeast Asia, and only a tenth in regional shops.

20. In Petersen's survey (1992), most maquila owners said they "regularly diverted profits to U.S. banks (and Korean banks)."

21. For example, Chile has yet to comply with ILO convention 35, which specifies employer contributions and non-profit administration of worker pension plans (ILO 1995a).

22. Interview with author, June 1995.

23. AFL-CIO, "Petition on Peru," 1992, quoted the U.S. State Department Country Report on Human Rights (1991) to the effect that worker rights were routinely violated;

there were legal restrictions on the right to strike, bargain, and organize. No right to strike laws existed, despite the provision for such in the constitution. The executive branch decided on strike legality. "In spite of the constitutional right to strike, nearly all strikes in Peru are declared illegal." Workers fired are permanently replaced. The right to bargain is restricted in the public sector: unions cannot negotiate for wages, only for working conditions that do not adversely affect the national budget. Regarding discrimination in the workplace, the Human Rights Report continued, "Union activists are sometimes harassed by employers who threaten to fire them. Others are paid off to leave the enterprise." The loss of democracy increased after the April 5 coup by Fujimori in 1991.

24. The 1990 labor code also required employers to grant a day of weekly rest, but only if the person worked on Sunday (versus ILO convention 106).

25. The government insisted that officers and two-thirds of members be Colombian. It also was overly broad in defining essential services that were prevented from striking.

26. The ILO committee requested reform of the penal code to prevent violations of convention 105 (ILO 1995).

27. Report by the Colombian Section of the Andean Jurists, 1994; and Saldarriaga, "Ser Lideres Perder la Vida?" *El Colombiano*, April 30, 1995, cited in AFL-CIO, "Petition to USTR," June 1995.

Chapter 5: The Labor Petitions in El Salvador

Author's note: I am indebted to Benjamin Davis for his critical reading of this and the following chapter and for his other work on the GSP process in El Salvador (see Davis 1995). The quotations are from interviews the author conducted in El Salvador in March 1995, unless otherwise noted.

1. The Law of Unions, promulgated on August 9, 1950, and revised on August 13, 1951, recognized the right to collectively negotiate for trade, plant, and industrial unions.

2. The code was promulgated in January 1963; Organic Law, decree 455, November 27, 1963, set up the ministry structure, which remained in place until the 1996 reorganization.

3. Decree 15, July 23, 1972.

4. The labor code in force in 1982 prohibited campesino unions. Although it allowed industrial, trade, and company unions, the government passed a series of inhibiting decrees. Decree 296 forbade the unionization of public employees. Decree 544 froze wages and curtailed wage negotiations.

5. Ministry of Labor, Statistical Report, 1991. The U.S. Labor Department listed 400,000 union members by 1987, constituting 20 percent of the workforce (FLT 90-18:5). This figure included cooperatives affiliated with the Unión Nacional Obera-Campesina (UNOC) that routinely exaggerated their memberships (see Frundt 1995 with respect to similar figures in Guatemala).

6. The enormous amount of U.S. aid to El Salvador in the 1980s (totaling $5 billion) had much to do with keeping the government in power. Such aid was phased out in the

mid-1990s as U.S. policy became susceptible to neo-liberalist pressures and competing demands for funding in Eastern Europe. Increasingly the Salvadoran government was allowed to fend for itself.

7. The testimony of Americas Watch to USTR, October 1987, listed sixteen instances of abuses in 1986–87. The testimony chronicles twenty-seven cases of labor-union leaders and members who were arrested from September 1985 to March 1987, as documented in International Human Rights Law Group (1987). It also recounted the disappearance of several unionists and the March 1987 poultry workers strike thwarted by soldiers.

8. USTR response to congressional letter, August 14, 1987.

9. Americas Watch, "Petition before USTR," April 22, 1988. Also see Americas Watch (1988). ILRF followed with petitions in 1988, 1989, 1990, and 1991.

10. AFL-CIO/AIFLD, "A Critique of the Americas Watch Report on Labor Rights in El Salvador," June 10, 1988, which was directed primarily at Americas Watch as an organization, not to its reports on labor rights. See also Armstrong et al. (1987), which documents AIFLD's role in creating UNOC during 1980s as a counterinsurgent organization directed against UNTS and FENASTRAS.

11. Americas Watch, "Petition before USTR on Labor Rights in El Salvador," joined by the Massachusetts Labor Committee, the Labor Campaign for Unions in El Salvador, and the National STISSS Support Committee, March 1989. ARDE was portrayed as a newly formed death squad.

12. USTR, "Public Explanation of Decision to Reject Petition Request on El Salvador," August 4, 1989.

13. Interview with author, May 1995.

14. One petition, largely compiled by Benjamin Davis, was submitted by the International Union of Electrical Workers and the United Food and Commercial Workers. A virtually identical petition came from FENASTRAS, the Massachusetts Labor Committee, the New York Labor Committee, the Philadelphia Labor Committee, and the Labor Committee on Central America. The AFL-CIO filed its own shorter petition documenting the attacks on UNOC affiliates.

15. The U.S. State Department Human Rights Report (1989), and the threatened GSP action were partially responsible for El Salvador's passage in March 1990 of the Law Governing Free Trade Zones and Fiscal Precincts, Leg. Decree 461. In theory, section F guaranteed the five basic ILO rights. Article 33 specified fines and temporary suspensions but included no enforcement mechanism.

16. The petition also challenged USTR's "inherent difficulty in extrapolating from allegations of incidents of harassment or violence against individuals to allegations of broader classes of worker- or human-rights violations" (AFL-CIO, *Bulletin*, November 1991). See also Letter from Rudy Oswald, director of Economic Research, AFL-CIO, December 13, 1990, calling for GSP termination because worker rights were still not respected.

17. The State Department Country Report and several human-rights monitors, including the UN Human Rights Commission and the special rappauteur for El Salvador, agreed that there were fewer human-rights violations by both the El Salvador armed forces and the FMLN during 1990 than during 1989. USTR cited this as justification for its inability to verify the linkage between individual and institutional harassment.

18. According to the GSP Subcommittee, ASTTEL appeared to have representatives in collective negotiations and was cooperating with the telephone company (ANTEL). "The large number of allegations over a long period of time made the case extremely difficult to judge." USTR, GSP Subcommittee, "1990 GSP Annual Review, El Salvador," April 1991.

19. The labor code required several stages of direct bargaining before any strike was taken. An employer not being struck could not fire or transfer workers without approval. Once a strike occurred, pay was to continue (although this has never happened). Private-sector strikes could be terminated via agreement or arbitration, with stages of bargaining (and with workers being allowed five days to return). It could also be declared illegal, in which case there was retribution.

20. USTR, GSP Subcommittee, "1990 GSP Annual Review, El Salvador," April 1991. The subcommittee "pended" its decision, meaning that it held up the official review process to see if El Salvador improved its compliance.

21. From USTR, "1991 GSP Annual Review, Worker Rights Review Summary," June 1992.

22. ILRF and American University International Human Rights Clinic, "Pre-hearing Brief on Worker Rights in El Salvador," before GSP, September 23, 1992.

23. Murders of FEASIES night watchman; Miguel Angel Alvarenga, STITGASC (tourist workers union), Ivan Ramírez, FENASTRAS, José Alejandro Jaco Perez, ATMOP; death threats, ASTTEL. A walk out by 28,000 public school teachers grew to 100,000. Soon, 250,000 public employees walked. See ILRF and American University International Human Rights Law Clinic, "Pre-Hearing Brief on Worker Rights in El Salvador, before the General System of Preferences," September 23, 1992.

24. ILRF and American University, op. cit., citing research by the Venezuelan Research Center for Documentation and Analysis for Workers, July 1992; and ILO report, January 1992. A total of 61.4 percent of the country's 526,584 families lived in poverty, and 29 percent were indigent (1990 figures). President Cristiani himself estimated that a third of El Salvador's 5.5 million people lived in extreme poverty.

25. Article 47 stated all workers could form professional associations; article 48 gave the right to strike; article 39 provided collective contracts for all. Article 47 also promised union officials no dismissal. Articles 9 and 38 opposed the use of forced and child labor. Article 38 supported payment of the minimum wage.

26. Interviews with Mauricio Herrera and Sonia Caceres, USAID-El Salvador, July 3, 1996. Although FOES received its legal status in mid-1991, Caceres believed that its growth "came out of the Peace Accords, and discussions over the Labor Code."

27. INSAFORP replaced the Ministry of Labor's Dirección General de Formación Profesional (DGFP), which in 1992 had been the largest bureau of the ministry, with more than seventy employees, fourteen sections, and four departments. Begun in 1966 as a ministry training program, DGFP attracted considerable foreign funding and trained more than 1,500 workers, but it came to be judged as very ineffective. INSAFORP represented an improvement but also embodied a host of difficulties (see Shepard et al. 1994:23).

28. Ratified were no. 105 (prohibiting forced labor), which promised realignment in the Salvadoran penal code; no. 12 (Workmen's Compensation in Agriculture); no. 104 (Abolition of Penal Sanctions for Breaches of Contract of Employment by Indigenous

Workers); no. 107 (Protection and Integration of Indigenous); no. 159 (Vocational Reha-
bilitation and Employment of Disabled); and no. 160 (Labor Statistics). See also note 43,
this chapter.

29. Klayman and Associates, Washington, D.C., 20024, for the Government of El
Salvador, "Response to the Post-hearing Briefs of the AFL-CIO and Other Petitioners,"
1992. The response addressed specific cases. For example, SOICSCES conducted "an
illegal strike"; the government investigated the bombing of FENASTRAS headquar-
ters once the debris was cleared and they were allowed access; President Alfredo
Cristiani had shown "political courage and skill," as noted in the *Washington Post,*
November 13, 1992. (Notably, Klayman and Associates shared the same address as Free
Trade Enterprises, Ltd.)

30. USTR, "1992 GSP Annual Review," July 1993.

31. According to AIFLD regional director Michael Donovan, the outgoing legislature passed the code in March, 1994 "with little discussion one Friday morning. They
made significant changes in the final version which really did not follow the 49 points
agreed upon."

32. Interview with author, March 1995.

33. Interview with author, March 1995.

34. Interview with author, May 1995. "He even brought up several impressive
UNTS members to testify about an EPZ controlled by the Air Force. They spoke of how
they were forbidden to get organizers into the EPZs because it was declared as a 'national security' area."

35. Interview with author, March 1995.

36. Interview with author, March 1995.

37. Interview with author, March 1995.

38. Interview with author, March 1995.

39. Interview with author, March 1995.

40. Interview with author, March 1995.

41. "The only limit which might conceivably affect our proposal was in regard to
convention 87, since the El Salvador constitution states that high officials must be of
Salvadoran nationality. But Venezuela has the same requirement, and they received
approval from the ILO to maintain the limit while at the same time passing legislation
implementing the conventions." Interview with author, March 1995. Article 226 also
specified the right to negotiate collective contracts.

42. Interview with author, March 1995.

43. Common unionist assessment expressed in interviews with author, March 1995
and July 1996.

44. Interview with author, March 1995. The crucial conventions were nos. 87, 98, and
154 on the right to organize, supported by conventions 11 (right to associate in agriculture), 135 (choosing work representatives), 141 (rural organization), 144 (tripartite consultations), and 151 (work relations in public administration).

45. Interview with author, March 1995. Yet according to Davis, they had consensus
on eighteen articles, disagreed over nine, and did not discuss thirty-one. The reforms
violated constitutional articles 17, 58, 69, 107, 214, and 219. Articles 224 and 312 contravened constitutional articles 47 and 42. There were lower standards than before in
articles 221, 224, 227, and 248. Letter to Joe Damond, GSP, May 9, 1994.

46. Interview with author, March 1995.

47. Interview with author, March 1995.

48. Interview with author, March 1995.

49. Interview with author, March 1995.

50. Interview with author, March 1995.

51. Interview with author, March 1995.

52. Interview with author, March 1995.

53. Interview with author, March 1995.

54. In 1994, the assembly ratified conventions 10, regulating minimum work ages in agriculture; 77, providing medical exams for minors working in industry; 78, providing medical exams for minors for distinct activities; 81, for labor inspections; 88, for developing human resources; 99, for regulating minimum salaries in agriculture; 111, opposing discrimination in hiring etc.; 122, on employment; 129, on labor inspections in agriculture; 131, on rules for regulating minimum salaries; 138, on minimum ages for work; 142, on the rights of rural workers to organize; and 144, on creating tripartite consultations.

55. Davis, interview with author, May 1996. One example: "The government decided who constituted 'essential workers' rather than implementing a joint understanding."

Chapter 6: Structural Implications of GSP Pressure in El Salvador

1. Interview with author, March 1995.

2. Government policy prevented union organizers from entry into EPZs while also promoting blacklists and year-to-year contracts (Davis 1995). When worker dismissals came before USTR, the Salvadoran government described its severance pay to fired workers. ILRF argued it showed an absence of the reinstatement remedy. Not one of the EPZ unions touted in the government brief was currently functioning since the workers who organized them were fired in every case. ILRF, "Post-hearing Rebuttal Brief," November 1993, case 005-CP-93, November 17, 1993.

3. Gross 1995 export earnings from maquila exports represented 39 percent of overall export earnings, but approximately 43 percent of maquila export earnings are expended on imported inputs (see Petersen 1992).

4. Interview with author, March 1995.

5. Interview with author, March 1995.

6. See Ruiz and García 1996:36ff. and materials produced by the NLC for a full account. The GAP contract was arranged by the Apparel Consortium Charter Group from Hong Kong.

7. For example, on October 5, 1994, Mandarin fired 900 persons for joining the union. These workers immediately blocked the exit until their employers agreed to negotiate. In mid-November, the owners finally agreed to hold negotiations. In mid-February 1995, once again Mandarin fired a large group of workers because of union affiliation. The San Marcos zone workers revived their protest until the head of security at Mandarin savagely beat one worker. Demonstrations rekindled in April. As union members reentered the plant, they found that the owners had formed their own "worker committee." Although the two groups held a tense negotiation with the minister of economy and the procurator of human rights, conflicts persisted. In mid-May,

the union called for a work stoppage to challenge the previous firings and attacks. The plant "worker committee" showered blows on the protesters, requiring government intervention, and another promised accord. Worker interviews, 1995.

8. Interview with author, 1995.

9. Simon Henshaw, U.S. labor attaché, interview with author, March 1995.

10. Mark Anner, interview with author, March 1995. Twenty-seven signed, twenty-four of them Salvadorans, including María Julia Hernández from the archdiocese's human-rights office.

11. In addition to the influential *Women's Wear Daily*, Bob Herbert's editorials in the *New York Times* (October 9 and 13, December 22, 1995) also stimulated discussion. Contact the NLC for a full packet of media responses.

12. Mark Anner, interview with author, March 1995.

13. The SETMI union was originally part of the Christian Democratic Central de Trabajadores Salvadoreños, then affiliated with CTD, but because it received little assistance, it subsequently became independent.

14. The Consortium Charter Group is the major coordinating body for apparel maquila owners. GAP and other companies negotiate with the Charter Group for orders, and it in turn determines which among more than a thousand local companies are most suitable for order specifications. This layered structure adds a dimension to the corporate structural debate noted above.

15. They also kept independent monitoring. The agreement was signed by David Wang, Mandarin International; CENTRA, the Archdiocesan Human Rights Office; the Instituto de Derechos Humanos Universidad Centroamerica (IDHUCA); Lucia Albarado Portán, secretary general of a company-created union (ATEMISA); and Eliseo Castro Perez, secretary general of SETMI, the bona-fide union. GAP (via the New York–based Interfaith Center for Corporate Responsibility) and NLC each provided $2,500 for implementation. By mid-1996, conditions had improved dramatically. GAP orders had returned, but in insufficient amounts to rehire the union workers. Many were blacklisted, but some managed to find work elsewhere. By mid-1997, about eighty union members and former workers had been rehired.

16. González and Bustillo, interviews with author, July 1996.

17. Arriola (1995), citing data from a recent El Salvador private-sector survey done by the Salvadoran Development Fund (FUSADES). "Análisis de la rentabilidad privada y económica del sector industrial salvadoreño," Documento de Trabajo no. 31.

18. Article 38, no. 2: "Every worker has the right to enjoy a minimum salary which is periodically adjusted; to adjust the salary, the cost of living ought to be primarily considered, along with the disposition of labor, the different systems of remuneration, the distinct zones of production, and other similar criteria. This salary ought to be sufficient to satisfy normal living necessities of the worker in the material, moral, and cultural order."

19. In the survey by Ruiz and García, maquila workers spent 17 percent of their salaries on transport (1996:54).

20. Arriola suggested that these low wages reflected the confidential guide by Price-Waterhouse, "Sistema Empresarial de Informacion Salarial," designed to help larger firms in their salary calculations. In 1995, the median salary for a qualified Salvadoran

worker was 30,000 colones a year ($287.36/month); for a beginning worker it was 21,500 ($205.94/month) (1995:44–95). Agricultural wages were more dependent on fluctuations in export revenues.

21. Ministry of Labor statistics on salaries only include workers covered under social security, and other salary determinants are unreliable (Arriola 1995:31). Even at that, calculations by U.S. Embassy (FLT 94) and Montesinos and Gochez (1995) do not indicate any noticeable real salary increases between 1989 and 1993, with decreases most years.

22. Carlos Ochoa of UNTS estimated that only 15 to 20 percent of the economically active population was covered by any benefits plan, and that coverage is minimal: "The 10 percent withheld from monthly salaries is for basic pension and health coverage; it does not cover all accidents or special problems" (interview with author, July 1996). Workers in the formal sector did much better. A total of 66.4 percent of workers in large companies and 60.3 percent in medium-sized industry were covered by social security, but this dropped to only 29.1 percent of workers in small companies. Overall, 42 percent of industrial workers had no social security coverage (Arriola 1995:18). The number of companies registered in Social Security remained around 11,000 between 1982 and 1988 but increased to 15,000 by 1992 (*Informe Laboral* 1994).

23. Fuentes, UNTS, interview with author, March 1995. Prior to reforms in 1993, pensions were covered by two funds. "Unfortunately," said Fuentes, "subsequent changes in the Social Security law have not been implemented."

24. Arriola (1995:37ff.). Examples of firings in 1994–95 following efforts to unionize occurred at the ADOC and AGAPE manufacturing plants and at free-zone companies such as Satellite International and Corpak Apparel.

25. Arriola (1995). The ministry does not apply reinstatement requirements, and can remain silent indefinitely (CTCA 1996). In 1995, the Salvadoran liquor company, Licorera Salvadoreña, took advantage of this to force workers to renounce forming a union (Arriola 1995:n.15).

26. In the mid-1990s, company-sponsored solidarista associations emerged at Helados Pops, Mike Mike, Bon Appetit, and Beneficio Ateos. They attacked a section of the Sindicato de la Industria del Cafe (Arriola 1995:39).

27. Interview with author, July 1996.

28. Informe's assessment may have been linked to the labor minister's performance as attorney for the business sector at the Social and Economic Forum.

29. This was largely due to a recent arrangement between the construction workers organized by Freddie Vasquez, who broke away from the CTD and made a direct agreement with the business sector.

30. Legally required payments for so many months of service—for example, an extra month's pay at Christmas after six months' service.

31. Mark Anner, interview with author, July 1996.

32. In discussing the ministry and courts, Arriola argues that any type of ministry or court action only directly applies to the 40 percent of the labor market covered by social security (1995:42).

33. Its allocation for 1995 was 24,302,270 colones ($2.8 million). It received the same percentage share in 1996.

34. Shepard et al. 1994. The ministry was given a new building in 1997.

35. Interview with author, July 1996.

36. Mauricio Herrera and Sonia Caceres, USAID-El Salvador, interview with author, July 1996.

37. Historically, Salvadoran construction unions have formed beneficial arrangements with the government. For example, in 1993, the Sindicato de Trabajadores de Construcción and the Sindicato Unión de Trabajadores de la Construcción (SUTC) presented 260 requests for negotiation, the highest for any sector.

38. Interviews with author, March 1995.

39. Trainees in Sonsonate and San Miguel functioned (and were counted) as inspectors. The inspectorate also had an office in La Paz, staffed by a secretary, but the number working in agriculture had dropped from twenty (Shepard et al. 1994:33).

40. Interview with author, July 1996.

41. As the USAID study points out, U.S. inspectors only average ninety inspections per year, with an additional seventy-five conciliations. If the figures held for 1993, companies in El Salvador only paid 15.73 colones per inspection ($2.00), or 11,000 colons per inspector, and 348,148 colones overall in back wages (Shepard et al. 1994:35).

42. Ministry of Labor statistics do not clearly distinguish between disputes investigated on site (such as inspections) and disputes brought to ministry offices. They also do not separate out the beneficiaries of dispute resolution, except by indicating the number of abandoned and unresolved disputes. The latter are forwarded to the court as complaints.

43. Of sixty-three labor disputes in 1993, including thirty-three strikes and ten street protests, thirty-nine were in the private sector, most due to firings and labor-rights violations. Sixteen public-sector actions happened for similar reasons. The ministry addressed very few of these. Only eight public disputes involved salary improvements (*Informe Laboral* 1993).

44. Herrera and Caceres, interview with author, July 1996.

45. Court judgments are of three types: judgments by the labor court; judgments by a particular regional court; and direct judgments, which involve a pre-agreement between the parties. Slightly over half of the decisions result in sentences, and this has been increasing, with about 12 percent coming from conciliations, and the remainder left unresolved (desistida) (see data in El Salvador, Ministerio de Trabajo y Previsión Social 1991).

46. Author interview with Miguel Ramírez, Raul Rivas, Manuel Contreras, and other members of the FESTRAES executive committee, March 15, 1995. FESTRAES is composed of eight unions: SIDPA, SELS, SIRIFUSA, SGP, SITRACASA, SGTIO, SIP, and SETA. Ochoa was interviewed separately.

47. USAID overall allocations to El Salvador dropped from $250 million in 1992, to $210 million in 1993, to $57 million in 1994, to $66 million in 1995; and to $27 million in 1996. Henshaw, interview with author, March 1995.

48. Interviews with author, March 1995. Created by AIFLD during the 1980s to take a counterinsurgent role versus the UNTS and FENASTRAS, for a short time UNOC gained the interest of the Partido Democratica Cristiano (PDC) as a grassroots organization for the 1994 elections. But UNOC slipped out of AIFLD control in about 1990 and repeatedly questioned PDC conduct in the national assembly. The private sector

sought changes in UNOC, and the U.S. Embassy also wished to recuperate control to marginalize the left wing. These rightist forces allied with the Confederación General de Trabajadores and the Federación de Sindicatos de Industria, Construcción, Transportación, y Similares (FESINCONSTRANS); sugarcane co-ops; UNICANA; and CGT-CLAT—four of eight labor organizations represented in the Consejo, isolating UNTS, ADC, the Asociación General de Empleados Públicos y Municipios, and possibly another AIFLD-created union, the Unidad Popular Democrática, which could still cut a deal (see CIDAI, UCA, July 14, 1993).

49. Mike Donovan, AIFLD-Central America, interview with author, March 1995.

50. Interview with author, March 1995.

51. Interview with author, March 1995. To help move the dialogue along, early in 1995 ANEP created a post to deal with labor issues—"the only private sector association in Central America to do so." Vidal would encourage the Ministry of Labor to step up its role in conflict mediation.

52. Interview with author, July 1996.

53. Author interview with participants, May 1995. The business community overreacted to the USTR delegation. One representative from the Asociación Salvadoreña de Industriales (ASI), part of ANEP, held a lengthy, frantic television interview condemning its protection of U.S. jobs at the expense of those in El Salvador. USTR official Jon Rosenbaum then met with the group the next day, and said, "Perhaps if we want to understand the purpose of this visit, we should ask the ASI representative." ASI was caught in a great embarrassment. "When I hear such screaming when I enter a country, then I know there are problems," continued Rosenbaum. The delegation's official purpose had been to check on the protections for intellectual property rights and video protections (Rosenbaum, as quoted by Anner, interview with author, July 1996).

54. Interview with author, July 1996.

55. "It failed, unlike the consejo on national safety, which has been quite active and worked very well." Sonia Caceres, USAID, interview with author, July 1996.

56. Pino (1996).

57. Interview with author, July 2, 1996.

58. Letter from Neil Levine, USAID director for Central American Affairs, May 17, 1996.

59. Mauricio Herrera, interview with author, July 1996.

60. Interview with author, July 1996. For example, to spend the money in 1996, FOES brought thirty-six participants to the Center for Institutional Study in Nicaragua to work on conflict resolution and mediation and negotiation techniques. However, most participants were unaffiliated with unions.

61. Interview with author, March 1995.

62. Anner, interview with author, July 1996.

63. Interviews with author, March 1995.

64. Interviews with author, July 1996.

Chapter 7: The Guatemalan Case

1. The author wishes to thank Steve Coats, director of U.S./GLEP, for critically reviewing this and the following chapter.

2. Labor supporters filed annual petitions from 1986 through 1992. USTR then inaugurated a review, which it periodically renewed until May 1997.

3. See Frundt (1995) on CUSG. For a history of Guatemalan labor law, see U.S. Department of Labor (1962), López Larrave (1979), and Frundt and Chinchilla (1987).

4. See Frundt (1987a). In 1983–85, Guatemala paid out 10 percent of its export revenues for debt service.

5. See AFL-CIO, "Statement before the GSP Subcommittee of the Trade Policy Staff Committee on the Labor Rights Provisions of the Generalized System of Preferences," June 24–25, 1986, Washington, D.C. The AFL-CIO cited violations listed by the ILO in 1985. See also American Embassy, "Labor Trends in Guatemala," 1984, 12–13, which found little change from anti-union violence of the early 1980s "illustrated in management threats to dismiss workers and close plants when workers try to organize unions; in assassinations and abduction of trade union leaders; in the absence of many new unions and the dismantling of many of the old unions . . . union leaders are regularly killed prior to signing a collective bargaining agreement." Appended are the names of twelve who disappeared or were murdered between 1983 and 1984.

6. USTR, "General Review of the Generalized System of Preferences (GSP) Worker Rights," 1987. While the 1985 Guatemalan constitution included seventeen articles protecting labor, its labor code did not reflect all of the constitutionally specified rights.

7. ILRF petition, "Labor Rights in Guatemala," May 30, 1988. Data on killings and threats from Americas Watch (1988b:59). Lance Compa, then international counsel for the United Electrical Workers (UE), coordinated and wrote ILRF-related Guatemalan petitions through 1992.

8. Many violations are documented in an ILRF-sponsored study (Goldston 1989). The petition argued that the killings were politically motivated. Many victims were kidnapped well before their bodies appeared; bodies were mutilated but money was left intact. In consequence, no armed forces or police were disciplined or taken to court (see also Amnesty International 1987; for Coca-Cola worker Rolando Pantaleon's brutal killing and the widow's account, see Reed and Brandow 1996:141ff.).

9. Legally, labor-union recognitions must occur within thirty days. In 1986, the Ministry of Labor admitted that forty-seven still awaited action in 1986, eighty-seven in 1987, and thirty-one through May 1, 1988 (see also U.S. Embassy, "Labor Trends in Guatemala," August 1987). However, the Cerezo administration had granted "juridical personality" to seventy-two unions, twenty-six in the public sector, whereas only fifteen had received recognition between 1981 and 1985. Despite its commitment, the ministry only approved seven more unions over the following months, and they did not include workers at Bonin and the Ministry of Labor itself, which waited two years without recognition.

10. According to the National Federation of State Workers (FENASTEG), decree 71-86 permitting public-employee unions had been diluted by delays in processing applications.

11. See Section 207 and section 226(a) of the labor code (1949) and section 51 (12) (1) of legislative decree 24-82 of 1982. The government also strictly supervised union activities (sections 211(a) and 211(b) of the labor code).

12. See sections 241(c), 222(f), and 222(m) of the labor code (1947). With few exceptions, strikes by agricultural workers during the harvest were also prohibited (sections

243(a) and 249). The police could intervene in illegal strikes (section 255) and imprison offenders (section 257).

13. "Memorandum for Members of the GSP Subcommittee from Labor Member," U.S. Department of Labor, Bureau of International Affairs, November 4, 1986. Workers could be beaten or killed for supporting strikes by others (see account in Reed and Brandow 1996:36ff.).

14. See reports on the Consejo de Comunidades Ethicas Runujel Junam (CERJ) in Americas Watch (1989) and U.S. Department of State (1989), which verify ten kidnappings and additional threats that forced patrollers to flee to exile.

15. U.S. State Department (1989) reaffirms data from a government-sponsored (SODIFAG) study on the socioeconomic conditions of indigenous children.

16. Calculations by CUC (1989) showed that a minimum wage of 16.05 quetzals was needed for the basic necessities of five people, a multiple of the minimum agricultural wage of 4.50 quetzals, or the urban wage of 5.00–8.50 quetzals. Farmworkers additionally faced short-weighing or were paid by their "measure of effort."

17. Labor-code article 121 stated that workers should be paid time and a half for overtime. Article 122 stated that overtime could not exceed twelve hours a week. Both of these provisions were widely violated.

18. Labor and Employment Committee, National Lawyers Guild; UE, ILRF, "Petition and Request for Review of the GSP Status of Guatemala," June 1, 1990. See also Green 1989.

19. For example, GSP Subcommittee of the Trade Policy Staff Committee, "1990 GSP Annual Review," cases 006, 0010-CP-90, Guatemala, August 1990, which found that most of ILRF's evidence was "not sufficient or not clear that it fell within the statutory provisions."

20. As evidence of "taking steps," USTR found that Guatemalan courts had ruled that organizers at the army bank were not "army specialists" and union organizing could proceed; they fined a battery company for reopening under another name to avoid a union (USTR, "1990 GSP Annual Review," August 1990). But a handful of court actions did nothing to prevent continued violations, as Francisco Parades' dramatic account of a twenty-nine-month strike for reinstatement at the battery company demonstrated (Reed and Brandow 1996:14ff.). But USTR viewed such strikes as evidence of progress, since only one strike had been declared legal between 1947 and 1986, whereas the present administration had approved strikes at Auxilio Postumo, IGSS, and the Municipality de Solola.

21. Labor code article 207 forbade union participation in politics. USTR responded that the 1985 constitution dropped the prohibition for unions by guaranteeing such a right for individuals. Article 211 charged the minister of labor with "the strict supervision of unions." USTR response: In practice, the minister was not effective in supervising union affairs. Article 216 required a minimum of twenty to form a union. USTR response: Skilled employers from several businesses (or municipalities) could join a union, overcoming the twenty-member limit. Article 217 forbade the initiation of union activity without authorization of the Executive Branch, which is contrary to ILO standards. USTR response: Groups can obtain *acuerdos* (agreements) before they officially gain the juridical personality status that allows freer reign. Articles 218 to 221 detailed requirements for applying for juridical personality that, effectively gave the

government control over unions, and took much more than the 60 days specified. USTR response: This has not prevented approval of more than 25 percent of all *juridica personalidades* now in existence. Article 222 limited union leader terms to two years. USTR response: In practice union leaders rotate. Article 223 specified the minimum and maximum number of executive council members, who must also read and write. USTR response: Not denied. Article 226 permitted the minister of labor to dissolve unions involved in politics. USTR response: no minister of labor has ever required a dissolution. Article 321 prohibited elected leaders from representing unions in court for cases above 300 quetzals. USTR response: True. Article 242 imposed a government definition of a just strike. USTR response: Any legal strike is also just, and workers must receive pay. Article 243 prohibited strikes by agricultural workers. USTR response: Ignored in practice. Article 244 allowed termination of workers involved in an illegal strike. USTR response: Firings for illegal strikes have only been done with court order, and courts are slow to act. Article 256 permitted courts to suspend strikes for six months for "grave economic and social character." USTR response: Such suspension is legitimate. Articles 321 through 431 created labyrinthine procedures for collective bargaining that allowed delays. USTR response: Agreed.

USTR also responded to other allegedly anti-union labor code articles (see U.S. Department of State 1989).

22. According to USTR, voluntary patrol action was to augment the army effort to combat the thirty-year insurgency.

23. The U.S. Embassy reported a 12 percent increase in school attendance between 1985 and 1988, about equal the increase in rural birthrate. Only 38.6 percent of indigenous children attended school.

24. GSP Subcommittee, "1989 Annual Review," August 4, 1989.

25. Congressional decree 29-89, the Exports and Maquila Activities Development Law, article 33, stipulated that national labor law should be followed.

26. USTR, "1990 GSP Annual Review," August 1990.

27. ILRF, "Petition to USTR," Guatemala, June 1991.

28. Serrano continued several programs begun under Cerezo: short-term certificates of credit that paid high interest (which brought in approximately $350 million in profit repatriation) and a tax modernization plan that the private sector had refused Cerezo, with "indirect" taxes on consumption to make it more palatable. To meet immediate liquidity needs, the government required major businesses to purchase ten-year bonds at 8 percent interest (CAR, May 10, 1991). Such steps helped equalize the nation's balance of payments, resulting in a $400 million surplus in current account balances in 1991 compared to $40 million in 1990. Judicious Central Bank intervention with exchange rates generated funds to pay overdue debt to the Interamerican Development Bank, earning new lines of credit (CAR, October 11, 1991). It was an instructive lesson for developing economies. Business expansion brought a 25 percent decline in imports, an 8 percent increase in exports, and a 52 percent rise in tourism.

29. See SRI International (1990), which outlines forty-five policy steps to enhance nontraditional exports, including special credit lines for exporters, privately administered free-trade zones (legalized via decree 65-89), a reduction in bureaucratic procedures, infrastructure improvements, and an eventual elimination of protective tariffs

(Petersen 1992). USAID's "Economic Assistance Strategy for Central America 1991 to 2000" projected a "three-fold growth of non-traditional exports" to $4.7 billion, most accomplished through promotion due to private investment.

30. CAR, November 8, 1991. The budget allocated 75 percent for urban areas—where only 25 percent of the population resided.

31. For employment aspects, see Martínez and Infante (1992).

32. Strook, a wealthy Idaho rancher and former Yale roommate of George Bush, was an unlikely candidate for such blunt protest. However, Guatemalan authorities had failed to adequately investigate the death Michael Devine, a U.S. citizen with ties to the embassy (see also Harbury 1997). So the ambassador was more sensitive when businesspeople also dragged their feet in pursuing labor complaints.

33. Karen Brandow, report to U.S./GLEP, April 25, 1992.

34. Frederico Polo, secretary of CACIF, and Juan Sanchez, head of the Non-Traditional Exports Association to the ILRF/GLEP delegation, March 1991.

35. Frederic Polo and Juan Sanchez to the ILRF/GLEP delegation, May 6, 1992. When U.S./GLEP director Stephen Coats pointed out that there had been no unions registered in the maquila sector during the past year, Polo recognized "problems in the Korean sector, but these are exceptions. . . . Some workers don't seek unions, and have lost faith in leaders. . . . We want to see results, improved conditions. We have raised the minimum wages. Many firms have doctors, cafeterias, bathrooms. They improve because they want to."

36. Others included the Washington Office on Latin America, the National Council of Churches Human Rights Office, the United Electrical Workers, the International Ladies Garment Workers Union, the United Food and Commercial Workers, the Amalgamated Clothing and Textile Workers, the International Union of Food and Allied Workers-North America, and the International Union of Electrical Workers.

37. ILRF cited death threats to leaders from UNSITRAGUA, FENASTEG, and the Sindicato de Trabajadores de Instituto Guatemalteco de Securidad (six left the country after leader Lillian Elizabeth Juarez Escobar was killed); the abduction of leaders from the Sindicato de Trabajadores de Instituto Nacional de Electrición (STINDE) and the Ministry of Sports; the killing of Maria del Carmen Anavizca, who led a protest at the Olga Maria plantation; and four earlier killings. The petition challenged USTR's assertion that available evidence did "not establish a pattern of systemic attack on unionists," just as it admitted "threats and violence against unionists by members of security forces."

38. Labor code bill 786 was dead after it passed first reading. The 1992 AFL-CIO petition reminded USTR of its 1991 determination that the nation was "not taking steps" if it "did not make meaningful attempts to reform the labor code." With the U.S. State Department, "Human Rights Report, 1992" also acknowledging the ineffectiveness of labor courts, ILRF urged the subcommittee "to cease speculating as to the prospects for labor code reform, and confront the reality."

39. Ministry figures combined *personeria juridica* granted to individuals with *personalidad juridica* granted to organizations. In fact, between January 1, 1991, and May 19, 1992, only fifteen public-sector unions and four private-sector unions had obtained *personalidad juridica*. ILRF, "1992 Petition," pp. 16–17.

40. According to the AFL-CIO's 1992 petition, despite Labor Minister Solorzano's commitment to simplify regulations, the government conducted a lengthy process to verify the employment status of the Camisas Modernas' union executive committee. Notwithstanding any labor-code requirement, a local judge then had to validate that they had no prior criminal record, a procedure that committee representatives had to undergo every two years. In addition, the Labor Ministry had not approved a single union within the sixty-day limit required by article 217 of the labor code.

41. The Serrano government set up a single office to handle approvals for foreign investors and reduced waiting time from six months to twenty days (see also Wagner 1992).

42. Quoted in ILRF, U.S./GLEP, UE, ACTWU, UFCW, IUF-NA, "Petition to USTR and Request for Review," June 1, 1991, which also cited repeated violations of labor code articles 211, 216, 217, 218–21, 222, 223, 321, 242, 243, 244, and 256. Unionists claimed that delays still marked registrations. The petition demanded attention to the solidarista association obstructions.

43. Daram and RCA maquila workers told of child labor, excessive hours, and abuse, and Sportex workers of a competing employee association. Others reported on Confeccines Unidas (fired seventy-four with no remedy); Incatecu (closed, fired 200 unionized workers, then reopened); Compania Comercial Agronomo Pecuaria (fired 306 who had just demanded to bargain); army bank (prevented unionization); Corporación Financiera Nacional (fired eighty under an *emplazamiento*); National Tobacco (fired union workers); CUSG-affiliated banana plantations (fired workers subjected to military threats), La Torre plantation (fired a hundred unionists); San Gregorio plantation (fired 300 for forming a union); and municipalities of San Pedro Carcha, San Andres Xecul, and Mazatenango (fired workers, harassed unionists).

44. Prepared union statement, March 16, 1992. Four labor courts had served the capital for forty years: they lost files, missed deadlines, kept irregular hours, and failed to notify parties. Judges were unprepared, ill-informed, and inconsistent; judgments were rare and then not enforced.

45. For more than ten years, the ILO had also reported as contrary to convention 105, Guatemalan penal code sections 390(2), 396, 419, and 430 and legislative decree nos. 9 and 10, 1963, which cited penal code section 47. The provisions allowed work to be imposed as a punishment for expressing political opinions and participating in strikes (ILO 1995a:C105).

46. CUC survey, 1991 (internal document). CONIC and other groups reported similar conditions.

47. The government made similar arguments in 1991 and 1992: "Since the Constitution states workers may not be discharged for participating in the creation of trade unions ... any law which limits this is null. Public and private employees have the right to strike." A total of 955 trade unions are currently in existence. President of the government of Guatemala to GSP, June 1992.

48. *Siglo XXI*, January 11, 1992, citing ILO convention 161 and other measures passed by the Guatemalan congress.

49. Karen Brandow, report to U.S./GLEP, February 1992.

50. Human Rights Ombudsman pronouncement, April 6, 1992. See also U.S. Department of State (1992).

51. President Serrano promised to support routine inspections in the maquila sector (114 done in March 1992; 700 warnings issued). The government would establish a tripartite committee to oversee compliance, construct child care facilities, form a global policy for hygiene and security with the Garment and Textile Industry Commission, and investigate corruption within the Labor Ministry. It would coordinate policy with the Ministry of Interior to protect trade-union leaders from violence, even though "trade union leaders enjoy little credibility among the security forces." President of the government of Guatemala, statement to GSP, June 1992.

52. Pharis J. Harvey, executive director, ILRF, in support of petition no. 005-CP-92 regarding the worker-rights practices of Guatemala, before USTR, October 15, 1992. (June 21 was a day of special memory for Guatemalan workers kidnapped by security forces in 1981.)

53. President of the government of Guatemala, statement to GSP, June 1992.

54. The mobilization, largely by U.S./GLEP's calls and mailings, was carried out on an annual budget of less than $20,000, including staff salaries and transport expenses.

55. The Law of Economic Compensation for Time of Service (decree 57-90) remained on the books but was effectively replaced by article 9 of the Annual Bonus Law (decree 42-92) backed by the business sector.

56. Solorzano, statement to ILRF/GLEP delegation, May 1992.

57. Congressional document (undated). Notwithstanding this admission, Guatemalan unionists played a crucial role. CUSG secretary general Juan Francisco Alfaro, who also served in the Guatemalan congress, was the bill's key author and lobbyist.

58. CGTG, UNSITRAGUA, CUSG, FESEBS, FESTRAS-UITA; FENATRAM, FENASTEG, FENASEP, FECETRAG, CTC, "With Regard to Labor Rights Violations in Guatemala," presented to USTR, September 10, 1992.

59. Harvey, "In Support of Petition no. 005-CP-92."

60. Dueñas, interview with author, June 1994. Dueñas also cited labor code article 219, which strengthened article 102 in the constitution and empowered the Ministry of Labor to take action. Article 380 specified that a worker could not be fired without order of a judge or that worker must be rehired within twenty-four hours. However, businessmen would subvert these articles via endless court appeals (see below).

61. See ILO (1995) on code section 211. Other difficulties included Guatemalan nationality requirements for trade-union formation or office (sections 220(d) and 223(b)), the requirement that two-thirds of the workforce must agree before calling a strike and related provisions (sections 243(a) and 249 prohibited agricultural workers from striking during harvest; sections 243(d) and 249 prohibited strikes that the government decided would seriously affect the national economy; section 55 permitted summoning the national police to ensure work during an unlawful strike; penal code section 390(2) allowed sentencing of persons who disbursed enterprises that developed the national economy), and other requirements for union office (section 220(d) required the interim executive committee members to swear they had no criminal record and were active workers in the enterprise; and section 223(b) stated at least three must know how to read and write). The ILO Committee believed that this restricted people who had unrelated convictions and persons such as pensioners who had helpful abilities.

62. Joy Ann Grune, IUF, "Special Report to the U.S. Trade Representative on Find-

ings of a U.S. Trade Union Women Delegation for Workers Rights Review of Guatemala's GSP Status," March 25, 1993.

63. STINDE, UNSITRAGUA, CTC, U.S./GLEP, "Posthearing Evidence in Support of Petitions," to USTR, case no. 005-CP-92, February 5, 1993.

64. The agreement recognized "the socioeconomic impact that exclusion of Guatemala from GSP would signify . . . the parties . . . commit themselves to . . . a positive evolution of labor relations and the compliance with the law, and solicit that Guatemala not be eliminated from that system." March 8, 1993, signed: Hortencia Del Cid de Aguilar, CUSG; David Tzay, Adolfo Lacs, FESEBS; Rigoberto Dueñas, Jose Pinzon, CGTG; Manuel de Jesus Godinez, CTC; Luis Reyes Mayen, Humberto Preti, Mauricio Farchi, CACIF; Mario Solorzano Martínez, minister of labor. UNSITRAGUA did not participate. Issues debated but not included were a commitment not to work against current laws that protect workers, for example the law of compensation for service; improvement in achieving *personalidad juridica*; an end to *solidarismo;* a rapid solution to labor conflicts; fulfillment and improvement of minimum salaries; respect for free union organization in the maquila; just application in juridical decisions; increased administrative support in legal and labor areas; reforms to protect social security for workers; Ministry of Labor compliance with the strict obligation to protect and promote worker rights; *and* expansion of "tripartite" to include all elements of the labor sector.

65. STEG, UNSITRAGUA, FESTRAS-UITA, FENASTEG, SITRASS, CUC, UTQ, UTESP, STINDE, UTE, FUTG, UASP-Suchitepequez, to GSP, March 23, 1993; see also letter from UASP to USTR: "We decidedly support the requests of those unions . . . that you consider until the end of the year (December 1993), the review and supervision of those GSP benefits which permit genuine evaluation of the political will of the government and employers in Guatemala." Signed Consejo Nacional de Viudas Guatemaltecas, UNSITRAGUA, Comunidades del Pueblo en Resistencia, Consejo de Desplazados Guatemaltecos, STEG, Asociación de Estudiantes Universitarios, CUC, FENASTEG, Grupo de Apoyo Mutuo, UTE, UTQ, SITRASS, UTESP, UASP Suchitepequez, CERJ, Asociación de Educadores de Enseñanza Media (AEEM).

66. A May 28, U.S. State Department warning that GSP preferences could be lost "panicked" the business community into resisting Serrano's decree (*New York Times,* June 1, 1993, p. 4).

67. Juan Sánchez Botran, head of the Guatemalan Agricultural Exporters, "Statement before House Committee on Ways and Means, Subcommittee on Trade, HR 1403," June 24, 1993.

68. GSP Trade Policy Staff Committee, "1992 GSP Annual Review," case no. 005-CP-92, Guatemala, July 1993 (emphasis mine).

69. Compatible with the goals of macroeconomic stability, de León Carpio's wage and labor policy stressed "economic growth and the fight against poverty." Its basic objectives were to strengthen wage commissions and the Labor Inspectorate to implement wage and health and safety rules and "guarantee liberty for trade union affiliation." It sought a "National Labor Agreement which will contain basic decisions about income, prices, productivity, investments, employment and training." It would promote collective agreements, wage increases as a result of productivity, the moderniza-

tion and expansion of social security, and priority to the most vulnerable groups: new workers, women, handicapped, the young. See Guatemala, Presidency (1993).

70. See Guatemalan Ministry of Labor, Declaración of Xelaju, Quetzaltenango, September 2–4, 1993; Seminario Internacional, "Analysis of the Labor Situation of Undocumented Farm Workers, Guatemala-Mexico."

71. The minister revived public law 71-86, which regulated the establishment of unions for state workers and their right to strike. It also aided passage of public law 22-93, which implemented ILO convention 156 on equal opportunities and treatment between men workers and women workers and workers with family responsibilities, and public law 31-93, which approved convention 159 and recommendation 168 on professional readaptation and employment of the handicapped.

72. See "Training Course Guide to New Labor Inspectors," September 17–30, October 1–15, 1993; sponsored by USAID with the support of UNDP, project GUA/91/005, in which "American instructors under the auspices of AID" (1) familiarized inspectors with labor regulations, the Constitution of Guatemala, and relevant ILO Conventions; and (2) held workshops on issues like gender equality, labor mediation, hygiene and safety, underage workers, labor rights, and benefits.

73. Ministry of Labor, "Los Derechos de las Niñas y los Niños Trabajadores," 1993; "Comisión del Menor Trabajador," 1993. Pamphlets.

74. The Ministry of Labor took responsibility for an "employee's comfort . . . job conditions and social security." It would help employers set up Commissions of Health and Safety at Work, with two representatives elected by each group of twenty workers. Commissions would assure fulfillment of "General Rules about Health and Safety at work. IGSS would resolve disputes." Government of Guatemala, agreement no. 530-93, October 6, 1993, signed by Ramiro De León Carpio and Gladys Amardella Morfin. However, employers objected and the agreement was never enforced.

75. Acto Numero Uno, October 28 1993, created the Comisión Bipartita del Sector Publico to resolve labor issues and achieve greater harmony between government officials and unions. It was signed by Ramiro Antonio Calderón Reyes, vice minister of labor; Nery Hernández and Luis Lara, Instancia Unitaria de los Trabajadores del Estado; Dante Monterroso and Armando Sánchez, FENASTEG; Jorge Galindo and Felix Hernández, Federación Nacional de Servidores Publicos; Miguel Angel Vásquez and Carlo Hugo Pereira, Sindicato de Ministro de Finanzes Publicas y Sindicatos Independientes del Estado; and Labor Inspector Lic. Roberto Cruz Minera.

76. Representatives from major labor and business groups attended tripartite seminars on "Democracy, Economy, and Civil Society" in October and November 1993. They discussed respect for the constitution, free organization, effective functioning of the ministry of labor, courts, harmony with owners, and the dignity of work. Workgroups came to consensus about the need for a tripartite approach, national dialogue, and an action policy for mutually beneficial strategies and accords for mechanisms for accord verification; for a culture of dialogue in all media; for compromise in the following up on recommendations (see letter from minister of foreign relations to U.S. ambassador, October 22, 1993).

77. UNSITRAGUA, "Proposed Union Document in Relation to the Lifting of GSP Benefits," October 15, 1993. Labor minister Gladys Morfin appended this to her letter

to Ambassador Marilyn McAfee, October 22, 1993. The labor minister also described the "Second Tripartite Reunion" between CGTG, CUSG, UNSITRAGUA, FESEBS, and CACIF, October 13, 1993, in which "parties had agreed . . . to sign a document indicating good will . . . to find concrete solutions in the short and medium time for guaranteeing Guatemalans their rights and sources of work, indicating a change of attitude." However, the tripartite discussions broke down after October 18. Government and business partially retracted their earlier submission, and labor representatives refused to sign a modified agreement (see U.S./GLEP, "Post-hearing Brief," November 15, 1993). The minister then sent the ambassador the cleansed "tripartite" statement, which the Guatemalan government later submitted to USTR.

78. "Prehearing Comments of the Tripartite Commission, Government of Guatemala, Private Sector and Labor, opposing withdrawal of GSP Beneficiary Status, 1992 GSP Annual Review Continuation of Country Practice Reviews, Worker Rights Review of Guatemala, before USTR, Oct. 20, 1993." (See also identical document listed as prepared by the Government of Guatemala, Ministries of Foreign Relations, Finance, Labor and Economy on October 7.) The document responded to "Summary of progress re: issues raised by workers' right review summary published July, 1993 by USTR." It argued that improved negotiations, coordination of activities, and technical support of international organizations such as USAID manifested "political will," as did the de León Carpio administration's search for a firm and lasting peace and fight against poverty.

79. Luis Reyes Mayén, quoted in *Prensa Libre,* October 30, 1993.

80. For example, Jose Raul González Merlo, director for La Mariposa/Pepsi, denied all allegations of union interference, despite persistent complaints.

81. Willi Kaltschmitt, Summary of Oral Testimony to USTR opposing withdrawal of GSP Beneficiary Status, October 20, 1993.

82. USTR, "1993 GSP Annual Review, Worker Rights Summary," case 007-CP-93, December 1993.

83. Stephen Coats, executive director of U.S./GLEP, "Oral Statement for USTR, GSP Subcommittee," November 3, 1993. See also "Preliminary Statement by the US/GLEP Worker Rights Review on Guatemala," case 005-CP-92, October 7, 1993; letter from Arturo Cardona Maeda, secretary of conflicts, FESEBS, October 19, 1993; presentations by Saúl Octavio Martínes, secretary general, and Reynaldo González, secretary of cooperative social activities; and the "Documento del Sector Sindical en Relación al Tema de Revisión de Los Beneficios del SGP," Washington, D.C., November 3, 1993. These reports questioned impunity and court processes and labor-code reforms since the number of unapproved union applications had increased and it was taking more than a year for registration that should legally take twenty days. Workers in the Bank of the Army had waited six years. In addition, employers paid below-minimum salaries and had engaged in massive illegal firings and threats of death to the union leaders (such as those of the Union of Workers of the National Housing Bank). Employer-solidarity associations had destroyed unions at Mahler Foods and Bank of the Army.

84. CUSG, CTC, UNSITRAGUA, FESEBS, FENASTEG, CGTG, FESTRAS-UITA, FENASEP, and CENOC, "Statement to USTR," September 1, 1994, calling for six more months of review and asking for a bipartite commission within the Ministry of Labor

to document violations of the right to organize and bargain, realistic budget modifications to comply with the Conciliation and Arbitration Tribunals set up by code article 294 (see below), and the imposition of sanctions listed in articles 33(f) and 43(c).

85. ILRF/GLEP claimed that fourteen were coops and more than ten had been rendered ineffective by intimidations, failure to negotiate, and closings: "Post-hearing Brief, Case 007-CP-93, GSP Annual Review, Worker Rights in Guatemala," November 15, 1993.

86. ILRF/GLEP, "Post-hearing Brief." The labor inspector who investigated the Pepsi case also allegedly also worked for the company, gaining a double salary.

87. H. E. Salomon Cohen, Guatemalan vice minister of foreign affairs, "Statement to USTR," October 20, 1993.

88. The government claimed to do more than 275 investigations between January and October 1992 (see chapter 8).

89. U.S./GLEP, "Review of Steps Taken on Worker Rights in Guatemala since December 1993," May 27, 1994.

90. Lance Compa, ILRF, "Testimony of US/GLEP and ILRF before USTR, GSP Subcommittee," November 3, 1993. (Several groups also inaugurated a lawsuit against the state for not monitoring pesticide use on bananas.)

91. Unclassified telegram from U.S. secretary of state, Washington, D.C., to U.S. Embassy, Guatemala City, on GSP worker rights, March 14, 1994.

92. USTR, "1993 GSP Annual Review," case 007-CP-93, July 1994, citing U.S. Department of State (1993), which documented the below-minimum enforcement of the labor code and found that base wages were not paid "to significant numbers." USTR did commend the government for reducing the backlog of requests for union recognition and meeting the new timetables. Thirty-nine new labor inspectors had increased ex-officio visits by 100 percent in four months and had tripled lawsuits; two new courts had finally been established; and the ministry had created a Commission for the Underage Worker and a special unit for working women. It had translated and disseminated the labor code in four indigenous languages (in fact, most of this had yet to occur).

93. Wage standards usually specify the base salary and an incentive benefit (*bonificación*) equivalent to one day's pay after six days of work. After employees work for a year, employers must also pay bonificación 14 (an extra month due in July) and the Christmas bonificación (an extra month due in December).

94. Dueñas, interview with author, 1994. ANACAFE canceled its social-action program when coffee prices fell in 1995.

95. U.S./GLEP, "Supplementary Evidence of Failure to Advance Worker Rights—Guatemala GSP Review," October 6, 1994.

96. U.S./GLEP, "Analysis of Steps Taken to Respect Worker Rights in Guatemala from July 1 to August 31, 1994," September 16, 1994. See also "Supplementary Evidence," October 6, 1994.

97. Interview with author, July 1994. In the mid-1990s, Alfaro's spouse, labor attorney Thelma del Cid, headed a local ILO-sponsored project. She helped all labor centrals monitor what came out of the GSP process. They examined contract difficulties and legal compliances.

98. CUSG, CTC, UNSITRAGUA, FESEBS, FENASTEG, CGTG, FESTRAS-UITA, FENASEP, and CENOC, Union Submission to GSP, September 1, 1994. The plan included: (1) a *bipartite* commission within the Ministry of Labor on freedom of association, "to document violations" and produce reports; (2) budget allocations to implement the code's conciliation and arbitration functions; (3) compliance with worker protections outlined in decree 29-89 and articles 33(f) and 43(c); (4) obligatory bargaining (as per article 106, section 8 in the constitution); (5) the purging of corrupt inspectors.

99. Interview with Reynoldo González, FESEBS, February 1995. Article 1 of accord 776-94 specified this annual review.

100. A daily rate of 16 quetzals in the countryside; 18 in the city ($2.35–2.75 per day).

101. The ILO also sent a Direct Contacts Mission to Guatemala to investigate cases submitted to the ILO Subcommittee on Freedom of Association. In March, Guatemala's attorney general convened a meeting between various labor centrals and government agencies in response, and the labor minister called for related administrative and court reforms (see ILO 1995b).

102. U.S./GLEP, "Guatemala GSP Worker Rights Action Request," April 1995. It listed the killing and or assaults of seven maquila workers.

103. Some argued that sugar was the wrong target even within the limited choices available under GSP (see chapter 3). Beginning in 1993, sugar owners introduced new technologies and claimed to have improved worker conditions. However, others questioned worker improvements, especially for cane cutters (see Oglesby 1997; Forster 1996).

104. Interview with delegation members, January 1996. One member cautioned that "USTR was afraid of getting caught in the cross fire. There was no way they were going to investigate impunity 'so don't ask us to include this.'" Indeed, impunity was rampant within the U.S. Guatemalan mission, with the CIA doing protective wiretaps on the Ambassador (Harbury 1997). However, the U.S. Labor Department remained a firm supporter of U.S. sanctions.

105. Delegation member Gary Maymarduk, head of the U.S. State Department Central American Desk, statement to U.S./GLEP, January 1996. See also Avendaño and Mendoza (1995:38).

106. Carlos Arias, head of the apparel exporters association, reportedly told the Tripartite Commission that since Guatemala signed the accords, it did not have to do anything more on labor rights.

107. The request, dated January 23, 1996, suggested changes in five areas (see chapter 8).

108. ILO representative Thelma del Cid, interview with author, June 1996.

109. This extended beyond the legal stipulation that negotiated contracts were to be submitted so that the Ministry of Labor could make sure there were no reductions in labor rights.

110. In addition to the González investigation, U.S./GLEP specifically requested (1) resolution of 5 percent of cases currently pending before the labor courts; (2) establishment of courts outside of Guatemala City; (3) increased fines for violators in the export sector; and (4) vigorous enforcement of the law requiring reinstatement within twenty-four hours for workers illegally fired.

111. USTR had complained that petitioners kept shifting the "goalposts," so both

sides agreed to put together a clear set of guidelines that would measure progress on worker rights. S. Coats, interview with author, November 1997. See also U.S./GLEP, "Revised Draft of Proposed Six-month Benchmarks Demonstrating Guatemala's Progress on Worker Rights," January 20, 1996.

112. In August 1996, the Tripartite's Commission for the Textile and Apparel Industry endorsed the "Labor and Environmental Principles to be Complied with by Members of the Textile and Apparel Commission of the Association of Exporters of Non-Traditional Products." It affirmed four of the five basic rights, excluding the right to bargain (CTCA 1996).

113. Accord 196, June 24, 1996. According to ILO representative Thelma del Cid, this and the law to regulate the maquila, no. 29-89, were outcomes of GSP and ILO pressure. The accord nevertheless contained an ambiguity, stating that the labor minister will notify the minister of economy of a violation and proposed suspension after "the respective legal process is exhausted," which could make it more restrictive than earlier law.

114. Although inaccurate and incomplete, the reports provided some important information. Petitioners had also requested investigation of cases listed by the ILO, but no information on these was forthcoming, suggesting that the threat of sanctions brings more effective legal results.

115. González had returned in June to test security. Admitting that they had not pursued his case, the various government ministries and the national police eagerly inaugurated the evidence-gathering process. MINUGUA and the U.S. Embassy were less helpful. Labor attaché John Cushing stressed that the attacks against Reynoldo and others did not represent organized government repression against unions. If U.S. unions wished clarification about it, they should "write another letter to the embassy." Cushing was soon transferred. On the other hand, Guatemalan human rights procurator Jorge Mario García LaGuardia, who had received about 5,000 labor-related denunciations in 1995, did not believe conditions in Guatemala were safe for anyone, since the government would not confront the tremendous insecurity. Presentations to North American labor delegation accompanying González, June 1996.

116. The ILO office cited a number of constitutional violations of the anti-strike law, which was passed after security forces entered the congressional chambers at the order of President Arzú. AIFLD also lobbied and won removal of presidential authority in defining "essential service." The ILO's definition of essential services contravenes many of the areas stipulated in the bill, such as telephone, telegraph, postal service, court activity, transportation (ILO, Association Digest, 1985). The law also removes the right to emplazamiento from public-sector workers, making it easier to fire them (see chapter 2).

117. Interview with author, June 1996.

118. When the PVH workers presented the sufficient number of signatures, the company insisted on an open meeting in which those voting yes would step out and identify themselves (for the back-and-forth debate on the list and methods of verification, see Armbruster 1997; on organizing, see Frundt 1998). CACIF reportedly demanded the removal of Labor Minister Moscoso since his failure to resolve the issue helped extend Guatemala's probationary status under GSP, and President Arzú quickly complied.

119. Letter from Barbara Shailor, director of international affairs, AFL-CIO, et al., to Mr. Jon Rosenbaum, assistant U.S. trade representative, October 16, 1996. However, U.S./GLEP and Guatemalan unions expected that the review would soon be lifted. The latter held a press conference on October 31 to announce they would not oppose it given the government's progress on the peace accords. They so informed USTR, unaware of government foot dragging on PVH.

120. U.S./GLEP had persuaded Human Rights Watch, chaired by PVH CEO Bruce Klatsky, to investigate. It validated the workers' claim and also cited intimidation by local company officials and irresponsible follow-up by the Ministry of Labor (see Human Rights Watch 1997). In March 1997, Klatsky "agreed to begin negotiations, taking the union's proposed contract as a starting point." See Bounds (1997). See also U.S./ GLEP, *PVH Campaign,* update 8 (March 18, 1997).

121. Comments to author, December 1997.

122. Paid agents forcibly abducted three labor activists from Mi Kwang apparel and beat them in a nearby jail. Official investigators allegedly warned the victims not to pursue their case (*US/GLEP Labor Education Campaign,* update 19 [July 1997]).

123. On August 1 and September 23, 1996, the Presidential Commission on Human Rights reported on fourteen recent cases cited by GSP petitioners. It found "limited investigation and prosecution and no convictions of those responsible for committing violence against workers because of their trade union activity." U.S./GLEP, "Assessment of Guatemalan Government's Progress on Worker Rights under President Arzú," October 2, 1996.

124. USTR, press release, May 2, 1997. "A better approach is to keep them on notice that they could be reviewed in the future." Jon Rosenbaum, comment to author.

Chapter 8: Structural Residues in Guatemala

1. The brutal murder in April 1998 of the head of the Archbishop's Human Rights Office, Bishop Juan Gerardi, deeply tempers optimism. He had just documented the Army's responsibility for 85 percent of the atrocities of recent decades. However, in the days that followed, a huge public outcry mobilized the country, despite additional killings of community leaders and minimal government investigation.

2. Interview with author, June 1996.

3. The ministry also addressed severe internal discontent. It utilized PL480-funded computers to track company violations. Rivera, interview with author, March 1995.

4. Defining priorities "took time because of differing ideas, changes at the ministry, and the tripartite experiment but I think it is much better that they decide their needs, not us. . . . Besides, AID had done its own survey and come up with similar assessments." Priorities were also influenced by a study sponsored by the ministers of labor in Central America, with funding from the Spanish government prepared by the Instituto Superior de Central America de Relaciones Laborales (ISCREL), based in Costa Rica. The private sector endorsed the approach. While critical of GSP pressure, Carlos Arias, a maquila owner and head of the Non-Traditional Export Association, suggested that "foreign aid would move the government toward better law enforcement." Karen Delaney, the responsible USAID field officer in Guatemala, interviews with author, July 1994 and February 1995.

5. Lic. Francisco Rivera Friar, first vice minister of labor, and Lic. Carmen Lopez de Cáceres, second vice minister of labor, interview with author, March 6, 1995.

6. Delaney, USAID, interview with author, February 1995.

7. Interview with author, June 1996.

8. "Post-hearing Brief, Case 007-CP-93, GSP Annual Review, Worker Rights in Guatemala," November 15, 1993. Randall Peterson of USAID found statistics on new union registrations "more useful than others, but companies still set up phony unions since the law allows different unions in one plant. So a higher number of union registrations could indicate a *worsening* of labor relations." Interview with author, June 1996.

9. Interview with author, July 1994.

10. Figures for 1995 are valid through June. Unions represented 96 percent of this number, federations and confederations the rest.

11. The number of unions that remained in suspension pending approval of their application dropped from 376 in 1992 to 233 in 1993 but rose to 465 in 1994. Ministerio de Trabajo, *Boletin*, 1994, 1995.

12. Interview with author, June 1996.

13. Ministerio de Trabajo, *Boletin*, 1994, 1995. Each worker is also legally obligated to receive an individual contract. Ministry-approved contracts dropped from 88,592 in 1992 to 59,979 in 1993, increased to 72,887 in 1994, and declined to 64,344 in 1995 (less than 2 percent of Guatemala's more than 3 million employed workers). While the Ministry of Labor rejects 10 to 12 percent for not meeting minimum requirements, most employers disregard them altogether.

14. "The law obligates the ministry to check all collective pacts to determine if they are in compliance with the minimum rights of workers; for example the constitution declares that all workers have a right to a minimum fifteen-day vacation. No pact can reduce this. However, it could augment it, until the minister declared such illegal." CUSG denounced the minister's interference with negotiations to the ILO. The government also felt free to impose "the anti-strike law without discussion." Juan Francisco Alfaro, interview with author, June 1996.

15. "Investigations are prompted by a variety of factors, even anonymous notes." A *de oficio* visit occurs when inspectors visit on a surprise basis to check code compliance; other visits arise from *denuncias* made by workers, either due to an individual or collective conflict or a strike. The inspector will attempt an *expediente* which can lead to a conciliation, or the matter could be settled *extra judicio*. Author interview with Assistant Director General of Labor Inspections Carlos Moran, July 1996.

16. "This sanction is not specifically stated in the labor code, but a strategy we started in February 1996 based on an interpretation of obligation in the constitution. We had to do something to bring this powerful class into compliance, and since they have an 'obligation to attend' and violations of obligations are punishable, we could justify the sanction." Moran, interview with author, July 1996.

17. Op. cit. The inspector writes up the case, and then the judge gives it to an attorney of the Labor Ministry to follow up. To add to the complexity, the judge must ask the attorney general's representative to notify the offending company.

18. Edmond Mulet, Guatemalan ambassador to the U.S., "Post-hearing Submission by the Government of Guatemala to USTR," November 16, 1993. According to Rivera

(interview with author, July 1994), the number of inspectors rose from sixty-seven in June 1993 to 108 in October 1993. See also Government of Guatemala, "Addenda to the Prehearing Comments of the Tripartite Commission, including 1994–5 Agenda of Work, Regulations, and Concerns about Labor Rights in Guatemala," which listed eighty-two labor inspectors. Thirty-eight or 46.3 percent were assigned to Guatemala City, thirteen to Quetzaltenango/San Marcos, fifteen to Esquintla, ten to Zacapa, and eight were listed as vacant. In the new plan, thirteen more would go to Guatemala, six more to Quetzaltenango, and four more to Zacapa. The numbers roughly correspond, but since not all positions were filled, the actual number of inspectors remained at about ninety-five through 1997.

19. Interview with author, July 1994.

20. Interview with author, July 1996.

21. As outlined in "Training Course Guide to New Labor Inspectors," September 17–30, October 1–15, 1993, sponsored by USAID with the support of UNDP, project Gua/91/005, "Modernization of the Ministry of Labor."

22. Interview with author, March 1995. "Inspectors had investigated legitimate complaints on fincas," said Cruz Minerva. He was less kind to the public sector, where "sometimes claimed violations are simply registered by workers to protect their jobs. In fact, workers don't work adequately or efficiently."

23. Moran, interview with author, July 1996.

24. According to H. E. Salomon Cohen, Guatemalan vice minister of foreign affairs, the government investigated 1,085 worker complaints between July and September 1993. "Statement to USTR," October 20, 1993.

25. Inspector General Cruz Minerva reported two types of conflicts: individual and collective. "Individual conflicts (90 percent of total) refer to firings, non-payment of benefits, loans, etc. Collective conflicts involve union complaints. Prior to cases becoming denunciations that involve mediation and court action, we can resolve conflicts through conciliations, for example when an indemnization is paid. This terminates the labor relation situation." Interview with author, March 1995.

26. The Ministry claims to have conducted 275 maquila inspections from January to October 1992 that resulted in 99 *juicios punitivos*, but there is no way to independently confirm this.

27. In 1995, funds at stake declined to about 4.5 million quetzals.

28. Interview with author, June 1996.

29. Interview with author, February 1995.

30. Delaney, interview with author, February 1995.

31. Guatemalan Labor Ministry listing of cases, undated (about 1993). A typical write-up (for example, case 3) included no documentation of labor contracts, required statistical reports, salary payments, or the company's internal labor regulations, implying even greater lacunae in routine inspection reports.

32. Summary of Oral Testimony of Willi Kaltschmitt, COSOSCO and FUNDESA, to USTR opposing withdrawal of GSP Beneficiary Status, October 20, 1993. COSOSCO is a large trade organization representing agricultural, textiles, and manufactured goods. FUNDESA, the Guatemalan Development Foundation, is a private institution that promotes development. Ruckert and Walther, a law firm in Washington, D.C., coordinated Kaltschmitt's testimony.

33. Carmen López de Cáceres, vice minister of labor, interview with author, July 1994.

34. Also, women only represent 9.3 percent of all union members and 14.3 percent of industrial union affiliates. Official statistics indicate a surprising decline in their percentage share of the overall workforce, although their representation is up slightly in the industrial sector (see Ehlers 1990 for an alternate view; see also Smith-Alaya 1991).

35. Notes by U.S./GLEP, March 1995. Esprit was the only U.S. corporation that reportedly checked on worker and child labor conditions among its contractors. See also U.S./GLEP, "Findings of an Investigation of PVH Contractors in San Pedro Sacatepequez," September 3, 1996.

36. The settlement was facilitated by the intervention of U.S. Embassy, but until the Guatemalan government established permanent tribunals, no strike could be declared legitimate. See U.S./GLEP, "Review of Steps Taken on Worker Rights in Guatemala since December 1993," May 27, 1994.

37. Interview with author, February 1995.

38. General Inspector Cruz Minerva thought that companies should be required to deposit a security fund to cover such contingencies (for example, the case of Dong He, SA, a Korean firm that suddenly shut when 300 workers organized a union in March 1995). "We sent inspectors and examined the case, but when we can't locate the owners, we are powerless. The Ministry of Economy needs to regulate this [it can cancel their license]." Interview with author, March 1995.

39. Interview with author, February 1995.

40. M. Lutini of the Guatel Workers Union, interview with author, July 1994.

41. Interview with author, August 1994.

42. "In 1993, our budget was half what it is now. The increase depends on institutional support and economic investment," admitted Vice Minister Rivera (interview with author, February 1995). Such support stagnated from 1996 through 1998.

43. Interview with author, February 1995.

44. Interviews with author, July 1994.

45. See U.S./GLEP, "Analysis of Steps Taken to Respect Worker Rights in Guatemala from July 1 to August 31, 1994," September 16, 1994. See also "Supplementary Evidence," October 6, 1994. U.S./GLEP referred to the La Exacta case as an example of failed court functioning. Private police, led by an ex-colonel who masterminded the killings, received no penalty. Conflicts between the public minister and the minister of government hampered the investigation. The police chief of Quetzaltenango was briefly jailed, but he was not the primary instigator.

46. ILRF/GLEP, "Petition to USTR," 1993.

47. Jon Rosenbaum, comments to author, December 1997.

48. According to Guatemalan law, *incidentes* can arise in conjunction with the failures to negotiate or respond to general grievances, as well as with massive firings. After 1994, they took on an additional significance as employers disregarded the *emplazamiento* and code article 308, which unions had successfully utilized for twenty years to win rehiring of fired workers within twenty-four hours pending a full hearing. Technically, the *emplazamiento* allowed fifteen days for resolution, but employers now delayed its application by filing additional appeals, thereby assuring that the workers would not return (see also CTCA 1996).

49. Interview with author, June 1996.

50. The 1994 ILRF/GLEP mission located only two resolutions of the 300 collective cases pending since December 1992.

51. Interview with author.

52. Estimated by Judge Pimentel (interview with author, February 1995; numbers differ somewhat from table 8.9 because of 7th Court cases). Sub-Labor Inspector Moran verified that the poor quality of labor inspections and incomplete documentation may have provided a basis for rejecting 20 percent of the cases from 1994 to mid-1995, but since then, the office "has carefully submitted all required material [with no] more than four or five being sent back." Interview with author, July 1996.

53. Letter from CUSG, CTC, UNSITRAGUA, FENASTEG, FESEBS, FCG, and FESTRAS to Doctor Mario Aguirre Godoy, president of the Supreme Court of Justice, received January 23, 1996. They followed with a full meeting on February 5, 1996 (see U.S./GLEP, "Analysis of and Recommendations for Improving the Labor Courts," 1996).

54. D. Knight, quoted by R. Doumitt, U.S./GLEP representative, interview, February 1995. In 1993, another U.S./GLEP representative found it was nearly impossible to track case numbers or locate documents. The representative did identify four case files but was unable to determine their disposition. There could be sentences, but without fines or without enforcement.

55. Verified by the Sindicato de Trabajadores de Organización Judicial. No union interviewed had knowledge of any penalties imposed. When U.S./GLEP presented these findings to USTR in 1994–95, they were not challenged.

56. Mario Godlao Imrri Corrfa, letter to the Supreme Court, March 1, 1994.

57. Cesar Augusto Avila, clerk, Sixth Labor Court, interview with author, July 1994.

58. Brenda Alvarez, secretary of the Sixth Labor Court, interview with author, July 1994

59. Interview with author, July 26, 1994. Judge Pimentel said tribunals had been convened for the police, the Banco Immobilaria, and the Bandesa cases.

60. Brenda Alvarez, secretary of the Sixth Labor Court, interview with author, July 1994.

61. Interviews with author, June 1995.

62. For example, payment via *dietas,* or work per day in place of a full judge's salary; temporarily return to the former law for handling regional conflicts; or invocation of a temporary *accion amparo.*

63. Labor and business representatives were allocated *dietas,* but none had been convened. It remained unclear how they would be compensated for reviewing the case files.

64. Interview with author, July 1995.

65. After completing the three-year $1.5 million USAID contract, the Harvard University Center for Criminal Justice judged that the Cerezo government did not have the will to curb violence. Statement of Philip Benjamin Heyman before the Subcommittee on Western Hemisphere Affairs, U.S. House of Representatives, July 17, 1992.

66. K. Delaney, interview with author, February 1995.

67. Francisco Rivera, interview with author, 1996. According to Gary Maymarduk, then director of the Central American Desk, U.S. State Department, Guatemala's penal

code passed in mid-1994 gave investigative power to the public minister. USAID assisted through its program on the administration of justice, which supported judicial training schools and curricula and development for court personnel and public prosecutors (*fiscales*) in the Public Ministry. In the State Department's view, in 1996 the Arzú administration made new appointments that reconfigured the army and allowed prosecution of human rights cases. For past cases, the UN Historical Clarification Mission recorded atrocities and assisted victims without blaming individuals (see also Garst 1996).

68. Interview with author, February 1995. To some, the court decision to allow the elimination of the National Housing Bank was an example of court manipulation.

69. Interview with author, June 1996.

70. Interview with author, July 1995.

71. Interview with author, July 1996.

72. After a visit by this writer and Reynoldo González, the judge reprimanded Sr. Gonzalez and told his staff that if he visited again they should give the wrong information.

73. Interviews with author, June 1996.

74. Interview with author, July 1994.

75. Despite their tendency to corruption in local areas (see chapter 1 regarding Coca-Cola), the first level *juez de paz* or second level *juez de instrucción* are in a position to settle small collective cases. "Such judges supposedly are capable of handling all aspects of the law—civil, labor, etc. And there is nothing in the reforms that prevents the first-level judge from participating in the tribunals of conciliation in each department," emphasized Sergio Guzman. "The President of the Supreme Court has refused to discuss our proposal, but he refused." Interview with author, June 1996. Cases still bottleneck in the labor courts, administered by a *juez de sencencia* or trial judge.

76. Interview with author, February 1995.

77. Interview with author, July 1994.

78. Karen Delaney, USAID, interview with author, February 1995. Other approaches included bypassing the courts via administrative enforcement of the labor code and models for dispute resolution utilized by AIFLD/FOES in El Salvador (see chapter 6).

79. Interviews with author. In 1997, the commission held hearings and presented a full list of recommended steps. See also U.S./GLEP, "Review of Steps Taken on Worker Rights in Guatemala since December 1993," May 27, 1994.

80. See table 4.9 for GDP/wage correlations. Wages did rise in 1995 due to a shortage of workers in coffee production, but they evened out in 1996 as prices moderated.

81. Sergio Guzman and Byron Morales, interviews with author, July 1994.

82. Interview with author, July 1994.

83. The seven commissions include: press, agriculture, manufacturing, commerce, services, construction, and bread production (which has been well organized for years). Each commission involves nine people besides the secretary: two representatives from business, two from unions, and five alternates.

84. Maria Camelina Javier Sagastume, commission president, interview with author, July 1994. See also testimony by labor representative Reynoldo González, FESEBS (described in chapter 7).

85. Rafael Can Chabac and Francisca Chinik, CONIC, interview with author, July

1994. See also CONIC letter to Labor Minister Gladys Morfin, February 1, 1994, listing violations of minimum wages in eighteen fincas from Alta Verapaz, one from Baja Verapaz, twenty from Retalhuleu (with additional reductions in wages paid to women workers), ten from Suchitepequez, eight from Quetzaltenango, and three from Chimaltenango. Additional fincas were cited in CIEP documents prepared by Mynor Andrio, Carlo Lobos, and others.

86. Interviews with author, July 1994.

87. Sra. Sagastume, invoking Guatemala governmental accord 1319, no. 36, April 9, 1968, interview with author, July 1994.

88. Moran enthusiastically described a USAID-funded four-month project involving eight inspectors in Alta and Baja Verapaz that "went into many areas where a labor inspector had never been before with interpreters. Many spoke no Spanish, and sometimes people on neighboring fincas even spoke different languages." Interview with author, July 1996.

89. Thelma del Cid, interview with author, June 1996. Licda. del Cid has attempted to coordinate the Ministry of Labor and Ministry of Health plans for worker protection in agriculture.

90. Lance Compa, ILRF, "Testimony of U.S./GLEP and ILRF before USTR, GSP Subcommittee," November 3, 1993.

91. The health commissions only function if companies support them (see chapter 7, note 67). Non-traditional Export Association leader Carlos Arias: "We did away with the Acta on mixed health commissions in the workplace. It was unworkable, and we already had IGSS and the labor code, which handled the need. We have formed an industry pressure group to address noncompliance with the requirement for two bathrooms." Interview with author, February 1995.

92. Interview with author, July 1994.

93. Karen Delaney, USAID officer in charge, interview with author, February 1995.

94. "Tripartite activities need the help of CAIM and the Gremial. To qualify for the $3 million program, the government has to implement a four-point plan to encourage Guatemalan purchases of U.S. imports by February 1995: improve guarantees protecting intellectual property rights; legalize the business registration process [the single-stop procedure/office had been created, but was not yet approved by Congress]; and implement a dispute resolution procedure." Only after these reforms had been put in place could the Ministry of Labor access the $1 million in local currency budget support funds. Karen Delaney, interview with author, July 1994.

95. Delaney, interview with author, February 1995. USAID did sponsor more seminars conducted by the U.S. Labor Department and from the LUNA Cooperative Project of the University of Wisconsin. Representatives spoke to a gathering of 300 from the private sector, with members also from FENESEP, CUSG, and the public unions, but this time UNSITRAGUA did not attend.

96. Fernando Rivera, interviews with author, July 1994 and June, 1996. USAID then allocated funds for the ISCREL studies and for the University for Peace to offer courses in globalization and labor codes.

97. Interview with author, June 1996.

98. Interview with author, June 1996.

99. Interview with author, June 1996.

100. Interviews with author, July 1994. See Oglesby (1997).

101. Cushing cited the cases of Procter and Gamble, Colgate, and Kellogg as illustrative. "None of the plants have unions, but they have fine workers and want to keep them. [Unlike the sweat approach] as industrialization progresses they come to realize they must treat workers somewhat decently." USAID's Delaney agreed that in addition to GSP pressure, change came due to "international pressure because of competition: the owners want to produce better quality goods, and if they are to compete with others they must have a well-functioning and trained workforce." Interview with author, February 1995.

102. Interview with author, June 1996.

103. Interview with Carlos Arias, president, Maquila Exporters, July 1994.

104. CACIF representatives Rolando Acares, Francisco Bonapaz, and Mauricio Fachie, interview with North American labor delegation, June 20, 1996.

105. Interviews with author. Arias reported, "Sales are higher because we have increased our manufacturing quality. Unit volume has not increased. In 1994, we barely made quota in trousers and shirts. The marginality of our business is becoming more evident. If we have no new program, our exports will decline in dollars as well as units. By ECLAC figures, both Central America and Mexico experienced a 25 percent growth rate every year in their sales to the U.S. in dollar terms until 1993. CBI was helping us. Then, in 1994, Mexico shot up to 40 percent, Central America declined to 9 percent. We had a trade surplus with the U.S. in 1985, and since then it has dropped to a $2 billion deficit the last several years."

106. Interview with author, June 1996.

107. According to the Guatemalan Textile Association (VESTEX), in 1995, seventy-two firms closed but thirty-six opened, for a net loss of thirty-two. VESTEX did not explain what happened to the closed firms. Only four had moved to Mexico. Many may have been purchased by others. In any case, apparel exports to the U.S. increased by 15 percent between 1994 and 1995 and 16.7 percent between 1995 and 1996. Jobs in the sector remain steady. According to the local J.C. Penney manager, "the official line that 25,000 jobs have been lost is adopted to gain CBI parity. The unofficial reality is that it is somewhere between too early to tell, and baloney."

108. Interview with author, March 1995.

109. Interview with author, July 1994.

110. Interview with author, June 1996.

111. Interview with author, June 1994.

Chapter 9: GSP and Labor Changes in Honduras

1. Figures cited in FLT (89-28) and Pearson (1987).

2. This provision was later added to the original code.

3. AFL-CIO, "Petition to USTR," June 1995, p. 1.

4. In 1986, the government replaced the Colegio Profesional de Superación Magisterial Hondureño (COLPROSUMAH) teachers union with a state-sponsored federation. When COLPROSUMAH members marched into the union office, they were attacked by covert military troops, tear-gassed, abused and beaten (NLC 1991:34).

5. This happened despite the infusion of $1.3 billion in U.S. foreign assistance in the 1980s and $335 million in 1990–91.

6. USAID helped draft the privatization law (via USAID's "Privatization of State-Owned Enterprises Project," which promoted the move against more than twelve state companies). USAID also funded opening of an industrial park in 1989 (NLC 1991:29).

7. These included the Confederación de Trabajadores de Honduras (CTH, the AIFLD-sponsored confederation that included the Federación Sindical de Trabajadores Nacionales de Honduras, encompassing the banana workers, and the Federación Central de Sindicatos Libres de Honduras); the Federación Unitaria de Trabajadores de Honduras (FUTH), tied to the World Federation of Trade Unions; the independent Federación Independiente de Trabajadores de Honduras (FITH); and the CLAT-affiliated CGT, which withdrew from the pact after the Callejas election since it had attained a close association with the government.

8. These include: (1) The killings and torture of twenty members of the CNTC, the union of landless peasants that was occupying uncultivated lands. A hundred and twenty members were imprisoned. (2) The 1991 murder of five campesinos from ANACH, and wounding seven more who occupied 28 hectares of their own land near the Atlantic coast. Although they had received title from the 1976 National Land Institute, a Honduran colonel claimed the property. (3) The assassination of Ramón Briceño, a leader of the Sindicato de Trabajadores del Banco Central (to be noted later). (4) Killings in July 1989 of activist Solomon Vallecillos Andrade of FUTH and Jose Danilo Martínez and the bombing of the home of Gladys Lanza, head of STENEE. (5) The illegal firing in 1990 of leaders of the Asociación Nacional de Empleados Publicos, who sought to end the government's privatization program.

9. The following discussion, taken from New York Labor Committee, "Petition before the U.S. Trade Representative on Labor Rights in Honduras, May, 1991," is recapitulated in large measure in the more publicly available NLC (1991).

10. See reports by the Committee for the Defense of Human Rights and the International Commission of Jurists, cited by the New York Labor Committee (1991:3).

11. In one example, the Manufacturing Textiles Company in Puerto Cortés, which was owned by Michael Fayad and which produced "Union Jack" clothing for the U.S. market, was organized by FITH. The workers had obtained a contract for an eight-hour day with a reasonable piece rate; so Fayad closed the factory and reopened another named CAM. Instead of checking company behavior, police from the National Investigations Division kept union members under surveillance (New York Labor Committee 1991:9). This case illustrated the general difficulties of organizing in the free zones which, according to the U.S. Commerce Department, had been reputedly promised a "year of grace" from labor organizing drives.

12. Cited by the Committee for the Defense of Human Rights in Honduras (NLC 1991:29).

13. Unions even complained to the ILO, which sent a technical expert to offer recommendations for safe use. However, Honduras only provides one public hospital for every 265,000 of its people; it has few resources to implement ILO counsel.

14. Although minimum wages rose in 1992 by 14.35 percent, domestic inflation and exchange-rate fluctuations brought this drop in dollar-equivalency (see FLT 92-12:3).

15. Decree 133 (1989) applied the "labor code referring to public services, to avoid interrupting the company's production."

16. Honduran shipments to the U.S. reached $365 million in 1992, compared to $451 from Guatemala and $165 million from El Salvador (Moncada Valladares 1995 and chapter 4).

17. In addition to Puerto Cortés with twelve companies, EPZs were at La Ceiba (three), Tela (one), Choloma/Immobiliaria Hondureña (twelve), Choloma/Industrial Galaxy (five), and Empresas Independientes (eight). Most of the industrial parks were in various Cortés municipalities. Nearly all firms listed above assembled apparel products (Moncada Valladares 1995).

18. FESITRANH leader Claudio Villafranco, reporting on a meeting with the Korean manager of Galaxy, February 25, 1994, cited by AFL-CIO, "Petition to USTR," 1995, p. 1.

19. AFL-CIO, "Petition to USTR," June 1995, p. 7. This same employer strategy often effectively negated rights to bargain under article 465.

20. They would be kept in sealed envelope, jointly delivered by an inspector and union official, and opened upon notification.

21. Other cases included Textiles Maya, which fired forty on March 9, 1993, after a security guard twice blocked labor inspector entry; Seolim Co., which fired forty-five after a labor inspector who was first denied entry at the factory delivered it to the company's personnel director at home, who in turn refused to sign the receipt (September 10, 1993); Spring City Co., which fired fifty-two after a security guard, who called management, prevented inspector's entry (October 20, 1993); Industria de la Cal, which fired forty-five *and* the plant superintendent who signed the notification receipt. AFL-CIO, "Petition to USTR," June 1995, pp. 8–9.

22. Unless expressly indicated, the juridical review procedures for implementing the labor code must follow the *via ordinaria,* which takes much more time. However, courts had been in the practice of allowing companies this expedited procedure.

23. *El Tiempo,* October 1, 1993.

24. AFL-CIO, "Petition to USTR," June 1995, appendix 2 (Galaxy). The delegation included then AIFLD director Doherty and human-rights director David Jessup.

25. Moncada Valladares, quoted in *El Heraldo,* February 25, 1994; see also Moncada Valladares (1995).

26. *La Prensa,* March 25, 1994.

27. *Congressional Report,* May 4, 1994.

28. *El Tiempo,* November 25, 1994.

29. AFL-CIO, "Petition to USTR," June 1995, appendix 2, p. 7.

30. The first and second labor courts in San Pedro Sula reported a decrease in legal complaints from Choloma, dropping from 104 to 64 between 1993 and 1994. Those from La Lima and Villanueva remained the same, at 24 (Moncada Valladares 1995).

31. Interview with author, June 1994.

32. AFL-CIO, "Petition to USTR," June 1995, p. 1.

33. Interview with author, January 1996.

34. In one case, the company reinstated a pregnant union leader because the unionists threatened more testimony in the U.S. Congress; in another case, reinstatements

came after Liz Claiborne warned its Korean-owned supplier that it could lose its contract. AFL-CIO, "Petition to USTR," June 1995, p. 9.

35. Article 54 of the labor code obligated employers "to negotiate a collective contract with the union when requested," but there was no enforcement mechanism. The bargaining rule could result in one of three types of collective agreements: collective contracts, collective pacts (with a transitory association), or collective law contracts (with a branch company). The first needed a legal union, which adopted bargaining demands by majority vote in general assembly. It presented these demands to a labor inspection office in triplicate, with certified minutes, the names of the members of the negotiating committee, and request for employer notification. The inspectorate was required to accept the request, then nominate a specific inspector to notify the employer of the *emplazamiento*. The inspectorate would finally determine the date by which the owner must respond and begin bargaining. AFL-CIO, "Petition to USTR," June 1995, p. 10. See also table 9.1.

36. AFL-CIO, "Petition to USTR," June 1995, p. 11. The Labor Ministry has not published any penalty regulations to enforce this article 83.

37. Rosenbaum, USTR, and Zavala Méndez, Honduras, "Memorandum of Understanding." Tequcigalpa, November 15, 1995. Photocopy.

38. Interviews with author, December 1995.

39. Jon Rosenbaum, USTR, comment to author, December 1997. The Honduran Human Rights Commission had set up a monitoring program without full consultation with either the Labor Ministry or the unions, who should have been carefully incorporated into the process (see also Frundt 1998)

Chapter 10: Petitions in the Dominican Republic

1. Murphy (1987:266) argues that while the invasion brought local unions together, it also permitted U.S. labor and Samuel Gompers's involvement, enhancing divisions between professionals and laborers.

2. Law 288 required certain companies to pay 10 percent of pre-tax profits to their permanent workers.

3. Jeffrey Hermanson, UNITE, interview with author, January 1996.

4. The political divisions within the labor movement and the role of certain unions in manipulating popular sentiment and leadership lack a full account. In the Dominican, unions were much more aligned with political parties than in Central America (except in Panama). Here is a brief chart of relationships.

PRD: Founded the Unión General de Trabajadores Dominicanos (UGTD) in 1978. By 1985, the UGTD was in shambles, leading to the Central de Trabajadores Clasista (CTC).

Partido de Liberación Dominicana (PLD) of Juan Bosch: Divisions over the appropriate response to government policy also affected the CGT, also a leftist union, which spun off the Central de Trabajadores Mayoritaria (CTM), linked to the PLD and the World Federation of Labor.

PRSC (Partido Reformista Social Cristiana): The Confederación Autonoma Sindical Clasista (CASC) remained linked to the PRSC and affiliated to CLAT.

The PCD (Partido Comunista Dominicana) had ties to the Central Unitaria de Trabajadores (CUT), which also had relations with the PLD and was active with sugar workers. It also experienced internal divisions in 1985.

PRI (Partido Revolucionario Independiente): The Confederación Nacional de Trabajadores Dominicanos (CNTD). Its predecessor organization, the Confederación Nacional de Trabajadores Libres, had been tied to the PR (Partido Reformista—Balaguer's old party before merger with the PRSC in 1984) and AIFLD. It was known for its non-combative, class-collaborationist approach (Murphy 1987:282). However, after Balaguer's return to power in 1986, it grew considerably, attracting split-offs from more leftist confederations. It also maintained more neutrality toward the government, although for a time its general secretary was a PRI congressional deputy.

5. The CNTD, CGT, and CTC attempted a labor unification program in April 1987 (FLT 89-29).

6. CASC and CUT were the two confederations not participating in the June 1989 general strike. The PLD also opposed it. CASC participated in the subsequent negotiations.

7. The country cut off payments to commercial lenders but did not stop payments to multilateral institutions.

8. For several months, seven major confederations jointly met with the private sector, but negotiations stalled in September over a wage floor of 650 pesos. A union threat to resume the strike raised the agreement to 700 and won commitments for extending social security coverage, a freeze on rents, and a promise for permanent dialogue. But labor could not get the president to accept price controls on basic goods.

9. After widespread reports of election fraud, including from independent U.S. observers, analysts speculated that the U.S. held up investigations in exchange for further favors from Balaguer (see Cassá 1995; NACLA 1996). Meanwhile, the GNP dropped in 1990 (using fixed peso calculations). Sugar exports contracted, as foreign debt increased. Tourism and EPZs fared better. But inflation rose 101 percent (see FLT 91–41:4).

10. Interview with author, January 1996.

11. Letter from Holly Burkhalter, Americas Watch, to Carla Hills, USTR, May 29, 1991, opposing USTR's announcement, April 25, 1991, that the Dominican Republic had "taken steps."

12. NLC (1993:38–39), citing a February 8, 1991, letter from the U.S. Embassy's deputy chief in Santo Domingo to Commerce Secretary Robert Mosbacher inviting him to meet with Vice President Carlos Morales Troncoso and Manuale Enrique Tavares, owner of the Itabo Free Trade Zone and head of ADOZONA. Troncoso was also a shareholder in the Fanjul family's G&W operations. The Cuban-American Fanjuls had vacationed with Mosbacher and contributed heavily to Bush's election campaign.

13. Even in times of prosperity, the CEA had been used as a source of government loans. Now it faced lower prices, consolidations, and structural difficulties due to antiquated equipment.

14. Dominican Free Zones had officially existed since 1966. In 1990, law 8 set up the self-governing Asociación Nacional de Zonas Francas de Exportación (ADOZONA). It had no labor representation, but government officials could be invited. Dominican labor laws held. Companies had to give three month's notice if closing (article 44) (CTCA 1996; see also Kaplinsky 1993).

15. Investment in these sectors accelerated after CBERA's Special Access Program went into effect in 1987, playing a key role in creating the EPZ export platforms (see chapter 4). In 1991, seventy companies (thirty-three in apparel) began new operations in the Dominican Republic, with total new investments valued at $100 million. Of the sixty-one new investment projects inaugurated in 1992, forty were related to apparel or data processing services. The Dominican Republic also became the primary producer of footwear shipped to the U.S., as U.S. firms closed and expanded facilities in the Dominican to take advantage of the duty reductions provided in the 1990 changes in CBERA (USTIC 1994).

16. USTR, GSP Subcommittee, "Response to 1990 Petitioners," April 1991. See also Reyes Castro and Dominguez (1993) on impact of free zones.

17. USAID contributed at least $20.8 million to develop free trade zones in the Dominican Republic. Westinghouse and American Airlines had "unconscionably" shifted production operations from the U.S. to the Dominican "under conditions of high profit and guaranteed low wages targeted in the GSP law" (NLC 1993).

18. AFL-CIO, *Bulletin,* June 1991. See also AIFLD (1991).

19. See note 4, this chapter. The CTU was formed in May 1991 from a merger of the CTM, the CTC, the CTI, and the CUT.

20. Unions viewed the labor minister as "a good choice. Balaguer had to do something about labor rights yet did not wish to drive out investment. Alburquerque had the credentials: He represented the CNTD in the first free-trade-zone case (Westinghouse); he was honest, but also smart enough to make a deal. He came from a ruling-class family, but was known to business and labor alike." Jeffrey Hermanson, organizing director for UNITE, interview with author, January 1996.

21. Interview with author, June 1995.

22. The New York–based Interfaith Center for Corporate Responsibility and many other groups informed USTR of their support for the AFL-CIO's 1993 petition.

23. Rudy Oswald, AFL-CIO, letter to USTR, August 4, 1993.

24. Oswald, op. cit. According to the new code, labor courts were to be set up locally, but as in Guatemala they were not given any money to operate. Unlike Guatemala, they therefore still relied on justices of the peace, otherwise known as "courts of first instance," who were often subject to bribes.

25. AFL-CIO, "Rebuttal Brief to USTR," December 17, 1993.

26. Johnson, attorney for the Dominican government, letter to USTR, July 12, 1993, and Dominican Republic government rebuttal brief, December 29, 1993, which offered implementing regulations for the Dominican labor code, January 11, 1994. See also "Posthearing Brief," December 8, 1993; "Prehearing Brief," November 3, 1993.

27. Unions on the government list included Bibong, Westinghouse, Undergarment Fashions, Hanes, On-Time Caribe, H&J, Sylvania, Woo Chang, So Investments, Rayan, Importaciones y Exportaciones, Candelaria, Borinquena, Karson, and others where leaders in whole or part had been fired. AFL-CIO, "Rebuttal Brief to USTR," December 17, 1993.

28. Fuero sindical was the labor-code provision that protected union leaders from being fired during a specified time period without an adequate hearing.

29. Ambassador Ariza, letter to Joseph Damond, USTR, March 18, 1994.

30. Regulations of the Civil Service and Administrative Careers Act, March 29, 1994, section 142, para. 7: "the registration of organizations of public servants may only be quashed by a ruling of the Higher Administrative Tribunal when they engage in activities which are unrelated to their legal purposes." This was passed in response to the ILO concern over act 520, section 13 of December 1920.

31. Quoted by Jeffrey Hermanson, interview with author, January 1996.

32. Letter from Oswald to Joseph Damond, USTR, April 21, 1994.

33. Jeffrey Hermanson, UNITE's organizing director, interview with author, January 1996.

34. Letter of Minister of Labor Rafael Alburquerque, April 22, 1994, regarding sexual harassment complaints against Choiyng Gu of the Bibong Apparel Corp., April 1994.

35. Letter from Ambassador Carmen Ariza to Joseph Damond, USTR, April 28, 1994. The agreement also created an Educational Tripartite Commission to promote education and knowledge of labor legislation.

36. Johnson, Dominican attorney, letter to Damond, USTR, June 13, 1994.

37. Interview with author, June 1995.

38. "The union submitted 342 names; Bibong management said 435 didn't want a union; the union says it has a majority. The labor minister is going to verify the situation." Ambassador José del Carmen Ariza, letter to Damond, USTR, June 21, 1994.

39. Interview with author, January 1996.

40. GSP Subcommittee, "1993 GSP Annual Review," case 004-CP-93, Dominican Republic. Response to petition filed June 1993 by the AFL-CIO, July 1994.

41. Bobinas de Tabaco, SA, Moca; K.S.S.Enterprises, Santiago; Phil-More Dominicans, SA, Baní.

42. For example, Johnson, letter to Damond, September 13, 1994, citing Emily Donahue writing in the *Journal of Commerce,* September 2, 1994: "We believe that Ms. Donahue's assessment is accurate . . . (and the) evidence is conclusive." Bibong signed its contract on July 22, 1994; Caribbean Shoe, August 12, 1994.

43. Ambassador Ariza, letter to Daniel P. Shepherdson, chair, GSP Subcommittee, September 20, 1994.

44. Oswald, AFL-CIO, letter to Jon Rosenbaum, USTR, November 1994.

45. Interview with author, June 1995.

46. Interview with author, January 1996.

47. Johnson to Jon Rosenbaum, assistant U.S. trade representative, November 14 and December 6, 1994.

48. The government also reported to the ILO that between June 17, 1992, and October 1994 it had rejected no trade-union applications in EPZs. ILO (1995a).

49. Interview with author, January 1996.

50. Interview with author, June 1995. Even though new courts had been created, corruption was prevalent. The special courts only operated in four cities. Most *vocales* were unprepared (CTCA 1997).

51. Like Bibong, the Bonahan workers belonged to the Federación Nacional de Trabajadores de Zonas (FENATRAZONAS), which was part of the CNTD, by 1995 the DR's largest federation.

Hanchang had two other factories in the Dominican. One, with 750 workers, in the

Bonao Zone (also called Hanchang), had a sweetheart labor organization via the CGT, "like a solidarity association, with the management agreeing to provide loans, but a signed agreement that stipulated no economic benefits. After our successful bid at Bonahan, the union leadership wanted to affiliate with us." Hanchang's other factory employed 2,000 workers in the Daneen zone. It fired twenty workers in 1995, the day the company found out they were organizing a union. After Hanchang bribed a local justice with $50.00, "even the labor minister called it a miscarriage of justice, but we have appealed." Hermanson, interview with author, January 1996.

52. Hermanson, interview with author, January 1996.

53. Interview with author, January 1996.

54. Interview with author, January 1996. "ADOZONA was frantic to get parity resolved. Many already had cutting rooms set up in their plants, and would not have to pay any duty at all [or have labor-rights conditions if parity passed in the U.S. Congress]. Just when the strike was on, ADOZONA saw a last chance to push for parity. All the other confederations had signed an agreement supporting ADOZONA's parity request. They did not even mention labor-rights conditions. The FENATRAZONAS union said they would sign off on parity, but only if ADOZONA solved the [GSP principles concerning the] rights question. The CNTD and FENATRAZONAS took public positions stating the necessity for labor rights as a condition for supporting the agreement.

"The Labor Minister and ADOZONA claimed the country would lose tens of thousands of jobs because parity didn't pass. They used the seasonal layoff figures at Christmas to frighten people. In fact the zones continued to grow: employment was up by 25 percent; exports were up 25 percent [at the end of 1995]."

55. Hermanson, interview with author, January 1996.

56. See chapter 2.

Chapter 11: Regional GSP Efforts in Costa Rica, Panama, and Nicaragua

1. The author is grateful to Gene Miller of the Bildner Center for Western Hemisphere Studies, City University of New York Graduate Center, for his critical comments on the Costa Rica section.

2. Articles 368 and 369 severely restricted the right to strike, necessitating that 60 percent of the workers had to support the strike, register their names with a labor judge, and then agree to forty-five days of mediation before taking any action.

3. See García-Huidobro and Infante (1992). It is unclear how intentional this was since the IMF claimed that the 1984–86 wage-index system was linked to a distorted market basket of goods and services (though this was changed in 1986) see FLT 90-33:4.

4. The GNP hovered around 5 percent in 1987–89, dropped in 1990–91, and increased to 5 percent from 1992 to mid-1990s (see table 4.8 for GDP growth). See Honey (1994) for an analysis of the war-related economic impact of U.S. funding.

5. In 1991–92, production increased in concentrated orange juice, macadamia nuts, mangoes, melons, papayas, and pineapples. Twenty-nine new projects were reported in 1991, valued at over $33 million. Ten were in manufacturing. Investment to expand existing facilities totaled nearly $29 million, half of which was accounted for by a Hanes facility (Sara Lee Corp.) producing women's underwear. Rawlings Sporting Goods, a

U.S.-based firm, shifted its baseball production from Haiti. However, some textile manufacturing firms closed (USITC 1994).

6. Solidarismo was founded by Ernesto Martén, purportedly as a "Christian" effort to avoid class conflict. However, even the local archbishop, a major force behind the first Rerum Novarum labor federation, said "Martén had forgotten original sin." Labor organizations opposed *solidaristas* from the beginning. However, their explosive growth in the 1970s forced the *liberacionista* government to legalize them as a "fait accompli." Luis Alberto Monge, interviewed by Gene Miller, 1982.

The associations function like credit unions, offering savings plans and benefits. Both management and labor contribute between 3 and 8 percent of wages to the association, which sets aside a part of this for reinvestment in profit-sharing company-related enterprises. But, in fact, management's contribution is often what is owed workers as pension benefits. Management also usually controls appointments to the *solidarista* boards that oversee fund distributions. For a more complete picture of *solidarista* associations, see Wedin (1986); *Tico Times*, May 1, 1990 (exposé on such associations in the textile industry); Handler (1988).

7. This use of the *arreglo directo* caused a division between the Social School and the Movimiento Solidarista Constarricense, which represented two-third of the associations, mainly in urban areas, and said it did not want to see solidarity changed to an "anti-union tool" (FLT 91-19:8).

8. Between 1986 and 1990, the government had to pay more than 3 billion colons to comply with *laudos*. The teachers union and union of workers for the Ministry of Agriculture won *laudos* in 1989, and Sala IV (labor court) ruled against dismissals of school cooks in 1991 (FLT 91-19:10).

9. Quoted in AFL-CIO, "Worker Rights and the GSP: Petition to USTR," June 1993,

10. Quoted in AFL-CIO, "Worker Rights and the GSP: Petition to USTR," June 1993.

11. As determined by the legal advisor to the Centro de la Movimiento de los Trabajadores Costariquenses. Most legal strikes were against small businesses (FLT 94-43:8).

12. In August 1991, Costa Rica's three ICFTU affiliates, the Confederación Autentico de Trabajadores Democraticos, the Confederación Nacional de Trabajadores, and the Confederación Constarricense de Trabajadores Democraticos, merged to form the Confederación de Trabajadores de Rerum Novarum (CTRN), a revival of the earlier Rerum Novarum Confederation founded in 1943, and named from the 1891 papal encyclical on labor. The Catholic church meant the initial federation to serve as a counterbalance to communist-led unions, but it retained an independent character.

13. Interview with author, March 1995.

14. See Gregory and Davila (1993) for government evaluation of its code.

15. The CTRN signed with the CLAT-affiliated Central de Trabajadores Costarricenses (CTC), ANEP, and the left of center Confederación de Trabajadores de Costa Rica. The old Confederación Unitaria de Trabajadores, affiliated with the World Federation of Labor, had lost many affiliates since the mid-1980s (FLT 94-43).

16. Interview with author, June 1995.

17. Interview with author, March 1995.

18. Convention nos. 110, 140, 149, 151, 152, 153, 154, and 155 had also been submitted

for ratification during the 1980s, without success. The business sector still complained that conventions 110, 149, 151, and 154 were unconstitutional. Conventions not yet introduced included 158, 161, 162, 167, and 168.

19. The author is indebted to Susan Collazos Phillipps for her critical comments on the Panama section and for her larger study (1991; now out of print).

20. The primary confederations were the Confederación de Trabajadores de Republica de Panama (CTRP) related to AIFLD; the Central Panamena de Trabajadores del Transporte, an independent union of transport workers; the Central Nacional de Trabajadores de Panama (CNTP), affiliated with the communist World Federation of Trade Unions (WFTU); the Central Isthmia de Trabajadores, which split in 1992 into the General Autonoma de Trabajadores de Panama (CGTP) related to CLAT, and the Confederación Gremial de Trabajadores (CGT); and the militant but small Central Autentica de Trabajadores Independientes (CATI).

21. While the zone accounts for only 2 percent of the nation's employment, it has contributed a much higher percent of income.

22. Accolla (1982:2–3). The national commission appeared to have been the Consejo Nacional de Trabajadores Organizados, created by the 1972 labor code.

23. See the film *Panama Deception* for a clear demonstration of planned and persistent U.S. control over the Endara government.

24. In special circumstances, the government could also suspend collective agreements, and could order binding arbitration of conflicts that "cause serious economic difficulties." Parties could voluntarily agree to renegotiation.

25. AFL-CIO, "Petition to USTR on Panama," June 1992.

26. ILO report, March 1992, cited in AFL-CIO Petition, June 1992.

27. While some of the decline in union numbers was "due to the striking from the roles of unions that had become inactive," there was also a large drop in dues paying members, from 150,000 in 1988 to 73,345 in 1995, largely due to the 1993 decision by the Panamanian Supreme Court revoking the right for union bargaining-unit dues to be automatically deducted from paychecks (FLT 95-17:8).

28. Reform of the Social Security system appeared necessary, since the Caja de Seguro Social operating deficit rose from $67 million in 1988 to $187 million by 1991. Coverage was extended to 1.3 million, more than half the population, but only 425,000 paid into the system.

29. FLT 92-9:3–6. Reviving an old battle, the embassy repeated business arguments that mushroomed after the code's passage in 1972. Phillipps (1991) demonstrates that most of these arguments have little empirical foundation. Most changes in Panama's economy occurred for macroeconomic reasons.

30. In response to the huge outcry from labor, the government proposed the more moderate bill 27 to replace law 16, but it still eliminated jurisdiction of the national labor code in the free zones. Incentives in law 16, which exempted firms from collective bargaining, were still publicized to attract business investment (see *Global Production*, April–May 1992).

31. Interview with AIFLD supervisor David Jessup, June 1995.

32. Begun in 1992, the Fundación first involved representatives from the CTRP and later from the CNTP and CGTP.

33. The embassy drew upon a neo-liberal USAID-sponsored study (Gregory and Davila 1993) that questioned the usefulness of *any* minimum-wage legislation or labor code that contained significant employment protections. While the study demonstrated that the Panamanian code is stronger in most respects than codes in Chile, Costa Rica, Honduras, and Mexico, it offered little empirical evidence beyond employer statements that the code dissuades investment or shifts work to the informal sector. It made no effort to confront the careful challenge to these assertions in Phillipps (1991) or other business reports that did not find code requirements to have such detrimental economic impact.

34. For example, Panama still (tacitly) allowed police chiefs to sentence prisoners to work assignments on public projects, a violation of convention 29 (see ILO 1995a).

35. According to an unpublished study by Panamanian economist Juan Jované, the nation's labor legislation has not affected its GNP or rate of employment (University of Panama, 1994).

36. Before the August 12 agreement (see below), permanent workers fired for unjust cause were awarded an additional 50 percent of severance plus five months in back wages. For workers hired after the agreement, the additional payment would be 25 percent of severance plus three months in back wages.

37. CAR, August 18, 1995, and Susan Phillips, commentary to author, September 1995. The banana and construction unions never accepted the agreement and filed a complaint with the ILO.

38. Decree 1, January 1996, articles 8–13, dictated special labor conditions. Article 177 originally eliminated the obligation to collective contracts in the free zones. The revision accepted them "as long as these do not affect capital profits." The right to associate or negotiate was hardly guaranteed (CTCA 1996).

39. The author is indebted to Stahler-Sholk (1995) and that author's additional comments on the Nicaragua section.

40. The CST itself gained 130,000 members. Other FSLN-related unions included the Asociación de Trabajadores del Campo (ATC) with 60,000, primarily in state enterprises; the Unión Nacional de Empleados (UNE), representing 36,000 public employees; the Asociación Nacional de Educadores Nicaragüenses (ANEN); the Federación de Trabajadores de Salud (FTS); and the Unión de Periodistas Nicaragüenses (UPN).

41. See Americas Watch (1985), which found that the government helped peasants to unionize and respect labor rights, "unlike other L.A. governments." See also Booth (1985), Brown (1985), and Sklar (1988).

42. AFL-CIO, "Petition to USTR Regarding Nicaragua," 1985.

43. CPT received funding from AIFLD which encouraged its anti-Sandinista activities. The AIFLD-related CUSL, one of the smallest groups, was joined by the Central de Acción y Unidad Sindical formerly tied to the Nicaraguan Communist Party; the Confederación de Trabajadores de Nicaragua—Autónoma, formerly affiliated with CLAT; the Confederación General de Trabajadores—Independiente linked to the Socialist Party (PSN). In 1991, the CPT gained the Confederación Nacional de Maestros Nicaragüenses.

44. Author interviews of Sandinista labor leaders, 1983, 1984, 1989. Stahler-Sholk (1995) has added that in addition to assurances of rationed goods, day care, health

clinics, transportation, cafeterias, etc., they could invoke party help to obtain information and to resolve disputes with managers. They were also represented in the Council of State.

45. Stahler-Sholk pointed out that the USTR ruling was highly politicized by the war, the trade embargo, and a U.S. financial blockade. The International Court of Justice had just declared U.S. military hostilities against Nicaragua illegal. Commentary to author, July 1996.

46. Stahler-Sholk (1995) suggests that this change came from a new breed of Sandinista technocrats who implemented a much more orthodox economic program. Real wages declined subsequently (see also Ryan 1995).

47. In addition to election monies from the National Endowment for Democracy, the CPT received $1.2 million from USAID between 1990 and 1992.

48. As Stahler-Sholk outlined, the first strike in May 1990, really led by UNE, forced the rapid consolidation of the FNT itself. Because the government reneged on its promises, and because of the widening reaction created by antagonistic government policies, the "general strike" called in July 1990 verged on civil war. Daniel Ortega's intervention reinforced the FNT/FSLN separation, and it was soon followed by sixty labor conflicts, including twenty-one strikes.

COSEP eventually did not sign the agreements to protest selling any part of state enterprises to workers.

49. Letter from Francisco Rosales, minister of labor, Guatemala, and Emillo Periera Alègría, governor of the World Bank for Nicaragua, to Mr. Lewis T. Preston, president of the World Bank, April 14, 1994; see also World Bank 1993, chapter 9.

50. Pharis Harvey, ILRF; Jerome I. Levinson, Economic Policy Institute; Lance Compa, International Labor Rights Advocates; Lisa Haugaard, LAWG, "Memorandum" to Nancy Katz, interim U.S. executive director, World Bank, June 16, 1994. While Nicaragua was not trading within GSP, it was subject to the same regulations on labor rights via CBI, as explained in chapter 4.

51. *Barricada,* September 11, 1997. The new law 185 passed 79-0-2. Chamorro had vetoed an earlier version but a special tripartite commission subsequently reached consensus.

52. Prior to code reform, the 1991 Law of Free Trade Zone Industrial Exports offered EPZ workers limited protection. Chapter IV, Article 20 demanded that companies pay reasonable salaries, and benefits and that companies obey the laws of Nicaragua (this was its only reference to labor). In February, 1994, EPZ workers began forming a union at FORTEX apparel (see below). In August, a twenty-seven-day occupation of a gold mine which the government sold to Triton Canada brought further union recognition and a contract.

53. After a lengthy battle that required ILO intervention, FORTEX gained recognition and contract by December 1996. In turn, management illegally refused recognition, or contract negotiation. However, the victory motivated further organizing at Ecco Shoe (Italian), Nien Shing (Taiwanese firm contracting with J.C. Penney); and Foundation Cupid (U.S.), which contracted with Sears. In early 1997, management at the last two firms quickly fired union organizers, precipitating another international protest (letter from Pedro Ortega Mendez, Secretary of the Union of Textile, Clothing, Leather, and Footwear Workers, May 21, 1997).

54. Labor Minister Wilfredo Navarro welcomed investors from places "where unions are frightening investors." According to Ortega, the Minister provided an early warning to companies subjected to union organizing drives so they could fire members before the union gained legal status. In May 1997, he cancelled the legal recognition of the unions at Nien Shing and Foundation Cupid.

55. NLC/Hard Copy press release for airdate, November 11–13, 1997.

Chapter 12: Workers Evaluate Trade-based Labor Strategies

1. As Petchesky and Judd (1998) also discovered in researching women's rights in developing nations, often people do not use the language of rights but they do have a sense of justice and entitlement. Unionized women had a notably keen sensitivity.

2. Unless otherwise noted, quotations are from leaders' interviews with the author in 1995.

3. According to Luis Merida of UNSITRAGUA, "One of the difficulties with GSP was the formation of union demands. We would work on our own list to discuss with the government, but to be effective, we needed to develop positions not just from UNSITRAGUA but other confederations and sectors of the country." Interview with author, June 1996. For Roger Gutiérrez of FEASIES, taking advantage of the strategy was complicated, because "our movement is also very divided and dispersed, also a result of the war. Federations can be organized from any flotsam of unions (paper, construction, metallurgy all in the same federation). It is a crazy situation, and of course at times different interests are at stake that are difficult to reconcile and absorb much organizational effort." Interview with author, March 1995.

4. Interviews with author, March 1995. El Salvador's press had whipped up Vidal's hyperbole by misquoting a *Journal of Commerce* story announcing a new organizing campaign by UNITE, the amalgam of two major U.S. apparel unions, ACTWU and ILGWU.

5. Interviews with author, March 1995.

6. Michael Donovan, then AIFLD's Latin American field director stationed in El Salvador, interview with author, March 1995.

7. Notes by Rhett Doumitt, who accompanied reporter Bob Ortega (see Ortega 1995). "We saw a union coming, and immediately smashed it!" said the official. Meanwhile, Penney was contracting with Se Jan, a company illegally hiring children.

8. Interviews with author, July 1994.

9. Interviews with author, July 1994.

10. Delaney added, "The Guatemalan unions are now displeased with the code [as being] too specific. This results in bottlenecks, making it very difficult to work with." Interview with author, February 1995.

11. Enrique Alvarez, CIEP, interview with author, July 1994.

12. Interview with author, June 1996.

13. Interviews with author, March 1995.

14. Rodolfo Robles, UITA, interview with author, July 1994.

15. Rodolfo Robles, UITA, interview with author, March 1995.

16. Interview with author, February 1995.

17. Interview with author, February 1995.

18. Mario Lutini, secretary of conflicts, Guatel Workers Union, interview with author, August 1994.

19. Reynoldo González, FESEBS, interview with author, February 14, 1995; see also González (1997).

20. Interview with author, February 1995.

21. Lic. Juan Francisco Alfaro, interview with author, July 1994.

22. Interview with author, February 1995.

23. Interview with author, July 1994.

24. Mynor Andrio, CIEP, interview with author, July 1994.

25. Reynoldo González, FESEBS, interview with author, July 1994.

26. Interviews with author, March 1995.

27. Interviews with author, July 1994, March 1995.

28. Interviews with author, July 1994, March 1995.

29. Interviews with author, July 1994.

30. Rodolfo Robles, UITA, interview with author, March 1995. Robles spoke of good relations between UITA and Frigolifico de Guatemala, a large industrial group involved in meat and chicken export and fish production. Their various companies employed about 8,000, but only eighty were in the union.

31. Robles, Statement to the Labor Conference, "Jornadas de 21 de Junio," CAMI, Antigua de Guatemala, 1996.

32. Interview with author, March 1994.

33. Interview with author, July 1995.

34. Mazarieagos: "Sometimes I do not understand the union positions. They made many denunciations about the government and business sector in the press; but then, when it came time to vote, they refused to participate. The president had worked with unions as human-rights procurator. The workers often don't see that their struggle should be with the private sector, for example on taxes and lower electricity rates which the president supported." Interview with author, August 1994.

35. According to Vice Minister Rivera, in 1994 the ministry held three forums for the public unions, and in February 1994, it facilitated an accord with one of the telephone workers unions. Interview with author, July 1994.

36. Interview with author, July 1994.

37. Interview with author, June 1996.

38. Members of CACIF, presentation to U.S. labor delegation, June 1996.

39. Interview with author, July 1996.

40. Gilberto Ernesto García Dueñas of CENTRA, interview with author, March 1995.

41. Interviews with author, July 1996.

42. Gilberto Ernesto García Dueñas CENTRA, interview with author, July 1996. Also see CENTRA, "Resumen ejecutivo: Propuesta de las organizaciones de trabajadores sobre la reforma del estado y la privatización," March 1996, published in the Diario LatinoAmericano, July 28, 1996.

43. Interview with author, July 1996.

44. Sergio Guzman, UNSITRAGUA, interview with author, August 1994. Ministry investigation reported in El Grafico, July 27, 1994.

45. Byron Morales, UNSITRAGUA, interview with author, July 1994.

46. Interview with author, March 1995.

47. Interviews with author, March 1995, July 1996.

48. The demonstration on November 16, 1995, was precipitated by a letter signed on Consejo Superior de Trabajo, Sector Laboral stationery, with co-signers from FESINCONSTRANS, FEASIES, and FESTIAVTSCES/UNTC. But the latter two unions claimed manipulation and denied involvement or approval. Others who did not sign were FUSS, CGS, FESINTRABS, and FESTRAES. The last group split from FEN-ASTRAS in 1994, leaving it with only about 1,000 members. FENASTRAS had received funds from maquila owners, supposedly to protect Salvadoran jobs. A second potential group for filing GSP petitions, the CTD headed by Armanda Viatoro, had also suffered the loss of SUTC, the major construction union, in 1994. Sra. Viatoro also suffered a series of personal setbacks.

49. Interviews with author, July 1994, March 1995.

50. Interview with author, July 1994.

51. Luis Merida, UNSITRAGUA, interviews with author, March 1995.

52. U.S./GLEP, program report, Oct. 30, 1996.

53. Interviews with author, March 1995.

54. Former Guatemalan vice minister of labor Francisco Rivera, interview with author, June 1996. The effort was coordinated by Carlos Monge of Costa Rica.

55. Interview with author, June 1996.

56. See Romeo Fuentes (1994). This Fundación Friedrich Ebert-sponsored study includes Mexico and El Salvador. It examined the impact of neo-liberalism on the economy in El Salvador and demonstrated the lack of government interest in cooperating with labor unions.

57. Interviews with author, July 1994, March 1995.

58. Interview with author, July 1996.

59. Interviews with author, July 1994.

60. "ICIC includes unions from ORIT, COCENTRA, and CLAT although great tensions exist between them, and with unions affiliated with the WFTU Federación Sindical Mundial." Juan Francisco Alfaro, interview with author, July 1994.

61. Interviews with author, March 1995.

62. Interviews with author, March 1995.

Chapter 13: Conclusion

1. A 1996 survey by the U.S. Department of Labor, based on visitations of the Dominican Republic, El Salvador, Guatemala, and Honduras (as well as India and the Philippines) found that thirty-six of the forty-two largest apparel companies "had adopted formal standards prohibiting child labor." While enforcement remained a problem, child labor was "'not now prevalent' in the Latin American countries surveyed." Guatemala remained an exception (Meyers 1996).

2. In the early 1990s, the division's name was changed to include labor; its name was changed again to *remove* labor relations in 1996, although theoretically, coverage of these functions has continued. As an alternative, the UN has sponsored a project to improve labor relations that began in 1991 under the direction of Oscar Rivas; it offered concrete proposals such as Ministries of Labor levying fines directly, not going through the courts, and other changes in the labor codes.

3. Said to North American trade union delegation by Carlos Arias, Rolando Acares, Francisco Bonapaz, and Mauricio Fachie of CACIF, June 20, 1996, under the sponsorship of the Guatemalan office of the Friedrich Ebert Foundation.

4. CACIF members particularly objected if workers "went to the press about the difficult conditions of the country." It wanted to handle the problems internally (which it rarely did).

5. As chapter 2 mentioned, certain sociologists advocate network analysis as a useful approach to comprehend the persistence of these social configurations. When linked with class analysis, network construction can illustrate linkages between corporations and state agencies, but also counteractive formations between unions and among unions, religious, human-rights, consumer, and environmental groups. Differing graphical profiles of state policy responses to trade sanctions may provide insights about the effectiveness of trade-based labor-rights policy.

6. Interview with author, July 1994.

7. In Fall 1995, U.S./GLEP and the LAWG lobbied to strengthen worker rights conditionality in a new CBI parity proposal. While the bill did not pass, unionists felt their views had been heard during the CBI parity debate. According to a USAID spokesperson, a condition for receiving funds would have been that nations maintained eligibility for GSP benefits.

8. See Compa (1996) for multilateral issues involved in the NAFTA side agreement on labor.

BIBLIOGRAPHY

Accolla, Peter J. 1982. "Labor Profile: Panama." Washington D.C.: U.S. Department of Labor, Bureau of International Affairs. Photocopy.

———. 1989. "Privatization in Latin America." *Foreign Labor Trends* 89-20. Volume and number designation of the U.S. Department of Labor.

Accolla, Peter J., J. William Brumfield, Harold Davey, Glenn Halm, and Cleo Stallard. 1993. "International Child Labor Problems." *Foreign Labor Trends* 93-6.

Adams, Roy J., and Lowell Turner. 1994. "The Social Dimension of Freer Trade." In *Regional Integration and Industrial Relations in North America*, edited by Maria Lorena Cook and Harry C. Katz. Ithaca: Institute of Collective Bargaining, N.Y. State School of Industrial and Labor Relations, Cornell University.

AFL-CIO. *Bulletin*. Monthly.

———. Petitions to USTR. See endnotes for complete citations.

Aguilara Peralta, Gabriel. 1989. *El fusil y el olivo: La cuestión militar en Centroamérica*. San José: Departamento Ecuménico de Investigaciones y Facultad Latinoamericana de Ciencias Sociales.

AIFLD (American Institute for Free Labor Development). 1991. "Worker Rights in the Dominican Republic Free Trade Zones." Washington, D.C.: AIFLD.

Albizúrez, Miguel Angel. 1988. *Tiempo de dudor y lucha (Coca-Cola)*. Guatemala: Editor Local.

Alimonda, Héctor. 1994. "Mercosur, Democracy, and Labor." *Latin American Perspectives* 21, no. 4 (Fall).

Alston, Philip. 1996. "Labor Rights Provisions in U.S. Trade Law: "Aggressive Unilateralism?" In *Human Rights, Labor Rights and International Trade*, edited by Lance Compa and Stephen F. Diamond. Philadelphia: University of Pennsylvania Press.

Amato, Theresa A. 1990. "Labor Rights Conditionality: United States Trade Legislation and the International Trade Order." *New York Law Review* 65, no. 79.

Americas Watch. 1985. "Report on Human Rights in Nicaragua." New York: Americas Watch Committee (July).

———. Petitions to USTR. See endnotes for complete citations.

———. 1988a. *Organizing, Bargaining in the Private Sector*. New York: Americas Watch Committee (March).

———. 1988b. "The Reagan Administration's Record on Human Rights in 1987." New York: Americas Watch Committee.

———. 1989. *Persecuting Human Rights Monitors: The CERJ in Guatemala.* New York: Americas Watch Committee.

———. 1990. *Messengers of Death: Human Rights in Guatemala, November 1988–February 1990.* New York: Americas Watch Committee.

Amnesty International. 1987. *Guatemala: The Human Rights Record.* New York: Amnesty International.

ANEP (Asociación Nacional de Empresas Privadas). 1996. "El Manifiesto Salvadoreño." San Salvador: ANEP.

Arévalo, Rolando, and Joaquín Arriola. 1995. *Estudios de casos y educación obrera en zonas francas y empresas maquiladoras en paises del istmo centroaméricano y República Dominicana.* San Salavador: CENTRA/ILO.

Armbruster, Ralph. 1997. "Cross-Border Labor Organizing in the Garment Industry: The Struggle of Guatemalan Maquiladora Workers at Phillips Van-Heusen." Paper presented at a meeting of the Pacific Sociological Association, April 17–20.

Armstrong, Robert, Hank Frundt, Hobart Spalding, and Sean Sweeney. 1987. "Working Against Us: AIFLD and the International Policy of the AFL-CIO." New York: NACLA.

Armstrong, Robert, and Janet Shenk. 1982. *El Salvador: The Face of Revolution.* Boston: South End Press.

Arriola, Joaquín. 1993. *Los procesos de trabajo en la zona franca de San Bartolo.* San Salvador: Instituto de Investigaciones Economicas y Sociales.

———. 1995. "Diagnóstico económico del marco de relaciones laborales." San Salvador: CENTRA.

AVANSCO (Asociación Para el Avance de las Ciencias Sociales en Guatemala). 1994. *Apostando al futuro con los cultivos no-tradicionales de exportación I y II.* Guatemala City: AVANSCO.

Avendaño, N., and M. Mendoza. 1995. "El calvario laboral de los exportadores." *Crónica* 8 (December 1).

Banuri, Tariq. 1990. "Comments on Fields." In *Labor Standards and Development in the Global Economy,* edited by Stephen Herzenberg and Jorge F. Perez-López, 51–62. Washington, D.C.: U.S. Department of Labor, Bureau of International Labor Affairs.

———, ed. 1991. *Economic Liberalization: No Panacea: The Experiences of Asia and Latin America.* Oxford: Clarendon.

Banuri, Tariq, and E. J. Amadeao. 1988. "Worlds Within the Third World: Labor Market Institutions in Asia and Latin America." Helsinki: World Institute for Development Economics Research.

———. 1992. "Mundos dentro del Tercer Mundo: Instituciones del mercado de trabajo en Asia y America Latina." *Trimestre Económico* (Mexico) 59 (October–December).

Barry, Tom, and Deb Preusch. 1990. *AIFLD in Central America: Agents as Organizers.* Albuquerque, N.M.: The Resource Center.

Beneria, Lourdes. 1989. "Subcontracting and Employment Dynamics in Mexico City." In *The Informal Economy,* edited by Alejandro Portes, Manuel Castells, and Lauren Benton, 173–88. Baltimore: Johns Hopkins University Press.

Beneria, Lourdes, and Martha Roldan. 1987. *The Crossroads of Class and Gender.* Chicago: University of Chicago Press.

Benjamin, Media, ed. 1987. *Don't Be Afraid, Gringo: A Honduran Woman Speaks from the Heart.* San Francisco: Institute for Food and Development Policy.

Berger, Susan. 1992. *Political and Agrarian Development in Guatemala.* Boulder: Westview.

Bergquist, Charles. 1986. *Labor in Latin America.* Stanford: Stanford University Press.

———. 1996. *Labor and the Course of American Democracy.* New York: Verso.

Berryman, Phillip. 1984. *The Religious Roots of Rebellion.* Maryknoll, N.Y.: Orbis Books.

———. 1987. *Liberation Theology: Essential Facts about the Revolutionary Movement in Latin America and Beyond.* Philadelphia: Temple University Press.

———. 1995. *Stubborn Hope: Religion, Politics, and Revolution in Central America.* Maryknoll, N.Y.: Orbis Books.

Birkbeck, C. 1979. "Garbage, Industry, and the 'Vultures' of Cali, Columbia." In *Casual Work and Poverty in Third World Cities,* edited by R. Bromley and C. Gerry. New York: John Wiley.

Black, George, Milton Jamail, and Norma Stolz Chinchilla. 1984. *Garrison Guatemala.* New York: Monthly Review Press.

Blackwell, Ronald. 1988. Commentary delivered at the Symposium on Labor Standards and Third World Development, sponsored by the U.S. Department of Labor, Bureau of International Labor Affairs, and the Overseas Development Council, Washington D.C., December 12–13.

Bollinger, William. 1987a. "El Salvador." In *Latin American Labor Organizations,* edited by Gerald Michael Greenfield and Sheldon L. Maram, 307–88. New York: Greenwood.

———. 1987b. "Peru." In *Latin American Labor Organizations,* edited by Gerald Michael Greenfield and Sheldon L. Maram, 607–66. New York: Greenwood.

Bonacich, Edna, Lucie Cheng, Norma Chinchilla, Nora Hamilton, and Paul Ong, eds. 1994. *Global Production: The Apparel Industry in the Pacific Rim.* Philadelphia: Temple University Press.

Booth, John. 1985. *The End and the Beginning: The Nicaragua Revolution.* Boulder: Westview.

———. 1987. "Costa Rica," In *Latin American Labor Organizations,* edited by Gerald Michael Greenfield and Sheldon L. Maram, 213–42. New York: Greenwood.

Bounds, Wendy. 1997. "Phillips–Van Heusen, in Reversal, Plans to Negotiate with Union in Guatemala." *Wall Street Journal* (March 18).

Bowman, Scott. 1993. "The Ideology of Transnational Enterprise." *Social Science Journal* 30, no. 1.

Briggs, Barbara, and Charles Kernaghan. 1996. "The GAP and Sweatshop Labor in El Salvador." *NACLA Report on the Americas* 29, no. 4 (January–February).

Brocas, Anne-Marie, Anne-Marie Cailloux, and Virginie Oget. 1990. *Women and Social Security: Progress Towards Equality of Treatment.* Geneva: ILO.

Bromley, R. 1978. "Organization, Regulation, and Exploitation in the So-called 'Urban Informal Sector': The Street Traders of Cali Colombia." *World Development* 6, nos. 9–10: 1161–71.

Bromley, R., and C. Gerry, eds. 1979. *Casual Work and Poverty in Third World Cities.* New York: John Wiley.

Bronstein, A. S. 1994. "Regulaciones de salario mínimo: Normas internacionales y legislación nacional." *Relasur* (Montevideo) 3.

———. 1997. "Labour Law Reform in Latin America: Between State Protection and Flexibility." *International Labour Review* 136, no. 1 (Spring): 5–26.

Brown, Cynthia. 1985. *With Friends Like These.* New York: Pantheon.

Buchele, Robert, and Jens Christiansen. 1995. "Worker Rights Promote Productivity Growth." *Challenge* 38 (September–October): 32–37.

Bulmer-Thomas, Victor. 1987. *The Political Economy of Central America since 1920.* Cambridge: Cambridge University Press.

Burbach, Roger, and Patricia Flynn. 1984. *The Politics of Intervention: The United States in Central America.* New York: Monthly Review Press.

Burbach, Roger, Orlando Nuñez, and Boris Kagarlitsky. 1997. *Globalization and Its Discontents.* Chicago: Pluto Press.

Burnham, Bradford, Mary Clark, Elizabeth Katz, and Rachael Schurman. 1992. "Nontraditional Agricultural Exports in Latin America." *Latin American Research Review* 27, no. 2.

Cagatay, Nilufer. 1990. "Turkey." In *Labor Standards and Development in the Global Economy,* edited by Stephen Herzenberg and Jorge F. Perez-López, 123–40. Washington, D.C.: U.S. Department of Labor, Bureau of International Labor Affairs.

Caire, Guy. 1994. "Labour Standards and International Trade." In *International Labour Standards and Economic Interdependence,* edited by Werner Sengenberger and Duncan Campbell, 297–319. Geneva: ILO.

Cantor, Daniel, and Juliet Schor. 1987. *Tunnel Vision: Labor, the World Economy and Central America.* Boston: South End Press.

CAR (*Central American Report,* Guatemala). Weekly newsletter.

Carter, Brenda, Kevan Insko, Daved Loeb, and Marlene Tobias. 1989. *A Dream Compels Us: Voices of Salvadoran Women.* San Francisco: New Americas Press.

Cassá, Roberto. 1995. "Recent Popular Movements in the Dominican Republic." *Latin American Perspectives* 22, no. 3 (Summer): 80–93.

Cavanagh, John, et al. 1988. *Trade's Hidden Costs: Worker Rights in a Changing World Economy.* Washington, D.C.: International Labor Rights Education and Research Fund.

CEPAS (Centro de Estudios para la Acción Social). 1988. "El movimiento sindical: Un dilema entre lo viejo y lo nuevo." San José, Costa Rica: CEPAS.

CERIGUA (Centro de Reportes Informativos sobre Guatemala). 1997. *Peace in Guatemala: The Accords.* Guatemala City: CERIGUA. Special report 3, no. 1 (July).

Charnovitz, Steve. 1987. "The Influence of International Labour Standards on the World Trading Regime: A Historical Overview." *International Labour Review* 126, no. 5 (September– October).

———. 1992. "Environmental and Labour Standards in Trade." *World Economy* 15, no. 3 (May).

Chernick, Sidney. 1978. *The Commonwealth Caribbean.* Baltimore: Johns Hopkins University Press/World Bank.

Chinchilla, Norma, and Nora Hamilton. 1994. "The Garment Industry and Economic Restructuring in Mexico and Central America." In *Global Production: The Apparel Industry in the Pacific Rim,* edited by Edna Bonacich, Lucie Cheng, Norma Chinchilla, Nora Hamilton, and Paul Ong, 287–308. Philadelphia: Temple University Press.

CITGUA (*Ciencia y tecnología para Guatemala*). 1990. "El movimiento sindical en Guatemala, 1986–88, parte II." Mexico City: CITGUA (June).

Clymer, Adam. 1996a "Help Companies That Treat Workers Well, Kennedy Says." *New York Times* (February 9).

———. 1996b. "Clinton Is Cool to Democrats' Ideas on Shielding U.S. Workers." *New York Times* (February 29).

Coats, Stephen. 1991. "Phillips-Van Heusen Workers Organize." *Report on Guatemala* 12, no. 4 (Winter).

———. 1993. "Maquila Workers Campaign: Success Raises Questions." *Report on Guatemala* 14, no. 2 (Summer).

———. 1996. "Taking on Phillips-Van Heusen: Maquila Workers Fight for a Contract." *Report on Guatemala* 17, no. 4 (Winter).

———. 1998. "Reflections on the Issue of Independent Monitoring." Washington, D.C.: Campaign for Labor Rights Series on independent monitoring.

Cockcroft, James. 1995. *Mexico.* New York: Nelson Hall.

———. 1996. *Latin America: History, Politics, and U.S. Policy.* 2nd ed. New York: Nelson Hall.

Cogan, Doug. 1995. "Worker Standards for Non-U.S. Suppliers." Washington, D.C.: Investor Responsibility Research Center Background Report O (March 2).

Coleman, Kenneth M., and George C. Herring, eds. 1991. *Understanding the Central American Crisis.* Wilmington: Scholarly Resources.

Collier, Ruth Berins, and David Collier. 1979. "Inducements versus Constraints: Deregulating Corporatism." *American Political Science Review* 73, no. 4 (December): 967–86.

———. 1991. *Shaping the Political Arena: Critical Junctures, the Labor Movement, and Regime Dynamics in Latin America.* Princeton: Princeton University Press.

Collingsworth, Terry. 1989. "American Labor Policy and the International Economy: Clarifying Policies and Interests." *B.C. Law Review* 31.

———. 1997. "Child Labor in the Global Economy." Washington, D.C.: Institute for Policy Studies/Interhemispheric Resource Center. Foreign Policy in Focus brief.

Collingsworth, Terry, J. William Goold, and Pharis Harvey. 1994. "Time for a Global New Deal." *Foreign Affairs* (January–February).

Commission on the Future of Worker-Management Relations [Dunlop Commission]. 1994. *Report and Recommendations.* Washington, D.C.: U.S. Department of Labor, U.S. Department of Commerce.

Compa, Lance. 1993. "International Labor Rights and the Sovereignty Question: NAFTA and Guatemala, Two Case Studies." *American University Journal of International Law and Policy* 9, no. 1 (Fall).

———. 1996. "Another Look at the NAFTA Labor Accord." In *International Labor Rights and Standards after NAFTA: A Symposium,* Stephen Herzenberg, comp. New Brunswick: Rutgers Labor Education Center.

Compa, Lance, and Tashia Hinchliffe Darricarrère. 1996. "Private Labor Rights Enforcement Through Corporate Codes of Conduct." In *Human Rights, Labor Rights, and International Trade,* edited by Lance Compa and Stephen F. Diamond. Philadelphia: University of Pennsylvania Press.

Compa, Lance, and Stephen F. Diamond, eds. 1996. *Human Rights, Labor Rights, and International Trade.* Philadelphia: University of Pennsylvania Press.

Connelly, Patricia, and Martha MacDonald. 1995. *Trabajo, género y ajuste.* Guatemala: AVANSCO (June).

Cook, Maria Lorena, Morley Gunderson, Mark Thompson, and Anil Verma. 1997. "Making Free Trade More Fair: Developments in Protecting Labor Rights." *Labor Law Journal* 48 no. 8 August).

Cordova, Efren. 1984. *Industrial Relations in Latin America.* New York: Praeger.

———. 1996. "Commentary on the Study on Harmonization of Labor Codes in Central America." In CTCA, *Labor Code Harmonization in Central America,* 8–22. San Jose: CTCA .

Costa Rica. *Código de Trabajo.* 1993. San José: Provenir

Crahan, Margaret E., ed. 1982. *Human Rights and Basic Needs in the Americas.* Washington, D.C.: Georgetown University Press.

Craver, Charles B. 1995. *Can Unions Survive?* New York: New York University Press.

Crossborder Monitor. 1994. "MNC's Under Fire to Link Trade with Global Labour Rights. 2 (May 23).

CTCA (Confederación de Trabajadores de Centro América). 1996. *Labor Code Harmonization in Central America.* San José: CTCA.

Datta-Chaudhuri. 1990. "India." In *Labor Standards and Development in the Global Economy,* edited by Stephen Herzenberg and Jorge F. Perez-López, 155–72. Washington D.C.: U.S. Department of Labor, Bureau of International Labor Affairs.

Davies, R. 1979. "Informal Sector or Subordinate Mode of Production? A Model." In *Casual Work and Poverty in Third World Cities,* edited by R. Bromley and C. Gerry. New York: John Wiley.

Davis, Benjamin. 1995. "The Effects of Worker Rights Protections in U.S. Trade Laws: A Case Study of El Salvador." *American University Journal of International Law and Policy* 10, no. 3 (Spring): 1167–1214.

DeBray, R. 1975. "An Illustration of Nestle's Role in Developing Countries: Example of the State of Chiapas, Mexico." Vevey, Switzerland: Nestle Alimentana, S.A.

Delgado González, Maritza. 1994. "Workers' Education for Women Members of Rural Workers' Organizations in Central America and the Dominican Republic." In *Women in Trade Unions: Organizing the Unorganized,* edited by Margaret Hosmer Martens and Swasti Mitter, 115–26. Geneva: ILO.

Devroy, Ann. 1994. "Clinton Reverses Course on China: MFN Action Separates Human Rights and Trade." *Washington Post* (May 27): A1.

Deyo, Frederic C. 1993. "Beneath the Miracle: Labor Subordination in the New Asian Industries." In *The Political Economy of the New Asian Industrialism,* edited by Frederic C. Deyo. Ithaca: Cornell University Press.

Dietz, James L., ed. 1995. *Latin America's Economic Development: Confronting Crisis.* 2nd ed. Boulder: Lynne Rienner.

Dominican Republic. Secretaría de Estado de Trabajo. 1995. *Código de Trabajo.* Santo Domingo: Editora Lozano.

Donahue, Thomas R. 1994. "The Perspective of Labor." In *International Labor Standards and Global Economic Integration,* edited by Gregory Schoepfle and Kenneth Swinnerton, 46–48. Washington, D.C.: U.S. Department of Labor.

Donaldson, Thomas, and Patricia Werhane. 1995. *Ethical Issues in Business.* 5th ed. Englewood Cliffs, N.J.: Prentice-Hall.

Dorman, Peter. 1989. *Worker Rights and U.S. Trade Policy.* Washington, D.C.: U.S. Department of Labor.

Dosal, Paul J. 1995. *Power in Transition: The Rise of Guatemala's Industial Oligarchy, 1871–1994.* Westport, Conn.: Praeger.

Doyle, Frank. 1994. "The Perspective of Business," In *International Labor Standards and Global Economic Integration,* edited by Gregory Schoepfle and Kenneth Swinnerton, 43–45. Washington, D.C.: U.S. Department of Labor.

Edelman, Lauren B. 1992. "Legal Ambiguity and Symbolic Structures: Organizational Mediation of Civil Rights Law." *American Journal of Sociology* 97 (May): 1531–76.

Edelman, Lauren B., Howard Erlanger, and John Lande. 1993. "Internal Dispute Resolution." *Law and Society Review* 27, no. 3: 497–534.

Edgren, G. 1979. "Fair Labour Standards and Trade Liberalisation." *International Labour Review* 5.

Edwards, Richard. 1979. *Contested Terrain: The Transformation of the Workplace in the Twentieth Century.* New York: Basic Books.

———. 1993. *Rights at Work: Employee Relations in the Post Union Era.* Washington, D.C.: Brookings Institution.

———. 1994a. "Reshaping Employee Protections for a Global Economy." *Challenge* 37 (January–February).

———, ed. 1994b. *Working under Different Rules.* New York: Russell Sage.

Ehlers, Tracy. 1990. *Silent Looms.* Boulder: Westview.

Ehrenberg, Ronald G. 1994. *Labor Markets and Integrating National Economies.* Washington, D.C.: Brookings Institution.

Ehrenreich, Barbara. 1990. *Fear of Falling: The Inner Life of the Middle Class.* New York: HarperCollins.

Elmslie, B., and W. Milberg. 1996. "Free Trade and Social Dumping: Lessons from the Regulation of U.S. Interstate Commerce." *Challenge* 39 (May–June).

———. 1997. "Free Trade and International Labor Standards." *New Labor Forum* 1 (Fall).

El Salvador. Ministerio de Trabajo y Previsión Social. 1991–95. *Estadísticas de Trabajo.* San Salvador: Ministerio.

———. 1994. *Código de Trabajo.* San Salvador: Editorial Jurídica Salvadoreña.

Emmerij, Louis. 1994. "Contemporary Challenges for Labour Standards Resulting from Globalization." In *International Labour Standards and Economic Interdependence,* edited by Werner Sengenberger and Duncan Campbell, 319–28. Geneva: ILO.

Epstein, Edward. 1997. "Chilean Labor and Labor Rights under the Free Trade Area of the Americas." Paper presented at the 20th International Congress of the Latin American Studies Association, Guadalajara, April 17–20.

———, ed. 1989. *Labor, Autonomy, and the State in Latin America.* Boston: Unwin Hyman.

Epstein, Gerald. 1993. "Power, Profits, and Cooperation in the Global Economy," In *Creating a New World Economy,* edited by Gerald Epstein, Julie Graham, and Jessica Nembhard. Philadelphia: Temple University Press.

Ermann, M. David, and William H. Clements II. 1986. "The Campaign Against Marketing of Infant Formula in the Third World." In *Corporate and Governmental Deviance*

(3rd ed.), edited by M. David Ermann and Richard J. Lundman, 209–30. New York: Oxford University Press.

Escobar, Arturo, and Sonia Alvarez. 1992. *The Making of Social Movements in Latin America*. Boulder: Westview.

Escoto, Jorge, and Manfredo Marroquín. 1992. *La AID en Guatemala*. Managua: CRIES/ AVANSCO.

Espinal, Rosario. 1995. "Economic Restructuring, Social Protest, and Democratization in the Dominican Republic." *Latin American Perspectives* 22, no. 3 (Summer): 63–79.

Ezorsky, Gertrude, ed. 1987. *Moral Rights in the Workplace*. Albany: State University of New York Press.

Fallon, Peter, and Luis Riveros. 1990. "Macroeconomic Adjustment and Labor Market Response: A Review of Recent Experience in LDCs." In *Labor Standards and Development in the Global Economy*, edited by Stephen Herzenberg and Jorge F. Perez-López, 189–218. Washington, D.C.: U.S. Department of Labor.

Fantasia, Rick. 1988. *Cultures of Solidarity*. Berkeley: University of California Press.

Fernandez-Kelly, Maria. 1993. *For We Are Sold, I and My People: Women and Industry in Mexico's Frontier*. Albany: State University of New York Press.

Fields, Gary S. 1990. "Labor Standards, Economic Development, and International Trade." In *Labor Standards and Development in the Global Economy*, edited by Stephen Herzenberg and Jorge F. Perez-López, 19–34. Washington, D.C.: U.S. Department of Labor.

Flamm, Kenneth, and Joseph Grunwald. 1985. *The Global Factory: Foreign Assembly in International Trade*. Washington, D.C.: Brookings Institution.

Flanigan, Robert J. 1987. *Labor Relations and the Litigation Explosion*. Washington, D.C.: Brookings Institution.

FLT. *Foreign Labor Trends*, U.S. Department of Labor, various countries and numbers.

Forster, Cindy. 1996. "Guatemalan Labor Confronts Free Trade." *Report on Guatemala* 17, no. 3 (October).

Fox, James W. 1997. "Maquila Exports from the Caribbean Basin: Solution or Problem?" Paper presented at the 18th Annual Conference of the Middle Atlantic Council of Latin American Studies, Annapolis, Md., April 4–5.

Franklin, Jane. 1997. *Cuba and the U.S.: A Chronological History*. 2nd ed. New York: Ocean Press.

Freeman, Richard. 1994. "A Hard-headed Look at Labour Standards." In *International Labor Standards and Global Economic Integration*, edited by Gregory Schoepfle and Kenneth Swinnerton, 26–34. Washington, D.C.: U.S. Department of Labor.

French, John. 1994. "The Declaration of Philadelphia and the Global Social Charter of the United Nations, 1944–45." In *International Labour Standards and Economic Interdependence*, edited by Werner Sengenberger and Duncan Campbell, 19–28. Geneva: ILO.

French, John, and Russell E. Smith. 1995. "Labor, Free Trade, and Economic Integration in the Americas: National Labor Union Responses to a Transnational World." Miami: Center for Labor Research and Studies, Florida International University.

Friedman, Thomas L. 1994. "Trade vs. Human Rights." *New York Times* (February 6).

Frundt, Henry J. 1980. "Gulf and Western in the Dominican Republic." New York: Interfaith Center for Corporate Responsibility.

———. 1987a. "To Buy the World a Coke: Implications of Trade Union Redevelopment in Guatemala." *Latin American Perspectives* 14, no. 3 (Summer): 381–416.

———. 1987b. *Refreshing Pauses: Coca-Cola and Human Rights in Guatemala.* New York: Praeger.

———. 1990. "Guatemala in Search of Democracy." *Journal of Interamerican Studies and World Affairs* 32, no. 3 (Fall).

———. 1995. "AIFLD in Guatemala: End or Beginning of a New Regional Strategy?" *Social and Economic Studies* 44, nos. 2–3 (June).

———. 1996. "Trade and Cross-Border Labor Strategies in the Americas." *Economic and Industrial Democracy* 17, no. 3 (August).

———. 1997. "Central American Labor Responses to Free Trade." Paper presented at the 20th International Congress of the Latin American Studies Association, Guadalajara, April 17–20.

———. 1998. "Cross-Border Organizing in the Apparel Industry: Lessons from Central America and the Caribbean." Paper presented at the University and College Labor Education Association/AFL-CIO Conference, "Organizing For Keeps," San Jose, Calif., May 2.

Frundt, Henry J., and Norma Chinchilla. 1987. "Guatemala." In *Latin American Labor Organizations,* edited by Gerald Michael Greenfield and Sheldon L. Maram, 395–432. New York: Greenwood.

Fundación Myrna Mack. 1993. "La privatización y los derechos económicos y sociales." Guatemala City: Fundación Myrna Mack (November 5).

Gacek, Stanley. 1992. "Corporatist and Contracturalist Models of Labor Law: Brazil versus the U.S." Paper presented at the 17th International Congress of the Latin American Studies Association, Los Angeles (March).

García-Huidobro, Guillermo, and Ricardo Infante. 1992. "Costa Rica: Políticas para pagar la deuda social: Empleo, salarios y gasto social." PREALC Programa Mundial del Empleo, no. 366 (August).

García-Huidobro, Guillermo, et al. 1990. "La deuda social en Costa Rica." PREALC (paper series).

García-Rocha, Adalberto. 1990. "Mexico." In *Labor Standards and Development in the Global Economy,* edited by Stephen Herzenberg and Jorge F. Perez-López, 141–54. Washington, D.C.: U.S. Department of Labor, Bureau of International Labor Affairs.

Garst, Rachael. 1996. White paper on Arzu's military appointments. Washington, D.C.: Washington Office on Latin America.

Garver, Paul. 1989. "New Directions for Labor Internationalism." *Labor Research Review* 9, no. 1 (Spring): 61–70.

GAO (General Accounting Office). 1994. "Assessment of the Generalized System of Preferences Program." Washington, D.C.: General Accounting Office.

———. 1993. "U.S. Support for Caribbean Basic Assembly Industries." Washington, D.C.: General Accounting Office.

Gill, Henry. 1985. "Aspectos comerciales de la iniciativa estadounidense para la Cuenca del Caribe." *Capitulos del Sela* 9 (January–June).

Gindling, T. H., and Maria Crummett. 1995. "Maternity Leave Legislation and the Work and Pay of Women in Costa Rica." Report for USAID, Coopers and Lybrand, Contract PCE-0026-Q-00-3031-00 (May).

Gindling, T. H., and Katherine Terrell. 1995. "The Nature of Minimum Wages and Their

Effectiveness as a Wage Floor in Costa Rica, 1976–1991." *World Development* 23, no. 8 (August): 1439–58.

Gleijeses, Piero. 1991. *Shattered Hope: The Guatemalan Revolution and the United States, 1944–1954.* Princeton: Princeton University Press.

Goldston, James A. 1989. *Shattered Hope: Guatemalan Workers and the Promise of Democracy.* Boulder: Westview.

González, Mario Aníbal. 1990. *El desarrollo de la industria de la maquila en Guatemala: Estudio de casos de la ocupación de la mano de obra feminina.* Guatemala City: Facultad Latino-americana de Ciencias Sociales.

González, Reynaldo. 1997. "El medio de los sindicatos: Reconstrucción significa privatización." Paper presented at the 20th International Congress of the Latin American Studies Association, Guadalajara, April 17–20.

González Casanova, Pablo, coord. 1985. *Historia del movimiento obrero en América Latina.* Mexico: Siglo Veintiuno Editores, S.A.

Goodman, Louis W., William M. LeoGrande, and Johanna Mendelson Forman. 1990. *Political Parties and Democracy in Central America.* Boulder: Westview.

Green, Linda B. 1989. "Consensus and Coercion: Primary Health Care and the Guatemalan State." *Medical Anthropology Quarterly* 3, no. 3: 246–57.

———. 1997. "The Localization of the Global: Contemporary Production Practices in a Mayan Community in Guatemala." In *The Third Wave of Modernization in Latin America,* edited by Lynne Phillips, 51–65. Wilmington: Scholarly Resources.

Green, Mark, with Ralph Nader and Joel Seligman. 1976. *Taming the Giant Corporation.* New York: Norton.

Greenberg, Jerald. 1995. *The Quest for Justice on the Job: Essays and Experiments.* Palo Alto: Sage.

Greene, Graham. 1984. *Getting to Know the General.* New York: Simon and Schuster.

Greenfield, Gerald Michael, and Sheldon L. Maram, eds. 1987. *Latin American Labor Organizations.* New York: Greenwood.

Greenhouse, Steven. 1997a. "Accord to Combat Sweatshop Labor Faces Obstacles." *New York Times* (April 13): A1.

———. 1997b. "Sweatshop Raids Cast Doubt on Ability of Garment Makers to Police Factories." *New York Times* (July 18): A10.

Gregory, Peter, and Alberto Davila. 1993. "An Evaluation of the Panamanian Labor Code." Report prepared for the Government of Panama. Washington, D.C.: DEVTECH (Development Technologies, Inc.).

Guatemala. *Código de Trabajo.* 1993. Guatemala City: Ministerio de Trabajo y Previsión Social.

Guatemala. Ministerio de Trabajo y Previsión Social. 1991–96. *Boletin de Estadísticas.*

Guatemala. Presidency. 1993. "1994–5 Government Plan Agenda of Work." Guatemala City (September).

Gutiérrez Mayorga, Gustavo. 1985. "Historia del movimiento obrero de Nicaragua (1900–1977)." In *Historia del movimiento obrero en América Latina,* Pablo González Casanova, coord., 196–252. Mexico: Siglo Veintiuno Editores, S.A.

Hallett, Jeffrey. 1989. "Defining Rights in a Changing Economy." *Personnel Administrator* 34 (June).

Hamilton, Nora, Jeffry A. Friden, Linda Fuller, and Manuel Pastor Jr., eds. 1988. *Crisis in Central America*. Boulder: Westview.

Handler, Peggy. 1988. "Solidarismo: A Threat to the Labor Movement." *Report on Guatemala* 9, no. 3 (May–June).

Hansen-Kuhn, Karen. 1997. Presentation on free trade. National Guatemala Solidarity Conference, Washington, D.C., June 7.

Hansenne, Michael. 1994. "Promoting Social Justice in the New Global Economy." *Monthly Labor Review* 117, no. 5 (September).

Hansson, Gote. 1983. *Social Clauses and International Trade*. New York: St. Martin's.

Harbury, Jennifer K. 1997. *Searching for Everado: A Story of Love, War, and the CIA in Guatemala*. New York: Warner Books.

Harr, Jerry. 1990. "The Caribbean Basin Initiative: An Interim Assessment of the Trade Provision's Impact." *International Marketing Review* (UK) 7, no. 2: 21–27.

Harvey, Pharis J., and Lauren Riggin. 1994. *Trading Away the Future: Child Labor in India's Export Industries*. Washington, D.C.: ILRF.

Henk, Thomas, ed. 1995. *Globalization and Third World Trade Unions: The Challenge of Rapid Economic Change*. Atlantic Highlands, N.J.: Zed Books.

Hernández Alvarez, Oscar. 1994. "Latin America." In *Towards Social Dialogue: Tripartite Cooperation in National Economic and Social Policy-Making*, edited by Anne Trebilcock et al., 335–67. Geneva: ILO.

Herzenberg, Stephen, comp. 1996. *International Labor Rights and Standards after NAFTA: A Symposium*. New Brunswick: Rutgers Labor Education Center.

Herzenberg, Stephen, and Jorge F. Perez-López, eds. 1990. *Labor Standards and Development in the Global Economy*. Washington, D.C.: U.S. Department of Labor.

Honduras. 1992 [1959]. *Código de Trabajo*. Tegucigalpa: Graficentro Editores.

Hogness, Peter. 1989. "One More Hole in the Wall: The Lunafil Strikers in Guatemala." *Labor Research Review* 8, no. 8 (Spring).

Honey, Martha. 1994. *Hostile Acts: U.S. Policy in Costa Rica in the 1980s*. Gainsville: University Press of Florida.

Hooks, Margaret. 1993. *Guatemalan Women Speak*. Washington, D.C.: EPICA (Ecumenical Program on Central America and the Caribbean).

Hopkins, Thomas. 1994. "Workers' Rights Are the Gateway to Better Bottom Line." *Business First of Buffalo* 10 (June 13).

Horton, Susan, Ravi Kanbur, and Dipak Mazamdar. 1991. "Labour Markets in an Era of Adjustment: Evidence from 12 Developing Countries." *International Labour Review* 130, nos. 5–6: 531–58.

Human Rights Watch. 1997. "Corporations and Human Rights: Freedom of Association in a Maquila in Guatemala." New York: Human Rights Watch.

Humphrey, John. 1982. *The Brazilian Auto Industry*. Princeton: Princeton University Press.

ICCR (Interfaith Center for Corporate Responsibility). 1973. *Church Investments, Corporations, and Southern Africa*. New York: Friendship Press.

ILO (International Labour Organisation). 1992a. "Economic Restructuring and the World of Work." In *Report of the Director General*. Thirteenth Conference of the American States (September–October). Geneva: ILO.

———. 1992b. *General Survey of the Reports on the Minimum Wage-Fixing Machinery Convention #26.* 29th Congress. Geneva: ILO.

———. 1994a. *Lists of Ratification by Convention and Country.* Geneva: ILO.

———. 1994b. "Social Dimensions of the Liberalization of World Trade." Geneva: ILO.

———. 1995a. *Report of the Committee of Experts on the Application of Conventions and Recommendations.* Geneva: ILO.

———. 1995b. *Report by the Committee on Freedom of Association.* 263rd Session. Geneva: ILO (May).

ILRF (International Labor Rights [Education and Research] Fund). Petitions to USTR. See endnotes for complete citations.

———. *Worker Rights News.* Washington, D.C.: ILRF. Irregular serial.

———. 1986. "Background on the International Labor Rights Education and Research Fund." Washington, D.C.: ILRF (November 20).

———. 1991. *Worker Rights in a Changing International Economy.* Washington, D.C.: ILRF.

Immerman, Richard. 1982. *The CIA in Guatemala.* Austin: University of Texas Press.

Infante, Ricardo. 1991. "Labour Market Adjustment in Latin America: An Appraisal of the Social Effects in the 1980s." PRELAC Programa Mundial del Empleo, no. 357 (May) (paper series).

Informe Laboral 1993. 1994. San Salvador: Fundación Friedrich Ebert. Irregular serial.

Interhemispheric Resource Center (Albuquerque). 1997. "The Battle's On: Corporate Codes of Conduct." *Bulletin* 47–48 (October).

International Human Rights Law Group. 1987. "Waiting for Justice: Treatment of Political Prisoners under El Salvador Decree 50." Washington, D.C.: International Human Rights Law Group.

Irwin, Douglas A. 1996. *Against the Tide: An Intellectual History of Free Trade.* Princeton: Princeton University Press.

Johnson, Harold J., ed. 1993. *U.S. Support for Caribbean Basin Assembly Industries.* Washington, D.C.: General Accounting Office.

Jonas, Susanne. 1991. *The Battle for Guatemala.* Boulder. Colo.: Westview.

Jong-il You. 1989. "Worker Rights and Economic Development: What South Korean Experience Tells Us." Paper presented at American University, May 26–28.

———. 1990. "South Korea." In *Labor Standards and Development in the Global Economy,* edited by Stephen Herzenberg and Jorge F. Perez-López, 97–122. Washington, D.C.: U.S. Department of Labor, Bureau of International Labor Affairs.

Kammel, Rachael. 1990. *The Global Factory.* Philadelphia: American Friends Service Committee.

Kaplinsky, R. 1993. "Export Processing Zones in the Dominican Republic." *World Development* 21, no. 11 (November): 1851–66.

Keck, Margaret. 1992. *The Workers' Party and Democratization in Brazil.* New Haven: Yale University Press.

Keck, Margaret, and Kathryn Sikkink. 1995. "Transnational Issues Networks in International Politics." Paper presented at the 19th International Congress of Latin American Studies Association, Washington, D.C., September 28–30.

Kinni, Theodore. 1994. "The Empowered Workforce." *Industry Week,* no. 243 (September 19).

Kirkland, Lane. 1989. "Perspectives on Labor and the World: Toward a New Foreign Policy." Washington D.C.: AFL-CIO. Publication no. 185.

Kochan, Thomas, and William Nordlund. 1988. "Labor Standards and Competitiveness: An Historical Evolution." Paper delivered at the Symposium on Labor Standards and Third World Development, sponsored by the U.S. Department of Labor, Bureau of International Labor Affairs, and the Overseas Development Council, Washington D.C., December 12–13.

———. 1989a. *Reconciling Labor Standards and Economic Goals: An Historical Perspective.* Washington, D.C.: U.S. Department of Labor, Bureau of International Affairs (September).

———. 1989b. "Future Directions for American Labor and Human Rights Policy." *International Labor Relations Review* 44, no. 1.

Krueger, Alan. 1996. "Observations on International Labor Standards and Trade." In *International Labor Rights and Standards after NAFTA*, compiled by Stephen Herzenberg. New Brunswick, N.J.: Rutgers Labor Education Center.

Kuppers, Gaby, ed. 1994. *Compañeras: Voices from the Latin American Women's Movement.* London: Latin America Bureau.

Labor Institute. 1995. *Corporate Power and the American Dream.* Mt. Kisco, N.Y.: Apex Press.

LaBotz, Dan. 1995. *Democracy in Mexico: Peasant Rebellion and Political Reform.* Boston: South End Press.

LaFeber, Walter. 1984. *Inevitable Revolutions: The United States in Central America.* Expanded ed. New York: Norton.

Landau, Saul. 1995. *The Guerilla Wars of Central America.* New York: St. Martin's.

Langille, Brian. 1994. "Labour Standards in the Globalized Economy and the Free Trade/Fair Trade Debate." In *International Labour Standards and Economic Interdependence*, edited by Werner Sengenberger and Duncan Campbell, 329–56. Geneva: ILO.

LaRue, Frank. 1996. "Civil Society Must Be Strengthened." *Report on Guatemala* 17, no. 3 (October).

Latin America Labor News. 1992–93. "Labor and Free Trade."

———. 1995. "Labor and Free Trade." Special reports.

Lawyers Committee for Human Rights. 1989. *Worker Rights under the U.S. Trade Laws.* New York: Lawyers Committee.

Leary, Virginia A. 1996. "The Paradox of Workers' Rights as Human Rights." In *Human Rights, Labor Rights, and International Trade*, edited by Lance Compa and Stephen F. Diamond, 22–47. Philadelphia: University of Pennsylvania Press.

Ledogar, Robert. 1975. *Hungry for Profits.* New York: IDOC/North America.

Lee, T. 1996. "Trade Policy and Development: Spurning Good Growth." *Current History* 94, no. 604 (November).

Lee, T., and J. Schmidt. 1996. "Trade and Income Distribution: Theory, New Evidence, and Policy Alterntives." New York: Economic Policy Institute. Mimeograph.

Lernoux, Penny. 1982. *Cry of the People: The Struggle for Human Rights in Latin America—The Catholic Church Conflict with U.S. Policy.* New York: Penguin.

Levenson-Estrada, Deborah. 1994. *Trade Unionists Against Terror: Guatemala City, 1954–1985.* Chapel Hill: University of North Carolina Press.

Lim, Linda Y. C. 1987. "Export-Led Industrialization, Labour Welfare, and International Labour Standards in Singapore." In *Wages and Labor Conditions in the Newly Industrializing Countries of Asia,* edited by T. Addison and L. Demery. London: Overseas Development Institute.

———. 1990. "Singapore." In *Labor Standards and Development in the Global Economy,* edited by Stephen Herzenberg and Jorge F. Perez-López, 73–96. Washington, D.C.: U.S. Department of Labor, Bureau of International Labor Affairs.

López-Estrada, R. H., et al. 1993. "Como es y como actua la inspección de trabajo." Geneva: ILO.

López Larrave, Mário. 1979. *Breve Historia Del Movimiento Sindical Guatemalteco.* Guatemala City: Editorial Universitaria.

Loveman, Brian. 1987. "Chile." In *Latin American Labor Organizations,* edited by Gerald Michael Greenfield and Sheldon L. Maram, 129–78. New York: Greenwood.

Lustig, Nora A., and C. A. Primo Braga. 1994. "The Future of Trade Policy in Latin America." In *Integrating the Americas: Shaping Future Trade Policy,* edited by Sidney Weintraub. New Brunswick: Transaction.

Lyle, Faye. 1991. "Worker Rights in U.S. Policy." *Foreign Labor Trends* 91-54.

Lynd, Staughton. 1994. *Labor Law for the Rank and Filer.* Chicago: Charles H. Kerr.

MacLeod, Dag. 1994. "Guatemalan Maquiladora Workers in the Global Economy: Worker Rights in International Trade." Paper presented at the 18th International Congress of the Latin American Studies Association, Atlanta, Ga., March 10–12.

Maier, Heribert. 1994. "The Perspective of the International labor Organization." In *International Labor Standards and Global Economic Integration,* edited by Gregory Schoepfle and Kenneth Swinnerton. Washington, D.C.: U.S. Department of Labor.

Marshall, Adriana. 1994. "Economic Consequences of Labour Protection Regimes in Latin America." *International Labour Review* 33, no. 1.

———. 1996. "Employment Protection Reforms in South America: Effective Instruments to Manage Employment?" Focal/CIS Discussion Papers no. 1996-1. Toronto: Centre for International Studies, University of Toronto.

Marshall, Ray. 1987. *Unheard Voices: Labor and Economic Policy in a Competitive World.* New York: Basic Books.

———. 1994. "The Importance of International Labour Standards in a More Competitive Global Economy." In *International Labour Standards and Economic Interdependence,* edited by Werner Sengenberger and Duncan Campbell, 65–78. Geneva: ILO.

Martens, Margaret Hosmer, and Swasti Mitter, eds. 1994. *Women in Trade Unions: Organizing the Unorganized.* Geneva: ILO.

Martínez, Daniel, and Ricardo Infante, coords. 1992. "Guatemala: políticas de empleo e ingresos en el marco del pacto social." PREALC Programa Mundial del Empleo, no. 367 (September) (paper series).

Martinez, Lucio Miguel. 1994. "New Management Practices in a Multinational Corporation." *Industrial Relations Journal* 3 (June).

Maslow, Abraham H. 1954. *Motivation and Personality.* New York: Harper and Row.

Mead, Walter Russell. 1988. Commentary delivered at the Symposium on Labor Standards and Third World Development, sponsored by the U.S. Department of Labor, Bureau of International Labor Affairs, and the Overseas Development Council, Washington D.C., December 12–13.

Menchú, Rigoberta. 1984. *I Rigoberta Menchú.* London: Verso.

Menjívar Larín, Rafael. 1982. *Formación y lucha del proletariado industrial salvadoreño.* San José: Editorial Universitaria Centroamericana.

———. 1985. "Notas dobre el movimiento obrero salvadoreño." In *Historia del movimiento obrero en América Latina,* Pablo González Casanova, coord., 61–127. Mexico: Siglo Veintiuno Editores, S.A.

Menjívar Larín, Rafael, and J. P. Pérez Sáinz, comps. 1989. *Informalidad urbana en Centroamérica: Evidencias e interrogantes.* Guatemala City: FLACSO.

Meyers, Steven Lee. 1996. "Clothing Makers Taking Steps . . ." *New York Times* (October 21): A10.

Meza, Victor. 1980. *Historia del Movimiento Obrero Hondureño.* Tegucigalpa, Honduras: Editorial Guaymuras.

Moncada Valladares, Efraín. 1995. "Las dos caras de la maquila en Honduras." Tegucigalpa: OIT/Postgrado Centroamericano en Economía y Planificación del Desarrollo, Universidad Nacional Autónoma de Honduras.

Montesinos, Mario, and Roberto Gochez. 1995. "Política salarial y productividad en El Salvador." *Realidad Económico-social* 8, no. 44 (March–April).

Montgomery, David. 1996. "Labor Rights and Human Rights: A Historical Perspective." In *Human Rights, Labor Rights and International Trade,* edited by Lance Compa and Stephen F. Diamond. Philadelphia: University of Pennsylvania Press.

Moody, Kim, and Mary McGinn. 1992. *Unions and Free Trade: Solidarity vs. Competition.* Detroit: Labor Notes.

Monzán Fernández, Francisco. 1975. "La integración económica de Centroamérica y el movimiento sindical del área." *Mundo del Trabajo Libre, CIOSL [Free Labor World, ICTFU]* (February).

Munves, James. 1974. *Minding the Corporate Conscience.* New York: Julian Messner.

Murphy, Martin F. 1987. "Dominican Republic." In *Latin American Labor Organizations,* edited by Gerald Michael Greenfield and Sheldon L. Maram, 339–58. New York: Greenwood.

Myrdal, Hans-Goran. 1994. "The ILO in the Cross-fire: Would It Survive the Social Clause?" In *International Labour Standards and Economic Interdependence,* edited by Werner Sengenberger and Duncan Campbell, 339–58. Geneva: ILO.

NACDC (Netherlands National Advisory Council for Development Cooperation). 1984. "Recommendation on Minimum International Labour Standards." Recommendation no. 84. The Hague: Ministry of Foreign Affairs.

NACLA (North American Congress on Latin America). 1996. *Report on the Americas.*

Nader, Ralph, and Kate Blackwell. 1973. *You and Your Pension.* Washington, D.C.: Center for Responsive Law.

Nader, Ralph, et al. 1993. *The Case Against Free Trade.* San Francisco: Earth Island Press.

Navas Alvarez, María Guadalupe. 1979. *El movimiento sindical: Como manifestación de la lucha de clases.* Guatemala City: Editorial Universitaria.

New America Press. 1989. *A Dream Compels Us: Voices of Salvadoran Women.* Boston: South End Press.

Nicaragua. 1996. *Código de Trabajo.* Managua: Ley No. 185 [photocopy].

NISGUA (Network in Solidarity with the People of Guatemala). 1998. "Action Alert: Anti-Riot Police Invade Banana Plantations." Washington, D.C.: NISGUA. Press release.

NLC (National Labor Committee in Support of Democracy and Human Rights). 1983. "El Salvador: Labor, Terror, and Peace." New York: National Labor Committee.

———. 1985. "The Search for Peace in Central America." New York: National Labor Committee.

———. 1988. "Labor Rights Denied in El Salvador." New York: National Labor Committee.

———. 1991. "Worker Rights and the New World Order: El Salvador, Honduras, Guatemala." New York: National Labor Committee.

———. 1992. "Paying to Lose Our Jobs." New York: National Labor Committee.

———. 1993. "Free Trade's Hidden Secrets." New York: National Labor Committee.

———. 1995. "The U.S. in Haiti: How to Get Rich on 11¢ an Hour." New York: National Labor Committee.

O'Donnell, Guillermo, Philippe C. Schmitter, and Laurence Whitehead, eds. 1986. *Transitions from Authoritarian Rule: Latin America.* Baltimore: Johns Hopkins University Press.

OECD (Organization for Economic Cooperation and Development). 1996. "Report to the Council at Ministerial Level on Trade, Employment and Labour Standards." Paris: OECD (May 3).

Oglesby, Liz. 1997. "Labor and the Sugar Industry." *Report on Guatemala* 18, no. 1.

O'Kane, Trish. 1995. "New Autonomy, New Struggle: Labor Unions in Nicaragua." In *The New Politics of Survival,* edited by Morton Sinclair, 183–208. New York: Monthly Review Press.

Ortega, Bob. 1995. "Broken Rules: Conduct Codes Garner Goodwill for Retailers, But Violations Go On." *Wall Street Journal* (July 3): A1.

Osigweh, Chimezie. 1990. "Towards an Employee Responsibilities and Rights Paradigm." *Human Relations* 43 (December).

Otis, John. 1994. *Miami Herald* (March 24).

Otting, Albrecht. 1993. "International Labour Standards: A Framework for Social Security." *International Labour Review* 132, no. 2.

Otzoy, Antonio. 1996. "Guatemala: The Struggle for Maya Unity." *NACLA Report on the Americas* 29, no. 5 (March–April).

Overseas Development Council. 1986. "Third World Worker Rights and U.S. Trade Policy: Should They Be Linked?" Washington, D.C.: Overseas Development Council. Policy Focus Background Paper no. 6.

PACCA (Policy Alternatives for the Caribbean and Central America). 1984. *Changing Course: Blueprint for Peace in Central America and the Caribbean.* Washington, D.C.: PACCA.

Paige, Jeffrey M. 1997. *Coffee and Power: Revolution and the Price of Democracy in Central America.* Cambridge, Mass.: Harvard University Press.

Palomoes, L., and L. Mertens. 1993. "Cambios en la gestión y actitud empresarial en America Latina: Un marco de analysis." *Revista de Económica y Trabajo* (Santiago) (July–December).

Park, Young-Ki, ed. 1993. *Labor in Korea.* Seoul: Korea Labor Institute.

Panama. 1995. *Código de Trabajo.* Panama City. Photocopy.

Payne, Douglass W. 1993. "Dominican Labor and the GSP." *Journal of Commerce* (September 9).

Pearse, Jenny. 1982. *Under the Eagle: U.S. Intervention in Central America and the Caribbean.* Boston: South End Press.

Pearson, Neale J. 1987. "Honduras." In *Latin American Labor Organizations,* edited by Gerald Michael Greenfield and Sheldon L. Maram, 463–94. New York: Greenwood.

Pease, Donald J. 1994. "A View from a Former Congressman." In *International Labor Standards and Global Economic Integration,* edited by Gregory Schoepfle and Kenneth Swinnerton. Washington, D.C.: U.S. Department of Labor.

Peckenham, Nancy, and Annie Street, eds. 1985. *Portrait of a Captive Nation.* New York: Praeger.

Pedraja Toman, René de la. 1987. "Columbia." In *Latin American Labor Organizations,* edited by Gerald Michael Greenfield and Sheldon L. Maram, 179–212. New York: Greenwood.

Pereira, Anthony, and Cliff Welch, eds. 1995. "Labor and the Free Market in the Americas." *Latin American Perspectives* 22, no. 1 (Winter). Special issue.

Perez-López, Jorge F. 1990. "Worker Rights in the Omnibus Trade and Competitiveness Act." *Labor Law Journal* 41 (April).

Perez-López, Jorge F., and Greg Schoepfle. 1993. "The Informal Sector and Worker Rights." *Foreign Labor Trends* 93-9.

Petersen, Kurt. 1992. *The Maquiladora Revolution in Guatemala.* New Haven: Schell Center for Human Rights, Yale Law School.

Petchesky, Rosalind, and Karen Judd, eds. 1998. *Negotiating Reproductive Rights: Women's Perspectives Across Countries and Cultures.* London: Zed Books.

Phillipps, Susan Collazos. 1987. "Panama." In *Latin American Labor Organizations,* edited by Gerald Michael Greenfield and Sheldon L. Maram, 577–96. New York: Greenwood.

———. 1991. *Labor and Politics in Panama: The Torrijos Years.* Boulder: Westview.

Pino, Victor. 1996. "Entrampado el Consejo Superior del Trabajo." *La Prensa.* (June 29): 16A.

Piore, Michael. 1990. "Labor Standards and Business Strategies." In *Labor Standards and Development in the Global Economy,* edited by Stephen Herzenberg and Jorge F. Perez-López, 35ff. Washington, D.C.: U.S. Department of Labor, Bureau of International Labor Affairs.

———. 1994. "International Labor Standards and Business Strategies." In *International Labor Standards and Global Economic Integration,* edited by Gregory Schoepfle and Kenneth Swinnerton, 21–25. Washington, D.C.: U.S. Department of Labor.

Piore, Michael, Enrique Dussel, and Clemente Ruiz-Durán. 1996. "Adjustments in Mexican Industries to the Opening of the Economy to Trade." In *International Labor Rights and Standards after NAFTA: A Symposium,* Stephen J. Hertzenberg, comp. New Brunswick: Rutgers University Labor Education Center.

Plant, Roger. 1994. *Labour Standards and Structural Adjustment.* Geneva: ILO.

Portes, Alejandro. 1990. "When More Can Be Less: Labor Standards, Development, and the Informal Economy." In *Labor Standards and Development in the Global Economy,* edited by Stephen Herzenberg and Jorge F. Perez-López, 219–38. Washington, D.C.: U.S. Department of Labor, Bureau of International Labor Affairs.

———. 1994. "By-passing the Rules: The Dialectics of Labour Standards and Informalization in Less Developed Countries." In *International Labour Standards and Economic Interdependence,* edited by Werner Sengenberger and Duncan Campbell, 159–76. Geneva: ILO.

Portes, Alejandro, Manuel Castells, and Lauren Benton, eds. 1989. *The Informal Economy.* Baltimore: Johns Hopkins University Press.

Posas, Mario. 1980. *Lucha ideológica y organización sindical en Honduras (1954–65).* Tegucigalpa: Editorial Guaymuras.

Post, James E. 1978. *Corporate Behavior and Social Change.* Reston, Va.: Reston.

Potter, Edward. 1994. "International Labour Standards, the Global Economy, and Trade." In *International Labour Standards and Economic Interdependence,* edited by Werner Sengenberger and Duncan Campbell, 357–66. Geneva: ILO.

PREALC. 1991. "El salario minimo como señal para el mercado de trabajo." PREALC Programa Mundial del Empleo, no. 371 (paper series).

Puga. 1995. *Manual de trabajo.* Guatemala City: Ministerio de Trabajo y Previsión Social.

Pursey, Stephen K. 1994. "The Social Foundations of International Trade." In *International Labour Standards and Economic Interdependence,* edited by Werner Sengenberger and Duncan Campbell, 367–78. Geneva: ILO.

Rakowski, Cathy A., ed. 1994. *Contrapunto: The Informal Sector Debate in Latin America.* Albany: State University of New York Press.

Ramey, Joanna. 1994. "New Label Aims to Asure 'No Child Labor on Rugs.'" *Weekly Home Furnishings Newspaper* (October 24).

Ramírez, Nelson, Isidoro Santana, Francisco de Moya, and Pablo Tactuk. 1988. *República Dominicana: Población y Desarrollo, 1950–1985.* San José, Costa Rica: CELADE (Centro Latinoamericano de Demografía).

Ramírez, Werner Fernando. 1995. "Zonas francas e industrias maquiladoras en Guatemala." San José: Organización Internacional de Trabajo.

Ramírez, Werner Fernando, et al. 1994. *El significado de la maquila en Guatemala.* Guatemala City. AVANSCO.

Ramney, David. 1987. "Combating Plant Closings." *Journal of Ideology* (Winter).

Rawls, John. 1971. *Theory of Justice.* Cambridge, Mass.: Belknap Press.

Reed, Thomas, and Karen Brandow. 1996. *The Sky Never Changes: Testimonies from the Guatemalan Labor Movement.* Ithaca: Cornell University Press

Reich, Robert. 1994. "Keynote Address." In *International Labor Standards and Global Economic Integration,* edited by Gregory Schoepfle and Kenneth Swinnerton, 1–6. Washington, D.C.: U.S. Department of Labor.

Reyes Castro, F., and A. Dominguez. 1993. "Zonas francas industriales en la Republica Dominicana: Su impacto economico y social." Geneva: ILO.

Rifkin, Jeremy. 1995. *The End of Work: The Decline of the Global Labor Force and the Dawn of the Post-Market Era.* New York: G. P. Putnam's Sons.

Rodríguez, Roberto. 1994. *50 años de legislación laboral, 1994–1994.* Guatemala: Ministerio de Trabajo.

Rodrik, D. 1995. "Labor Standards in International Trade: Do They Matter and What Do We Do About Them." In *Emerging Agenda in Global Trade: High Stakes for Developing Countries,* edited by R. Lawrence et al. Washington, D.C.: Overseas Development Council.

Rohter, Larry. 1996a. "Hondurans in 'Sweatshops' See Opportunity." *New York Times* (July 18).

———. 1996b. "Costa Rica Chafes at New Austerity." *New York Times* (September 30).

Rojas Bolaños, Manuel. 1985. "El movimiento obrero en Costa Rica." In *Historia del movimiento obrero en América Latina*, Pablo González Casanova, coord., 253–81. Mexico City: Siglo Veintiuno Editores, S.A.

Rosen, Fred, and Deidre McFadyen, eds. 1995. *Free Trade and Economic Restructuring in Latin America*. New York: Monthly Review Press.

Rosen, Sumner. 1992. "Protecting Labor Rights in Market Economies." *Human Rights Quarterly* 14 (August).

Rothstein, Richard. 1993. *Setting the Standard: International Labor Rights and U.S. Trade Policy*. Washington, D.C.: Economic Policy Institute.

Ruiz, Marisol, and Gilberto García. 1996. "Condiciones laborales de mujeres y menores en las plantas de la maquila coreana y Taiwanesa en El Salvador." San Salvador: CENTRA.

Ruthrauff, John, and Teresa Carlson. 1997. "A Guide to the Inter-American Development Bank and World Bank: Strategies for Guatemala." Washington, D.C.: Center for Democratic Education.

Ryan, Phil. 1995. *The Fall and Rise of the Market in Sandinista Nicaragua*. Montreal: McGill-Queen's University Press.

Safa, Helen. 1995. *The Myth of the Male Breadwinner: Women and Industrialization in the Caribbean*. Boulder: Westview.

———. 1997. "Where the Big Fish Eat the Little Fish: Women's Work in the Free-Trade Zones." *NACLA Report on the Americas* 30, no. 5 (March–April): 31–36.

Sanderson, Steven E. 1992. *The Politics of Trade in Latin American Development*. Stanford: Stanford University Press.

Sanford, James. 1993. "Continental Economic Integration: Modeling the Impact on Labor." In *Free Trade in the Western Hemisphere*, edited by Sidney Weintraub. Special issue, *Annals of the American Academy of Political and Social Science* 526 (March): 92–110. Newbury Park, Calif.: Sage.

Sanz, Frederico. 1989. "Development, Crisis, and Prospects of the Central American Economy." In *Culture, Human Rights, and Peace in Central America*, edited by George F. McLean, Raul Molina, and Timothy Ready, 83–109. Lanham, Md.: Council for Research in Values and Philosophy.

Schilling, David M. 1997. "A Step Toward Eliminating Sweatshops: The White House Apparel Industry Partnership Report." *Corporate Examiner* 25, no. 9 (May 9).

Schoepfle, Gregory, and Kenneth Swinnerton, eds. 1994. *International Labor Standards and Global Economic Integration: Proceedings of a Symposium*. Washington, D.C.: U.S. Department of Labor.

Schor, Juliet. 1992. *The Overworked American*. New York: Basic Books.

Schor, Juliet, and Jong-il You, eds. 1995. *Capital, the State, and Labor: A Global Perspective*. New York: Edward Elgar.

Schoultz, Lars. 1981. *Human Rights and United States Policy toward Latin America*. Princeton: Princeton University Press.

Schulz, Donald, and Deborah Sundloff Schulz. 1994. *The United States, Honduras, and the Crisis in Central America*. Boulder: Westview.

Sciolino, Elaine. 1998. "Clinton Argues for 'Flexibility' over Sanctions." *New York Times* 147 (April 28).

Sengenberger, Werner, and Duncan Campbell, eds. 1994. *International Labour Standards and Economic Interdependence.* Geneva: ILO.

Sengenberger, Werner, and F. Wilkinson. 1994. "Globalization and Labour Standards," In *Managing the Global Economy,* edited by J. Michie and J. Grieve-Smith. Oxford: Oxford University Press.

Servais, J. 1989. "The Social Clause in Trade Agreements: Wishful Thinking or an Instrument of Social Progress?" *International Labor Review* 128, no. 4 (July–August).

Shepard, Robert B., coord; Peter Accolla, Danilo Jimenez, Ricardo Muniz, Gary Russell, Jeffrey Smith. 1994. "An Assessment of the Ministry of Labor of El Salvador." Washington, D.C.: U.S. Department of Labor/USAID. Photocopy.

Shepherd, Philip. 1988. *The Honduran Crisis and U.S. Economic Assistance.* Boulder: Westview.

Simpson, William R. 1994. "The ILO and Tripartism: Some Reflections." *Monthly Labor Review* 117, no. 9 (September): 40–45.

Sims, Beth. 1992. *Workers of the World Undermined: American Labor's Role in U.S. Foreign Policy.* Boston: South End Press.

Sims, Calvin. 1998. "Free-Trade Zone of the Americas Given a Go-Ahead." *New York Times* (April 20): A1.

Singh, Ajit. 1990. "Southern Competiton, Labor Standards, and Industrial Development in the North and the South." In *Labor Standards and Development in the Global Economy,* edited by Stephen Herzenberg and Jorge F. Perez-López, 339–364. Washington, D.C.: U.S. Department of Labor, Bureau of International Labor Affairs.

Sklair, Leslie. 1993. *Assembling for Development: The Maquila Industry in Mexico and the United States.* San Diego: University of California Center for U.S.-Mexican Studies.

Sklar, Holly. 1995. *Chaos or Community.* Boston: South End Press.

Slaughter, Jane. 1987. "Which Side Are They On? The AFL-CIO Tames Guatemala's Unions." *Progressive* 51 (January).

Smith-Ayala, Emilie, ed. 1991. *The Granddaughters of Ixmucané.* Toronto: Women's Press.

Sonnenberg, Frank. 1993. "An Employee's Bill of Rights." *Supervisory Management* 38, no. 10 (November).

Southhall, Roger, ed. 1988. *Trade Unions and the New Industrialization of the Third World.* Pittsburgh: University of Pittsburgh Press.

Spalding, Hobart. 1977. *Organized Labor in Latin America.* New York: New York University Press.

———. 1988a. "U.S. Labor Intervention in Latin America: The Case of the American Institute for Free Labor Development." In *Trade Unions and the New Industrialization of the Third World,* edited by Roger Southhall. Pittsburgh: University of Pittsburgh Press.

———. 1988b. "AIFLD Amok." *NACLA Report on the Americas* 22, no. 3 (May–June).

———. 1993. "The Two Latin American Foreign Policies of the U.S. Labor Movement." *Science and Society* 57, no. 1 (Spring).

SRI International. 1990. "National Export Plan for Guatemala: Guatemala Millions." Final report to USAID (January).

Srinivasan, T. N. 1994. "Labor Standards Once Again!" In *International Labor Standards and Global Economic Integration,* edited by Gregory Schoepfle and Kenneth Swinnerton, 34–40. Washington, D.C.: U.S. Department of Labor.

Stahler-Sholk, Richard. "Nicaragua." 1987. In *Latin American Labor Organizations*, edited by Gerald Michael Greenfield and Sheldon L. Maram, 549–76. New York: Greenwood.

———. 1995. "The Dog That Didn't Bark: Labor Autonomy and Economic Adjustment in Nicaragua under the Sandinista and UNO Governments." *Comparative Politics* 28 (October).

———. 1996a. "Structural Adjustment and the Labor Movement in Nicaragua." Paper presented at the annual meeting of the Industrial Relations Research Association, San Francisco, January 5–7.

———. 1996b. "Structural Adjustment and Resistance: The Political Economy of Nicaragua under Chamorro." In *The Undermining of the Sandinista Revolution*, edited by Gary Prevost and Harry Vanden, 74–113. London: Macmillan.

Swepston, Lee. 1994. "The Future of ILO Standards." *Monthly Labor Review* 117, no. 9: 16–23.

Swinnerton, Kenneth, and Gregory K. Schoepfle. 1994. "Labor Standards in the Context of a Global Economy." *Monthly Labor Review* 117, no. 9: 52–58.

———. 1997. "An Essay on Economic Efficiency and Core Labor Standards." In *The World Economy: Global Trade Policy 1997*, edited by Sevn Arndt and Chris Milner. London: Blackwell.

Tardanico, Richard, and Rafael Menjívar Larín, eds. 1997. *Global Restructuring, Employment, and Social Inequality in Urban Latin America*. Boulder: Lynne Rienner.

Terrell, Katherine D. 1984. "Labor Mobility and Earnings: Evidence from (Ladino) Guatemala." Ph.D. diss., Cornell University.

Thrupp, Lori Ann. 1995. *Bittersweet Harvests for Global Supermarkets*. Washington, D.C.: World Resources Institute.

Tiano, Susan. 1990. "Maquiladora Women: A New Category of Workers?" In *Women Workers and Global Restructuring*, edited by Kathryn Ward. Ithaca: ILR Press.

Tolkman, V. E., ed. 1992. *Beyond Regulation: The Informal Economy in Latin America*. Boulder: Lynne Rienner.

Tonelson, Alan. 1996. "Protecting Ourselves: Cancel China's Most-Favored-Nation Status." *New York Times* (May 16): op. ed.

Torres Rivas, Edelberto. 1989. *Repression and Resistance*. Boulder: Westview.

Trebilcock, Anne, et al., eds. 1994. *Towards Social Dialogue: Tripartite Cooperation in National Economic and Social Policy-Making*. Geneva: ILO.

Trudeau, Robert H. 1993. *Guatemalan Politics: The Popular Struggle for Democracy*. Boulder: Lynne Rienner.

Tucker, Stuart, Jorge F. Perez-López, and Stephen Herzenberg, coords. 1988. "Beyond Subsistence: Labor Standards and Third World Development." Report on a symposium co-convened by the Bureau of International Labor Affairs of the U.S. Department of Labor and the Overseas Development Council, Washington, D.C. (December). Washington, D.C.: U.S. Department of Labor.

Tussie, Diana. 1993. "Bargaining at a Crossroads: Argentina." In *Developing Countries in World Trade*, edited by Diana Tussie and David Glover, 119–38. Boulder: Lynne Rienner.

Tuyuc, Rosalina. 1994. "From Grief Comes Strength: Indigenous Women's Resistance." In *Compañeras: Voices from the Latin American Women's Movement*, edited by Gaby

Kuppers, 111–15. London: Latin America Bureau.

United Nations. Comisión para la Verdad en El Salvador. 1993. *De la locura a la Esperanza: Informe de la Comisión de la Verdad de El Salvador.* New York: United Nations (March).

United States. Department of Commerce. 1990a. "Foreign Economic Trends and Their Implications for the United States." Washington, D.C.: U.S. Department of Commerce (February).

———. Department of Commerce. 1990b. *U.S. Foreign Trade Highlights.* Washington, D.C.: U.S. Department of Commerce.

———. Department of Labor. 1962. *Labor Law and Practice in Guatemala.* BLS Report no. 223. Washington, D.C.: Government Printing Office.

———. Department of Labor. 1996. "The Apparel Industry and Codes of Conduct: A Solution to the International Child Labor Problem?" Washington, D.C.: Government Printing Office.

———. Department of Labor, Bureau of International Labor Affairs. 1984. "Labor Profile: Honduras." Photocopy.

———. Department of Labor, Bureau of International Labor Affairs. 1990. "Worker Rights in Export Processing Zones." Washington D.C.: U.S. Department of Labor. Special report, summarized in *Foreign Labor Trends* 90-32.

———. Department of State. 1986. "The U.S. and Central America: Implementing the National Bipartisan Commission Report." Special Report no. 148 (August). Washington, D.C.: U.S. Department of State.

———. Department of State. 1989. "Human Rights Report: Guatemala." Washington, D.C.: Government Printing Office.

———. Department of State. 1992. "Human Rights Report: Guatemala." Washington, D.C.: Government Printing Office.

———. Department of State. 1993. "Country Report on Human Rights Practices: Guatemala." Washington, D.C.: Government Printing Office.

———. House of Representatives. 1984. "Report 98-1090" (2nd session). Washington, D.C.: Government Printing Office.

———. National Bipartisan Commission on Central America. 1984. *Report of the National Bipartisan Commission on Central America.* Washington, D.C.: Government Printing Office.

UNOC (Unión Nacional Obrera-Campesina). 1994. "Analysis de la propuesta del Doctor Bronstein y de las acutales reformas al código de trabajo." San Salvador: UNOC (June).

U.S./GLEP. Briefs to USTR. See endnotes for complete citations.

———. 1997. *Labor Education Campaign* 19 (July).

———. 1998. *Labor Education Campaign* 21–22 (April).

USITC (U.S. International Trade Commission). 1994. *Impact of the Caribbean Basin Economic Recovery Act.* Washington, D.C.: USITC.

Valésquez, Eduardo. 1993. "Efectos de la privatización en la empleo." Report of public panel. Guatemala City: Fundación Myrna Mack (November 5): 21–34.

Valticos, Nicholas. 1979. *International Labour Law.* Geneva: ILO.

van Adams, Arvil, et al. 1992. "The World Bank's Treatment of Employment and Labour Market Issues." Washington, D.C.: World Bank. Technical Paper no. 177.

van Liemt, Gijsbert. 1989. "Minimum Labour Standards and International Trade: Would a Social Clause Work?" *International Labor Review* 28, no. 4.

Vargas-Lundius, Rosemary. 1991. *Peasants in Distress: Poverty and Unemployment in the Dominican Republic.* Boulder: Westview.

Vida Soría, José. 1993. "ILO Report on El Salvador." (September 27). Photocopy.

Vilas, Carlos. 1986. *The Sandinista Revolution.* New York: Monthly Review Press.

Vogel, David. 1978. *Lobbying the Corporation: Citizen Challenges to Business Authority.* New York: Basic Books.

Vogel, Thomas. 1997. "Central America Goes from War Zone to Enterprise Zone: Economic Reforms in Guatemala May Set Pace for Other Nations." *Wall Street Journal* (September 25).

Wagner, Jan. 1992. "Guatemala, a Leader Again." *International Business Chronicle* (May 10).

Walker, Thomas. 1985. *Nicaragua: The First Five Years.* New York: Praeger.

————. 1997. *Nicaragua Without Illusions: Regime Transition and Structural Adjustment in the 1990s.* Washington, D.C.: Scholarly Resources.

Waterman, Peter. 1995. "Global Civil Solidarity." In *Globalization, Communication, and the Transnational Public Sphere,* edited by Sandra Braman and Annabelle Sreberny-Mohammadi. Creskill, N.J.: Hampton Press.

Weaver, Frederick Stirton. 1994. *Inside the Volcano: The History and Political Economy of Central America.* Boulder: Westview.

Wedin, Ake. 1986. "International Trade Union 'Solidarity' and Its Victims: The Costa Rican Case." Research Paper no. 43. Stockholm: Institute of Latin American Studies.

Weinberg, Bill. 1991. *War on the Land: Ecology and Politics in Central America.* London: Zed Press.

Weinrub, Al, and William Bollinger. 1987. *The AFL-CIO in Central America: A Look at the American Institute for Free Labor Development.* Oakland: Labor Network.

Weintraub, Sidney, ed. 1993. *Free Trade in the Western Hemisphere.* Special issue, *Annals of the American Academy of Political and Social Science* 256 (March).

Westin, Alan, and Stephan Salisbury, eds. 1980. *Individual Rights in the Corporation.* New York: Pantheon.

Wiarda, Howard, and Harvey F. Kline. 1985. *Latin American Politics and Development.* Boulder: Westview.

Williams, Robert G. 1986. *Export Agriculture and the Crisis in Central America.* Chapel Hill: University of North Carolina Press.

Wilson, Richard. 1995. *Maya Resurgence in Guatemala: Q'eqchí Experiences.* Norman: University of Oklahoma Press.

Wood, Elisabeth, and Alexander Segovia. 1995. "Macroeconomic Policy and the Salvadoran Peace Accords." *World Development* 23, no. 12 (December): 2079–99.

World Bank. 1993. *Nicaragua: Country Economic Report.* Washington, D.C.: World Bank (October 22).

WTO (World Trade Organization). 1996. "Ministerial Declaration." Singapore (December 12).

Yates, Michael. 1991. *Power on the Job: The Legal Rights of Working People.* Boston: South End Press.

Index of Names

Flores, Hernol, 95
Forster, Cynthia, 158
Franco, Rafael 95
Franklin, Jane, 3
Freeman, Anthony, 42, 47, 69–70, 222
French, John, 38
Fujimori, Alberto, 97

Galvez, Juan Manuel, 193
García, Juan José Antonio, 17–19
García, Manuel, 195
García Dueñas, Gilberto Ernesto, 124–26, 139
García-Huidobro, Guillermo, 230
García-Rocha, Adalberto, 44
Garver, Paul, 68
Genovez, Edito, 135–36
Gifford, Kathie Lee, 1, 9
Gindling, T. H., 230
Gingrich, Newt, 1
Gleijeses, Piero, 3
Goldman, Francisco, 189
Goldston, James A., 142
Gómez, Efraín Recinos, 18
Gómez, Yovany, 157
González, Reynoldo, 157–59, 176, 258–59, 271
González, Rodin, 164
González, Nelson, 27–28, 123
González Méndez, Carlos, 29
Goodman, Louis, 79
Green, Linda, 7
Greene, Graham, 79, 246
Greenfield, Gerald Michael, 73
Greenhouse, Steven, 48
Gregory, Peter, 240
Grunwald, Joseph, 90
Guerrero, Francisco, 196
Gutiérrez, Roger, 114, 116–17, 121, 135–37, 256–57, 263, 272
Guzman, Sergio, 30 156, 159, 172, 175, 260, 264, 267, 271–72

Hamilton, Nora, 4, 191
Hannson, Gote, 64

Hansenne, Michael, 62
Harbury, Jennifer, 155, 197
Harkin, Thomas, 47
Harvey, Pharis, 148
Henshaw, Simon, 113, 115–16, 120, 134, 138, 255
Hermanson, Jeffrey, 212, 222, 224–26
Hernandes, Ignacio, 225
Herrera, Mauricio, 129, 137
Herzenberg, Stephen, 9, 73, 254
Hogness, Peter, 145
Horton, Susan, 51
Howard, Alan, 157, 159, 204–6
Hurtado, Carlos, 28 116–17, 129, 135, 255, 257, 268, 272

Immerman, Richard, 5
Infante, Ricardo, 84, 230
Irwin, Douglas A., 56

Jessup, David, 95–97, 136, 191, 202, 204–5, 217, 221, 224, 232, 235, 240
Johnson, Harold J., 4
Jolón, Tomas, 22
Jonas, Susanne 5, 141, 283
Jong-il You, 45, 50

Kaltschmitt, Willi, 153
Kammel, Rachael, 90
Kantor, Michael, 34
Keck, Margaret, 75
Kirkland, Lane, 69
Kissinger, Henry, 6, 86
Knight, Donald, 174, 181, 183–81, 187, 256, 267, 285
Kochan, Thomas, 43, 49
Krueger, Alan, 61

LaBotz, Dan, 99
LaFeber, Walter, 5
Lamport, Pedro, 160
Landau, Saul, 5, 105, 247
Langille, Brian, 57–58
LaRue, Frank, 160, 173
Ledogar, Robert, 231

Index of Subjects

CBI (Caribbean Basin Initiative), 7, 9, 86–89, 251, 253, 268, 274, 287–90; benefits and drawbacks, 70, 86–90; Central America's role, 87; ILO standards, 62; leading exporters, 287–90; Special Access Program, 7, 88
CENTRA (El Salvador), 118, 126, 263
Central America:
—economy, 76, 84–92; exports to U.S., 87; informal sector, 84; lost decade and employment, 84, 92; non-traditional exports and employment, 88–91
—labor legislation, 10, 79–82, 90, 269–70, 283; ILO conventions ratified, 81
—integration of, 266; social clause, 269
—peace process, 84, 91, 256
—state's role in union separation, 79–82
—worker action, 269–70
CGTG (Guatemala), 142, 188, 257
child labor, 78, 110, 123, 173, 191; continued misuse of, 25, 53, 61; enforcement of standards 47–48, 52, 61, 343n.1. See also specific countries—labor conditions
Chile, 69, 80; GSP petitions, 94–95
China, 7, 9, 46, 59
Chiquita (United Fruit Co.), 20, 197–98
CIA, 5, 193, 239
CIEP (Guatemala), 21 184, 256
class analysis, 4, 134, 139, 282–86
CNT (Guatemala), 21, 142
CNTD (Dominican Republic), 211, 216, 220–22
Coca-Cola, 21, 46, 163; union (Guatemala), 21–22, 141–42
COCENTRA, 271–72
CONIC (Guatemala), 21, 184
coffee, 85; Anacafe agreement, 155–56, 271
Columbia, 51, 98
corporate behavior, 74; dislocation, 8; employee codes, 46; GSP petitions,

98. See also independent monitoring
COSEP (Nicaragua), 249–50, 285
Costa Rica
—business attitudes, 234–35
—economic conditions, 230; middle-sector adjustment, 230; non-traditional export production, 88, 336n.5
—government (in)action, 233–35
—GSP petitions: action threat, 232; filing, 233; withdrawal and backtracing, 235–37
—ILO relations, 62, 231, 236; convention violations, 233; ILO ratifications, 234, 337n.18; Regulation on Union Freedom signed, withdrawn, 231
—labor conditions, 82; blacklistings and firings, 233; free-zone conditions, 233, 237; lack of rights in private sector, 236; right of association, 234; right to bargain, 231–32, 234, 237; right to strike, 233, 235, 336n.2; for public employees, 229, 233–34; union growth, decline, 228, 233, 237; wage bargaining versus CPI, 92–94, 230
—labor confederations and actions, 233–34, 337nn.12, 15
—labor legislation and codes; early history, 80, 229; key provisions of 1993 agreement, 235; later code reform, 234; poor implementation, 236; use of arreglo directo, 229, 231, 337n.7
—Labor Ministry, 237; admission of ineffective sanctions, 232
—solidarista associations, 228, 337n.6; growth, 230–32; legal abuses, 231; reduced legal status, 235
—U.S. embassy resistance, 236
—women workers, 229–30, 236
CPT (Nicaragua), 248–50
CST (Nicaragua), 247–50, 252
CTCA, 270, 272
CTD (El Salvador), 122, 139, 266
CTH (Honduras), 196, 201
CTRN (Costa Rica), 233